ANTIQUE FIREARMS

ANTIQUE FIREARMS

By

FREDERICK WILKINSON

Guinness Superlatives Limited
2 Cecil Court, London Road, Enfield, Middlesex

Second impression 1977
Published in Great Britain by
Guinness Superlatives Limited, 2 Cecil Court,
London Road, Enfield, Middlesex

ISBN 0 851121 64 0

Colour Separations By
Newsele Litho Limited, London and Milan

Printed and bound in Great Britain by
Redwood Burn Limited, Trowbridge & Esher

CONTENTS

INTRODUCTION

THE series of monographs combined here in a single volume traces the history of the firearm from its introduction to Europe in the 14th century through to the appearance of the modern repeating rifle. It is a fascinating story, and one whose many areas of obscurity still offer worthwhile opportunities for continuing research.

The study and collection of antique firearms has become very popular in the last generation; and to the outsider it may seem that this is evidence of a peculiar and suspect taste, since firearms are engines of violence designed purely to maim and kill. As such they would hardly seem to justify the study and care that they receive today from so many thousands of enthusiasts. It is arguable that the attitude of collectors is one of deliberate self-deception, but in fact they seldom consider the original purpose of the weapons, seeing them simply as articles of beauty and craftsmanship devoid of any violent overtones.

Prior to the 19th century the great majority of firearms were the result of the skills and combined talents of perhaps ten or fifteen craftsmen, each an expert in his own field. Every weapon was unique, each differing subtly from others of the same basic type. Some satisfy the eye with their graceful, almost stark lines and their simple functional design; others, such as the wheellocks of the 16th century, are examples of the highest standards of design, craftsmanship, and artistic taste of their period.

For the more mechanically minded collector, many of these firearms offer a multitude of ingenious and occasionally positively dangerous systems intended to improve their action. Thus there are facets of the subject to please almost every taste, and this is undoubtedly one of the reasons for the enormous growth of interest over the past few decades. From being a rather specialised and restricted taste, the study of firearms has grown rapidly and consistently until today it is one of the more popular fields in the antique world. Increased demand has stimulated further research, and newly acquired knowledge has encouraged new collectors, in a continuing spiral of interest. The greater demand has unfortunately but inevitably led to a general rise in prices and has set gun collecting among the more expensive hobbies open to the public but although this has restricted many enthusiasts to an academic approach to the subject, it has not reduced interest to any great degree. It is hoped that both the active collector and the student will find something to interest them in these pages.

Friends have helped in many ways in the production of this book, not least by lending valuable items to be photographed and I gladly record my debt to them. Particularly valuable has been the professional skill and patience of Paul Forrester, who took so much trouble over the colour plates. The superb quality of his work speaks for itself.

Frederick Wilkinson.

BIBLIOGRAPHY

THE following is a list of the principal sources consulted in writing these *Signatures*:

J. A. Atkinson
Duelling Pistols, London, 1964.

H. L. Blackmore
British Military Firearms 1650-1850, London, 1961.

H. L. Blackmore
Royal Sporting Guns at Windsor, London (H.M.S.O.), 1968.

H. L. Blackmore
Guns and Rifles of the World, London, 1965.

C. Blair
European and American Arms, London, 1962.

C. Blair
Pistols of the World, London, 1968.

G. Boothroyd
Gun Collecting, London, 1961.

A. M. Carey
English, Irish & Scottish Firearms Makers, Reprint, London, 1967.

J. Dunlap
American, British and Continental Pepperbox Firearms, San Francisco, 1964.

W. B. Edwards
The Story of Colt's Revolver, Pennsylvania, 1953.

R. E. Gardner
Small Arms Makers, New York, 1963.

W. W. Greener
The Gun and its Development, London, 1910.

J. Hayward
European Firearms, Victoria & Albert Museum, London, 1955.

J. Hayward
The Art of the Gunmaker, (2 volumes), London, 1963 and 1965.

R. Held
The Age of Firearms, New York, 1957.

H. J. Kauffmann
Early American Gunsmiths 1650-1850, Pennsylvania, 1952.

J. D. Lavin
A History of Spanish Firearms, London, 1965.

T. Lenk
The Flintlock: Its Origin and Development, London, 1965.

M. Lindsay
One Hundred Great Guns, London, 1968.

Sir J. Mann
Wallace Collection Catalogue of European Arms and Armour, London, 1962.

W. K. Neal
Spanish Guns and Pistols, London, 1955.

W. K. Neal & D. H. L. Back
The Mantons—Gunmakers, London, 1967.

G. C. Neumann
The History of Weapons of the American Revolution, New York and London, 1967.

H. Ommundsen & E. H. Robinson
Rifles and Ammunition, London, 1915.

J. E. Parsons
The Peace-Maker and its Rivals, New York, 1950.

H. L. Peterson
Book of the Gun, London, 1963.

H. L. Peterson, Ed.
The Encyclopedia of Firearms, London, 1964.

H. Ricketts
Firearms, London, 1962.

P. Riling
The Powder Flask Book, Pennsylvania, 1953.

C. H. Roads
The British Soldier's Firearm 1850-64, London, 1964.

J. E. Serven
Colt Firearms 1836-1960, California, 1960.

"Stonehenge" (J. M. Walsh)
The Shotgun and Sporting Rifle, London, 1859.

A. W. F. Taylerson
Revolving Arms, London, 1967.

A. W. F. Taylerson
The Revolver 1865-1888, London, 1966.

F. Wilkinson
Small Arms, London, 1965.

F. Wilkinson
Flintlock Pistols, London, 1969.

H. F. Williamson
Winchester—The Gun that Won the West, Washington D.C. 1952.

L. Wilson
Samuel Colt Presents, Hartford, Connecticut, 1962.

L. Winant
Early Percussion Firearms, New York, 1959; London, 1961.

L. Winant
Firearms Curiosa, New York, 1955; London, 1961.

1

Matches and Powder

BLACK was the colour of the devil; all accounts of him speak of his sulphurous smell, and hell was a place of fire and smoke. It is not surprising, therefore, that to the people of the Middle Ages gunpowder was indeed an invention of the Antichrist. Not only was it a black powder, but it also contained sulphur—what further proof was needed? With a loud roar and a dense cloud of smoke, a small projectile of metal or stone could be sent hurtling through the air to bring death and destruction over a wide area. The introduction of gunpowder into Western Europe dramatically changed the face of warfare. Prior to the 14th century a soldier or an archer needed to practice in order to acquire some skill with weapons; but the new firearms required little actual skill, only a measure of good luck. With this new weapon in his hand the clumsiest, most wretched peasant could strike down the mightiest and best armed knight in the land.

The origin of this terrible discovery has long been debated by firearms historians. Its first use has been erroneously dated by some of the earlier writers as going back to the Ancient Greeks, or the early Hindus; and even today, taking into account the latest research, the early history is still not at all certain. The problem is bedevilled by a lack of written evidence, and the confusion over the interpretation of some terms used by very early chroniclers writing on war and its weapons. To the early researchers artillery meant only one thing—cannon; but in fact the term was used to cover any form of missile-throwing weapon, be it catapult, *trebuchets* or large crossbow. There was similar confusion over technical terms used by writers in Chinese and Arabic; thus many of the early writers were led into errors of fact through mistranslations.

Distinction must first be made between gunpowder and incendiary materials, for compounds of various kinds had been used to start fires by the armies of the ancient civilisations. The most renowned was that known as Greek Fire which, despite its name, came not from Greece but from Byzantium. Early references suggest it was first used in the 7th century A.D. but, despite exhaustive research, its composition is still not agreed today. It probably contained some form of petroleum, and tradition has it that it could be extinguished only by vinegar, urine or sand. However there is no evidence to suggest a link between Greek Fire and the later gunpowder.

The most extensive modern research, particularly that by Professor J. Partington, indicates that gunpowder (or at least a mixture of saltpetre, sulphur, charcoal and other chemicals) was known to the Chinese in the early part of the 11th century. Its explosive power was very limited and it would seem unlikely that it was used as an effective propellant but rather to provide noise, flash and smoke. However, once the

Fig. 1: A crude Oriental three-barrelled hand gun; a wooden stock fitted into the rear of the breach. The large touchhole is clearly visible. Overall length, 7 inches. (*See Plate 2.*)

concept had been grasped the inventive Chinese naturally began to experiment and about a hundred years afterwards, sometime around 1130, they produced their *Hou Chi'ang*, which was some form of tube. Made of paper or bamboo and reinforced by binding or metal bands, the cylinder could be packed with crude gunpowder, topped with a projectile and the powder ignited by some means, to form a very simple firearm. Experiments continued, and by the middle of the 13th century it is fairly certain that the Chinese were using gunpowder composed of proportions of saltpetre, charcoal and sulphur very similar to those used later in Europe. The Chinese also seem to have produced (quite independently, for contact between the East and West was very limited) a form of cast iron cannon dating from *circa* 1356.

IF gunpowder was discovered in China, how did knowledge of it first reach Europe? It would seem that the Arabs were largely responsible for this important contact. One Arabic document dating from the first half of the 14th century is illustrated with drawings of soldiers using a tube-like weapon to discharge either balls or arrows. The shapes correspond closely with the earliest form of firearm in this country. Thus it seems likely that the knowledge of gunpowder reached Europe via the Arabs; but if this is the case, when did it happen? The answer is not at all clear. Some works by Mark the Greek, who is supposed to have lived during the 8th century, contain formulae which used saltpetre, but there are very good reasons for believing that these references were, in fact, inserted at a much later date. In 13th century Cologne lived Albertus Magnus, who wrote a book on the marvels of the world which proved a best seller and ran into numerous editions in the 15th century. Few editions correspond exactly and there is every indication that many of the formulae for gunpowder included are later amendments.

Another name which is frequently mentioned in discussions on the early history of gunpowder is that of Roger Bacon, an Oxford lecturer who wrote several scientific books around the middle of the 13th century. In a printed version of one of his books dating from 1618 there appears a section which one historian interprets as containing an anagram for the formula of gunpowder. However, the chapter in question does not appear in the earliest recorded version of Bacon's work, and another manuscript dating from the 15th century contains a different version of the anagram, so again the

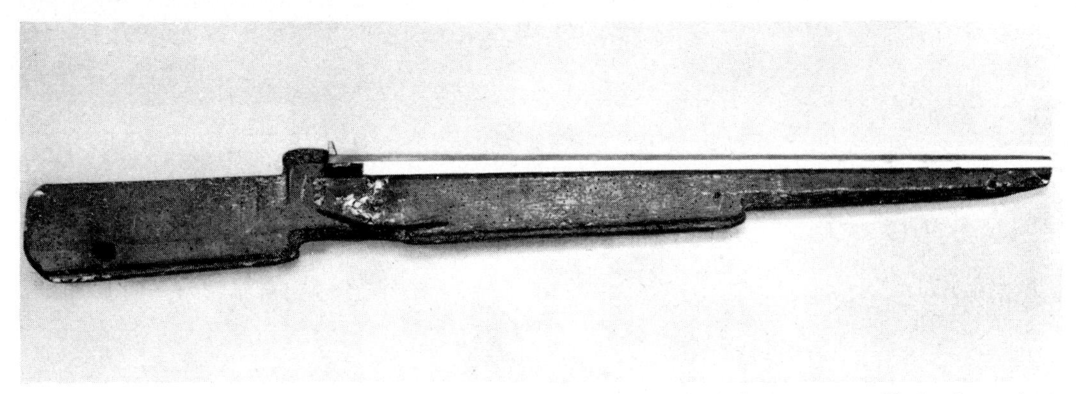

Fig. 2: An early 16th century matchlock of very basic design, with a bronze barrel; note that the lock is missing from this early example. Overall length, 42 inches; barrel, 29½ inches. (Tower of London.)

matter is open to doubt. Despite this confusion over the question of the anagram, it is apparent from Bacon's comments that he was familiar with the effects of gunpowder. He states that if a mixture of saltpetre, sulphur and hazelwood charcoal is enclosed in a parchment tube and fired it produces a loud noise and a terrible flash. He also explains that if the container is made of more solid material the explosive force is much greater.

Although there are good grounds for believing that the explosive properties of gunpowder were well understood by the middle of the 13th century there is no indication that this knowledge was successfully applied to the production of firearms for at least 60 years. In China this delay between the acquisition of the knowledge and the application of its powers was even longer. The commonest version of the origin of the gun is one which has been current since the 15th century. This legend describes dramatically how a monk, Berthold by name, was working in his laboratory when he pounded together the ingredients of gunpowder. An accidental spark was struck which ignited the powder, and the explosion blew the pestle from his hand, thus implanting the idea of using this power to send a projectile through the air. The story is a good one but recent research casts serious doubts on the very existence of the monk himself, although he is honoured by a statue erected in Frieburg.

It is Italy that supplies the first irrefutable evidence of the use of firearms, for in 1326 it is recorded that the City of Florence authorised the employment of two men whose job was to produce cannon, metal bullets and arrows for the defence of towns and villages within the republic of Florence. In the same year the learned Chaplain of Edward III, Walter de Milemete, produced two manuscripts for the instruction of the king. One was a copy of a book by Aristotle and the second was a hand-book on the nobility and wisdom of kings. In the borders of both manuscripts appear the earliest pictures of a firearm, although the text carries no mention of them. The two vase-shaped weapons are shown resting, apparently unsecured on some form of trestle table and from the open necks protrude arrows—in one the head only is visible, in the second the entire arrow can be seen. By comparing them with the knights in the picture the length of one may be estimated at about four feet while the other seems to be some six or seven feet long. In both cases mailed knights are shown firing the weapon by means of a long thin rod. At first glance the shape might seem to be imaginative

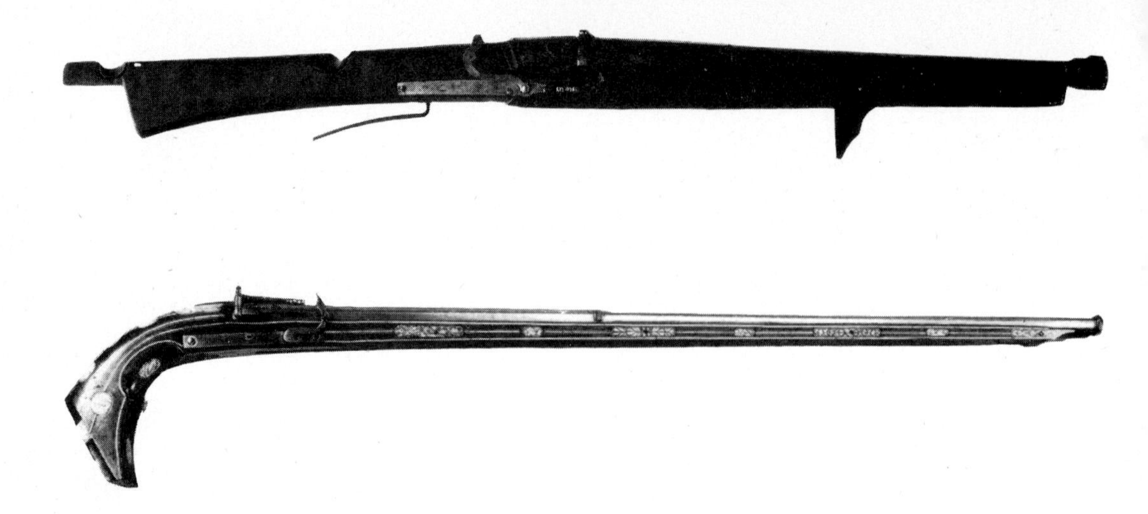

Top, *Fig. 3: Matchlock with bronze barrel and hooked stock, the match-holder operated by a lever. Overall length, 35½ inches. (Historiches Museum, Berne.) Fig. 4 shows a French matchlock of about 1595; this very heavy piece would have been used with a rest. Barrel, 50½ inches. (Tower of London.)*

and distinctly odd, but references in both Italian and French documents offer supporting evidence for this shape. Even more striking evidence was provided by the discovery of an actual example in Sweden in 1861. The Swedish gun is very much smaller than those in the Milemete illustrations, only some 12 inches long; it is cast in bronze and was presumably intended as a handgun, which would suggest that it is of a later date than those illustrated, for reasons we shall see later.

FROM 1340 onwards European records carry an increasing number of references to firearms of various types. Since these references merely use the word "cannon" it may reasonably be assumed that the writers thought everybody would understand exactly what was meant. This implies that cannon were not, at that date, strikingly unusual or else some further details might have been included. Thus one may deduce that firearms probably made their first appearance during the first quarter of the 14th century and were no longer great novelties by the end of this period. It is interesting to note that in 1346 there is a reference in the English Privy Wardrobe Accounts which speaks of guns with "tillers". In crossbows the word tiller was applied to the long wooden central arm, so this reference implies that by 1346, in England at least, there was some primitive form of handgun comprising a barrel fitted to a wooden stock. It must be pointed out that the term "handgun" has not been traced as occurring any earlier than 1388. The earliest form of handgun seems to have been a small version of the cannon cast in bronze or wrought iron and secured with iron bands or leather thongs to the end of a long pole. The earlier vase shaped barrel was soon replaced by a more cylindrical type and as the century progressed no doubt it became apparent that the length of barrel had some bearing on the accuracy of the weapon, and the illustrations indicate that the barrels were gradually lengthened. Early illustrations show

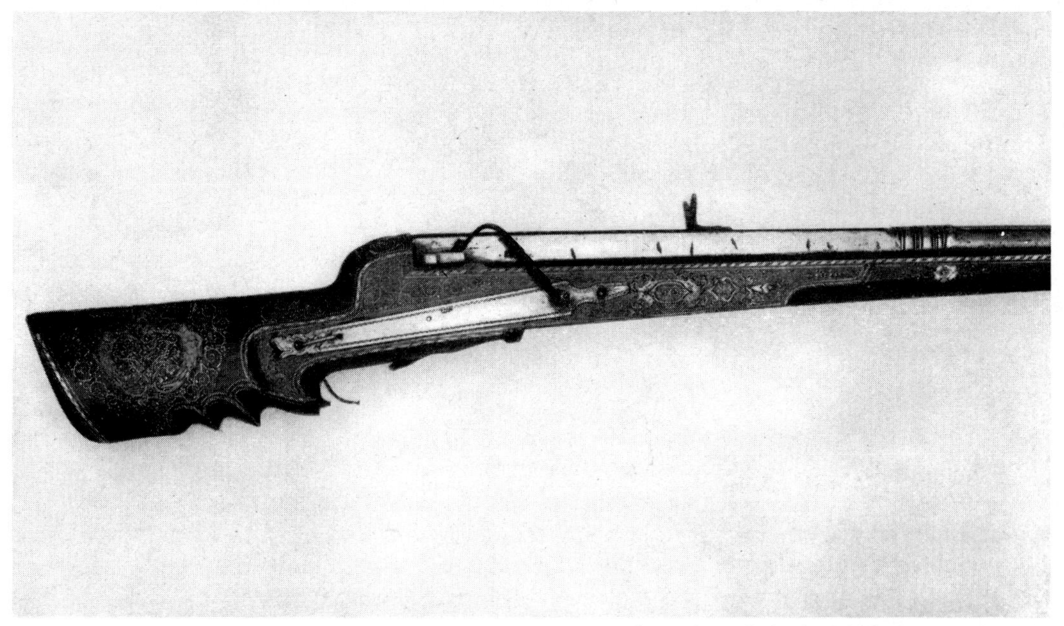

Fig. 5: A harquebus of the late 16th century, the stock decorated with ivory inlay. Barrel, 48 inches. (Tower of London.)

them with stocks that are quite straight, which must have made aiming almost impossible. By the end of the 15th century the stock had begun to acquire a butt. Soldiers are shown firing the weapon from the shoulder, which suggests that they must have been able to take some sort of aim.

A more sophisticated variety of the handgun was the all-metal single-piece weapon. Here the wooden stock was replaced by an extension to the breech which often terminated in a ring through which a cord might be passed, allowing the weapon to be slung around the neck when not required. A third type of handgun was affixed to the wooden stock by means of a socket at the breech into which the tiller was fastened; some of these were cast in elaborate forms to judge by extant examples.

Most early forms of handgun had a downward projecting hook fitted to the stock or beneath the barrel, and this was to allow the firer to rest the weapon over a wall or pallisade while firing. The hook reduced and absorbed a great deal of kick back, or recoil. The German name for such weapons was *Hakenbusche*—hook gun—from which the English word "arquebus" was derived.

It was no easy matter to load and fire one of these weapons. Powder was first poured down the barrel, and then a wad or the ball itself was rammed firmly down on top of the powder. From the centre of a small saucer-like depression on the outside of the barrel a tiny hole connected with the main charge of powder inside the barrel; a small pinch of fine gunpowder, the priming, was placed in the depression. A glowing spark or hot wire was then touched to the priming, the powder flared up, the flame passed through the touchhole to the main charge inside the barrel, which then exploded expelling the bullet. In the case of stationary artillery the firing of the priming was done by means of a piece of red hot coal or a heated rod or wire. For the foot soldier this presented a serious problem; after all it is no easy matter to go into battle holding a

Fig. 6: This German matchlock rifle of 1598 has peep sights, and elaborate inlay decoration on the stock. Overall length, 48½ inches; barrel, 38 inches. (Reproduced by permission of the Trustees of the Wallace Collection.)

red hot iron which, of course, would cool just at the moment it was needed. It seems likely that the Milemete knights are using such a heated iron to fire their gun, but how the ordinary infantryman coped is not known. Possibly a piece of smouldering coal, tinder, or moss was placed inside the end of a tube to provide the means of ignition.

The early gunner not only had to carry his rod, which was awkward enough, but he had to keep it alight. Some unknown genius, probably late in the 14th century, thought of using a slow-burning match to ignite the priming. This was nothing more or less than a piece of cord which had been soaked in one of a variety of solutions, most of which contained saltpetre. When the dry match was lit it burnt very slowly with a glowing end. This meant that the gunner was now able to move about independent of any sources of fire other than his match. There still remained the problem of handling the match and placing the end into the priming at the crucial moment, not an easy task if the wind was blowing or the hand was shaking! At an unknown date another nameless inventor introduced the idea of a mechanical positioner, which consisted simply of an S-shaped piece of metal fastened at the side of the stock. One end was split so that the match could be clipped into place. The arm was pivoted at the centre, and the lower half of the "S" projected beneath the stock. When the lower end was pressed back and upwards it caused the other end to tilt forward and downwards and deposited the glowing end of the match in the priming. This arm, because of its sinuous, snake-like shape was named the "serpentine". When it was first introduced is not known, but it is illustrated in a manuscript of 1411.

Now that the gunner had both hands free it was easier to aim the weapon, and there was a gradual improvement in the shape of the stock to make it sit more comfortably against the shoulder; it was for this reason that the flattened part of the stock, the butt, was given a curved end. But however comfortable the stock might be, it was no easy matter to aim the weapon, for in the early guns the touch hole and the match were positioned on top of the barrel. A natural step was to place the touch-hole and priming at the side of the barrel, but in order to do this an extra platform or lug had to be fastened to the side of the barrel, the touch-hole terminating at this lug which now held the small saucer-like depression. There was still one problem to be overcome, for the fine powder used in the priming was subject to the least breeze; and quite early on a pan cover was fitted which could be slipped over the priming when it was not required. Prior to firing, the pan cover was pushed aside, allowing a clear passage for the glowing end of the match.

The serpentine represented a considerable improvement but it was not without

Plate 1 *A bronze hand gun found at Loshult in Sweden. Early 14th century. Length, 11¾ inches. (National Historical Museum, Stockholm.)*

Plate 2 *A rare three-barrelled hand gun, originally mounted on a short wooden pole. Length, 7 inches; barrel, 3¾ inches. (Blackmore Collection.)*

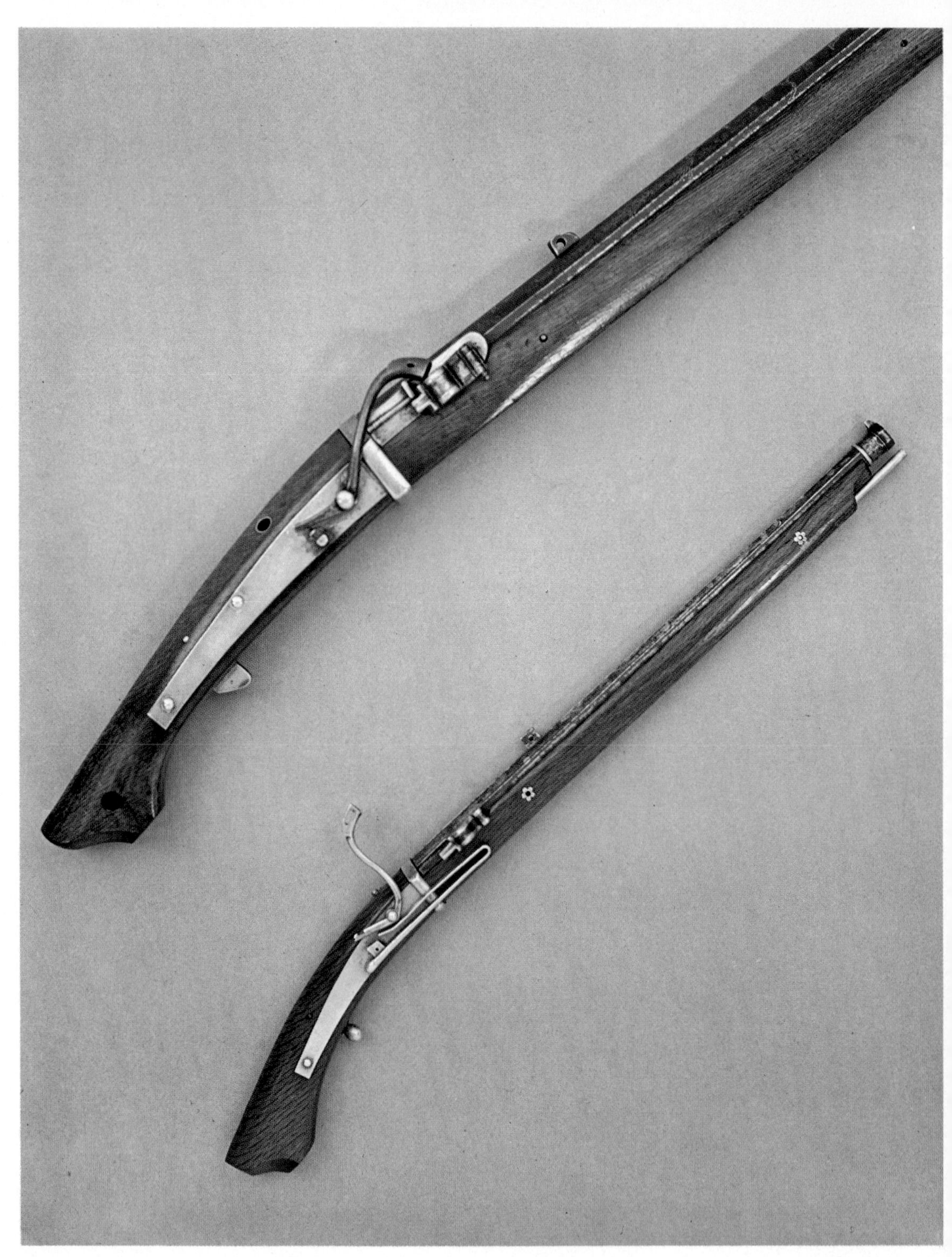

Plate 3 *Two Japanese matchlocks; rather thick barrels and short, stubby stocks and butts are typical characteristics of early Japanese firearms. As on the mainland of Asia, the matchlock continued in widespread use in Japan long after the system had been abandoned in the west.* (*Durrant Collection.*)

its drawbacks, the angle of movement required to swing the match into the priming being quite considerable, so that it was a natural step to devise ways to reduce the movement required. In the last quarter of the 16th century there appeared two types of lock which required only the movement of a finger to depress the match into the priming.

The snaplock was a potentially dangerous system, for the top section of the serpentine which held the match (the cock) was at rest with the match pressed into the pan. When the match was glowing nicely it was fastened into the cock, which could then be pulled back and locked in place by a simple spring and catch arrangement. The pan was then primed and the gun was ready for firing. To release the cock a small stud, usually situated in a recess under the stock, was pressed and the catch was withdrawn. The spring then pressed the cock forward and down to engage the burning match with the priming. The entire mechanism was mounted on a separate metal plate which was attached to the stock, the latter being recessed to house the internal mechanism. The obvious danger of accidental discharge with the snaplock soon made it unpopular and a second system, the ordinary matchlock, became the most common. In this system the cock was normally at rest in the raised position, away from the pan; the cock was connected, internally, to a small link which was in turn coupled to a long arm. The lower section of this arm projected below the stock, and gentle pressure on this longer lever arm was sufficient to tip the cock down into the priming. This system was not without its disadvantages, for the long projecting sear required only slight pressure to cause an accidental firing. There was also a certain amount of difficulty in fitting the mechanism into the wooden stock, and soon it was replaced by the trigger mechanism. The pivot of the arm was moved forward so that a smaller movement by the trigger, a separate unit, was sufficient to activate the cock.

Fig. 7: The lock of a very fine early 17th century matchlock; note the peep sights, the pivoted pan cover and the mother of pearl inlay work. (Perry Collection.)

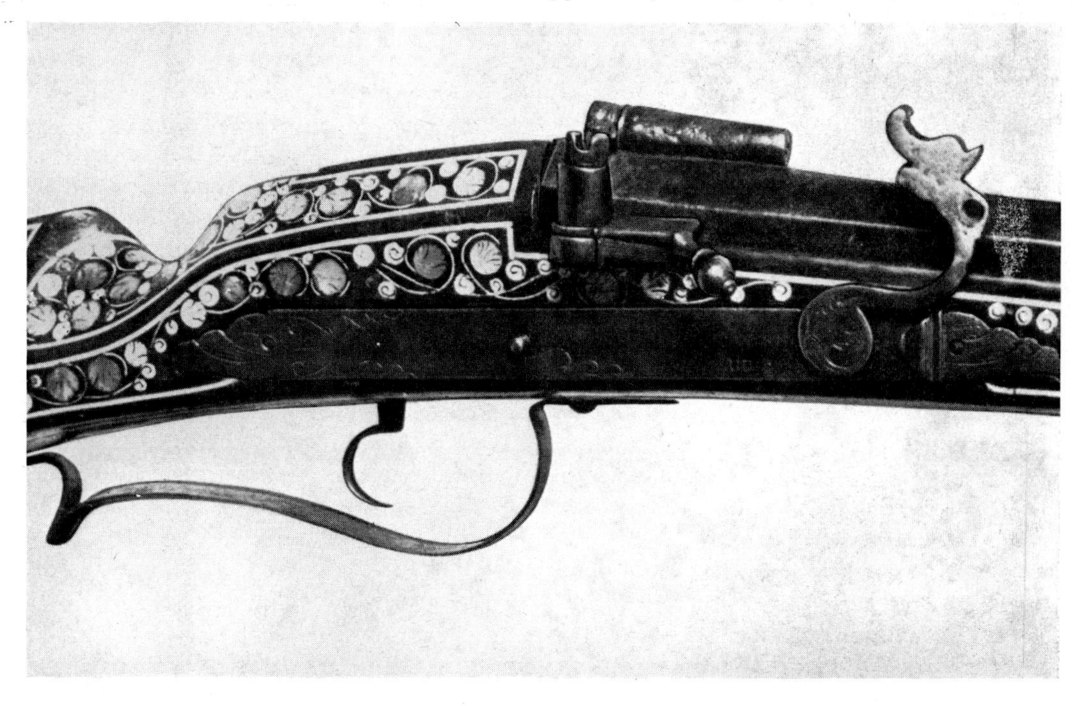

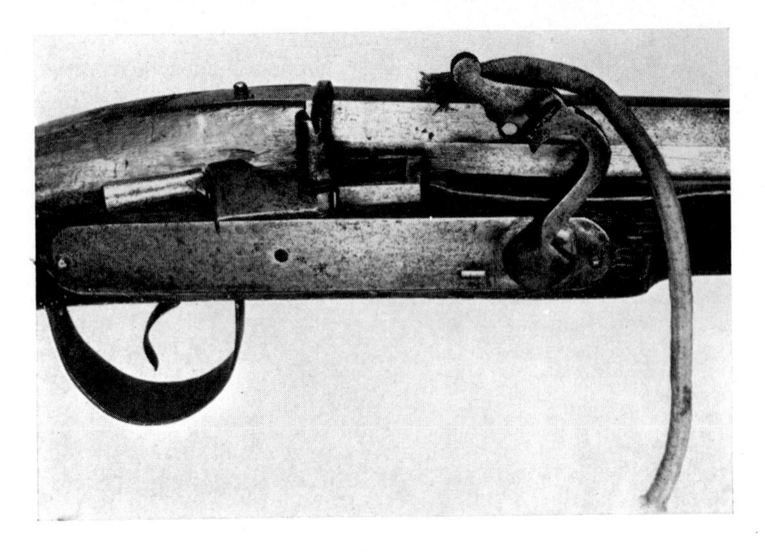

Fig. 8: The simple lock of an early 17th century military matchlock; compare with Fig. 7. (Dominion Museum, New Zealand.)

The smaller trigger was far less susceptible to accidental knocks and further protection was given by the introduction of a trigger guard—a bar of metal shaped to curve around the trigger. The trigger guard remains in use on most firearms up to the present day.

THE matchlock mechanism as described above remained basically unaltered for the whole of the period for which it continued in use. There were minor improvements in design; the cock was improved by the addition of a threaded screw which could be adjusted to hold the match firmly in position, and triggers were altered slightly in shape. Most European matchlocks have the cock situated at the front of the lock plate and swinging backwards towards the butt, whereas with most Asian and African weapons the reverse is the case. One important development in the 17th century was the fixing of the pan and pan cover to the lock plate instead of the barrel, which was now completely free of any extraneous projections apart from the sights. These were often of the peep type with a small tube fitted above the breech of the barrel. The method of securing the barrel had altered; instead of it being secured to the stock by external bands, small lugs were brazed to the underside which fitted into recesses cut into the top of the stock, a pin passed through the stock and the lug holding it firmly in place. This method of fixing was to remain in general use in England until well into the 19th century, although in America and parts of Europe there was a return to the external band system.

The matchlock was essentially a simple weapon to produce and use and was, therefore, provided in quantity for the majority of the European armies. Weapons were produced in a variety of sizes and it is not easy to be sure about the names of the various classes of weapons, for contemporary writers themselves disagree. Best known was the musket, and this is generally taken to refer to the heavier type of portable firearm—portable in the sense that it was not used for wall defence; weapons for this purpose were usually known as the *arquebus à croc* and were very large indeed. The derivation of the word musket has also been disputed, but the majority opinion is that it derives from the Italian word meaning a hawk (*moschetto*). The musket was heavy enough to require some form of support, and this was provided by a pole fitted with a U-shaped metal arm at the top and a spike at the bottom. The musket first appeared

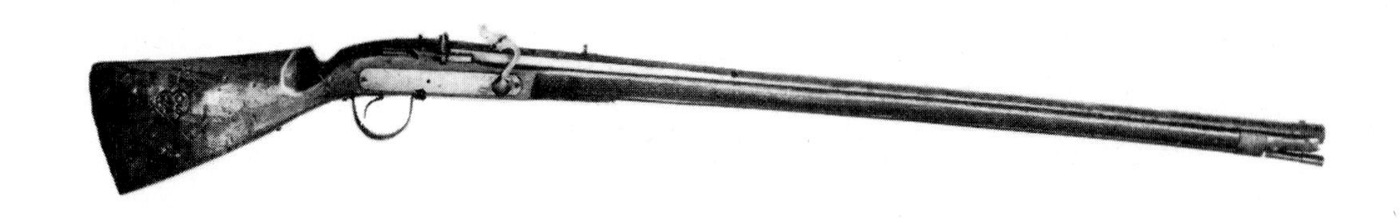

Fig. 9: Overall view of the arm illustrated in Fig. 8; this weapon is typical of matchlock muskets of the period. (Dominion Museum, New Zealand.)

during the latter part of the first quarter of the 16th century. The barrel of the musket was some four feet long, and it fired a ball which was approaching one inch in diameter—12 balls weighed one pound. Smaller in size, with a 39 inch barrel, was the "caliver"; the shorter, lighter barrel allowed the firer to dispense with the rest. In 1630 official regulations were set down defining the size and bore of the various weapons, and two smaller weapons are listed; the "harquebus", which had a 30 inch barrel but fired the same size ball as a caliver; and the carbine, or "petronel", which had the same size barrel as the harquebus but fired a smaller ball.

The wooden body or stock was of two main types. The so-called French style closely resembled a hockey stick, with the butt curving down at a fairly acute angle. Such weapons were aimed with the end of the butt resting on the chest and were known originally as petronels, but this term was increasingly used for any light firearm carried by a horseman. Differing greatly from the French stock was the "Spanish" style which had an essentially straight line with the butt drooping only slightly and the waist (that part of the butt just behind the breech) recessed to allow the thumb to sit comfortably over the top. This recess was gradually deepened, and the stock began to acquire the more or less conventional shape, with the butt wide at the heel, tapering towards the small of the butt just behind the trigger and the stock continuing straight along under the barrel.

The majority of matchlocks were plain and lacked any special decoration. A few, particularly those belonging to special groups such as bodyguards or the "trained bands" of towns and cities, were often decorated with inlaid sections with patterns of stag horn or mother of pearl. A few, apparently made for rich patrons, were further decorated with elaborate chiselling on the barrels and decorations on the stock.

THE musketeer of the 17th century had an unenviable task, as his equipment was heavy and cumbersome. The musket measured well over five feet in total length and the caliver some four and a half feet. Since the musketeer carried a rest as well as his heavy musket it was no easy matter to march for any distance. He needed a supply of gunpowder, and this he carried in a powder horn which was made from a section of cow-horn which had been softened by boiling and then pressed into a narrow, flattened, open-ended shape. One end was closed by a block of wood or metal cover and to the

IDGheyn in
1

Opposite, *Fig. 10:* 'The Musketeer'—*drawn by Jacob De Gheyn in 1607; this print shows the gunner's full equipment including powder and priming flasks, bullet bag, spare match, bandolier and rest.*

narrow end was fitted an ingeniously designed spout, which allowed just the right amount of powder through each time a side spring was pressed. These powder horns were suspended from a cord around the neck to hang down to one side of the musketeer. An alternative method of carrying gunpowder consisted of a number of wooden containers each holding just the correct amount of powder for one charge, suspended from a leather belt across the musketeer's chest. Bandoliers such as these were convenient but noisy, as any movement of the musketeer made them rattle one against the other. In addition to the main-charge gunpowder the musketeer required a supply of finer grained powder for the priming, and this was normally carried in a small powder flask also suspended from a sling across his shoulder. The bullets were carried in a leather pouch or loose in the pocket. When going into battle speed was likely to be essential, and the musketeer often placed several bullets in his mouth. By the early 17th century the majority of bullets were lead balls, but this had not always been the case; earlier hand guns had fired iron, steel and brass balls. These had not always been spherical, as experiments had flourished and many bullets had been of distinctly unusual shapes. Lead offered certain advantages in that it had a moderately low melting point and therefore did not present too great a problem to the musketeer when casting the bullets.

As may be imagined the loading and firing of the musket and the caliver were very complicated matters. Before going into action the musketeer carefully lit both ends of his match, to be on the safe side. The working end was clipped into the serpentine and the musketeer was ready. Once the charge in the musket had been fired there was a long and complicated sequence to be followed. In order to prevent accidents the glowing match was detached from the serpentine and was now gripped between the fingers of the left hand. The musketeer poured down the barrel the correct charge of powder, then the ball was forced home with the ramrod or scouring stick, which was normally housed in a recess cut in the wooden stock beneath the barrel. The ball had to sit firmly on top of the powder because a space here was likely to have dangerous consequences, possibly bursting the barrel. The scouring stick was then removed from the barrel and returned to its recess in the stock. Now the pan cover was opened and a pinch of the finer priming powder placed inside and re-covered, any spare grains of

Fig. 11: A fine Italian arm with combined wheellock and matchlock mechanism; this gun, which has some curious decorative work on the stock, is reputed to have belonged to Louis XIII of France. Overall length, 44 inches; barrel, 32¾ inches. (Wallace Collection.)

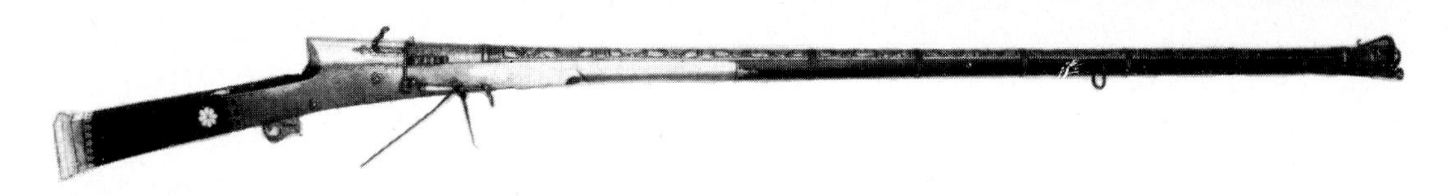

Fig. 12: An Indian matchlock of the 18th century. The matchlock ignition system continued in use in the Orient until quite recent times. Overall length, 64 inches. (Wallace Collection.)

powder being carefully blown away. The match was returned to the serpentine and blown or trimmed until it was glowing nicely; the spare end was also checked and trimmed, and the musketeer was now ready for the second shot. However, if there was any appreciable delay between the loading and firing then he would almost certainly need to adjust and check the match; as it burned down it was essential to pull it further through the jaws of the serpentine, or it would extinguish itself. This whole procedure had to be repeated on every occasion the weapon was fired.

Obviously this long and complicated process occupied some considerable time even with the best training in the world, and during this time the musketeer was completely defenceless and open to attack by cavalry or enemy infantry. In order to give him some protection it became the custom for groups of pikemen armed with 16 and 20 foot spears to be stationed in groups amongst the musketeers to guard against charges by the enemy cavalry.

Difficult as all this process was for the musketeer standing firmly on the ground, it would have been as nothing to the problems of handling such a weapon on horseback. Even if the weapon were reduced in size to some 18 or 20 inches length the problems of dealing with the glowing match were too severe to be overcome with any ease. This restriction meant that very few matchlock pistols were made. There were exceptions, however; for example Henry VIII (1509 to 1547) equipped his bodyguard with pistol shields. These comprised a metal buckler, or round shield, through the centre of which protruded the barrel of a small matchlock pistol. Just above the pistol was a barred opening in the shield through which the bodyguard could aim the rather elaborate weapon. It is interesting to note that the pistols in these shields were also breech loading, a system which did not come into common use for another 200 years. These pistols are listed in an inventory of 1547 and a number still survive.

One of the problems facing an army commander in the 17th century was the question of smoke. When the weapons were fired they produced a great deal of thick black smoke and given certain weather conditions, the pall of smoke could quickly cover an entire battlefield. Most of the illustrations of the time show two distinct clouds of smoke, one from the priming in the pan and the other from the barrel.

A more immediate problem for the musketeer was in keeping his match burning at all times when there was any risk of action, no simple task in wind or rain. The only solution produced was a tube pierced with a number of holes which was fitted over the end of the glowing match. It helped, but did not solve the problem. If one end of the match were extinguished then the musketeer could, of course, relight from the other end; but should both ends be put out then it meant stopping, taking out the tinder box, striking sparks and rekindling, all of which took time and might well cost the commander crucial moments of initiative in a battle. Again, the glowing match was a sure indication to the enemy of your size and direction of march. It was practically impos-

Fig. 13: A magnificent German gun of about 1565, with combined wheellock and matchlock mechanism and intricate inlay decoration. Overall length, 46 inches; barrel, 33 inches. (Wallace Collection.)

sible to carry out a night attack, since even ten glowing matches were difficult to miss. The glowing end of the match was a constant danger to all concerned, with powder lying about in barrels or cartridges, or with loose grains scattered on the floor. During a battle the musketeer might well empty his powder flask or the charges in his bandolier. In the heat of the moment it happened more than once that an excited musketeer rushed forward, took his flask or container in his hand and dipped it into the barrel completely forgetting that between his fingers he also held a length of glowing match—a mistake he was unlikely to repeat! Even those with bandoliers were not immune from such accidents and it is recorded on several accounts that musketeers whose carelessly applied match discharged one charge on a bandolier, started off a chain reaction and so demolished not only the bandolier but the musketeer as well!

MANY of the musketeers carried a sword but this was essentially a "last resort" weapon, and if attacked the musketeer was at a considerable disadvantage. True, the pikemen were there to help, but even so the musketeer with his empty weapon was a liability. During the middle of the 17th century the bayonet made its appearance in an attempt to provide the musketeer with some means of defence. The origin of the bayonet is somewhat obscure; the usual derivation given is that of the town of Bayonne which was well known for a kind of knife. Legend has it that during one action the excited inhabitants of the town of Bayonne stuffed the hilts of their knives into the barrels of their useless muskets and rushed forward using them as spears or pikes. There could well be a degree of truth in this story. The earliest reference in Britain occurs around the 1660's, and the bayonets of this period are usually described, from their method of use, as plug bayonets. The blades were normally broad at the base, tapering to a point; some have a flamboyant or wavy edge and most have a cross guard, often of brass and frequently terminating in "angels" or heads. The grip is of polished wood belling out at the guard and tapering towards the far end which again may well be capped in brass. The blades may be inscribed with certain patriotic sentiments. Many were privately made and these tend to be far more elaborate with ivory grips and elaborately carved quillons, cross guard and pommel.

The matchlock was to remain in general use until the latter part of the 17th century, when newer systems of ignition replaced it.

2

Wheels and Keys

THE matchlock was mechanically simple, the only moving parts of the lock mechanism being a simple spring, two or three levers and a link. This made it cheap to produce and capable of repair by almost anybody with some skill in metalwork. It was easy to use and maintain, and therefore recommended itself to the ordinary citizen interested in hunting. However, as has been shown it was subject to several disadvantages both from a military and a civilian point of view. Its efficiency was subject to weather conditions, it was cumbersome, and, above all, it could not be brought into action quickly; in a sudden attack the musketeer could offer no resistance until he had taken out steel and flint and kindled his match.

One solution to the problem was some form of mechanical ignition—a means of producing a flame or spark that did not involve continuous combustion. Man's early discovery of fire was probably accidental but it may safely be assumed that it was not long before he discovered that if certain objects were banged together they could produce a spark. Certainly the possession of such spark-making implements was considered essential for a journey, including the longest journey of all—for in many prehistoric tombs pieces of pyrites and flint have been found buried with the body, sometimes actually in the hand. Flint was to figure prominently in the history of firearms at a slightly later date but first it was the turn of the pyrites. Pyrites is a mineral, a form of sulphide of iron, which occurs in areas all over the world. Its name comes from the Greek word for fire, and it must have been discovered in very early times that when struck with a hard object such as flint it produced a number of sparks glowing dull red. Later, when man had discovered the secret of making iron, the pyrites was replaced by a piece of steel. Flint and steel were to remain in general use as the main method of fire-making until well into the 19th century.

This domestic system of producing a spark was a fairly obvious line of development for the gunsmith and the earliest form of mechanical system was the so-called Monk's gun which was, by tradition, invented by Berthold, the legendary father of European firearms. It consists of an 11-inch barrel thickened slightly at the breech; beneath the barrel there is a hook so that it may be hung from the belt when not in use. On the left side of the barrel is a metal box the rear end of which forms the priming pan. Secured to the forward end of the box is the cock with its long slender neck terminating in two jaws between which was placed a small piece of pyrites. The cock was swung forward until the pyrites was resting on the pan at the end of the side-box. A thin steel rod, notched and roughened on one side like a file, was then pushed into the box parallel with the barrel. The pyrites now rested against one end of the roughened side of this steel rod. After the gun had been loaded and primed the barrel was gripped firmly and a finger slipped through the ring at the end of the steel rod. This was then pulled back quickly making the roughened face rub against the pyrites, producing sparks to ignite the priming and fire the charge. The dating of this unique piece (which is in the Dresden museum) is a difficult matter but it was probably made at some time between the third quarter of the 15th century and the middle of the 16th century. Its action must have been erratic and its accuracy negligible—certainly the jerk as the arm was pulled back must have thrown the thing completely off aim if, indeed, any aim had been taken originally. The entire weapon, if such it be, seems to be unique and it is considered by most students to be a blind alley rather than a step in the main development of the wheellock.

The early history of the wheellock is still uncertain but it would seem that the invention may be credited to Leonardo da Vinci. As is well known, this paragon of the "Renaissance man" was an accomplished musician, artist, architect, sculptor, mechanic, philosopher and engineer. Amongst his many activities was a spell as military advisor to the Duke of Milan, and during his service he sketched and considered a number of militarily feasible schemes. One of his collections of works, known as the

Fig. 14: Three decorative German wheellocks of the late 16th century. The stocks are inlaid with plaques of stag's horn and all have the large ball butt typical of the period. Lengths, 19 to 20 inches. (Reproduced by permission of the Trustees of the Wallace Collection.)

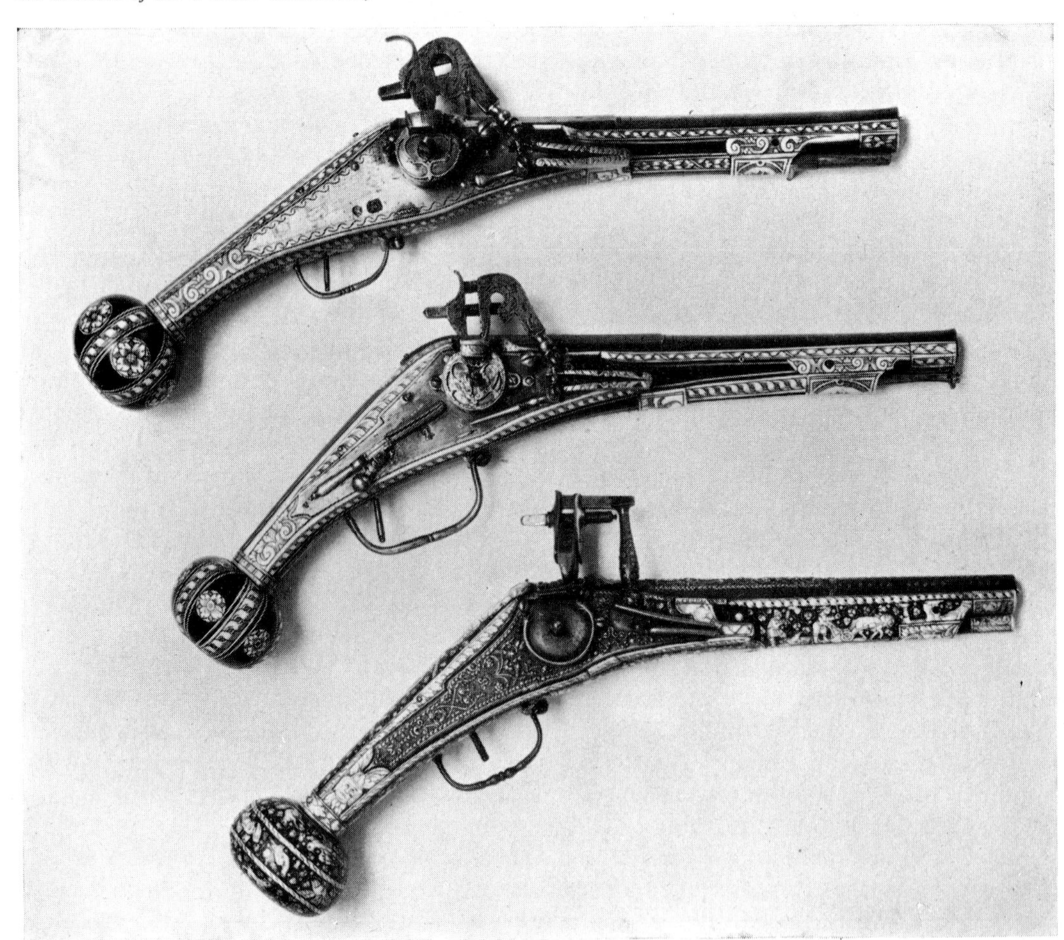

Codex Atlanticus, contains a large number of drawings. Amongst this mass of material are two illustrations which show designs for producing sparks by mechanical means; these may, on good evidence, be dated to about 1500. Whether they were ever made is not known, but modern facsimiles have functioned with reasonable efficiency. The drawings show two mechanisms; one of these consists of a wheel against which is pressed a piece of pyrites. As the wheel was rotated it compressed a coiled spring at which point a small arm, the sear, clicked into position to hold the wheel locked. Pressure on a trigger withdrew the sear allowing the spring to expand and this rotated the wheel so that the friction between the wheel and the pyrites produced a stream of sparks. There is at least one wheellock pistol in Madrid, fitted with this type of coiled spring-lock. However, this is a slightly unusual form and the second system bears a closer resemblance to the wheellock mechanism that was incorporated into firearms of all types. In place of the coiled spring there is a large V-shaped spring, and the sear lever is fitted to the outside of the lock plate. There is a simple lever trigger rather similar to the early matchlock release mechanism; pressure on this forces it against a

Fig. 15: An impressive pair of double-barrelled all-steel wheellock pistols made in Nuremberg, Germany in about 1570. The single trigger fires both locks one after the other. Overall length, 20 inches. (Wallace Collection.)

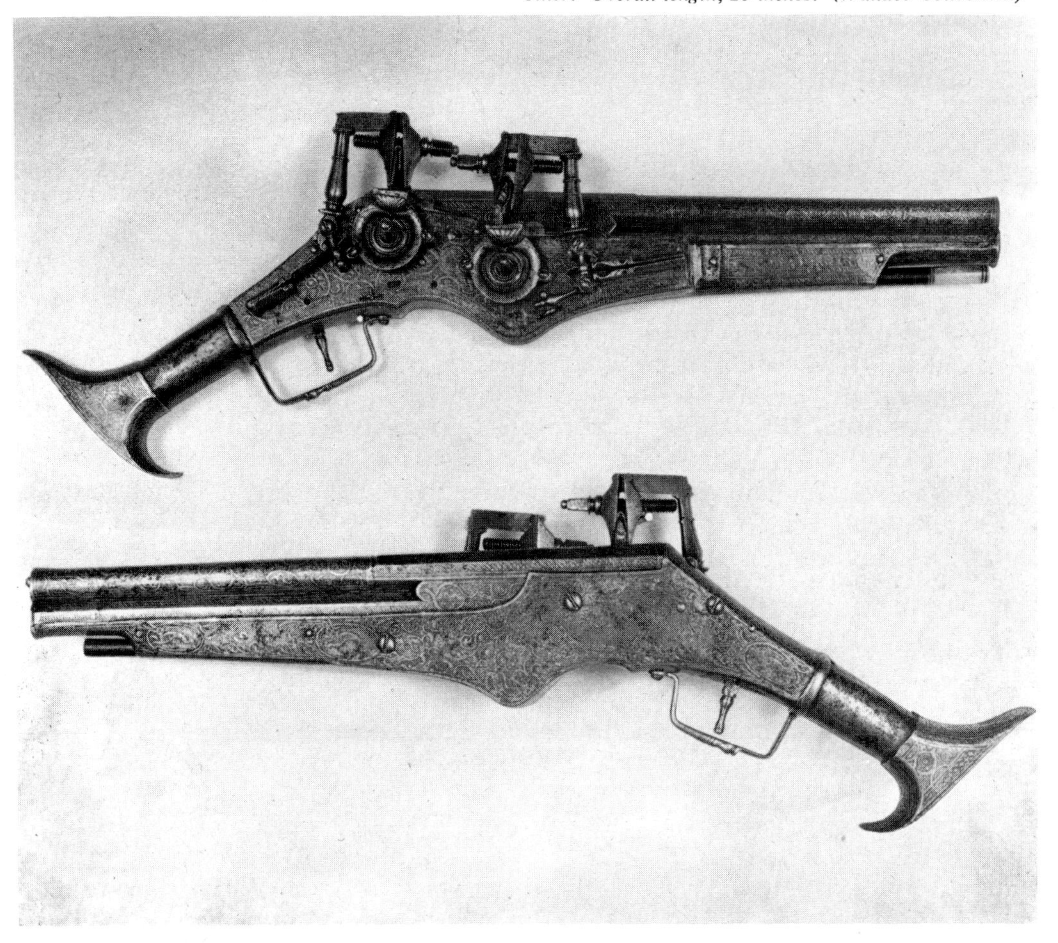

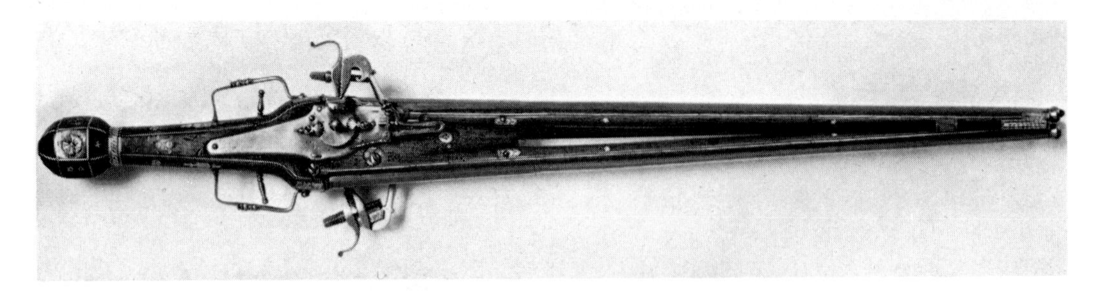

Fig. 16: Double-barrelled wheellock pistol with separate locks and triggers. There is a long steel hook for suspending it at the saddle. This weapon was made in Nuremburg in about 1600. Overall length 34 inches; barrels, 24½ inches. (Wallace Collection.)

triangular shaped section which in turn withdraws the sear and releases the wheel, allowing it to rotate. The pyrites is held between two jaws at the end of a gracefully curved, slim cock.

These are not the only drawings of wheellock mechanisms, for two others occur in a manuscript which was written either for or by a German living in Nuremberg, by name Martin Löffelholz. He died in 1533 but the manuscript bears the date 1505, or to be exact, bore this date, for unfortunately the manuscript has now disappeared. The illustration in question showed two tinder lighters both of which worked on the wheellock principle. One is very simple, with an L-shaped box fitted with wheel and cock holding a piece of pyrites. The motive force for the wheel is provided by a length of string which was wound around the axle as the wheel was turned; a quick jerk on the cord caused the wheel to rotate and so produced sparks from the pyrites. The other tinder lighter or wheellock shown in the Löffelholz manuscript is far more complicated but has many points of similarity with that designed by Leonardo da Vinci. The basic mechanism is the same, with a U-shaped spring, but this time the trigger has been replaced by a small leather thong.

The earliest discovered reference to wheellocks occurs in 1507 when the steward of the Bishop of Zagreb—in present-day Yugoslavia—ordered from Germany a gun which was "kindled by a stone", a description which seems to suggest some form of mechanical lock. The next relevant reference would seem to be one of 1515, when a young man at Augsburg in Germany, apparently wishing to impress a lady of the town,

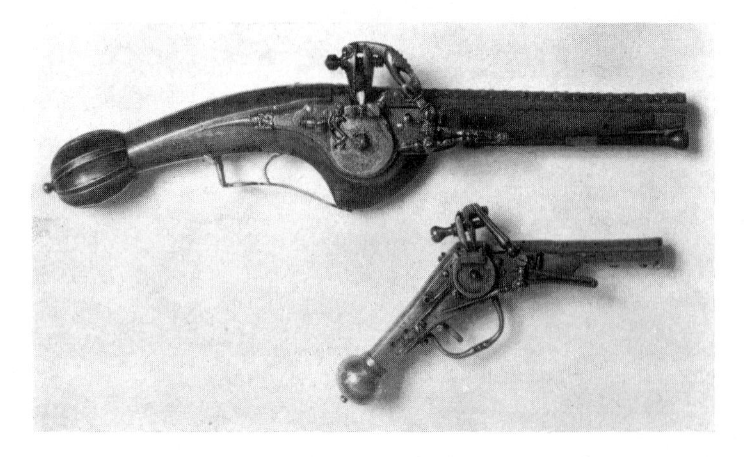

Fig. 17: **Top,** *Wheellock pistol of about 1615 with a silver-decorated barrel; unusual in displaying signs of both French and Italian influence, this piece was probably made in France. Overall length, 13½ inches; barrel, 7¼ inches. (Wallace Collection.)* **Bottom,** *all-steel pocket wheellock pistol made in Augsburg, Germany,* circa *1580. Overall length, 7 inches; barrel, 4¾ inches. (Wallace Collection.)*

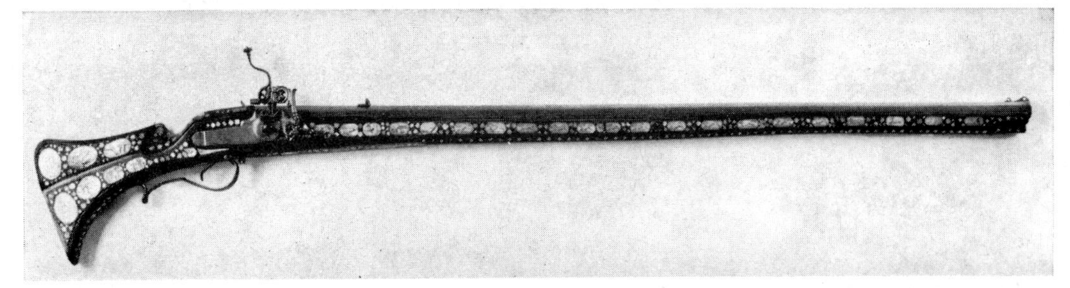

Fig. 18: Long wheellock gun with a Dutch or Flemish barrel dated 1624 but a German lock of about 1680; the shape and style suggest that this was originally a matchlock. Overall length, 60¾ inches; barrel, 48¼ inches. (Wallace Collection.)

was demonstrating to her his latest acquisition—one of the new firearms. He accidentally pressed the trigger and the gun, described as "igniting itself", went off and wounded the woman. It proved an expensive accident, for the woman received some 40 florins compensation and an annual pension of another 20 florins for life, whilst the doctor and other expenses cost a further 77 florins. Since the term "ignited itself" would hardly apply to a matchlock the inference is that some mechanical method of ignition was being used.

The earliest surviving wheellock firearms are Italian and are in the Palazzo Ducale at Venice; they are dual purpose weapons, crossbows fitted with wheellock mechanisms which are screwed to the "tiller" or wooden stock of the crossbow. Unfortunately it is not possible to be certain as to the date but it would appear likely that they were made about 1510 and the style of decoration seems to confirm this dating.

Surprisingly enough the next earliest reference occurs in 1517, when the Emperor Maximilian I (1493—1519) issued an edict which forbade the carrying, in Hapsburg territory, of hand guns "which ignite themselves"—again an apparent reference to wheellocks. Why ban them? The answer lay in the compact readiness of such weapons. The matchlock required considerable preparation and even when loaded, primed and with match glowing it still required attention. The wheellock, once it had been loaded and primed and the dogshead set, remained ready for use for an indefinite period. It was now fairly easy for an assassin to conceal the small pistol and use it at

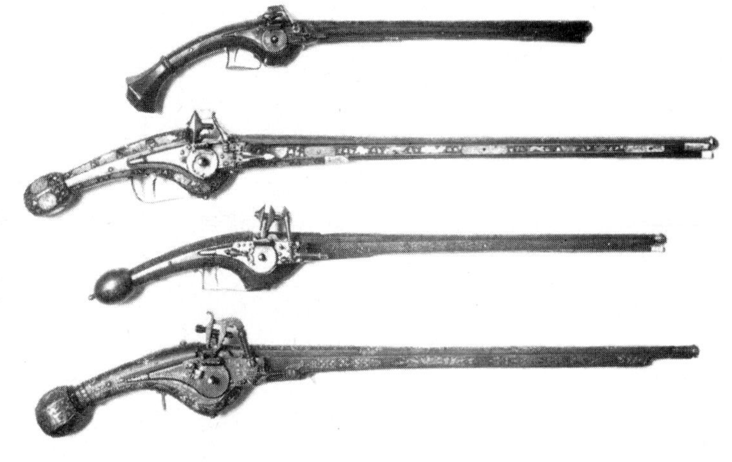

Fig. 19: Four French wheellocks of the early 17th century. **Top to bottom:** *Pistol with octagonal butt and silver wire inlay,* circa *1615; overall length, 22½ inches; barrel, 15½ inches. Wheellock with mother of pearl and stag's horn inlay,* circa *1620; lengths 33¼ inches/25 inches. Pistol of about 1610, originally in armoury of Louis XIII, made by brother of Marin le Borgeoys (see* Signature 3*); lengths 27 inches/19¼ inches. All-steel pistol of about 1600 with gold and silver inlay; lengths 33¾ inches/23¼ inches. (Wallace Collection.)*

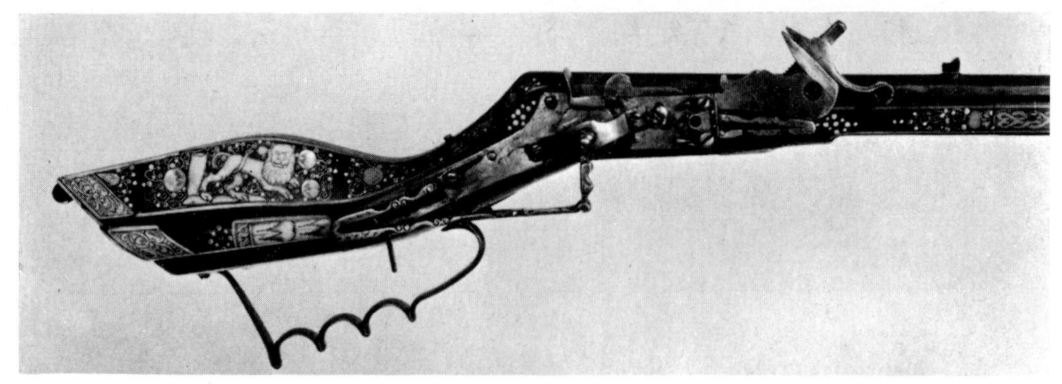

Fig. 20: Graceful Tschinke *of about 1670, with rifled barrel; the mainspring is clearly visible. Overall length, 48 inches; barrel, 37¼ inches. (Tower of London).*

the opportune moment without warning; hence this prohibition. Similar prohibitions are recorded in 1522 in the City of Ferrar, and several other Italian city-states.

By the 1530's the mechanism had acquired most of the features which were to stay in general service for the entire period that wheellocks were used. The mechanism was mounted on a fairly large flat lock plate and on the exposed side could be seen a small V-shaped spring pressing firmly upwards against the tip of an angled arm, at the top of which were two adjustable jaws holding a piece of pyrites. This was the cock, or dogshead, normally fairly simple in design although later examples were sometimes fashioned in rather fantastic forms. The other features sometimes seen on the outside of the lock plate were a variety of studs and knobs which operated some of the sundry safety devices attached to the inside mechanism. This, incidentally, is a reasonably good guide to the date of a wheellock, since the earlier onces tend to have a profusion of knobs and buttons which were gradually reduced in number until weapons made in the latter part of the 17th century have an almost completely uncluttered lockplate.

Inside the lock was the rather complicated mechanism. Although differing in detail, the majority of locks comprised a wheel, probably some quarter of an inch thick, the edge of which was groved and notched. This wheel was secured to a spindle, frequently squared off; one end protruded through the lockplate, the other was secured to a support on the inside. This wheel was attached by means of a small link chain to a large V-spring. A key, with a squared hole, fitted over the exposed end of the spindle and was rotated for approximately three quarters of a revolution. As the wheel turned it compressed the spring until a small spring-loaded arm, the sear, clicked into a recess on the inside of the wheel, locking it in position. The lock was now said to be "spanned". The edge of the wheel formed, in effect, part of the bottom of the priming pan, in which a small amount of priming powder was placed. A sliding lid or cover was pushed over the pan to cover the priming and hold it securely and safely in place. The cock holding the piece of pyrites was now swung forward and down until it rested on top of the pan cover, and the lock was now ready for firing. Pressure on the trigger withdrew the retaining sear; the tension of the spring was transferred via the small link chain to the wheel, which rotated quickly. At the same time another arm automatically pushed clear the pan cover allowing the pyrites to press down on the edge of the wheel. Friction

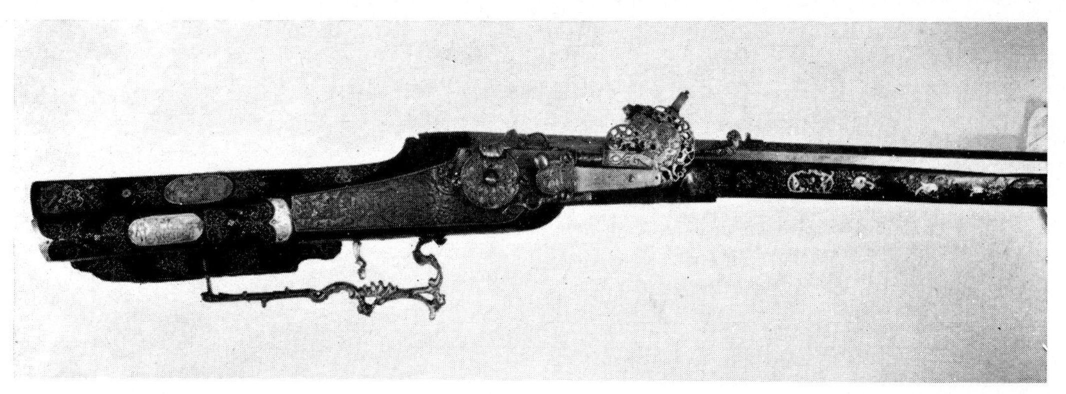

Fig. 21: Superbly decorated wheellock, probably made in Poland; circa *1640. The stock is elaborately inlaid with silver wire, and the trigger guard is intricately fashioned. Note the downwards projecting cheek-piece on the left of the butt. Barrel length, 39½ inches. (Tower of London.)*

between the roughened edge and the pyrites created a shower of sparks which ignited the priming and thence, through the touchhole, the main charge in the barrel. The action was quick and certain but in addition it had the tremendous advantage that the weapon could be loaded, primed, spanned and put to one side ready for action at any time. Leaving loaded weapons about could obviously be dangerous; apart from various safety devices incorporated in the mechanism of some locks, the safest method was simply to swing the dogshead clear so that even if the trigger were pressed and the wheel rotated the pyrites was not in contact and no sparks were produced.

The wheellock was technically somewhat complicated but it could be made in any size. This meant that the gunmaker was no longer restricted to the large, long arms, and could now produce small weapons that fitted comfortably into a pocket. The pistol may have become a practical device, but it still did not become a common weapon, for the mechanism was an expensive item and the cost was a limiting factor. Until this time the cavalry had been prevented from using firearms by the sheer physical inconvenience of trying to manage a large matchlock on a plunging horse. Wheellock pistols could be managed quite easily on horseback although expense prevented general issue and only certain select groups such as bodyguards or other élite units were provided with a pair of wheellocks. The general tactic was for ranks of cavalry to charge the enemy and when within close range to turn, discharge their pistol, swing round and fire the second and then gallop away reloading as they went. This procedure could, in theory, be repeated any number of times.

THE variety of sizes, shapes and designs of wheellock pistols and guns was enormous. As the invention spread from Northern Italy to Germany and the rest of Europe, many countries began to develop an individual national style of their own, recognisable by characteristics of decoration and design. Germany was probably the main producer of wheellock weapons and examples of their exports may be seen in museums all over the world. Although the majority of wheellock pistols were probably made in Germany the name "pistol" is generally taken to derive from the city of Pistoia in Italy, although some hold that it is derived from the name of a coin, or from a Bohemian hand gun known as a *pistala* or pipe. German wheellock pistols are of two main types; the earliest had an almost completely straight stock and butt which often terminated in a small oval-shaped pommel, usually six sided. The second common type has a very sharply angled butt, almost an L-shape and these were frequently fitted with extremely large ball-shaped butts. The butts may be as much as seven inches in diameter but, despite their apparently solid construction, they were in fact very light and secured to the main stock by, at the most, a peg or two. This clearly shows that the old tale of using the butt as a club if the gun failed or when it was empty has little or no foundation. Since most of these wheellock pistols were for horsemen it is far more likely that the large ball was fitted to enable the horseman to draw the weapon from the holster with greater ease and less fumbling.

The stocks of most wheellock pistols tend to be rather fragile. Early lockplates were extremely large but as the makers acquired greater skill the mechanism was reduced in size, as was the lockplate. However, the stock had to be cut to accommodate this mechanism. There was naturally a weakness in the wood at this point and some German makers overcame this problem by constructing the entire stock of metal to give it additional strength.

The great majority of wheellock pistols are beautifully decorated and the plainest group are the military ones used during the 17th century. In fact wheellock pistols had been used by the cavalry as far back as the 1540's, but the plain, everyday weapon only became common during the early part of the 17th century. Such weapons were used by both sides during the English civil wars, 1642-1648, although the high cost of them probably restricted the numbers carried by Parliament's soldiers. Many of these weapons were made in Northern Europe and there is evidence to suggest that very few

Fig. 22: Two German wheellock guns, the top one very plain and the other decorated with stag's horn inlay work depicting foliage and hunting dogs. Circa *1630. (Tower of London.)*

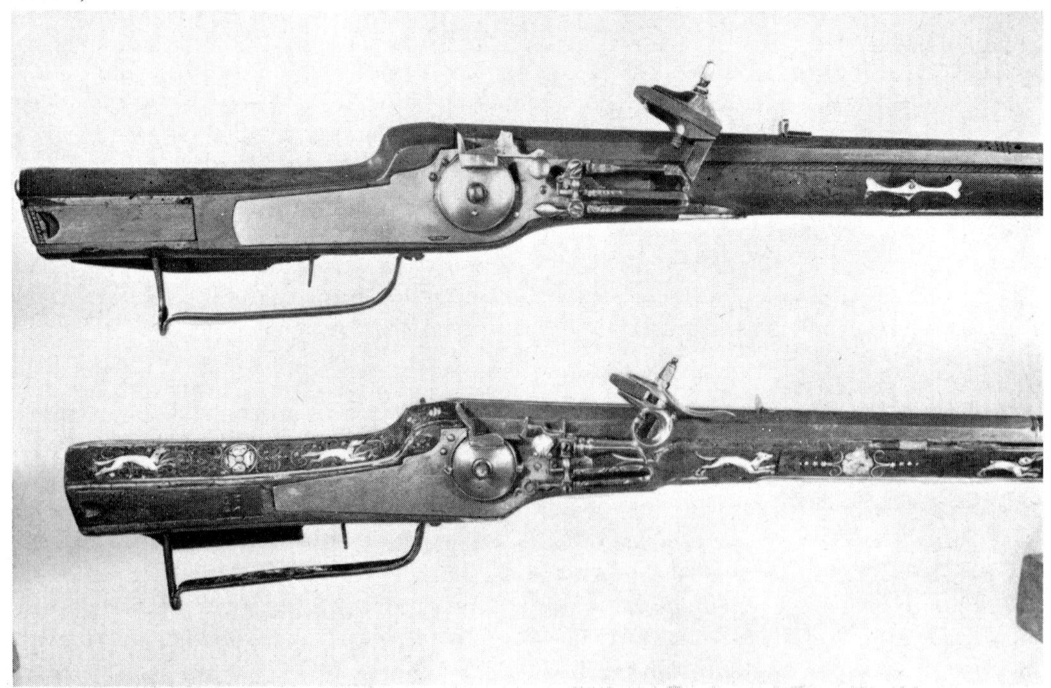

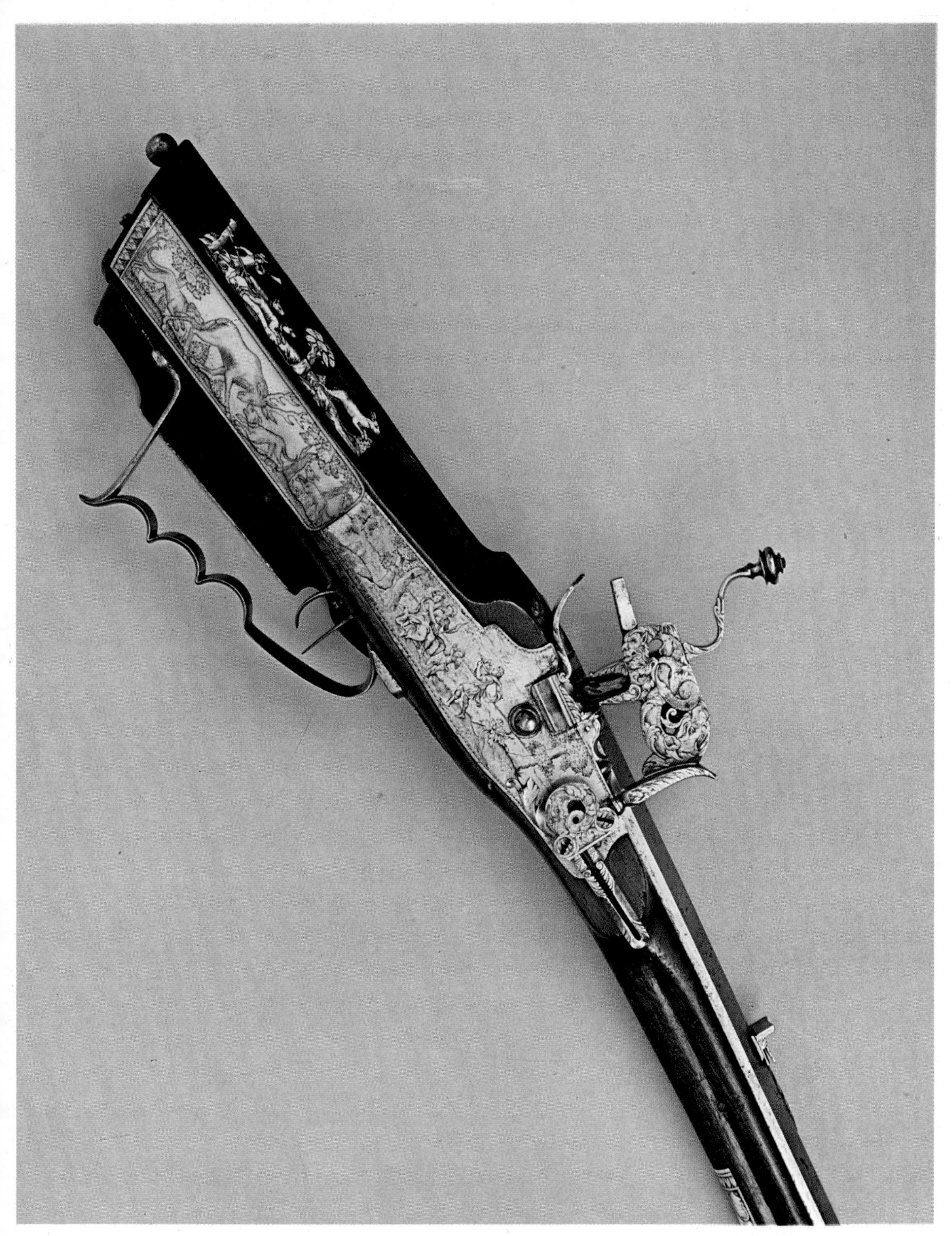

Plate 4 *Lock and butt of a fine wheellock hunting rifle made in Germany late in the 17th century: note that this weapon is fitted with a set or "hair trigger". The steel lockplate and dogshead are chiselled, and the stock is decorated with engraved stag's horn inlay. Overall length, 44 inches; barrel, 33 inches.* (*Gyngell Collection.*)

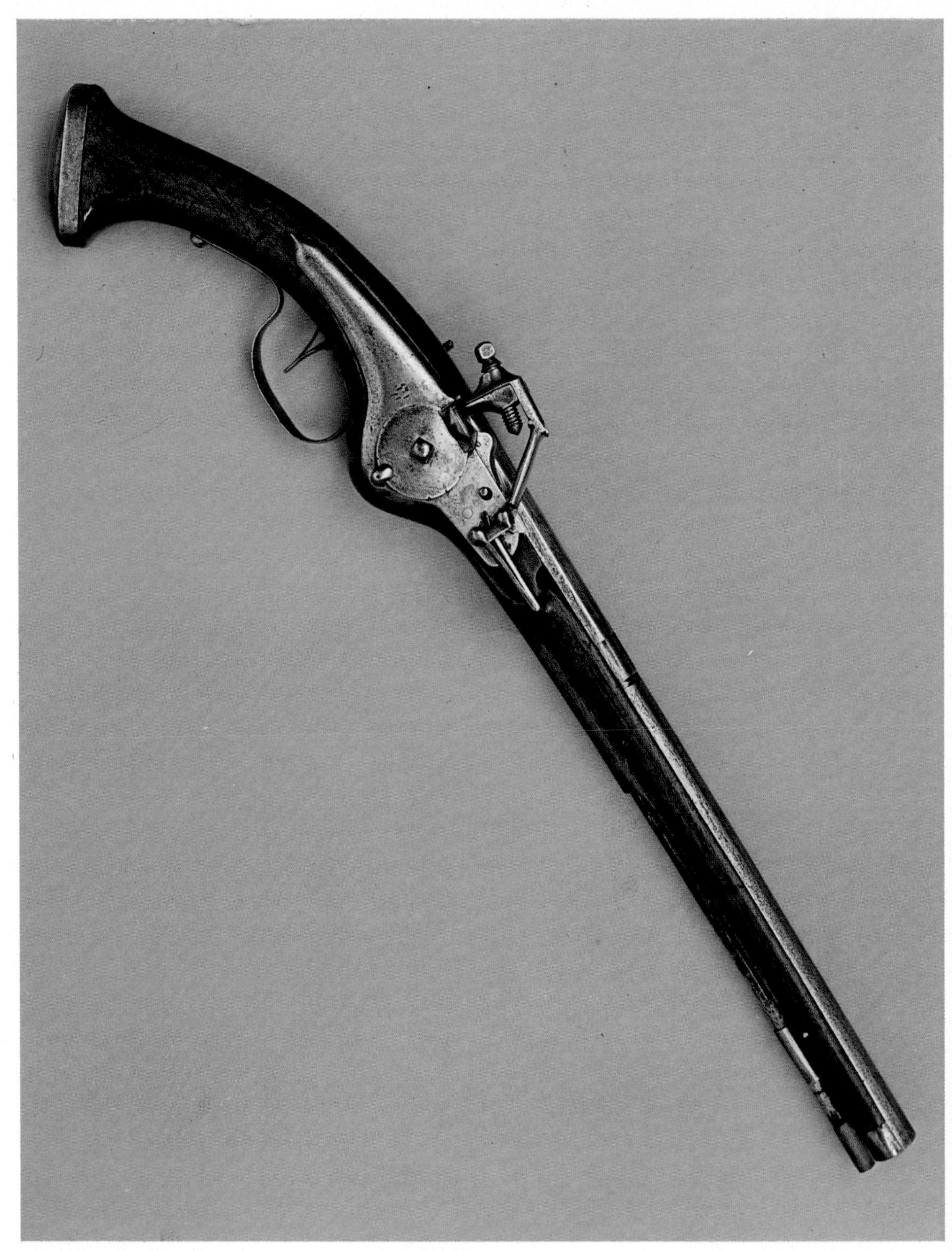

Plate 5 *A plain military wheellock holster pistol of about 1640; the type of weapon with which Cromwell equipped his formidable "Ironsides" of the New Model Army. Each trooper would have carried a pair of these pistols in leather holsters slung on each side of his saddle-bow. Overall length, 20½ inches; barrel, 14 inches. (Gyngell Collection.)*

Fig. 23: Combined wheellock key and spanner. (Gyngell Collection.)

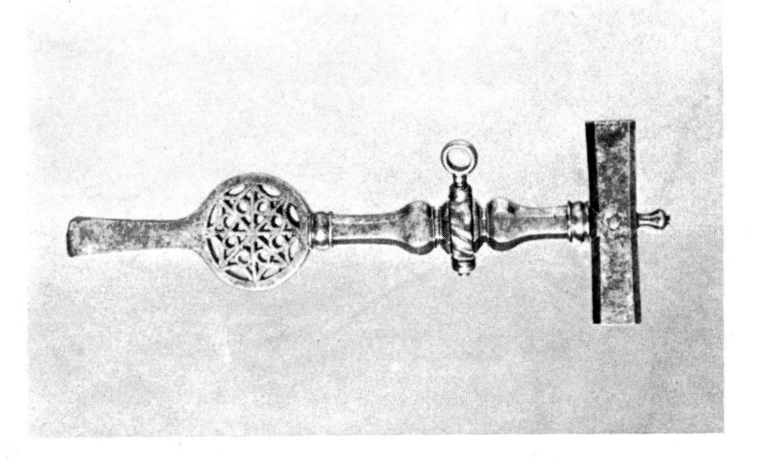

were manufactured in England. Stocks were usually quite plain with a slightly down-curving butt which normally terminated in a flattened swelling strengthened by a metal band. Some are slightly more elaborate with pan covers in gilt, and some of the studs and pan releases were also gilded. Barrels on the whole tend to be very simple and lack decoration. One rather special group of pistols should be mentioned here. The Dutch seem to have acquired a penchant for working in ivory and quite a number of wheellock pistols were produced with beautifully carved ivory butts and stocks.

ALTHOUGH wheellock pistols as a group are decorative, the long guns are even more eye-catching. The owner of a wheellock could usually afford to demand the best and naturally where there was a demand the gunsmith sought to satisfy it. If his patron wanted a highly elaborate, striking piece with which to impress his friends, to offer as a gift to his sovereign, or for any other reason, then cost was of little consequence. The gunmaker could offer improved accuracy by rifling the barrel and a very large percentage of wheellock sporting weapons are, in fact, fitted with rifled barrels. The principle of spinning the ball to make it accurate was no new invention and had been understood, although dimly, from the earliest times. The barrels themselves are usually fairly heavy because a heavy barrel helped to reduce the amount of recoil. It was on the stock that the gunsmith was able to express himself fully, and often the finished weapon was the result of the combined skills and talents of half a dozen craftsmen and artists. The barrel maker was proud of his skill and often his initials will be found stamped somewhere on the (usually octagonal) barrel. The lockmaker would likewise sign his work, and such locks were frequently chiselled; in some cases the dogshead was fashioned into a variety of rather unusual shapes. Rifles still exist with Doctors of Divinity, stags and dragons holding the pyrites in their hands or jaws. The stock was embellished in a variety of ways, but the most popular style was inlay. Delicately engraved plaques of horn, mother of pearl, gold or silver were inset into the stock. The themes of such decorations were, not unnaturally, often of hunting or classical scenes. The stocks will often repay a very close study, for the design was sometimes worked out to the customer's requirements, and some are distinctly unusual; our forefathers' lusty enthusiasm for the pleasures of life is demonstrated in many of the objects they left behind.

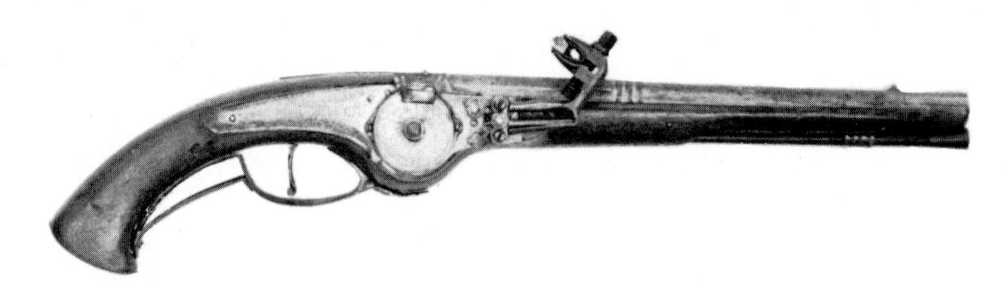

Fig. 24: A wheellock military pistol of about 1640. Although of much better quality than most (see Fig. 25) *this weapon is representative of the type of holster pistol used by both Royalist and Parliamentary troops in the English Civil War. Overall length, 19 inches; barrel, 11¾ inches.* (*Bennett Collection.*)

Many of the wheellock sporting rifles are fitted with the so-called German butt in which the stock continues in a straight line with just a slight dip to the rear of the lock, and there is no recess to fit over the shoulder. This is hardly surprising since the weapons were designed to be fired from the cheek, and the butt is recessed to fit snugly against the face. The shape of this cheek piece is another aid in dating such weapons, for in the middle of the 16th century the line was quite straight and the cheek piece was fairly small. Towards the end of the 16th century this cheek piece was extended downwards so that, in fact, it hangs below the main line of the butt. At the same time the step from the breech down to the butt became much clearer and bolder. A majority of these weapons also have a small box with a sliding or spring cover cut into the stock. These boxes held tools or, frequently, the patches of material which were put round the lead ball before it was pushed home into the barrel. This ensured that the ball fitted snugly against the rifling of the barrel. As so much skill amd money had been lavished on the stock decoration of the wheellock it was obviously desirable that it should not suffer any undue damage and in order to protect the forgetful owner against such hazards a round ball, often of steel, was screwed to the flat end of the butt so that the weapon could be rested without fear of damaging the stock or inlay.

One easily recognisable and quite distinctive form of stock is the delicate, graceful and gently curving butt of the *Tschinke*. The name is derived from Teschen, a town on the northern border of Bohemia where these rifles were most commonly made. The majority are of 17th century manufacture and they are peculiar in retaining the old system of fitting the mainspring on the outside of the lock. This had been the practice on early wheellocks and had the advantage of reducing the size of the recess cut into the stock to house the lock mechanism. This meant that the stock could be lighter and slimmer as there was less weakness. On the *Tschinke* the mainspring is visible beneath the bend of the butt, as is the chain running up towards the wheel. Since there was obviously a danger of catching ones finger in the mainspring a brass cover is fitted near the trigger guard where the fingers were most liable to damage. The *Tschinke*, and indeed almost all wheellock long arms and pistols, were fitted with very long trigger guards. Some are simple and straight, many others have shaped finger grips; only the index finger was placed inside the guard to operate the trigger.

French wheellocks exhibit one feature which seems to be peculiar to the gunmakers of France. The mainspring of most wheellocks is normally attached to the inside of the lockplates but the French, apparently seeking to reduce the amount of cutting required to inset the lock mechanism, came up with the idea of making the mainspring separate. In French wheellocks the mainspring is secured to the stock, not the lockplate, by means of a long sturdy pin. The spindle of the wheel passes completely through the lockplates and sits into a metal recess on the opposite side of the stock. Another national characteristic which is of assistance in dating and identifying wheellocks is the Italian preoccupation with metal inlay. By and large the Germans preferred to inlay materials such as horn or mother of pearl whereas the Italians rather favoured steel and silver; they also frequently carved the stock in a very delicate and attractive fashion, something seldom seen on the German wheellocks.

As mentioned above, since expense was frequently no object when ordering a wheellock, extras were often fitted. Some may seem rather bizarre but, in fact, had a very practical value. When any of these early firearms were discharged there was a cloud of smoke from the priming, a slight, but appreciable delay, and then the main charge fired. The puff of smoke from the priming could betray the presence of a hunter to his quarry and possibly cause him to miss his shot. This was a problem which bothered shooters until the introduction of the percussion system in the early 19th century, but one solution offered by the designers of wheellocks was a small pivoted chimney situated above the pan. When not in use it lay flat along the barrel but when the weapon was to be fired the chimney was raised to a vertical position to carry the

Fig. 25: Detail of the lock of the pistol illustrated in Fig. 24, showing the engraved gilt wheel cover and gilt-ended studs. The degree of decoration suggests that the weapon may have been the property of an officer of considerable means. (Bennett Collection.)

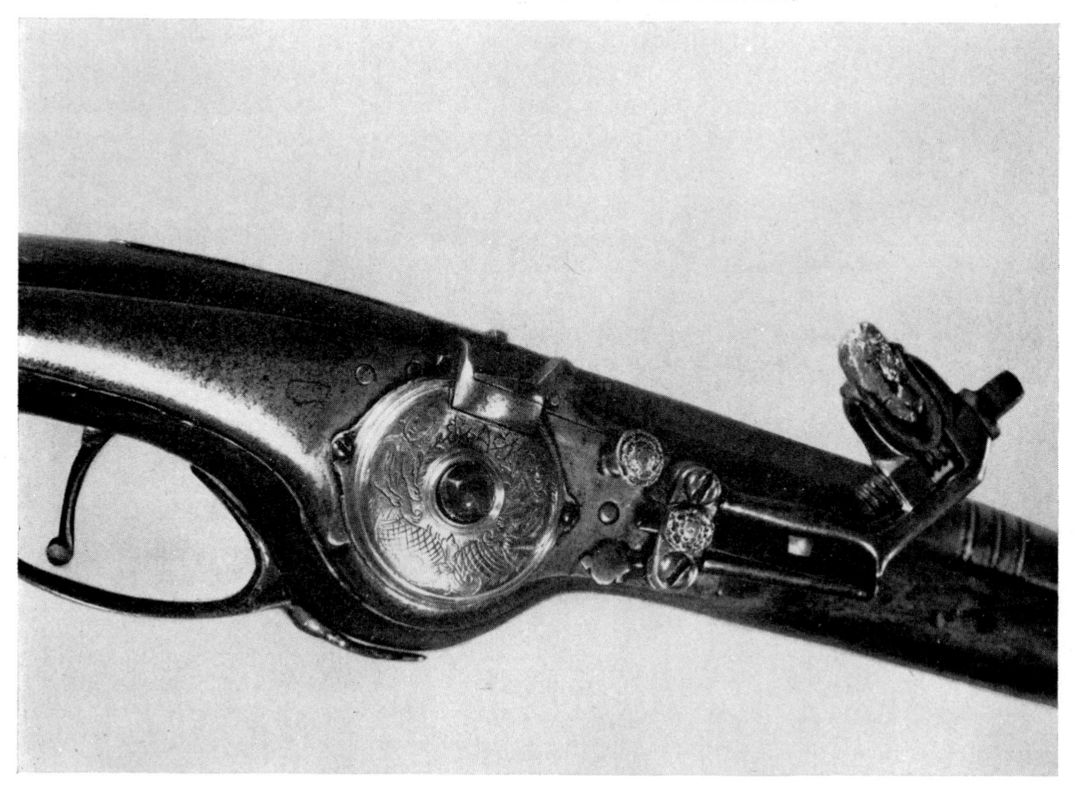

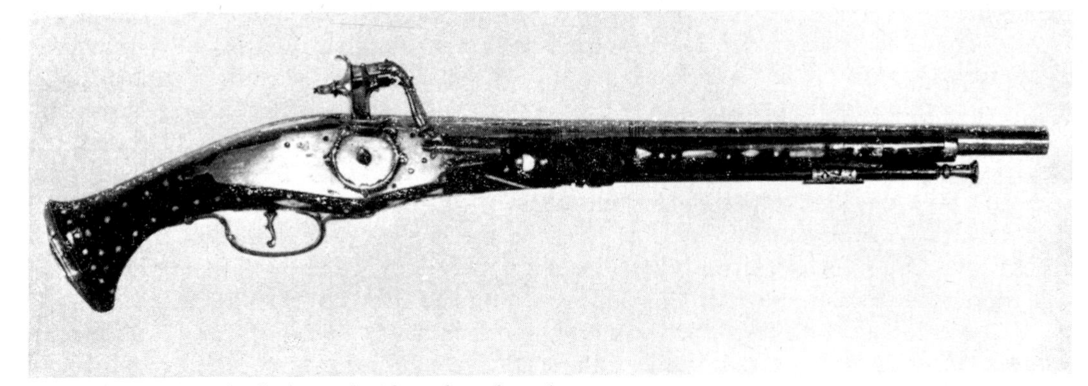

Fig. 26: An Italian wheellock pistol with mother of pearl inlay and steel fittings; early 17th century. Overall length, 20¾ inches; barrel, 15 inches. (Gyngell Collection.)

smoke away from the firer's face, besides helping to conceal the give-away flash. This rather grotesque idea was in practice quite sensible. There were numerous other refinements offered, such as self-spanning wheellocks in which the wheel was rotated by the movement of the cock or, in certain cases, by the trigger guard, so that the key or spanner was dispensed with. For the pessimistic hunter some wheellocks, particularly the early ones, were made with a combined matchlock and wheellock mechanism so that if one failed the second might be pressed into service. However, when the wheellock had proved its reliability such novelties were dispensed with.

As mentioned above most wheellock sporting guns are fitted with very heavy barrels; this meant that it was not easy to hold the heavy weapon in the aiming position for any longer than was absolutely necessary. Since the barrel was rifled, if full use was to be made of its potential accuracy the shooter had to guard against lowering or jerking the weapon when firing, and in many of the early examples the trigger pull was heavy enough to lead to a risk of pulling the weapon off aim. As early as the last quarter of the 16th century some weapons had been fitted with a hair, or set, trigger. This was a system of springs and levers which could be adjusted so that only the tiniest pressure on the trigger was required to withdraw the sear and allow the mechanism to operate. These are most commonly seen on wheellock sporting guns and have the appearance of a very thin, almost wire-like trigger set in front of the normal trigger. When the wheellock was spanned, primed and ready for firing the small hair trigger would be adjusted to bring the set mechanism into action.

The wheellock in all its shapes and forms represented a very considerable technological advance in the field of firearms design, but it was not without its faults. Matchlocks had been simple, and any half-skilled blacksmith could repair a matchlock mechanism. In the case of a wheellock the problem was far more complicated; tiny and delicate chains, hard springs and links required some considerable skill and a degree of technical knowledge that was beyond the capabilities of the ordinary soldier. Thus a comparatively minor accident could render the weapon completely useless. Then, too, the pyrites was a constant source of trouble for as a mineral it is rather crystalline and tends to break into small pieces. It was very easy for a piece of broken pyrites to slip down under the pan or into the mechanism itself and so jam the action completely. Diagnosing the cause of trouble was one thing, but its removal was another. Again, there was the constant problem of rust; it needed only a spot on the wheel or chain links to seize up the entire mechanism. This particular problem exercised the ingenuity of

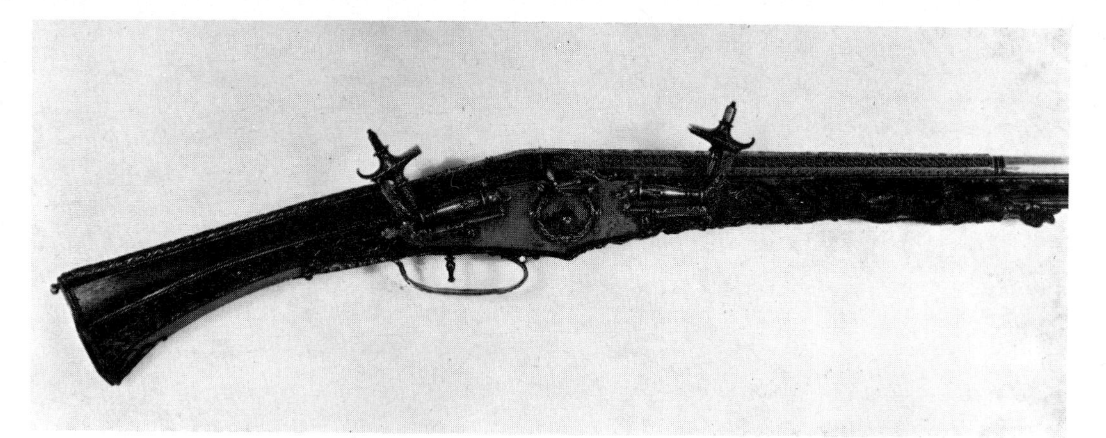

Fig. 27: Italian wheellock gun of the mid-17th century; this weapon has a duplicate "standby" cock in case the pyrites should break. Overall length, 46½ inches; barrel, 33½ inches. (Wallace Collection.)

many of the great craftsmen and some very ingenious locks were produced which, theoretically, would operate no matter how wet the conditions. Expense was another limiting factor, and the gunsmith was constantly on the lookout for a simple, reliable and efficient means of using a spark which did not require such complicated mechanism.

When eventually the gunsmith did find a simpler and more efficient method, the flintlock, it did not mean that the wheellock was discarded overnight. Its grace and beauty and possibly even its mechanically complicated mechanism endeared it to the hearts of many sportsmen and a few were still being made as late as the 1720's; at least one is known which bears the date 1726. The later wheellock weapons had a simpler and plainer lockplate and also a very large volute-like curving projection from the top of the cock which was gripped firmly when pulling the cock forward to the firing position or pushing it clear to the safety position. Although by the middle of the 18th century wheellock production in Europe was virtually at an end, odd specimens were still made to customers peculiar requirements and there is one recorded pistol by a French maker, Le Page, which is dated 1829; at first glance it looks very like the normal flintlock or percussion pistol of the period.

There has been a growing interest in wheellocks, for they are comparatively rare and almost invariably attractive in shape and design. Naturally the growing demand has resulted in rising prices and this, in turn, has stimulated a number of less scrupulous dealers and collectors to produce examples which are of questionable pedigree. Since the cost of a wheellock pistol or long arm is so exorbitant today collectors hoping to acquire one would be very well advised to seek a second opinion before investing large amounts in one weapon.

3

Flint and Steel

Foot of page, *Fig. 28: The lock of a fine English "snaphaunce" dated 1590 and embellished with gold and silver decoration. Overall length, 67½ inches; barrel, 52½ inches.* (*Tower of London.*)

MATCHLOCK firearms were easy to use, reasonably reliable, and above all, very cheap to produce. Wheellock firearms were less easy to use, quite reliable, could be left prepared for use, but had the serious disadvantage of being complex, difficult to make and repair, and therefore costly. What was wanted was a weapon which offered the advantages of the wheellock with the cheapness and simplicity of the matchlock. The direction of future development had been pointed by the wheellock and it was essentially the same system, production of sparks by friction, that was to provide a very satisfactory solution to the problem.

The solution lay in the use of the flintlock mechanism. There is some difference of opinion over the exact definition of a flintlock; however, ignoring the finer distinctions, basically the flintlock mechanism produced sparks by striking a piece of flint against steel. It was, in fact, a mechanical equivalent of the domestic way of producing fire. The flint was held between two jaws which were arranged at the end of an arm (the cock) in such a way that when impelled by a strong spring, it was swung in an arc to strike the steel at just the right angle to slide down its length and break

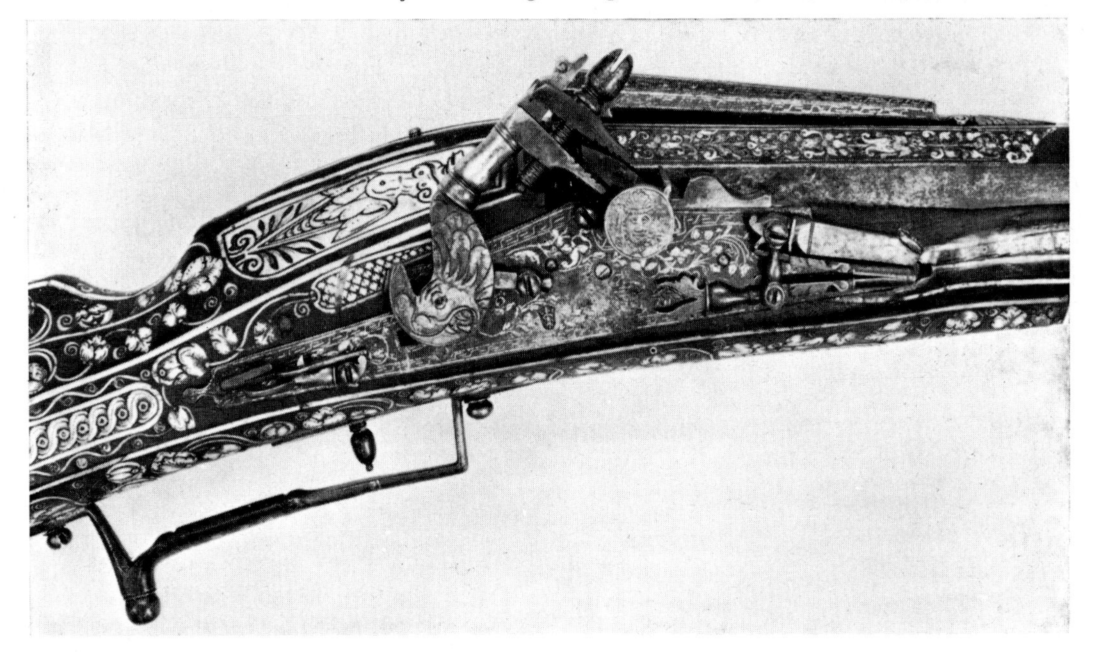

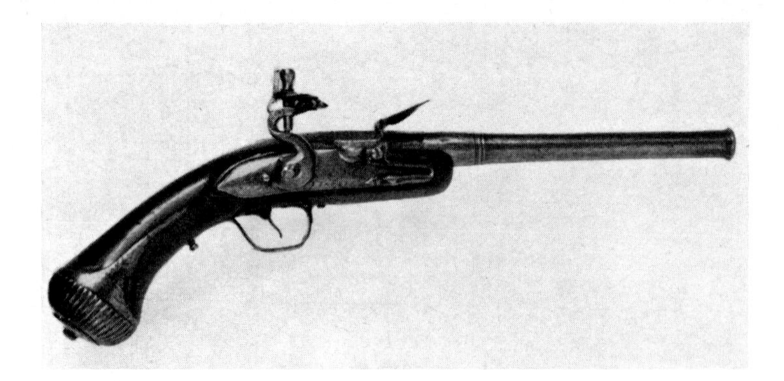

Fig. 29: English flintlock pistol of about 1660 made by J. Tarles; the barrel unscrews for loading. Overall length, 14½ inches, barrel, 8½ inches. (Gyngell Collection.)

off tiny pieces of incandescent steel which ignited the priming and so fired the weapon.

The flintlock in this basic sense seems to have appeared not very long after the wheellock, although it did not emerge as a generally accepted method of ignition until much later. In fact the early distinction between the wheellock and flintlock is very vague, for terms such as "self igniting guns" and "stone guns" could have applied equally well to both the flintlock and the wheellock. One strong piece of evidence supporting the belief that the wheellock appeared first lies in dated weapons that have survived. Whilst there are a number of wheellocks dating from 1530 the earliest flintlock is one which was probably made in 1556. The earliest reference to a flintlock is to be found in an Italian document from Florence, dated 1547, which refers to a gun with flint; and there is another reference in the same year in Swedish accounts. Although this second document actually refers to a snaplock the context suggests that it was some form of flintlock.

The early flintlock mechanism was naturally very similar to the wheellock. Both mechanisms contained a strong V-shaped mainspring which might be mounted either on the inside or the outside of the lockplate. In all early flintlocks it pressed against some part of the cock which, like that of the wheellock, had two jaws holding in this case a shaped piece of flint. There was also a small priming pan, although in the flintlock it was a single piece of metal with a slight depression cut into it. There was a pan cover which could be moved either manually or automatically by means of connecting

Fig. 30: Dutch flintlock pistol with solid ivory stock, the butt carved in the shape of a helmeted head; circa *1660. Overall length, 21 inches; barrel, 12½ inches. Fine ivory work was a characteristic of Dutch pieces of this period. (Reproduced by permission of the Trustees of the Wallace Collection.)*

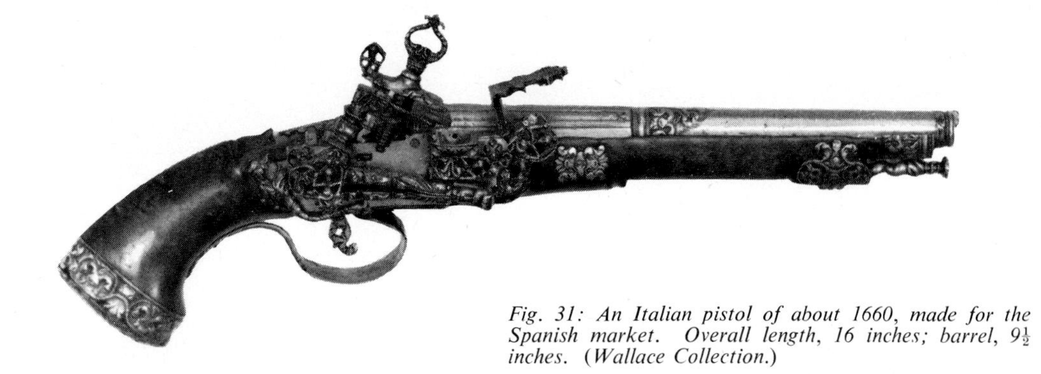

Fig. 31: An Italian pistol of about 1660, made for the Spanish market. Overall length, 16 inches; barrel, 9½ inches. (Wallace Collection.)

levers. Above this was a pivoted arm at the end of which was a flat steel plate. To prepare the flintlock for firing it was only necessary to pull back the cock, thus compressing the mainspring. An arm, the sear, engaged with the cock and locked it in position with the spring under tension. To fire the flintlock one loaded and primed it in exactly the same fashion as both matchlock and wheellock. A pinch of priming powder was placed in the pan, a cover closed and the arm with the steel at the end was moved into position so that it stood vertically at the front of the pan. Pressing the trigger withdrew the sear, so allowing the spring to force the cock quickly through a quarter turn; the flint struck downwards at an angle against the face of the steel which, being pivoted, was pushed clear by the impact. The sparks so produced dropped into the priming, the pan cover having already been removed either manually or automatically.

This was the basic flintlock mechanism which, in the 16th century was described as a "snaphance" or "snaphaunce". This title seems to be derived from the Dutch or Flemish *Snap Hann*, which meant, literally, "snapping hen". Numerous stories

Fig. 32: A high quality pair of Italian flintlock pistols, circa *1660, with steel mounts and chiselled locks. Overall length, 19 inches; barrels, 12½ inches. (Wallace Collection.)*

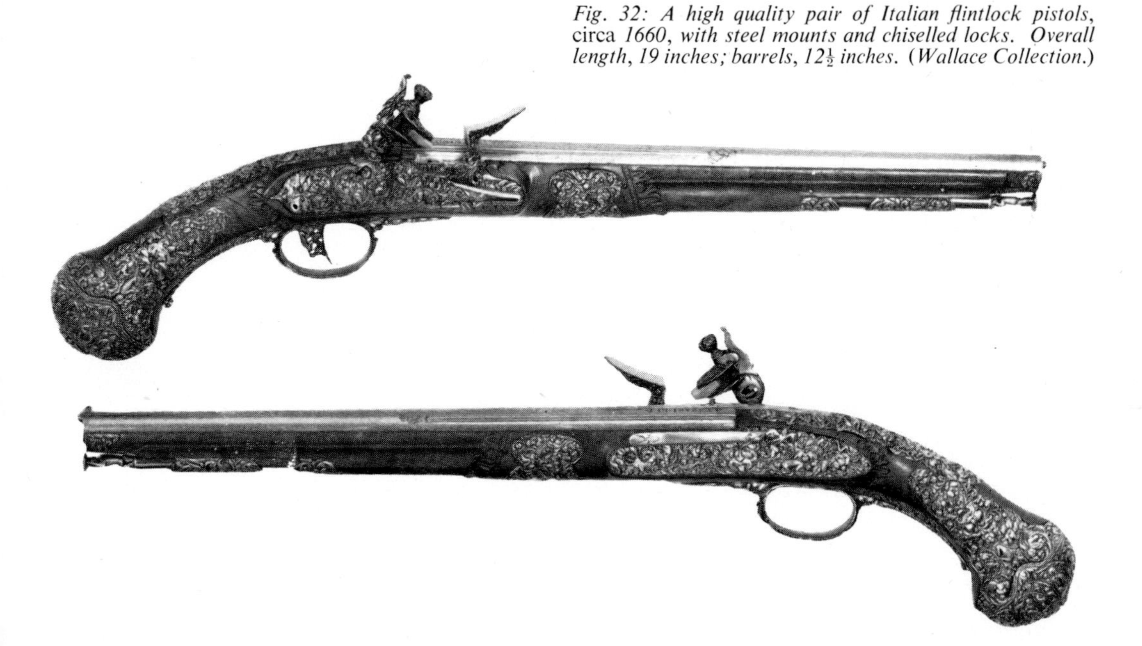

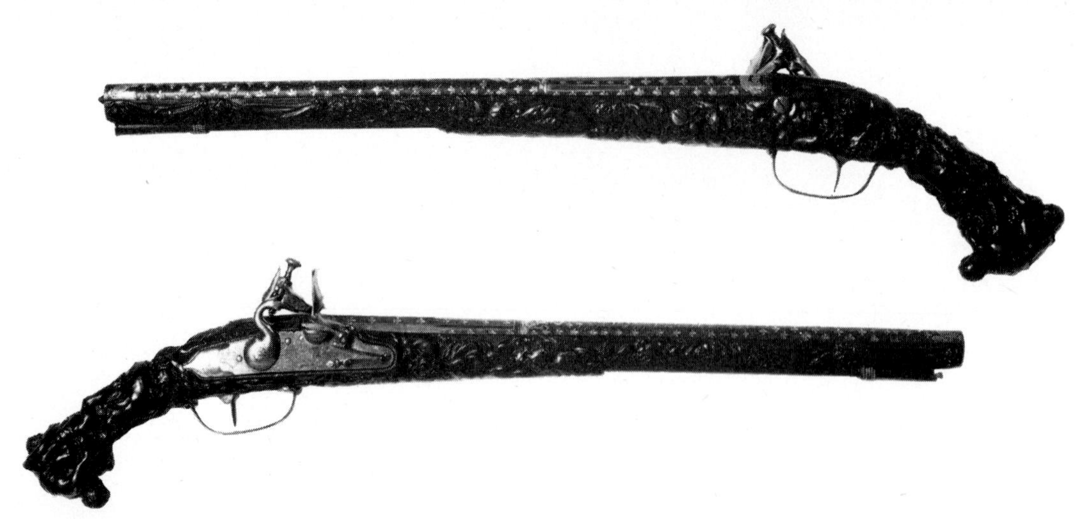

Fig. 33: A pair of pistols made in France in about 1670 for King Louis XIV. The walnut stocks are carved overall. Overall length, 23½ inches; barrels, 16½ inches. (Wallace Collection.)

were invented to explain why this name was chosen. The most frequently repeated theory is that the thieves in the Low Countries intent on grabbing the farmers' chickens were greatly troubled by the fact that their matchlocks glowing in the darkness gave them away, and in seeking some method which would not betray them eventually came up with the snaphaunce or flintlock! However, it would seem far more likely that the movement of the cock with a quick "pecking" action, similar to that of a chicken, was responsible for the name. It is of interest to note that the word snaphaunce did, by a process of association, come to mean a footpad or thief. The term is unquestionably an old one; the first recorded use of it is in 1539.

The term snaphaunce originally applied to any form of flintlock but in collecting circles it has become generally limited (erroneously perhaps) to the type of lock where the steel and the pan cover are separate. The term flintlock, in the collectors' sense (though many experts would disagree) applies to the form of mechanism where pan cover and steel are combined in a single L-shaped piece; but in fact, this development was not to appear for some little time yet.

It is an interesting fact that the flintlock appears to have developed on a somewhat regional basis; areas such as the Baltic, the Mediterranean, Europe and England seem to have produced locks which at one time or another exhibited characteristics peculiar to that area. The earliest mention of the snaphaunce concerns some weapons in the Royal Armoury at Stockholm and these were described in 1556 as being fitted with "snaplocks". The type of snaplock was probably that described by students as the Baltic lock. Early examples are comparatively rare but easy to recognise; the cock is of a distinctive shape, being very long, slender and rather gracefully curved. The early examples all have the mainspring fitted on the outside of the lockplate; the long end of the mainspring bears directly on to the lower end, or heel, of the cock. When the cock is pulled back the heel is locked into position by a sear fastened on the inside of the lockplate, the nose of which passes through the lockplate to engage with the cock.

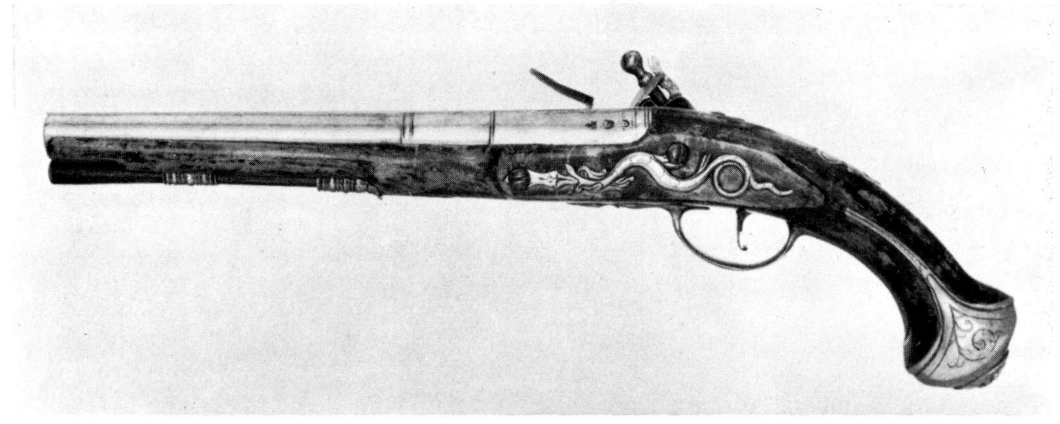

Figs. 34 and **(foot of page)** *35: Both sides of one of a pair of attractive English flintlocks made in about 1680 by I. Hall; the fittings are in brass. Overall length, 18 inches; barrel, 11¼ inches. (Knowles Collection.)*

One further feature of these early locks is that one spring is made to serve two purposes; not only does it provide the motive force for the cock but it also supplies the tension to hold in position the arm to which the steel is attached. This type of flintlock suffered one serious disadvantage in comparison with the wheellock. When cocked and primed there was a grave risk of accidental discharge. One method of overcoming this problem was to make the steel separate and attach it to the arm in such a way that it might be swivelled to an angle at which the flint could not strike sparks from it. This Baltic lock continued in use until the 19th century on cheaper hunting weapons and the design altered but little, so that it is sometimes difficult to date specimens with any certainty. The Baltic lock does not seem to have been restricted entirely to the immediate area, and examples are known in Russia.

Around the Mediterranean there appeared two other types of flintlock, similar in certain respects but differing in others. The Italian lock, also known as the Roman lock, has the mainspring mounted externally on the lockplate. A hook-like termination at the end of the spring presses on the front portion, or toe, of the cock. The opposite side, or heel of the cock, has a small rearward facing lug. When the cock is

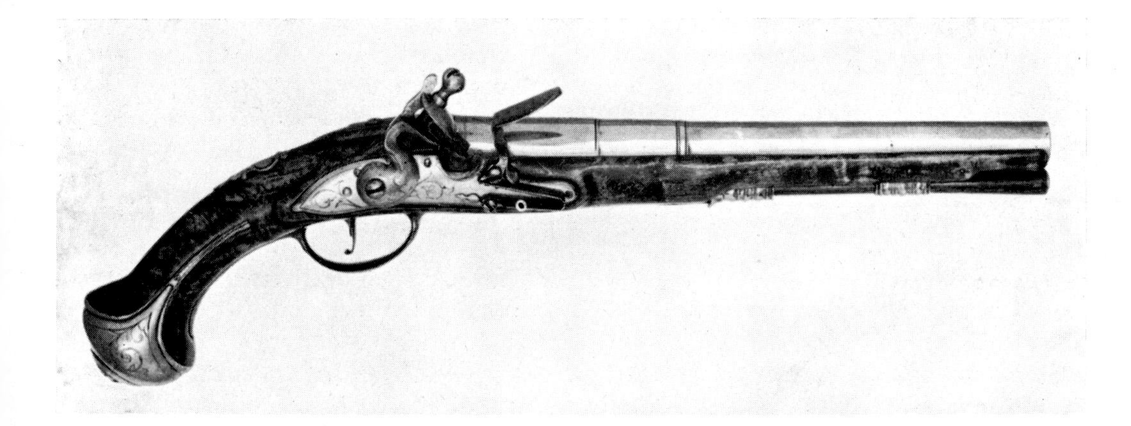

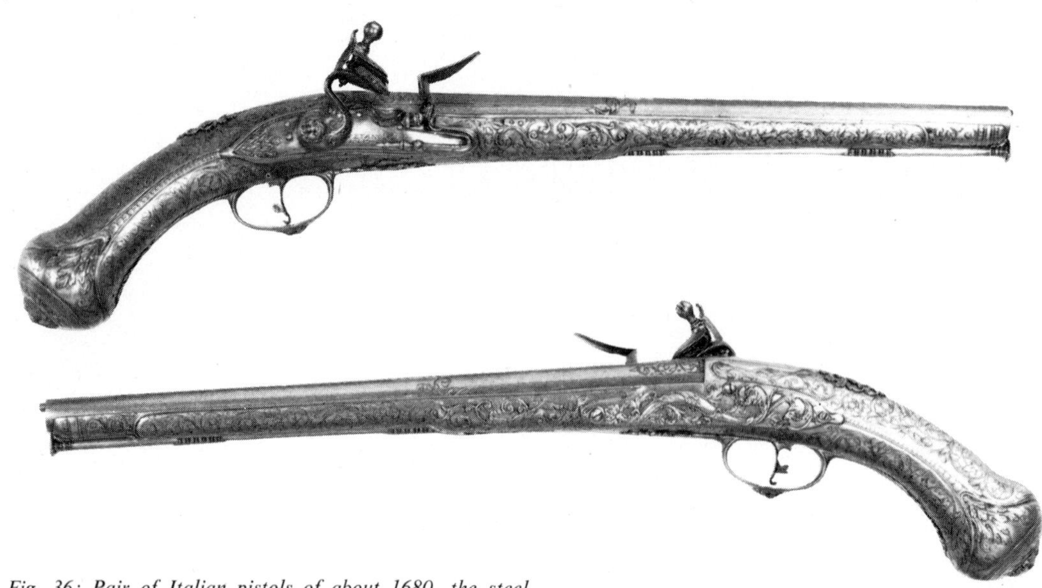

Fig. 36: Pair of Italian pistols of about 1680, the steel stocks covered with engraved floral work and heads. Overall length, 20 inches; barrels, 13 inches. (Wallace Collection.)

pulled back a small spring-operated sear projecting through the lockplate engages with the cock to hold it locked in position.

Somewhat similar is the Spanish lock, usually called a Miguelet; although the mainspring, also mounted on the outside of the lock, presses up on the rear of the cock rather than down on the toe. This type of lock is easily recognisable since the cock itself is normally quite squat and the jaws are usually rectangular and broad, while the steel is vertically groved. Since the movement of the cock is less than that on other types a very strong mainspring is fitted to provide enough force to strike sparks. This spring makes it difficult to cock the action, and the top of the cock is often fitted with a ring through which the forefinger may be passed to obtain a good grip. A double curved bar may also be found fitted to the top jaw screw, again to afford a good grip.

Sometime early in the 17th century the French gunsmith Marin le Bourgeoys of Lisieux, a small Normandy village, produced what was to become the more or less standard pattern of flintlock for the next 200 years. The so-called French lock as produced by le Bourgeoys incorporated several established features and one new one. First, he used a single L-shaped piece of metal which combined steel and pan cover, pivoted just in front of the pan, and a small V spring set below held it closed. This was not an original idea since examples of combined pan covers and steel occur as early as the second half of the 16th century, and indeed some Baltic and Italian locks are so fitted.

It did offer one tremendous advantage in that when the pan cover was closed the steel was automatically in the correct position. This combined pan cover and steel is usually referred to as the "frizzen" or "battery". As the flint struck the steel it pushed it back, so uncovering the pan and priming at the same time. This allowed a more simplified mechanism; no longer were arms and levers needed to open the pan cover.

To prepare the flintlock the cock had to be pulled back and locked into position by an arm or sear. In the case of the Miguelet and Roman locks the sear had operated

Fig. 37: One of a pair of French flintlocks of circa *1680; the mounts are silver, the stock beautifully marked walnut. Overall length, 21 inches; barrel, 14 inches.* (*Wallace Collection.*)

laterally through the lockplate and engaged directly on to the cock. In the French lock of Bourgeoys the mainspring was mounted internally and it pressed, not directly on the cock, but onto a tumbler, a small block of metal fitted to the same pivot as the cock. This tumbler was so shaped that as it rotated with the cock the sear pressed against the edge until the end engaged with a slot cut therein and so locked the cock in position. This was probably the most important feature, for the sear acted directly on the tumbler inside the lock and no longer pierced the lockplate; in other words it was a vertically acting sear rather than a lateral one as had been the case on almost every previous type of lock.

This new lock was not without its drawbacks, particularly as far as safety was concerned. In both the wheellock and the snaphaunce perfect safety could be ensured by leaving the dogshead, or steel, clear of the pan. However, with this combined L-shaped piece once the pan cover was closed the steel was automatically in the firing position. If the cock was in the rear, or full cock, position then there was obviously a serious danger of accidental discharge. This problem was overcome by cutting a second notch into the face of the tumbler. As the cock was rotated the sear engaged with the first notch and in this position the trigger could not withdraw the sear. The cock was safely held in what was known as the "half cock" position. All that was needed was a slight backward movement of the cock which disengaged the sear from the first notch and allowed it to slip into the second one from which the trigger could withdraw it.

This, then, was the lock produced by le Bourgeoys, probably between 1610 and 1615. The most important contribution that he made was in the vertically operating sear, and to some experts this is the distinguishing feature of a true flintlock. Most collectors, however, mark the distinction by the combined pan cover and steel.

The new French lock in a variety of forms spread over most of Europe. In England it produced the more or less typical English dog lock with its flat plate and rather angular cock; but with the distinctive feature of a small pivoted hook fitted behind the cock. Evidently, with true British conservatism, the English gunmakers did not altogether trust this new sear and tumbler arrangement for the half cock position, and a good solid hook was fitted which engaged with a notch cut in the back of the cock. In the half cock, or safety position, this hook was pushed into place holding the cock upright. When the cock was rotated to the firing position the hook was

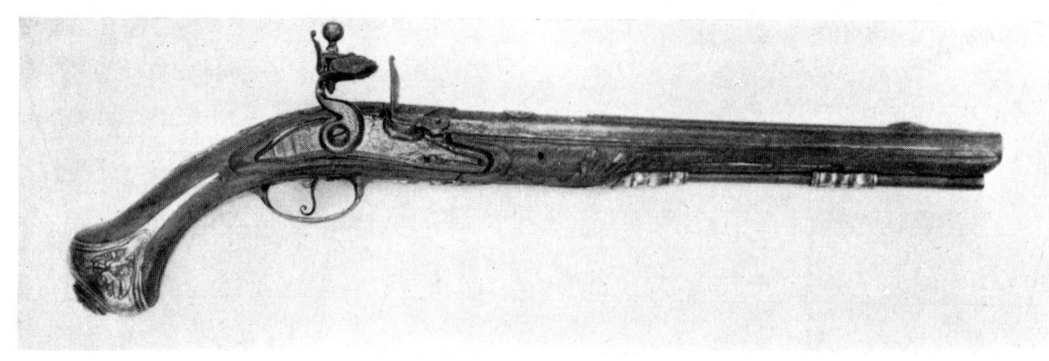

Fig. 38: One of a pair of Flemish flintlocks made in the first quarter of the 18th century. Overall length. 21 inches; barrel, 13½ inches. (Bennett Collection.)

automatically disengaged. The English lock often had a buffer or metal block fitted just to the rear of the pan to prevent the cock from swinging too far forward.

THE new style of lock soon replaced earlier types and by the end of the 17th century was in general use throughout most of the Western world, although Spain always resisted it and continued to use the Miguelet lock until well into the 19th century. The flintlock was pressed into use for every type of weapon; large holster pistols, small pocket pistols, large military flintlocks and delicate fowling pieces. The basic design was to remain unchanged throughout the next two centuries, but modifications to improve its general efficiency and reliability were not long in coming. The purpose of many of these variations was to reduce friction; thus a small roller was fitted to either the tip of the frizzen where it engaged with the spring or to the frizzen spring, so that when the steel struck it pushed the frizzen clear quickly to ensure a good crisp firing action. Similar rollers were fitted to the end of the mainspring to ensure that the friction between tumbler and spring was reduced. Another method of reducing friction was by using a link coupling between the tumbler and the end of the mainspring, thus reducing the size of the bearing areas. Gunpowder of the period was often rather impure and its burning produced "fouling", corrosion which could block the touchhole and erode the pan. To prevent this many of the better class weapons had a thin coating of gold or platinum in the pan. Similarly, a plug of the same metal was fitted into the barrel at the breech and the touchhole drilled through the plug.

As the flintlock continued in use for such a long period—up to around 1840—it might be expected that dating flintlock weapons is likely to be difficult. Fortunately there are some general indications which help in deciding on the approximate date. In the case of pistols the shape and style of the stock is a useful guide. Early stocks from the middle of the 17th century tend, quite naturally, to be similar to those of wheellocks in appearance. Butts were straighter than in later models and they normally terminated in a slight swelling cut straight across and often strengthened by a band of metal. As the century progressed the butt tended to become a little more acutely angled; the end became more ball-like in shape and in place of the single edging band the entire pommel or end of the butt was encased in steel or brass. During the early part of the 18th century brass butt caps were common and were fitted with long spurs which extended up both sides of the butt to afford extra strength. By the middle of the century these spurs were being reduced in size and by the early 19th century most pistols had either discarded the butt cap completely or had one with only very attenuated spurs at the sides. Early flintlock pistols also have carving on the stock around the breech and the lockplate and the retaining screws on the opposite side of the stock. There was a general tendency for the stock to become plainer as the century progressed. The so called "Queen Anne pistol" although produced long after the death of that monarch in 1714 were of very pleasing shape decorated with designs of inlaid silver.

As the flintlock was so much simpler to construct, and thus cheaper to produce than the wheellock it was naturally pressed into service for "mass produced" weapons. Armies discarded their old fashioned matchlocks and flintlock weapons became the order of the day. In the early part of the 18th century there first appeared that veteran of military firearms, the so-called "Brown Bess", which was to do sterling service for the British army for well over a century. Rugged and yet graceful, simple and yet sturdy, this weapon saw service in every continent of the world; and although barrel and stock were altered during its lifetime, the lock was virtually unchanged.

The hunter was well served by the new lock and double-barrelled long arms became far more common. Punt guns, in effect small cannon designed for shooting wild fowl, were introduced with the flintlock. Pocket pistols had been made during the 17th century, but were another type of weapon that became commonplace during the 18th and early 19th centuries. Many pocket and Queen Anne pistols, indeed all types of flintlock pistols, had what is known as a boxlock. Basically the action was identical with the usual flintlock, but the cock was mounted centrally above the breech rather than at the side. This arrangement made for a much cleaner line, since priming pan, frizzens and springs were less exposed and projecting. This was obviously a very desirable feature for pocket pistols, which could so easily snag on clothing and pockets at the crucial moment.

Naturally almost every matchlock, wheellock and flintlock suffered from the same disadvantage—they were single shot. Double barrelled weapons had been intro-

Fig. 39: Pair of "snaphaunce" pistols with steel fittings, made in Northern Italy in about 1660. Overall length, 21 inches; barrels, 15 inches. (*Wallace Collection.*)

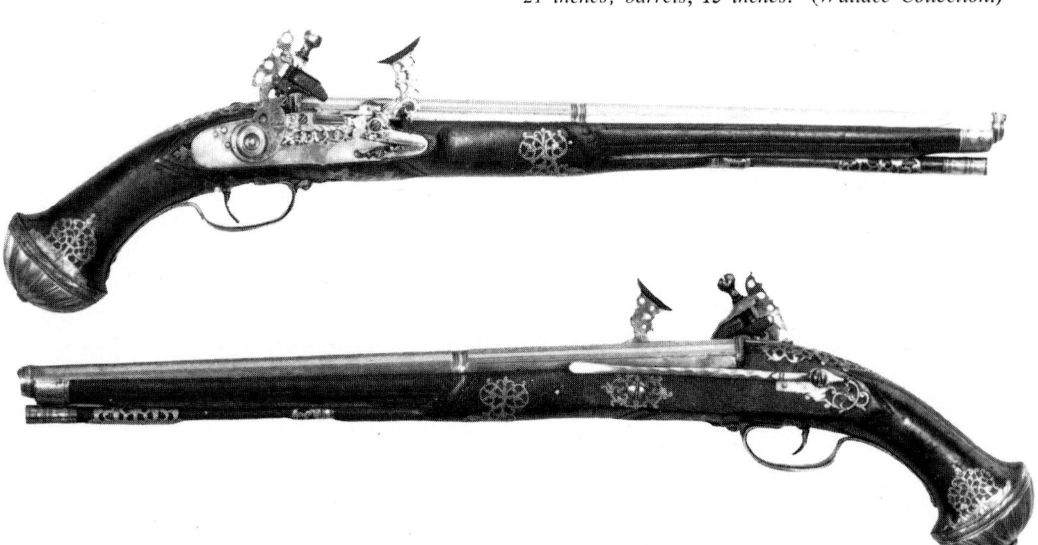

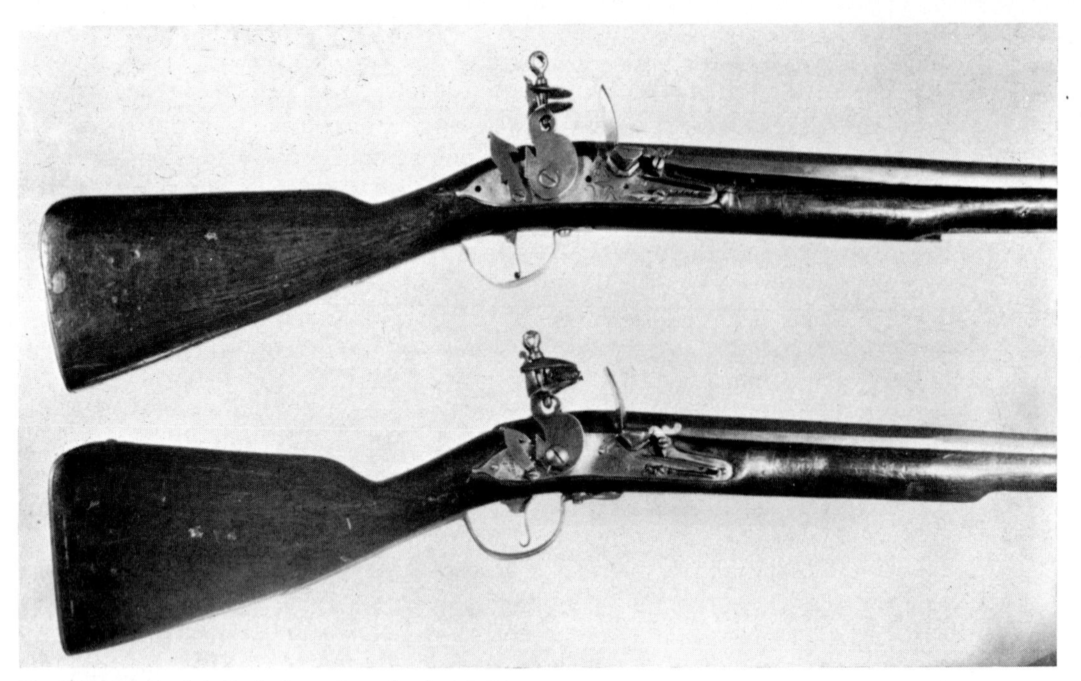

Fig. 40: Two English flintlock muskets fitted with "dog-locks"; both pieces date from the early 18th century. Barrel lengths, 46 inches and 45 inches. (Tower of London.)

duced from the earliest times but with the advent of the flintlock mechanism the gunsmith was able to experiment with three, four, five, six and even seven barrelled pieces. Weapons with two barrels mounted side by side or one above the other, the so-called "over and under" system, were common; three barrels are rare, and four barrels equally so in the case of flintlocks, although percussion weapons of this configuration are not so scarce.

The sizing of pistols is always a difficult task for collectors, and contemporaries never quite agreed, but generally speaking the smallest are pocket pistols and the largest are holster pistols. The latter group, as the name implies, were intended to be carried in holsters, but the holsters were carried by horsemen and were situated just at the back of the horse's neck. Personal holsters did not appear until the 19th century. Should a man wish to carry a pistol then it would have been either a pocket pistol or a larger pistol fitted with a belt hook which was simply a shaped bar of steel fastened to the side of the stock which could be slipped over a sash or belt. There are a number of intermediate sizes and these are usually described as overcoat pistols or travelling pistols, but there is little agreed standardisation in nomenclature. Travelling was a hazardous business and some form of protection was a real necessity. In order to deter the highwaymen—"the Gentlemen of the Road"—many of the coaches carried a guard armed with flintlock pistols or a flintlock blunderbuss.

The flintlock pistol of the 18th century often bears a number of marks and these can be a great help in dating and identifying the pistol. In 1637 The London Company of Gunmakers was given its charter; fortunately most of its records have survived and

Plate 6 *A pair of Spanish "miguelet" flintlock pistols of the mid-18th century, decorated with brass and silver. Overall length, 10½ inches; barrels, 6½ inches; bore, ·7 inch.* (Gyngell Collection.)

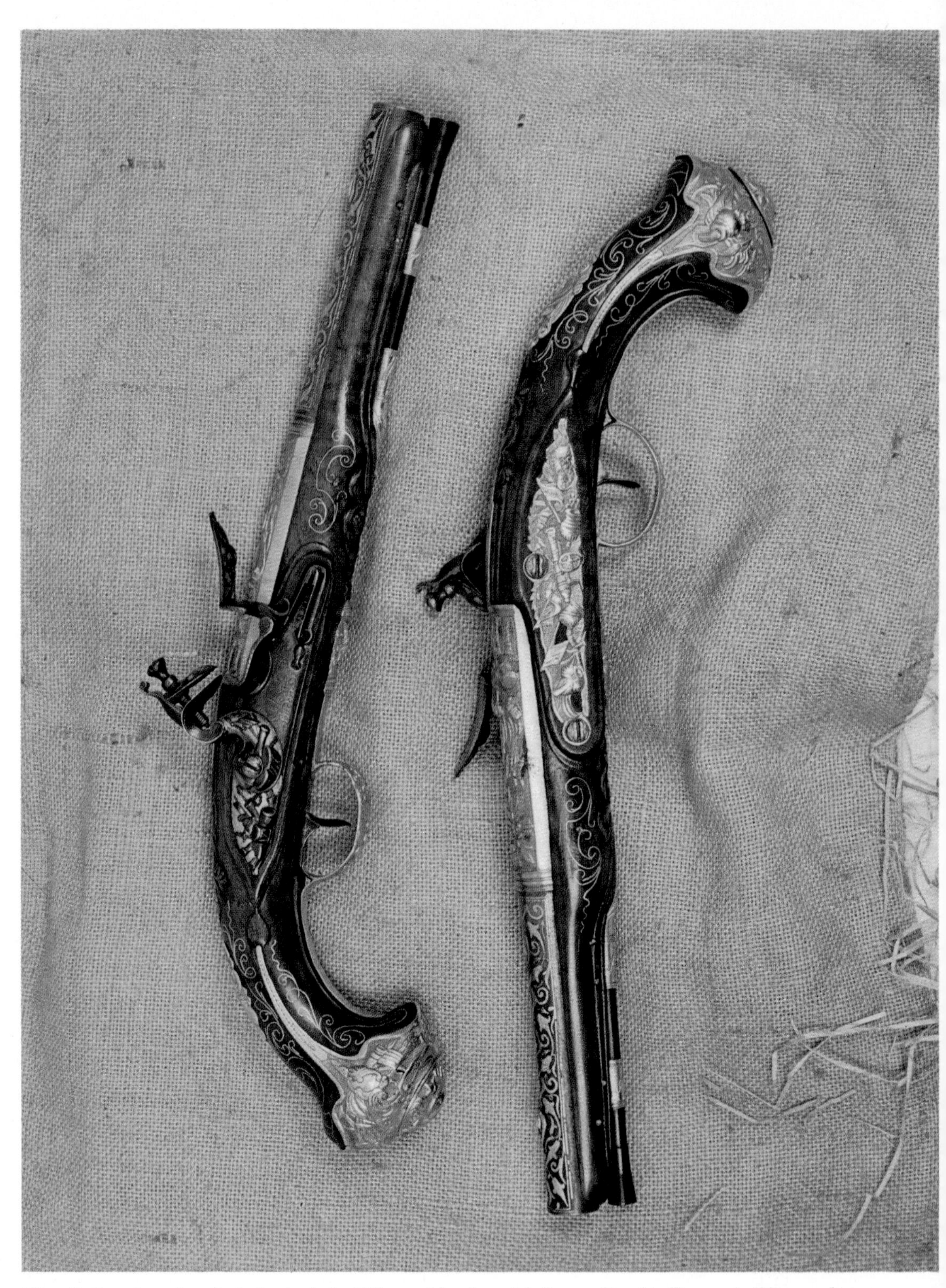

Plate 7 *Superb quality flintlock pistols by Wilson of London with fine quality chiselling and gilding on hammer, barrel, side plates and pommel. Circa 1760.* (*R Thornton*).

Fig. 41: An Italian "snaphaunce" of the late 18th century, one of a pair both fitted with belt hooks. Overall length, 12 inches; barrel, 7 inches. (Wallace Collection.)

from these it has been possible to identify many of the better known London gunmakers whose initials appear on a number of weapons. Not only were there means of identifying the maker of the barrel, but the barrels themselves often bear marks and these marks mean that the barrel has been proved. With any explosive there is always an element of danger, but the danger can be minimised; and to ensure that there were few burst barrels it was laid down by law that every barrel had to undergo a test. They were usually grossly overloaded with a charge of powder far above their normal load, which was then ignited, and the barrel closely examined. If the violent explosion had not split the barrel or exposed any weaknesses or pinholes then the barrel was stamped with the proof mark and could now be sold and fixed to stock and lock. Two official proof houses existed, one in London and later one in Birmingham; and the information conveyed by these marks can be extremely useful. Many of the makers of flintlock pistols marked their wares on the lock or the barrel or on both. Some gave merely their surname, others put not only their full name but the address as well. In the case of military weapons the lockplate and barrel may well bear additional marks and on British weapons the most common is the broad arrow and the crown indicating that it was a government weapon. In the case of many pistols and long arms the initial or number of the regiment was engraved on some part of the pistol. It is interesting to note that Government weapons up to 1764 bore the word Tower and the date; but it was found that, quite naturally, officers and men were reluctant to accept old dated stock and wanted the latest weapons, so that items tended to get left in store. In order to overcome this problem it was decided that in future no locks would be dated and the practice was indeed abolished in 1764.

AROUND the 1780's there appeared "the perfection of pistols," the duelling pistols prepared by some of the master gunmakers of London; men like Manton, Wogdon, Nock, Egg and Parker. Duelling pistols had to be accurate, easy to aim and very reliable. The usual basic formation of a flintlock dueller comprised a heavy octagonal barrel (heavy to give it stability); a very comfortable stock; and a carefully designed

Fig. 42: A good quality English flintlock with a very large bore, made by the famous gunsmith Henry Nock.

trigger guard which enabled the firer to bring his hand up and line up on his target almost without thinking. To this end many trigger guards had an extended spur which enabled the firer to get his fingers round this extra curve to ensure a really good grip. These pistols were sold in a wooden case complete with many accessories such as a powder flask, bullet mould, screw driver and cleaning rods. The cases were of mahogany, walnut or oak and the inside was divided into sections each designed to hold one of the accessories. Inside, lid and case were usually covered with green baize or similar material and affixed to the inside was to be found the maker's trade card, often illustrated with a small line engraving and bearing name and address and some testimonial. Naturally such complete items as this are in great demand and realise very high prices.

An empty pistol was obviously useless, and from the later 18th century onwards some pistols were fitted with a spring bayonet which could be used as a last resort in self defence. The blunderbuss and pocket pistol were the most common weapons to display this feature; the bayonet was fitted beneath, above or to one side of the barrel. It was held in place by some form of sliding catch, and releasing this clip allowed the bayonet, impelled by a spring, to swing forward and lock into position on a small lug situated at the end of the barrel. The idea seems reasonable but so far very few references to its actual use have been discovered.

The soldier of the 18th century, like his predecessor, was issued with a bayonet to fix to his musket. The method of attachment had been considerably improved and in place of the old plug bayonet which had simply been pushed into the barrel, the weapon now had a tube-like attachment which slotted over the outside of the muzzle. This locked into position and allowed the musket to be fired even when the bayonet was fixed. The bayonet was carried in a sheath suspended from a cross belt.

Powder flasks had largely been abandoned by the armies, and the majority of European troops carried a wooden or japanned metal box hung from their shoulder

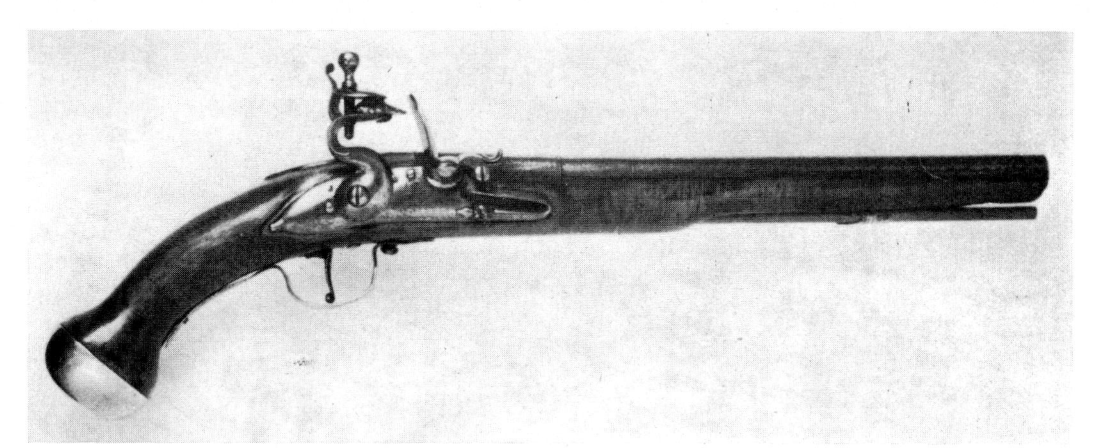

Fig. 43: An English military flintlock pistol of about 1680, with plain brass butt cap. Overall length, 18¼ inches; barrel, 11½ inches. (Gyngell Collection.)

belt in which were placed a number of cartridges. A piece of stiffish paper was carefully rolled around a former and one end sealed by tying or twisting; powder and ball were then inserted, and the other end tied. When in action, the soldier bit or tore the end off the cartridge, and after putting a pinch of powder in the pan poured the rest down the barrel and then with his ramrod, or scouring stick, forced the powder and ball firmly down the musket's barrel. The soldier also had a supply of spare flints, for the quality of flints was rather subject to luck. Many believed that the dark blue, almost black flint provided the best sparks, but in most cases the flint could be relied on with fair certainty to give a maximum of some 30 to 40 shots before it had to be changed. A large proportion of the flints came from an ancient mine in Norfolk, England.

The flintlock was basically a very sound and reliable mechanism, but like both previous systems of ignition it had its disadvantages. Flint and steel was not the most efficient method of ignition and the percentage of occasions on which it failed to produce sufficient sparks was quite high. The priming in the pan was, of course, subject to weather conditions; rain or strong wind could easily prevent the flintlock weapon from firing, and even if the priming fired the main charge might fail to ignite, with only "a flash in the pan". There was an appreciable delay, known as the "hang fire", between the pressing of the trigger and the firing of the weapon. This delay was quite a serious matter for the hunter who had to make due allowance for this time lag when aiming; and in battle this hang fire could well cost a man his life. The answer to these problems lay in the invention of a chemical system of ignition to take the place of the mechanical process, and this was to come early in the 19th century.

Flintlock weapons in general and pistols in particular are very popular collector's items, for they possess special attractions. Each is unique, for all were hand made, and even with pairs there are small differences. They have a grace of their own, and a rather romantic image which endears them to many. Their variety is enormous and offers the collector opportunities to specialise in any one of a number of fields—period, country, style of decoration, type of weapon or the products of a particular maker.

4

Chemicals and Caps

THE flintlock remained in general use for something over 200 years, but by the early 19th century it had reached its ultimate point of development. Its action had become as crisp, smooth and reliable as it was possible to make it under normal circumstances; but it still did not quite satisfy all the requirements of an ideal lock. It was necessary to use priming powder, and this made the action susceptible to all the vagaries of wind and weather. Success was dependent upon the action of a piece of flint which might equally well supply a shower of sparks or none at all. Even if the sparks fired the priming it might just be "a flash in the pan" and not fire the main charge. If the weapon was in constant use the flint wore down the steel which sooner

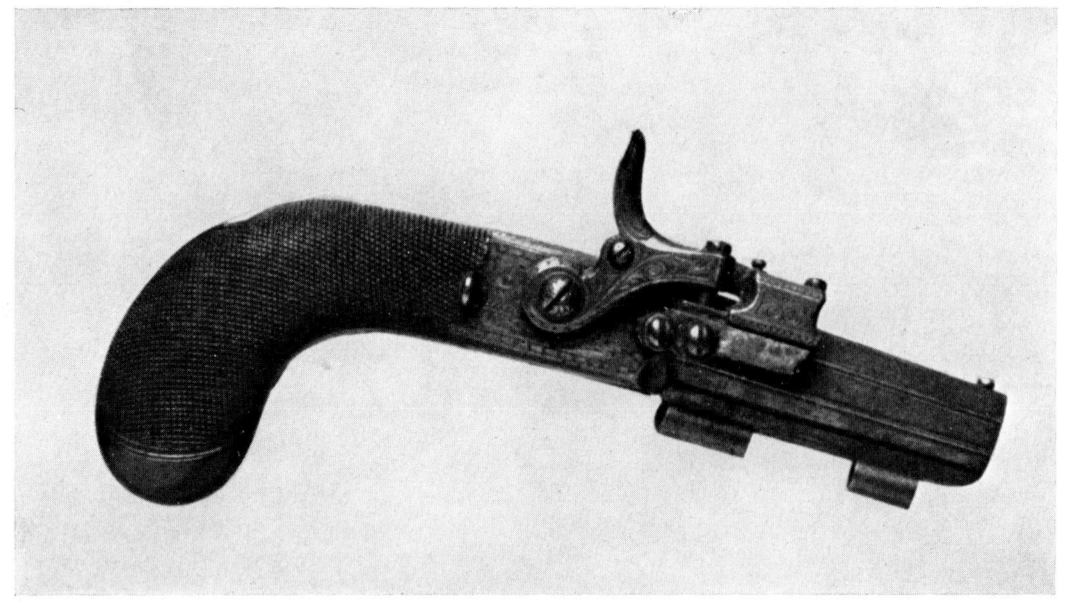

Fig. 45: Small magazine primer using pills, seen here fitted to a pocket pistol. (Perry Collection.)

Opposite, *Fig. 46: Lock of a fowling piece made by Samuel Nock, using small fulminate pellets for ignition. (Bubear Collection.)*

or later had to be replaced. The real solution lay not in further refinements to the system but rather in a completely fresh approach. Basically the problem was how to supply a means of ignition for the main charge. In the matchlock this had been achieved by actual combustion and in both the wheellock and flintlock by sparks produced by friction.

The line of development which was to supply the answer had its origin back in the 17th century, but ironically the motive behind the original research was the improvement of the quality of the explosive force of gunpowder. The ever-expanding horizons of science during the 16th and 17th centuries encouraged men of vision to experiment, and they tried out a whole host of new ideas. Often the research was inspired rather than planned and some of the formulae savour more of necromancers' spells than scientific experiments. However, among the exotic and highly fanciful mixtures tested were some of those very unstable chemicals known as fulminates; Samuel Pepys mentions in his diary a demonstration of gold fulminate. Research in this direction was limited by the difficulty of producing fulminates in any quantity, although French and German chemists were certainly familiar with mercury and gold fulminate. In 1799 an easier method of producing fulminate of mercury was discovered and the powder was again used in an attempt to improve or replace the explosive qualities of gunpowder. Needless to say the results were violent and very nearly disastrous, and that line of development was very soon dropped.

Fortunately for the gun trade, amongst those who read of the new chemicals and experiments was a rather obscure Scottish clergyman. On the east coast of Scotland, just a little to the north of Aberdeen lies the small village of Belhelvie, and to this small village in 1791 was appointed the man who was to change the entire system of firearms ignition. John Alexander Forsyth was an unusual minister of the Scottish church; he was keenly interested in science—sufficiently so to have had a

paper published in the Journal of Natural Philosophy—and an extremely keen shot. It is recorded that he had many times suffered the annoyance of missing a good shot because the flash of the priming and the hang fire had given the quarry warning and enough time to avoid the shot. Forsyth became sufficiently interested in the problem to experiment with methods of overcoming it. One of the solutions he is supposed to have tried was fitting a hood over the pan—a system not dissimilar to the chimney fitted to some of the early wheellocks—but his success was limited. It was about this time that he combined his scientific interest with his shooting. He had no doubt read or heard of the new experiments with fulminates, and it seems that this enterprising cleric sought some way to utilise this knowledge in producing a gun which would fire quickly and also obviate the tell-tale flash of the priming. For a long time he persevered with his experiments; his parishioners must have been extremely tolerant, for it is reported that he spent many hours walking on the seashore pondering the problem. At first he tried to use the fulminate in place of gunpowder, but like all his predecessors met with no success. Then at some time or other he apparently hit upon the idea of replacing the priming altogether, and by 1805 he had produced a workable solution using fulminates.

One of the biggest problems he had to overcome was the means of using fulminate in the only form in which it was obtainable, that is as a powder. He had to devise some means by which small amounts of fulminate could be measured out and no doubt he suffered many disappointments; but at last he felt he had the answer. He appears to have been ambitious, for he was not content to keep the invention to himself and undertook the long journey to London to see if he could interest the British army in the new and improved system of ignition. Forsyth arrived in London and met the

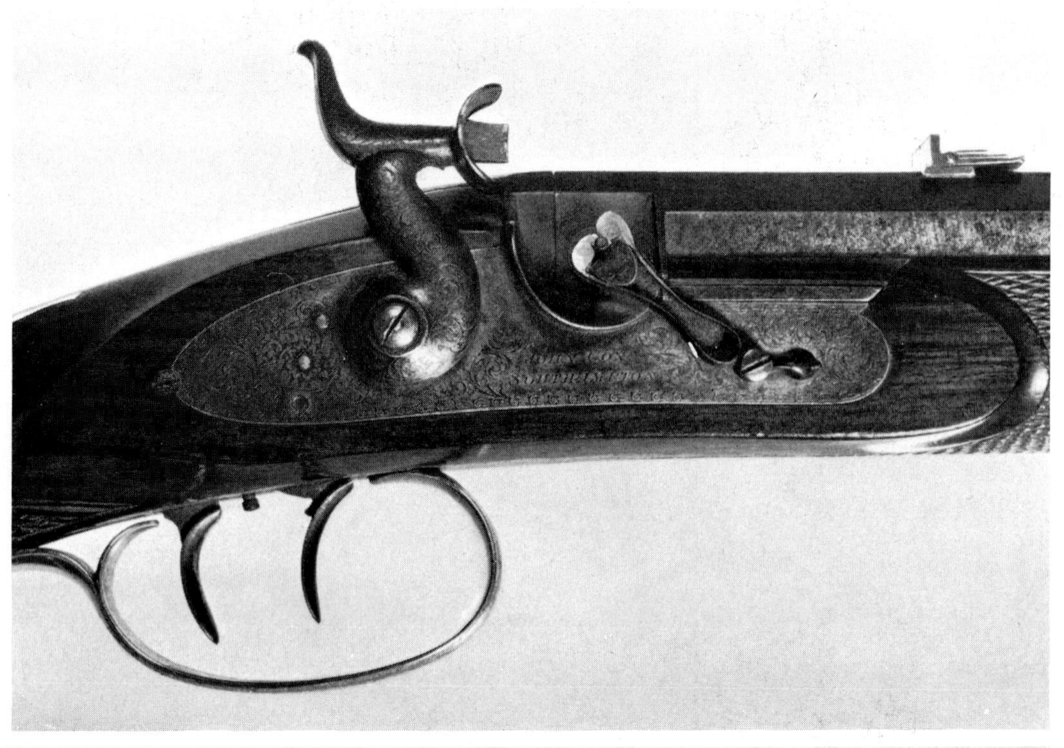

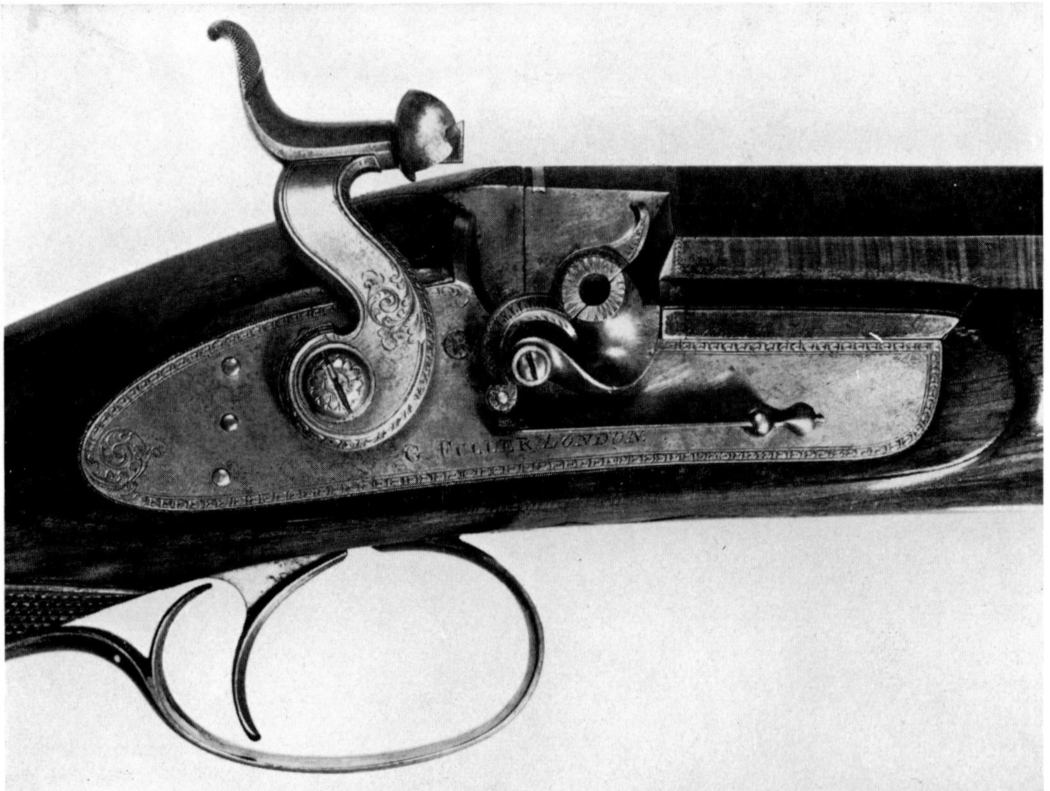
G. FULLER LONDON

Left, *Fig. 47: Tube lock by John Cox of Southampton,* circa *1847. Note the silver mounts and set trigger.* (*Bubear Collection.*)

Master General of Ordnance, Lord Moira, who was sufficiently impressed to offer him facilities for continuing his research and experiments in the Tower of London.

No doubt one of the factors which persuaded Lord Moira to offer some official support was the fact that the existing flintlock weapons could be adapted to the new system. Basically Forsyth's system involved the removal from the lock of the pan, frizzen and frizzen spring and the substitution of a hammer in place of the cock; the internal mechanism of the lock was unchanged. The only other modification was in the barrel; the small touchhole was enlarged to take a small round plug through the centre of which was drilled a small hole terminating in a tiny saucer-like depression. Pivoting around this plug was a small metal container. Seen from the outside it had a key-hole shape and resembled the bottles used at that time for perfume, and was soon referred to as "Forsyth's scent bottle". One end of the "scent bottle" held a small quantity of fulminating powder; the plug acted as a seal to this section of the scent bottle. At the other end was a small plunger, and when the scent bottle was at rest the plunger was seated above the small depression in the breech plug. To prime the mechanism the scent bottle was rotated so that the longer section now came to the top and a few grains of fulminating powder fell into the depression at the end of the touch-hole tunnel. The scent bottle was then returned to its original position so that the striker was in position above the fulminate. If the lock were now cocked and the trigger pressed the hammer swung forward and struck the spring-loaded plunger, which detonated the fulminate. The flash from the fulminate passed via the small touchhole into the main charge. This system was practical but rather delicate, for the construction of the scent bottle was quite complex and it had to be very accurately assembled. Forsyth and his Tower workmen produced two locks, one to fire a carbine and one to fire a cannon. Some official tests were carried out at Woolwich, near London, but the results were very disappointing. In the meantime a new Master General of Ordnance had been appointed; apparently a man of little vision, he was not at all impressed with the results of Forsyth's work and the Scotsman was asked to leave, taking with him his "rubbish".

SUCH a disappointment might well have deterred a lesser man; but in 1807 Forsyth took out what was, in effect, a master patent for all percussion detonating systems. So shrewdly was it worded that Forsyth was able to bring successful actions against several gunmakers who infringed on his patent. In 1811 Forsyth set up a shop in Piccadilly in London, trading under the name of Alexander Forsyth & Co. In his patent he illustrated three systems using his idea, but he seems to have preferred the scent bottle, for the few existing examples of his work nearly all incorporate the scent bottle in some form or another. Forsyth's patent only applied to Great Britain, and on the Continent a number of French gunmakers produced their own versions of his lock.

Forsyth's system had one basic weakness in that it used loose fulminate powder; this represented a serious safety hazard. The scent bottle had to be constructed to quite strict limits of accuracy and both these handicaps prevented its widespread adoption. However, the system was basically sound and the big problem was to find

Left, *Fig. 48: Tube lock by George Fuller of London, 1820.* (*Bubear Collection.*)

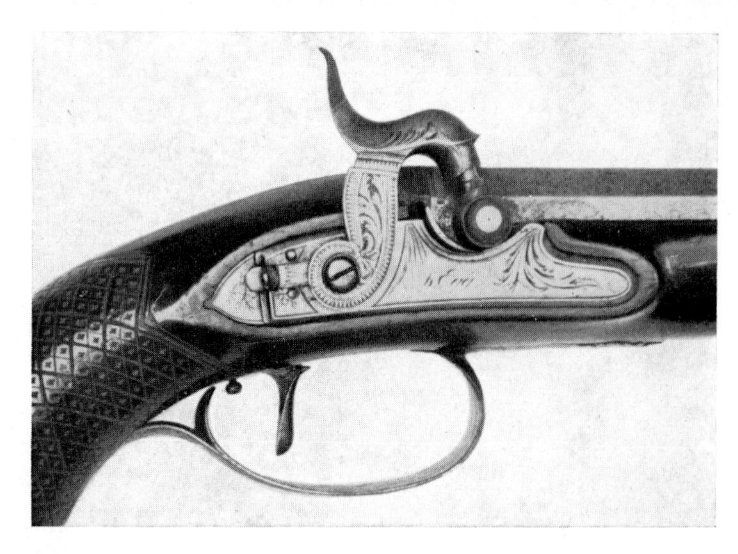

Fig. 49: Converted lock of a duelling pistol by the renowned Durs Egg—note the platinum block.

a way of converting the powder into some more manageable form. One system was to mix it with some binding agent so that it could be fashioned into small pills or pellets. This rather obvious solution was developed simultaneously by a number of gunmakers in America and Europe. Wax was one of the binding agents used but this was not very satisfactory as any warmth softened the pellets and when placed into containers they tended to stick together in a single sticky mass.

In America a Doctor Samuel Guthrie also hit upon the idea of pills, using potassium chlorate mixed with gum arabic. His system is usually referred to as the punchlock, and tradition has it that it acquired this name because Dr. Guthrie while demonstrating his new idea fired a cannon by placing a pill into the vent and then hitting it with an ordinary metal punch to detonate it and fire the cannon. Realising that few soldiers were likely to have a hammer and punch with them Dr. Guthrie further developed his idea, and soon produced a workable punchlock. The frizzen was removed, the pan reduced in size until it was just big enough to hold one pill, and the hammer was modified by the addition of a sharp pointed iron striker. The system worked quite well and the lock was patented by one William A. Hart of New York in 1827. An interesting feature of these locks was a return to the sliding pan cover first seen on wheellocks. The weapon could be primed by placing a pill into position and the cover was then slid over, to be automatically removed when the hammer was cocked.

In England Joseph Manton, the well known London gunmaker, patented a pellet or pill lock in 1816; in his design the pill was placed into a small tube which was fitted on the hammer. The pill was held in place by a small plunger and when the hammer fell the plunger struck the pill and detonated it. Manton also patented another idea using a small conical wooden plug, which was placed into a shaped cavity over the touchhole. A small pellet was dropped into the plug and was detonated by an iron pin which was banged down by the hammer. Other systems particularly favoured in Europe involved placing the pellet in a small recess near the touchhole where a pivoted cover held it in place.

One development made possible by the production of the pill or pellet was that of automatic priming. A number of systems were invented and the majority of them comprised some form of magazine holding a number of pellets which were allowed, one at a time, to fall into the cavity over the touchhole. Despite improvements which

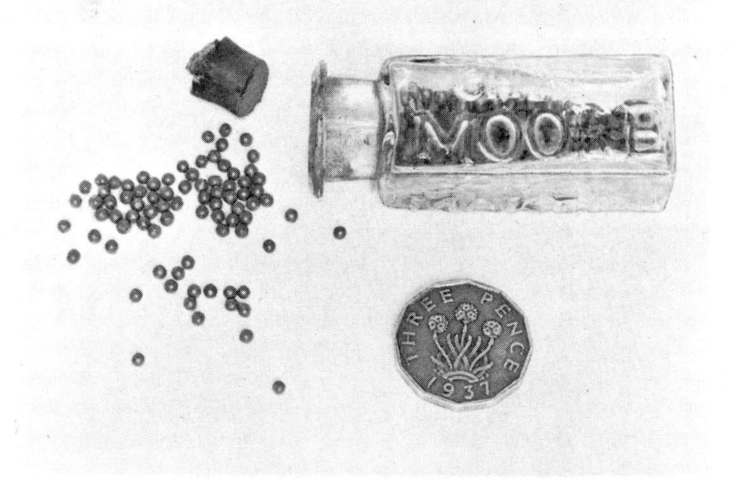

Fig. 50: Bottle of mercury fulminate priming pellets made by Charles Moore—each about 2 mm. in diameter. (The coin is ·8 inch in diameter.)

soon rendered the pellet obsolete a number of enthusiasts still advocated their use and patents were taken out as late as 1853 for pellets of various compositions.

One of the most serious handicaps in all pellet systems was the sheer physical size for they were so tiny that they were extremely difficult to handle in the field. Many gunmakers sought to make them more manageable, and one method was to fit the tiny pellets into a holder of some kind; soft metal, paper and card were all used with this object in view. Small pellets of the fulminate were mounted at the centre of discs or squares and the patch was usually covered by a thin layer of wax to render it waterproof. Some of the lock systems using patches had the cap fitting into the hammer while in others they were placed in position over the touchhole. A number of patents were taken out including one for a magazine priming using discs, which was granted in 1852 to an American, Christian Sharps; a name that was later to become famous in gun-making circles. He used small copper discs stored in a spring-loaded tube by the side of the touchhole; as the hammer fell it automatically pushed the top disc into position. Systems using discs and patches were never widely exploited by gunmakers and examples of such weapons are comparatively scarce.

Another approach to the task of making it easier to handle the priming powders was the so-called "tube lock", in which the fulminates were fitted into tubes of hollow metal or quills which could be slipped into position at the touchhole. In many ways they were more convenient to handle than the patches or pellets, but there was a tendency for them to send a small jet of flame sideways or even to blow out of the touchhole. Some gunmakers overcame this serious hazard by fitting a shield on to the hammer, so reducing the dangers to anybody standing by the side of the shooter. Joseph Manton patented such a lock in 1818, and although it was considered an infringement of Forsyth's master patent many weapons using it were made. Another means of avoiding these unpleasant possibilities was to make the tube wedge-shaped, so that it dropped into a specially shaped pillar nipple. The hammer struck down directly on the top of the nipple, holding the tube firmly in position even when it exploded.

A further development in this direction was tape priming; two long, thin strips of paper were stuck together with small pellets of fulminate placed between them, centrally along the entire length. Continous lengths of priming obviously had advan-

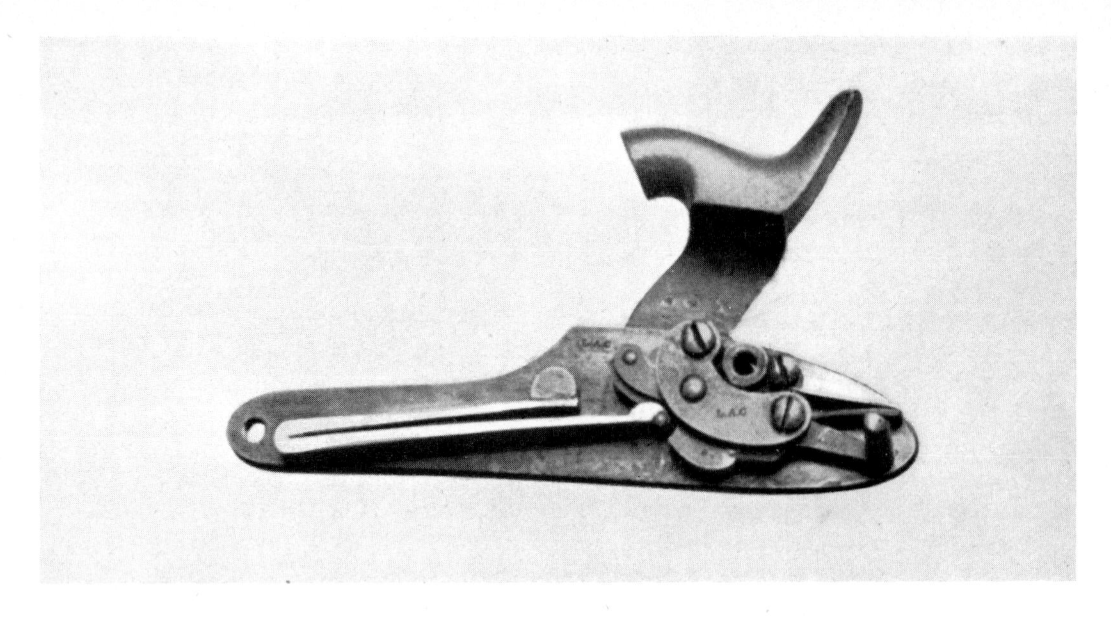

Fig. 51: Interior of a percussion lock from an Enfield rifle of about 1850.

tages for magazine or self-priming weapons. In 1845 a Doctor Edward Maynard, an American dentist, patented such a tape primer in which a coil of the tape was placed in a small compartment near the nipple. As the hammer was cocked a cogged wheel pushed the tape up so that one of the pellets was placed over the nipple. When the trigger was pressed the hammer exploded the fulminate and also cut the tape. The process was naturally repeated each time the hammer was cocked. The tape primers were fitted to a variety of weapons, both pistols and long arms.

ALL these systems had advantages, but none of them attained the success or the general adoption that distinguished the copper percussion cap. As with so many firearm developments, the origins of the copper cap are obscure. Many famous gun-makers and shooters have laid claim to being the true originator of these extremely useful little devices, but none has presented an irrefutable case. The truth of the matter is probably that a number of people were engaged in perfecting the same idea more or less simultaneously. On balance modern students give the credit for the invention to an English landscape painter who emigrated to America, by name Joshua Shaw. Although Shaw was not granted a patent until 1822 and there were French patents for the cap which predate this, he always claimed that he had used the copper percussion cap at least seven years before. Even the patent of 1822 is unrecorded but Shaw must have had a good case, for he was able to persuade the American Government that his claim was strong enough for him to receive the very large sum of 18,000 dollars as compensation for the use of his invention by the United States Army. Henry Wilkinson, writing in 1841 in his book *Engines of War*, says that he was told by Shaw that in 1814 he had invented a steel cap containing detonating powder which, having been used, could be primed again. Shaw himself claimed that the idea of caps occurred when he was experimenting with a paste of fulminate stored in a small steel tube. One of these

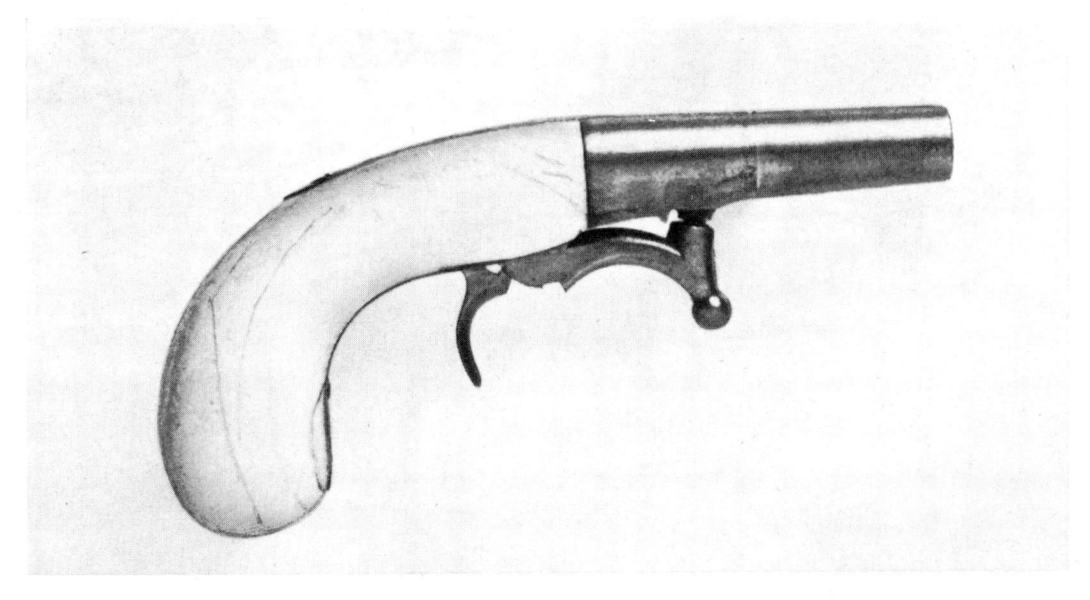

Fig. 52: Underhammer percussion pocket pistol with ivory butt. (Gyngell Collection.)

tubes was fitted over the end of an artist's pencil and was knocked or dropped. The charge exploded, and started Shaw on the design of caps. The story is somewhat reminiscent of the invention of cannon by Black Berthold! In the same book it is stated that Shaw used a pewter cap in 1815 which was intended to be used but once and then discarded. In the following year, 1816, he produced a copper cap which was the prototype for all later examples. Shaw claimed that he had not applied for a patent at that time because he was advised that Forsyth's master patent would preclude any such grant to him. Shaw emigrated to Philadelphia, U.S.A. in 1817 and for some unexplained reason he did not apply for a patent until 1822. Those French patents recorded for 1818 and 1820 are no proof that Shaw's idea was not the original one: the French gun trade was well known for its pirating of foreign patents!

The percussion cap consisted of a small copper tube closed at one end and shaped rather like a top hat, with a small deposit of a detonating composition inside the top, covered by a thin layer of silver foil and sealed into place with a drop of shellac. The cap fitted over a small tube known as the nipple; when it was struck by the hammer, the flash travelled straight through the nipple to the main charge. The cap was not an immediate success as the copper had a nasty habit of splitting into small pieces. In the case of pistols the result could be painful but not dangerous, but for the shooter with the lock close to his face the splinters could have very serious effects. John Mills, writing in 1845, said that many an eye had been lost particularly in the case of French caps, which were apparently made with very thin metal and so had a tendency to shatter easily. Some experts also claimed that they were a serious health hazard!

The early detonating compounds also had a corrosive effect upon the metal, but in 1823 a further improvement was made when E. Goode Wright proposed the substitution of mercury fulminate as being far less corrosive. One of the London chemists—Frederick Joyce—was soon producing caps with this compound and claiming to be the inventor of the anti-corrosive gun cap. The name Joyce is often to be found on old

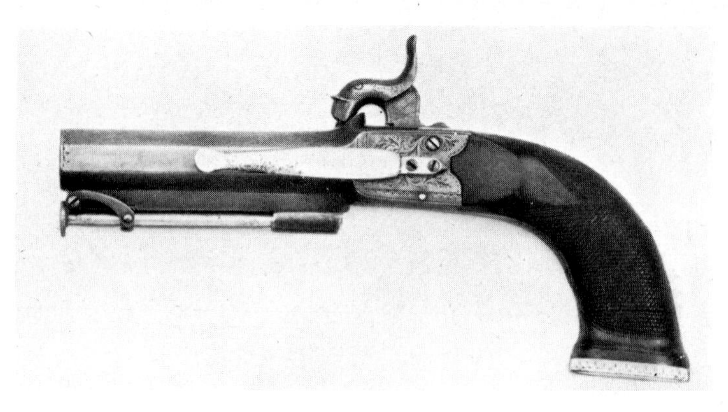

Fig. 53: One of a pair of percussion pistols with concealed triggers and belt hooks; the trigger slides out as the pistol is cocked. Overall length, 8 inches; barrel, 3½ inches. (Tower of London.)

percussion cap tins with this description included on the label. The danger from shattering caps was overcome by two simple methods. First the copper casing was made slightly thicker and ridged vertically, resulting in its splitting into four large pieces. In addition the hammer was made with the nose recessed so that it fitted over the nipple, thus enclosing the cap completely.

If the civilian was slow to take up the percussion cap, the military were even slower. This was not due entirely to conservatism but to a necessarily cautious appraisal of the problems involved. While a system might work beautifully for a hunter with time to spare, under no pressure, and able to carry out careful maintenance of his weapons, it might break down under the harsh conditions and rough usage of the battlefield. Most nations began experiments and trials with the percussion system in the 1830's, and France actually issued some percussion arms in 1829, but it was not until the early 1840's that most European and American armies were equipped with weapons using the percussion system. The British Government started their tests in 1831 but did not officially adopt the new system until 1838. A number of the old faithful Brown Bess muskets were converted to the new system, but soon specially designed weapons were in use. The caps were normally carried in a small pouch attached to the belt but it was not always easy for the soldier to slip his fingers into the pouch, pick out the cap and place it firmly over the nipple ready for firing. For the hunter in cold weather the problem of handling such small items while wearing gloves was equally frustrating, if not so potentially fatal. One solution offered by many gunmakers was to supply cap dispensers which were simply spring loaded devices which delivered one cap at a time. There were also numerous attempts to design a magazine for percussion caps, but none was ever really successful.

Like all new departures the percussion cap was not immediately taken up by every gunmaker and shooter in the world. For some years flint was still supreme, but gradually the apparent advantages of the percussion system won more converts. Some of the gunmakers manufactured locks which could be used, with only a simple adjustment, for flintlock ignition or percussion, and these double locks are another unusual item which do occasionally appear on the antique market. Many firearms owners, won over by the new system's simplicity and certainty, had their own weapons converted to percussion. It is not uncommon to find fowling pieces, military muskets and pistols converted from flint to percussion by the simplest method of removing the unnecessary appendages of the lock and substituting for the touchhole a small drum fitted with a nipple. Usually the conversion can be spotted, for there are tell-tale holes in the lockplate which have been filled in but will still be visible on close examination. The general style of the weapon will also naturally be earlier than one would expect for percussion. For the collector it is a tragedy that so many weapons were converted, for flintlock pistols converted to percussion are far less popular than any other type. It is an interesting comment on the long working life of some of these weapons that it is not uncommon to see pistols of the early 18th century converted to percussion. This argues that the weapon had been in use for something like a century before it was converted and probably continued in use for a further 20 or 30 years. In the case of boxlock pistols the conversion was very simple and many of the pocket pistols simply had the frizzen removed and a nipple screwed directly into the breech where the touchhole had been. In one or two cases it may be found that the flint is replaced by a small metal hammer head and these will be the only actual changes carried out; in other weapons the cock was removed and a hammer substituted.

From 1820 to 1850 there was a great deal of rather academic discussion as to the relative virtues of flintlock and detonating or percussion systems for hunting weapons, and each system had its own supporters. Generally it was agreed that the percussion fired faster and with greater certainty, while others maintained that the flintlock gave less recoil and was more reliable in other ways. Most of the shooting books of the time devote considerable space to this vexed question. Certainly flint gave less recoil, for some of the gas from the explosion was able to escape easily through the touchhole. With the percussion system the only escape was through the nipple, fairly firmly capped by the exploded percussion cap and the hammer, so there was a tendency to a greater kick. A simple remedy was found for this by drilling a tiny pin hole into the breech through the plug so that enough gas escaped to make the recoil far less drastic.

Lt. Colonel P. Hawker, a renowned shooter of the early 19th century, wrote a book entitled *Instruction to Young Sportsmen* which ran to numerous editions. In the sixth edition (1830) he discounts the percussion system, claiming that the gun trade were promoting it because the detonating system shook the guns to pieces and wore them out quicker, thus creating more trade. He also published the results of tests he had carried out showing that a flintlock gave a better pattern of shot and penetration. However, his final conclusion was a general, rather grudging, approval of the new system. He stated that percussion guns needed to be stronger than flintlocks, and heavier to withstand the recoil.

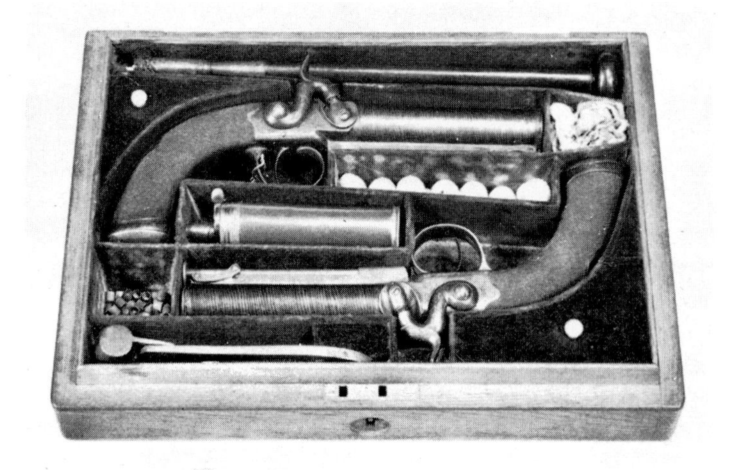

Fig. 54: A cased pair of percussion pistols complete with all accessories.

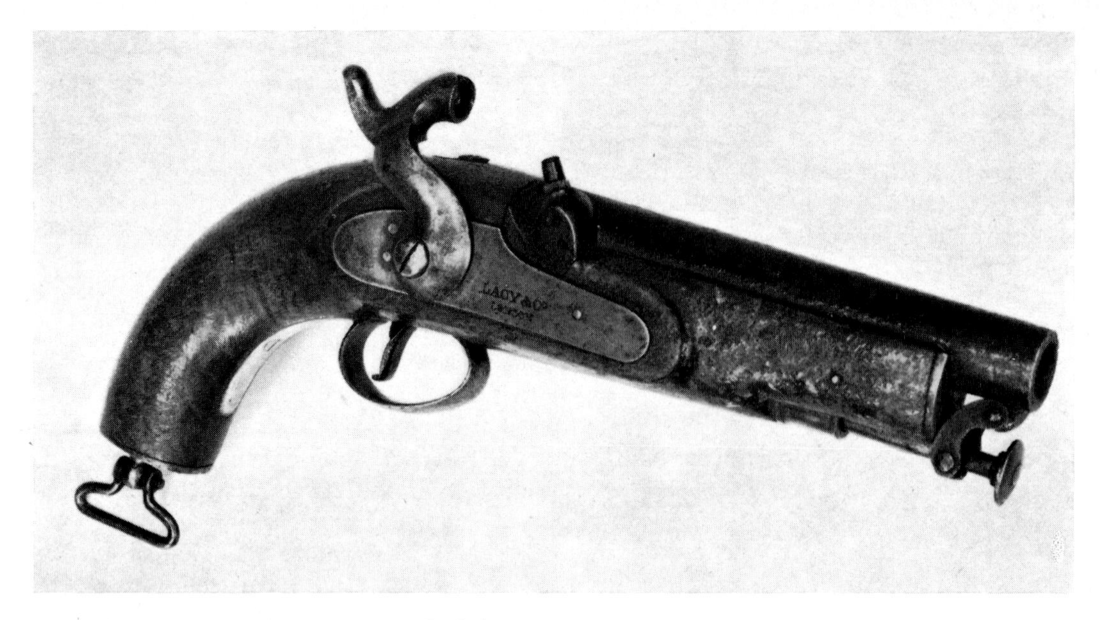

Above, *Fig. 55: A typical percussion pistol of about 1840, with swivel ramrod and lanyard ring.* (*Dominion Museum, New Zealand.*)

The simplicity of production and design made the percussion lock firearm cheap to produce, and this encouraged a number of smaller gunmakers to enter the field. Large numbers of cheap and rather nasty percussion pistols were produced in Birmingham, England and Liège, Belgium. Most are of the pocket pistol type but shotguns, double barrelled pistols and revolvers were also made in quantity. Most are easily recognisable by their rather inferior workmanship, and the lack of makers' names and proof marks.

Every type of weapon made in flintlock was also produced with the percussion lock; military, pocket, sporting, multi-barrelled, all were supplied in bulk. There were certain fresh departures as in the under-hammer guns and totally enclosed locks, but far more important were the new possibilities offered by the introduction of the system. Repeating weapons became for the first time a practical possibility.

REVOLVING weapons had been produced as early as the 16th century, but they were always rather clumsy and too complex to be really useful. Now the cap enabled men like Samuel Colt of the U.S.A. to produce revolvers which were reliable, practical and simple to use. During the 18th century and early 19th century the most common weapons for personal defence were the blunderbuss and the pocket pistol, but now the percussion revolver began to replace both these weapons. Some percussion blunderbusses were produced and a number were converted from flintlock, but as a group they were discarded. In England and France the pepperbox, a simple form of revolver, was very popular but by the middle of the century revolvers were in general use. Apart from the hand-held revolvers many manufacturers produced revolving carbines and long arms for, until the advent of the metal cartridge, the revolving cylinder was the most satisfactory method available for repeating weapons.

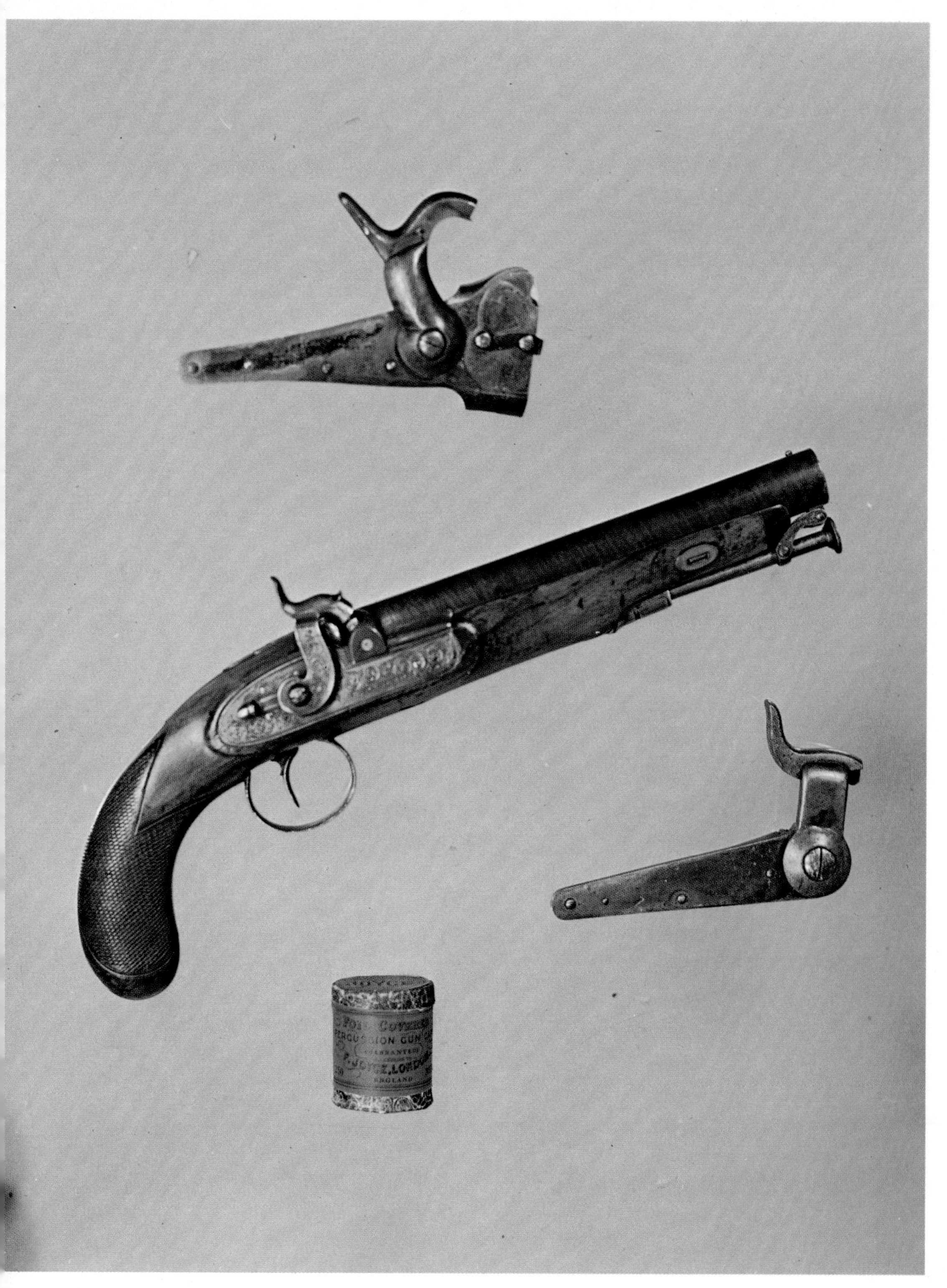

Plate 8 *Percussion pistol, and two separate locks with caps.*

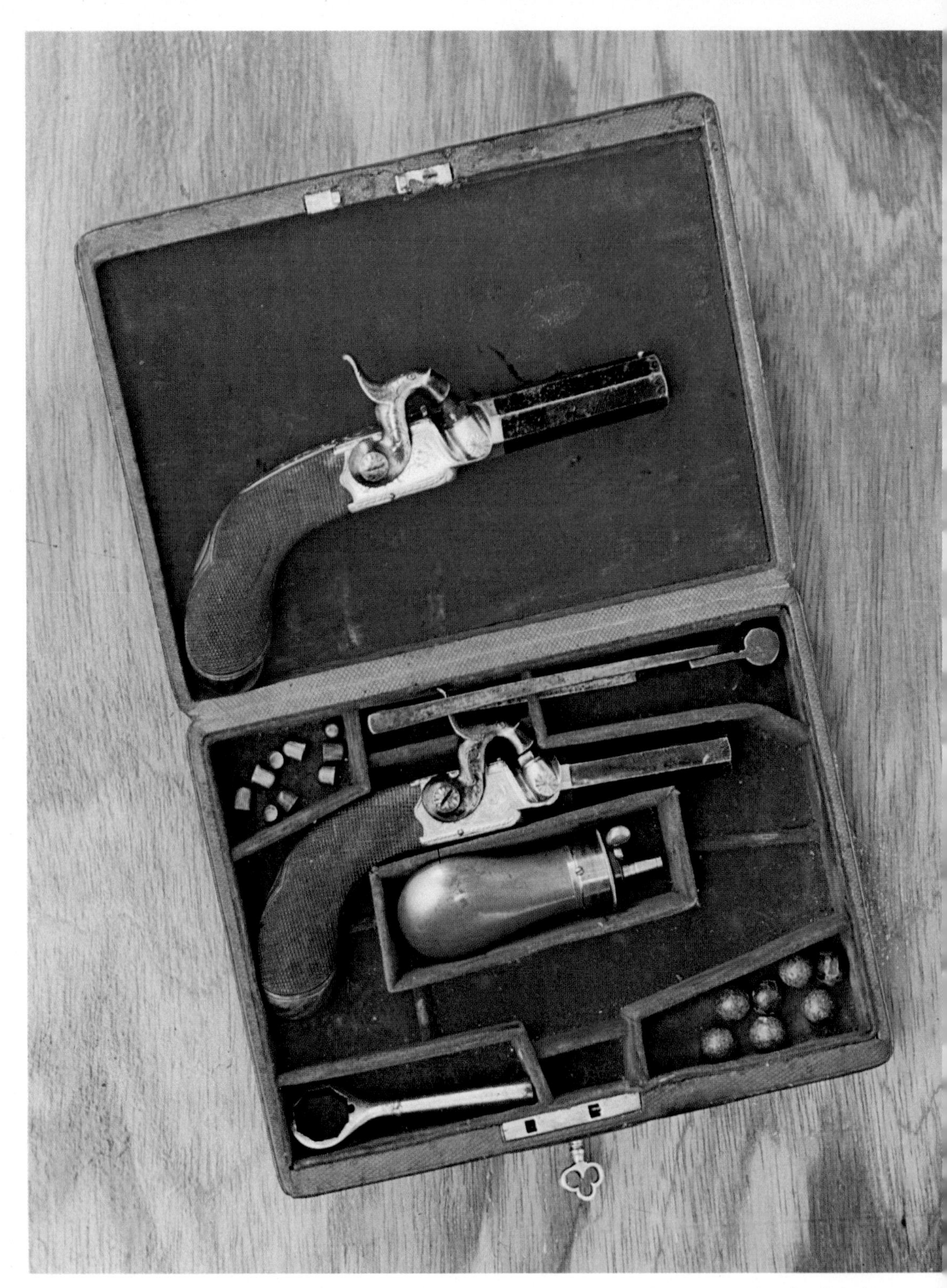

Plate 9 *Cased pair of percussion pistols by Conway of Manchester. Overall length, 5½ inches; barrels, 2¾ inches; bore, ·36 inch.* (*Gyngell Collection.*)

Fig. 56: Colt revolver of the "Dragoon" type bearing London proof marks, circa *1853; these weapons are extremely popular with collectors, both for their historical associations and for their superb lines. Barrel, 7½ inches; ·44 calibre. (Dominion Museum, New Zealand.)*

The percussion system was also to make possible the introduction of breech-loading cartridge weapons, but this development did not take place until the middle of the 19th century and is a fascinating study in its own right. At about the same time rifles became more or less general issue to the armies of the world.

Basically the lock mechanism remained unaltered throughout the percussion period apart from one inovation—the back-action lock. In this mechanism the main-spring was fitted to the rear of the tumbler and cock instead of beneath it as in normal locks. Lt. Colonel Hawker mentions these weapons in 1830 and says that they were good in that they ensured that the corrosive effects of the fulminates were less likely to affect the mechanism. Joseph Manton did not approve of them since they spoiled the line and convenience of the stock. Despite this they were used on a variety of weapons.

Percussion weapons were not, as a group, quite as popular with collectors as flintlocks. However, this state of affairs has changed, for the already strong and constantly rising demand for flintlock weapons is raising the price above the level of many collectors' pockets. Collectors of antique firearms are turning their attention towards these more mundane weapons. One of the factors which had somewhat reduced their interest in the eyes of enthusiasts was that they were produced on a larger scale than the flintlocks and lack their individuality. This argument does not seem to have prevented the massive interest in percussion revolvers produced in large quantities by Colt in the U.S.A. and England, for their value increases almost daily. English percussion revolvers are also beginning to climb in value although still lagging behind American examples.

For the collector prepared to consider the percussion weapon on its own merits there is much to please. Certainly the long arms of the first half of the 19th century are of great interest, for so many makers were experimenting with ways of producing breech-loading weapons using percussion caps that the number of variations on the theme is enormous.

5

Military Firearms

It might well be argued that all firearms are "military", but in the collector's world the term is usually understood to apply only to officially issued weapons or those of a type known to have been carried by organised forces. This definition is, of course, imprecise and there are a number of fringe weapons, especially the earlier examples, which might well be included. One might well feel that the term "Regulation Weapon" is preferable for it suggests an overall authority setting down a pattern. As a distinct and separate group military firearms may be said to date only from the late 16th or early 17th century. Prior to this date armies and bodies of troops were raised and equipped on a very personal basis by the officer commanding or the feudal tenant-in-chief. There was consequently little, if any, uniformity of equipment or dress. With the introduction of gunpowder and the development of new tactics there was a gradual but positive change towards a system of standard arms and uniforms.

There had always been a degree of uniformity in the case of certain élite troops or bodyguards; Henry VIII's bodyguard was equipped with pistol shields, while certain cavalry units were issued with regulation wheellocks. Ceremonial guards were often equipped with identical pole arms or swords, but these cases were exceptional and atypical. Prior to the 17th century most armies were a motley collection of soldiers with little uniformity of equipment, but where there were "standard" weapons ownership was usually indicated by the inclusion of a coat of arms somewhere on the weapon itself. Frequently these arms were engraved, etched or even chiselled into the lock or barrel; but such weapons are extremely rare, and it will be a very lucky collector who finds any examples of military firearms pre-dating the 17th century.

Any uniformity implies some control of manufacture, and prior to the 16th century armourers, swordsmiths and gunmakers were, broadly speaking, free from any such control. In the England of Henry VIII the firearms trade was largely, but not exclusively, in the hands of foreigners encouraged to settle here by the king. Many were established in the neighbourhood of the Tower in what was known as the Minories, and this remained the case until the late 18th and early 19th centuries. London was the principal centre of firearms production although there were a few provincial makers. When the English Civil War broke out in 1642 it was the gunmakers of London who

Fig. 57: Typical matchlocks of the 16th century, with long lockplates and peep sights above the breeches. Both have lever-type action (Tower of London.)

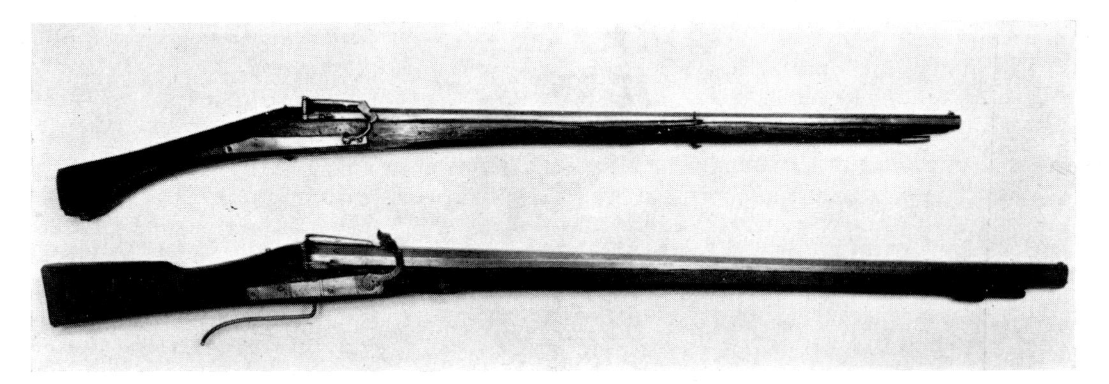

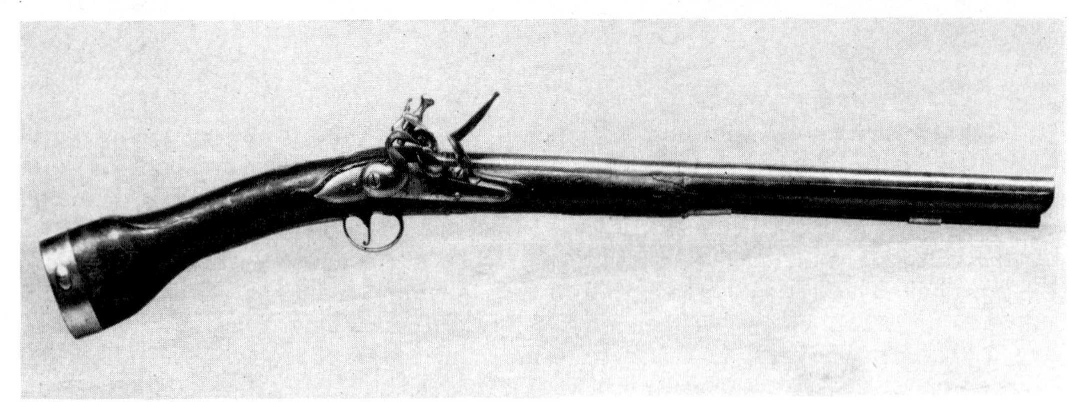

Fig. 58: Pistol-carbine of the late 17th century; the butt plate can be extended to form a long butt when firing from the shoulder. Overall length, 26½ inches; barrel, 16¾ inches. (Glasgow Art Gallery and Museum).

were largely responsible for the collection, repair and supply of firearms. Efforts were made to persuade some of them to settle in the provinces by the offer of certain privileges. Around 1630 Birmingham's gun trade began to develop, and by 1643 it had expanded sufficiently for it to be supplying firearms to the Parliamentary armies.

Civil war brought about rapid strides in the setting up of a more uniform system of arms supply and the official body known as The Council of War drew up certain rules specifying details of the weapons to be supplied to the armed forces. However, the majority of these specifications define nothing more than barrel length, size of ball or overall length so that it is not possible to be certain that any particular weapon was indeed a government military issue.

The military firearms of the 17th century were, of course, almost exclusively matchlocks, some with barrels four feet long and others six inches shorter. Most of the 17th century military firearms bear no identifying marks to distinguish them as being officially ordered and frequently the contract only stipulates that they shall be "full bore and proof and 4 feet longe" and makes no mention of any marks apart from the initials of the armourer. Thus in 1645 Walter Benge was ordered to stamp his weapons with a W.B., William Watson with W.W. and William Fell with a W.F. Weapons ordered by the official supply body, The Ordnance, were tested for strength and were then described as Tower Proof. Later this procedure was modified and from the time of the later Stuart monarchs, British Military firearms bore (usually on the lockplate) the Royal Cypher, the crown and initials of the sovereign.

DURING the later part of the 17th century the process of conversion from matchlock to flintlock was well in hand and the majority of the troops carried a large flintlock musket. By the early 18th century the British Army flintlock had taken on what was to remain its basic shape for the next 200 years. A large bore barrel (about .75 inches) 46 inches long was fitted to a plain wooden stock with a chunky, but pleasing, shaped butt. In a slot cut into the stock beneath the barrel was housed the ramrod. The fittings and furniture were usually of brass and comprised a band of brass around the stock beneath the muzzle, the fore end; the trigger guard; ramrod pipes which helped secure the rod; a brass plate screwed to the end of the butt; and a side plate which helped strengthen the stock and housed the screws securing the lock.

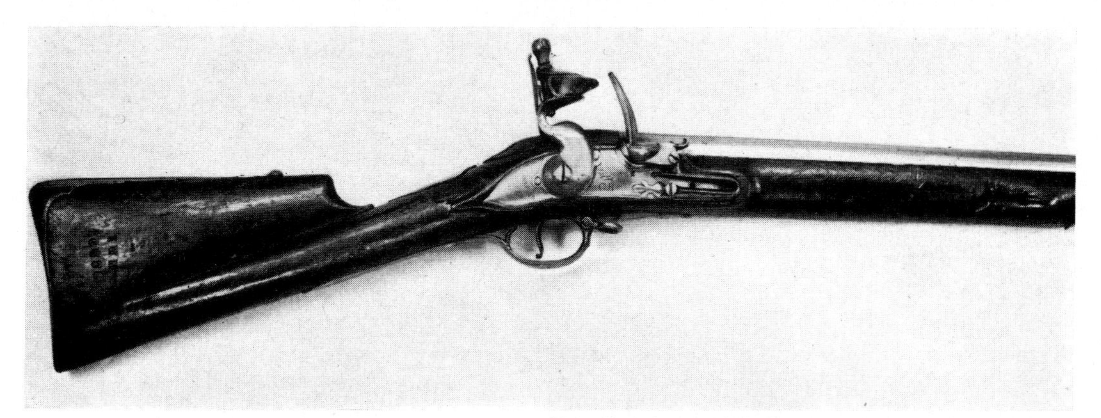

Fig. 59: Butt and lock of an early military flintlock musket; the lockplate bears the Royal cypher (G R below a crown), the maker's name RANSFORD and the date 1717. (Tower of London.)

Locks were usually large, about seven inches long, and lacked all decoration although the maker's name and date of manufacture were usually engraved at the rear end. Changes in lock design are useful pointers in dating weapons; those of the early part of the 18th century are most often flat with a somewhat drooping appearance and frequently have a dog catch fitted—a small flat metal hook fitted to the rear of the cock. This could be engaged with a notch cut into the back of the cock to hold it locked into the safe position. On weapons of this date the trigger guards are thin and rather crude, while the screw which engages with the tang or metal bar extending back from the barrel is so arranged that it traverses the stock from the bottom through to the top. This method of attachment was abandoned in the early 18th century and henceforward the tang screw was fitted from above passing down through the tang and into the stock. A further pointer is the style of stock, for on very early matchlocks and snaphaunce muskets the wooden stock beneath the barrel extended to the muzzle. When socket bayonets were introduced early in the 18th century the stocks were modified, a small section being cut from the end and a flat brass fore end fitted so that the bayonet could slide over the end of the barrel.

Not all lockplates were flat, and there seem to have been two distinct varieties; one with the flat lockplate and dog lock and another with a rounded lockplate. Many of the latter type show clear signs that they were originally fitted with the dog catch but that it had been removed and the screw hole filled in.

Many of the regiments were still being equipped at the discretion and whim of their colonel, but this profusion of weapons was gradually reduced and in 1722 it was decreed that in future all arms should be made "according to the said pattern and proved and viewed by the Proper Officers of the Ordnance". The final distillation of design was to produce the well known "Brown Bess"; this name is applied to a number of muskets of varying pattern but which retain basically the same shape and style. Why Brown? Why Bess? These questions have exercised the talents of amateur and professional etymologists for some time. Some argue that Bess is a corruption of Buchse (German-"gun") and the brown is said to refer to the stock; others would argue that the brown referred to the barrel, which was indeed browned. It is a dispute unlikely to be settled to everybody's satisfaction. The term "Brown Bess" is not recorded before the late 18th century, but the musket was in service from about 1720 to 1840.

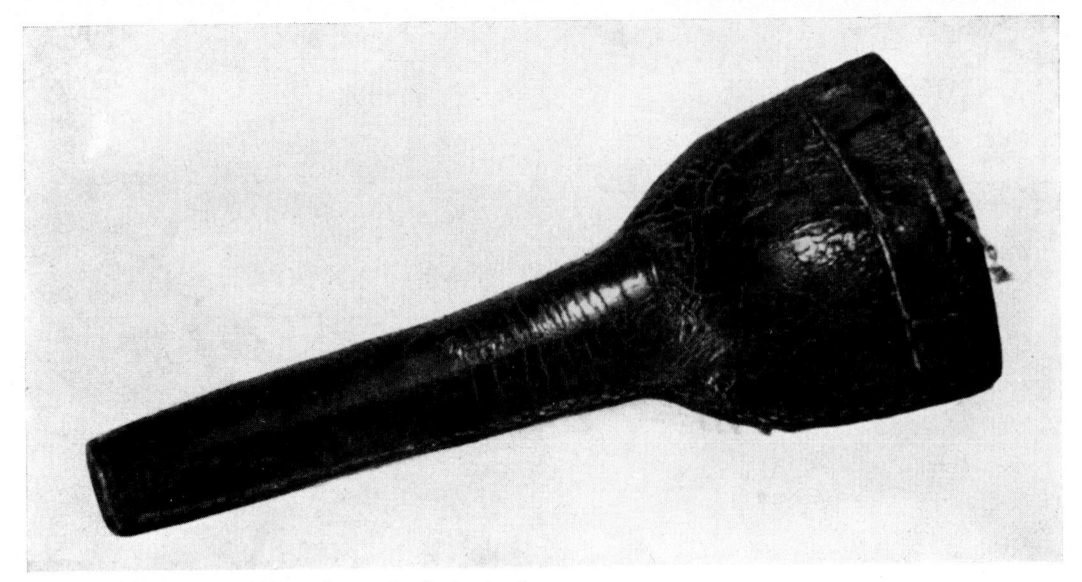

Fig. 60: Black leather holster for a wheellock pistol; a pair of these would have been carried at the horse's neck. (Woollacott Collection.)

The earliest form of Brown Bess was basically the same as the musket described above with a 46 inch barrel; it had brass furniture and was fitted with a wooden ramrod. The lock was slightly drooping and some seven inches long. From around 1740 there are increasingly common references to the Short Land Musket which was basically identical but was fitted with a barrel six inches shorter. These two forms of musket, Long Land and Short Land, were to remain in general use until the 1780's with only minor modification such as the introduction of the steel ramrod which was certainly in use as early as 1724. Steel ramrods were obviously less liable to damage than wooden ones but they did not seat as tightly in the ramrod pipes; this necessitated some slight modification in the stock in that a small spring was fitted on the inside of the last ramrod pipe to grip the ramrod firmly and hold it in position.

Whilst a long barrel might conceivably afford some improvement in accuracy (and experiments cast doubt on this assumption), there is no doubt that a 46 inch or 42 inch barrel could be a great hindrance under certain conditions. Certainly for horsemen or artillerymen they represented a considerable encumbrance; for these and others a shorter version of the musket was produced. This type of weapon was known as a carbine and normally fired a smaller diameter ball. Carbines were usually carried suspended from a shoulder belt fitted with a spring clip which engaged with a sliding ring mounted on a bar at the side of the stock.

Pistols were essentially weapons for the cavalry and for officers and were not generally regarded highly. In the case of officers they were most frequently privately purchased, but cavalry troops received issue weapons. Much of their story is uncertain for pistols are less well documented than long arms. Most have a very similar appearance and differ only in barrel length: Heavy Dragoons, 12 inches; Life Guards, ten inches; and Light Dragoons, nine inches. Stocks, usually of walnut, were plain and fitted with brass furniture and a wooden ramrod. The butt terminated in a brass cap with spurs extending along the sides of the butt and in early pistols these spurs were very long, but as the 18th century progressed they were reduced in size until in the early part of the 19th century they were mere curves on the butt cap. Some pistols are marked with the initials of the regiment, e.g. R.H.G.—Royal Horse Guards; and both pistols and muskets prior to 1764 will be found to carry a date engraved on the lockplate. The practice was discontinued in that year because officers and men were often very reluctant to accept articles which were apparently several years old whereas, in fact, they were almost certainly brand new, never having been issued. Collectors of military firearms must surely regret this decision more than any other made by the Ordnance.

THE outbreak of the Napoleonic wars and the spreading conflict throughout Europe increased the overall demand for firearms so much that the normal suppliers were unable to keep pace with demand. Birmingham turned out brass furniture, trigger guards, butt caps and pipes by their thousands. Components produced in Birmingham were shipped to London where they were assembled by the local gunmakers, but even they were unable to supply the enormous demands of the Ordnance. Those components sent to the Tower were assembled under the control of the staff of the Small Gun Office. There was also a heavy demand from private bodies such as the East India Company which maintained considerable armed forces. Thus much of the gunmakers' output did not find its way directly to the Ordnance. Efforts to overcome the shortages were made by ordering large numbers of weapons from Belgium, particularly from Liège, but this was not a very satisfactory solution for the work was not up to standard and supply was slow. Eventually the situation became so difficult that it was decided that an approach should be made to The East India Company requesting permission to purchase their entire stock of new weapons. In 1794 the Court of Directors of the East India Company agreed to this sale and the Ordnance purchased a very large number of

Fig. 61: An unusual military weapon, used for discharging small grenades; the lock bears the name JOURSON and the weapon probably dates from the mid-18th century. (*Tower of London.*)

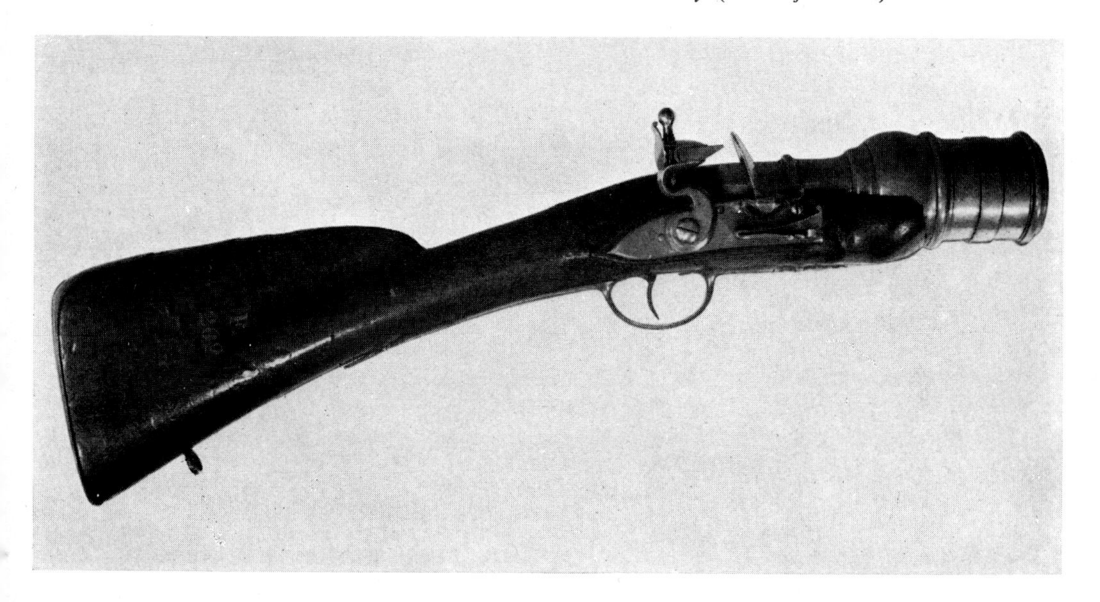

the East India pattern musket. The India pattern musket was slightly inferior on most counts—the barrel was shorter, only 39 inches; the brass furniture was plainer and simpler, whilst the wood used for the stocks was of second grade quality. However, having acquired such enormous numbers of these weapons the Ordnance felt that they might as well become a general pattern and so the musket with the 39 inch barrel was adopted as more or less standard in 1797.

In 1802 the Ordnance produced its own type of India pattern musket which was dubbed the New Land Model. It consisted of a plain wooden stock with a 42 inch barrel and was, in effect, simply a better made India pattern weapon. The lockplate was flat, some six and a half inches long, and the graceful swan-neck cock was replaced by a flat ring-neck cock, often with a very full belly. Later a second model was produced with a 39 inch barrel and fitted with sights and a scroll to the trigger guard, both designed to ensure a better performance for the marksman.

Pistols had remained basically unchanged apart from the introduction of the

Below, *Fig. 62: Small contemporary print showing two stages of arms drill in the mid-18th century. In the left hand view, the soldier is withdrawing his ramrod from its pipes prior to loading his musket.*

Plate 10 *A pair of leather, brass-mounted holsters of the late 18th century, with a pair of brass-barrelled officer's pistols by Bond of London. Overall length of pistols, 11 inches; barrels, 6 inches; bore, ·55 inch.* (*Durrant Collection.*)

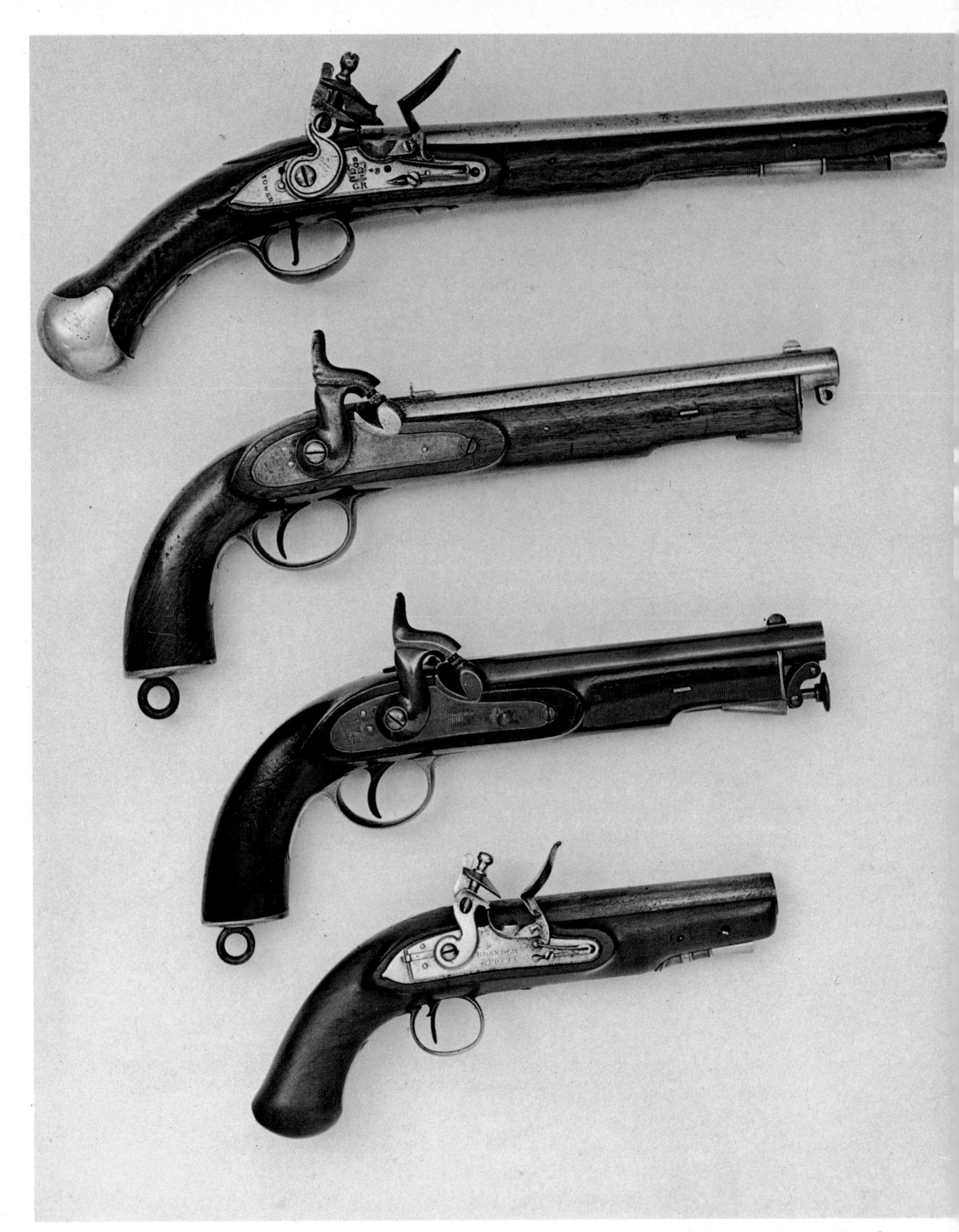

Plate 11 (Top to bottom) *Long Sea Service flintlock pistol of 1805, overall length 19¾ inches, barrel 10 inches, bore ·6 inch; Enfield Rifle pistol of 1859, overall length 15 inches, barrel 10 inches, bore ·58 inch; a smooth-bore cavalry pistol made for Indian service in 1871, overall length 14 inches, barrel 8 inches, bore ·65 inch; and a small flintlock pistol by Brander & Potts, overall length 11¼ inches, barrel 6 inches, bore ·69 inch.* (*Durrant Collection.*)

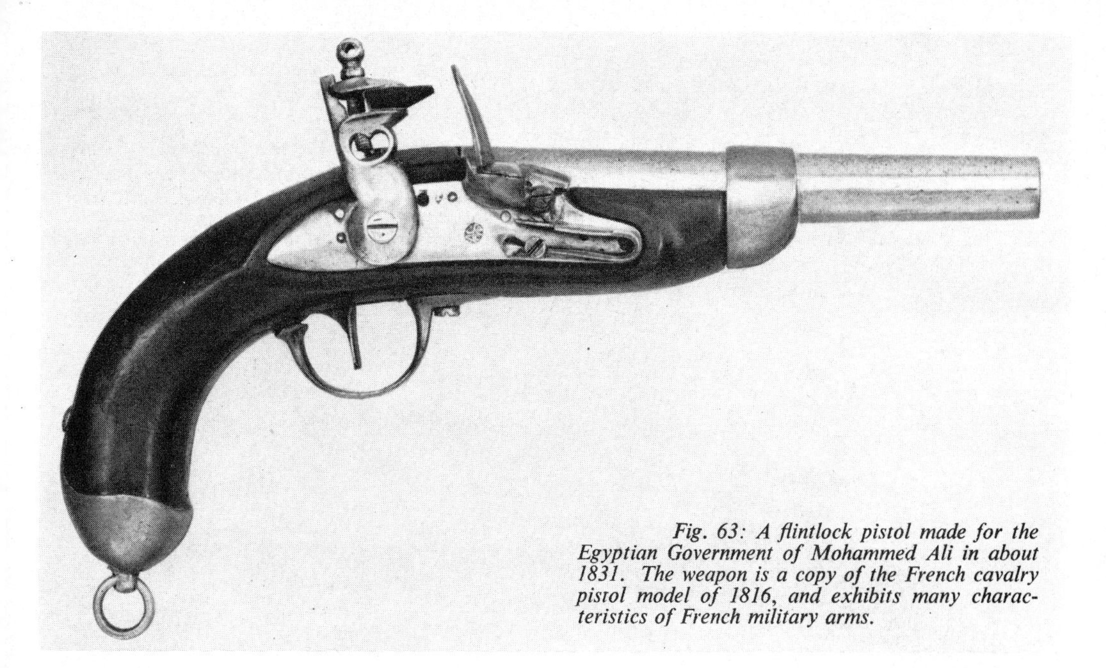

Fig. 63: A flintlock pistol made for the Egyptian Government of Mohammed Ali in about 1831. The weapon is a copy of the French cavalry pistol model of 1816, and exhibits many characteristics of French military arms.

pivoted steel ramrod. One of the hazards with the separate ramrod had been the danger of losing it in the heat of action. Towards the end of the 18th century a square lug was fitted beneath the muzzle of the barrel and a simple but ingeniously designed link was fitted to the lug. It held the ramrod captive although still allowing it to be used freely.

During the Napoleonic Wars the danger of invasion aroused an enormous patriotic fervour in Britain and a great citizen army of volunteers sprang up. The rate of growth was particularly marked after the Peace of Amiens and the fresh outbreak of war in 1803, and a large number of cavalry, infantry and artillery groups were raised. Some of these units were equipped by the Ordnance but others purchased their weapons privately so that collectors will find that many a musket which superficially appears to be a 39 inch India pattern or 42 inch New Land Model is, in fact, a privately made weapon lacking Ordnance marks but bearing a well known gunmaker's name. Weapons supplied by the Ordnance were stamped on the lock with the word TOWER and the Crown and G.R., whilst on the butt cap was engraved an initial and a V for Volunteer—thus E.V. indicates Essex Volunteers. Unfortunately with the letter C—Cambridge, Cornwall, Cheshire, Cumberland—there is no way of knowing which was the county of origin.

This series of muskets and pistols were to be the last of the flintlocks, for by 1830 the Board of Ordnance were seeking guidance as to whether the percussion system might be adopted by the British Army. Although the system had much to recommend it military authorities were loath to rush into any costly commitments before they were assured of its superiority over the flint. A further problem was the enormous stock of flintlock muskets already held in store or issued to the troops; the authorities wished to utilise a scheme that would allow these flintlock muskets to be converted to the new system. These early tentative steps in the direction of percussion stimulated many gunmakers to produce a great variety of weapons which were offered to the Ordnance for their examination and approval. A number of these weapons were tried out by the

Left, *Fig. 64: Portion of the lockplate of a Long Sea Service pistol, illustrating typical markings found on British military weapons after 1764.*

Below, *Fig. 65:* (Top to bottom) *Long Sea service pistol with 12-inch barrel; a flintlock pistol with a nine-inch barrel as originally specified for Light Dragoon units, and a belt hook; a New Land Pattern pistol with a swivel ramrod; and a percussion Coastguard pistol of about 1840.* (*Tower of London.*)

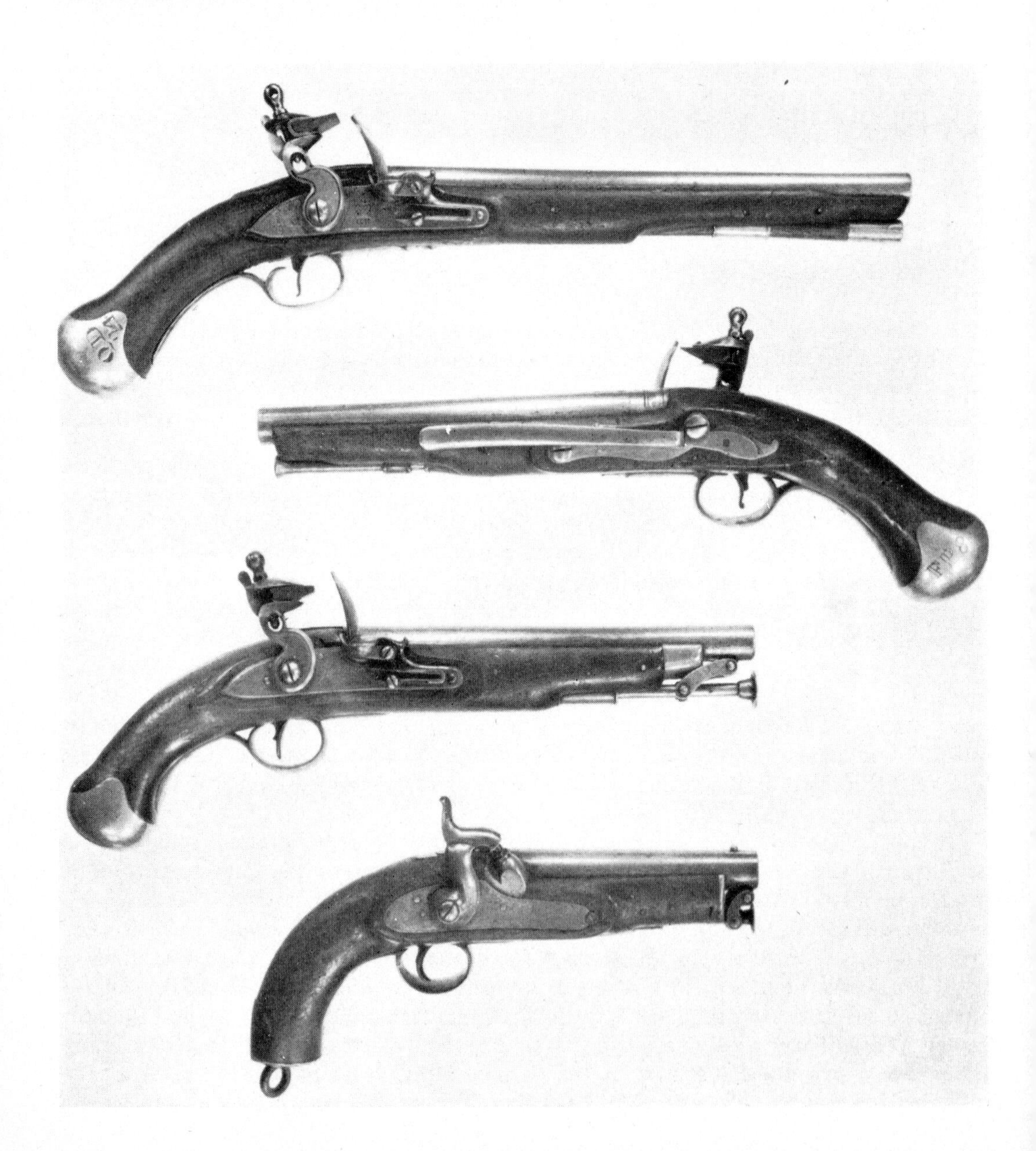

Ordnance Boards and after prolonged tests both in the field and under controlled conditions, the results were examined and discussed. Some very peculiar styles were tested but in the end the one which gained most approval was a back action musket designed by George Lovell, storekeeper at the Enfield Arms Factory; and in 1831 200 of his muskets were ordered to be set up. Many of the muskets held in store were converted to percussion by the simple expedient of fixing a nipple directly into the barrel. The lock was modified by removing the pan, frizzen and frizzen spring and substituting for the cock a large offset hammer.

During the 19th century technical advances in all fields of engineering and design had made possible the mass production of items which had previously been considered the metier of the individual craftsman. The old system of volley firing by large bodies of men was being abandoned in favour of a system of accurate fire by individuals. Accuracy with a smooth bore weapon was very much a haphazard affair and it had long been realised that rifling was the only way to ensure really accurate aiming. Even under ideal conditions a fired musket would distribute its shots over a not inconsiderable area. During the American War of Independence (1775—1783) the army had realised, to its cost, the deadly effect of aimed rifle fire, especially from the long-barrelled Pennsylvanian rifle. There was therefore a growing emphasis on the use of rifles in place of the old smooth bore musket. George Lovell himself was interested in this project and he examined a number of weapons which were submitted for his approval and consideration. Among the examples submitted was one designed by the Field Adjutant, Captain Berners, of the Duke of Brunswick's staff. Into the inside of its 39½ inch barrel were cut two deep grooves which completed one full turn in the length of the barrel. The lead bullet was made with a raised belt running around it and the bullet was fitted into the barrel so that the belt engaged with the two grooves and thus a spin was imparted to the ball as it left the gun. Lovell was impressed with this rifle's performance and produced his own version with this two-groove rifling which offered some considerable improvement in minor detail over the original weapon. Again his weapon proved to be the most successful and it was agreed that it should be adopted. In 1837 there was a bulk order for 1,000 of this pattern, henceforward known as the Brunswick Rifle. This model Brunswick had been fitted with Lovell's back action lock but in 1841 he reverted to a side action lock as used on the original weapon, and this type of lock was to remain in general use until the end of the percussion era. By the early 1850's the Brunswick rifle was going out of fashion and in 1852 it was decided that no new ones would be ordered although those parts in stock would be made up. In 1853 the Rifle Corps handed in their Brunswicks and received in place the Minie rifle or pattern 1851 rifle musket. The Brunswick was never a very popular weapon for it was heavy and, despite its rifling, not as consistently accurate as might be expected. As was the common practice the Brunswick rifles withdrawn from the regular Regiments of the Line were placed in stock and then issued to Militia regiments which were, in effect, second line troops intended for home defence.

One of the problems with rifles was to ensure a good fit for the ball into the barrel and in the Minie rifle the close fit was achieved by a special bullet. The flat end of the lead bullet was hollowed out and into this space went a small iron cup; as the expanding gas formed by the explosion forced the bullet along the barrel it also pushed the cup into the base and so expanded the bullet slightly. This expansion forced the lead firmly into the grooves of the rifling, although since the bullet was of a slightly smaller diameter than the bore it could be loaded very easily. The Minie rifle proved

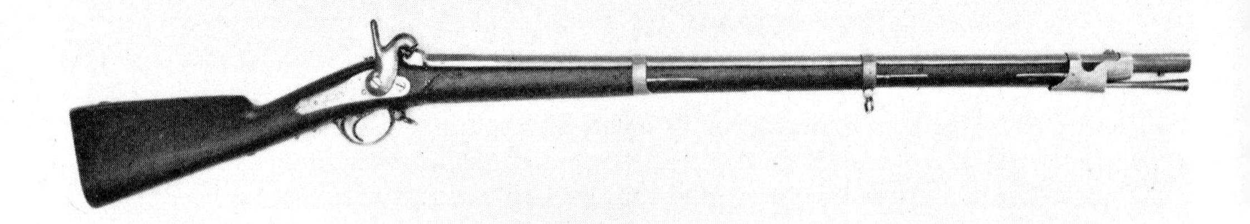

to be superior to others in tests and in 1851 it was adopted as the standard weapon of the British Army, becoming general issue for all troops.

The new Minie rifle was not without its drawbacks and sighting seems to have been one of the most common causes of complaint. Some regiments reported that the sights varied in their position along the barrel and others that they were not accurately lined up with the muzzle. In 1852 the Board of Ordnance decided to test weapons with a smaller calibre, for the majority of long arms were still using a bullet with a diameter around .7 of an inch. A great many rifles were submitted for testing and the Committee decided that there should be two experimental rifles and they were to fire bullets of .577 inches diameter. Extensive tests of the weapons submitted by almost every well known maker of firearms in England finally resulted in the adoption of the so-called 1853 Pattern Rifled Musket, known to most collectors as the Enfield Rifle.

Although the Enfield rifle soon proved to be a highly successful weapon, experiments were not discontinued and the famous engineer Sir Joseph Whitworth was invited to discover ways to improve accuracy using a new system of rifling. Two years of extensive experimentation were undertaken and in 1857 a Whitworth rifle was being tested at the Army School of Musketry at Hythe in Kent. The important difference in the Whitworth rifle was in the design of the rifling, and although the new system was found to be extremely successful it was soon discovered that it suffered from very severe fouling in the barrel. As a result the Whitworth rifle was never generally adopted as an issue weapon.

IN 1848 the Prussian army had adopted a revolutionary new weapon and its superiority was shown by the victorious campaigns waged by this highly successful army. The essential feature of this new system was a breech loading bolt action which allowed

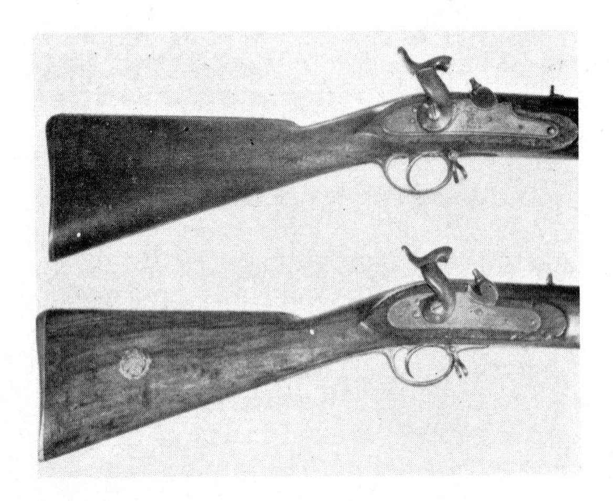

Head of page, *Fig. 66: Percussion musket of French Dragoon pattern, model of 1853 (although this example is dated 1857). Barrel, 36 inches. (Tower of London.)*

Left, *Fig. 67:* (Top) *Military Land Regular Musket, pattern of 1839.* (Bottom) *A "sealed pattern" of 1842—i.e., the pattern on which all production examples must be based. (Tower of London.)*

Head of opposite page, *Fig. 68: Martini Henry lever-action rifle, officially adopted by the British Army in 1871. Barrel, 33 inches; bore, ·45 inch.*

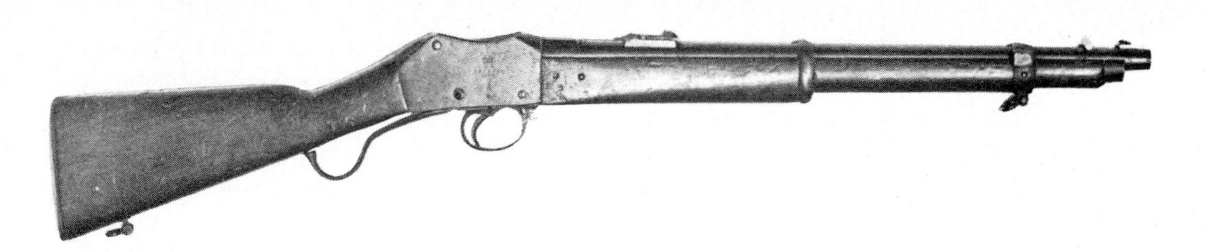

rapid and easy loading. A paper cartridge was inserted not from the muzzle, as was the case with almost all other military weapons, but by an opening at the opposite end, the breech. This cartridge contained a percussion cap which was ignited by a long needle-like rod—hence the title of the Needle Gun. In the case of this weapon the opening of the breech was achieved by a cylindrical metal block which could be withdrawn to open the breech and then locked shut for firing.

Probably the most important feature of this weapon was its demonstration that a cheap, reliable breech loading weapon was a practical possibility; and in 1864 a Select Committee was set up to consider the adoption of a breech loading rifle for the British Army. It was felt that one of the factors which should influence the choice was that the system chosen would enable existing stocks to be converted without too much trouble. Gunmakers were once again invited to submit their designs for converting existing muzzle loaders to breech loading. Tests were again carried out and in 1867 the decision went in favour of an American, Jacob Snider. His action consisted of a block fitted at the breech and pivoted so that it could be swung open to allow access directly to the chamber. A cartridge was then inserted and the block replaced and held in position by a strong spring. Detonation was produced by a striker which passed through the block and projected up in roughly the position previously occupied by the nipple. The blow of the hammer caused the striker to drive forward and detonate the percussion cap contained within the Snider cartridge. Although the adoption of the Snider action was a stop-gap measure aimed at the conversion of existing arms to the breech loading system, the Ordnance had not lost sight of the fact that an entirely new weapon was really required; and in 1867 yet another committee was set up to consider the selection of a specially designed breech loading rifle. Again there were tests and reports which were carefully studied, and the committee's choice fell upon the breech action of Frederich Von Martini of Switzerland combined with a barrel designed by a Scotsman, Alexander Henry. Martini's action was operated by a lever situated beneath the small of the butt; when the lever was depressed the breech block dropped down allowing direct access to the chamber; and by returning the lever to the closed position the breech block was lifted back into place and locked in position. The barrel was 33 inches long with a bore of .45 and seven groove rifling.

The Martini Henry rifle was officially adopted in 1871 and was to see many years of service in campaigns all over the world. It was not entirely successful and one of its most serious weaknesses was in the extraction of the spent cartridge, which frequently jammed. In 1883 yet another committee was formed with the object of seeing what improvements could be effected in the Martini Henry rifle. In 1886 this committee recommended that the calibre be reduced to .402 and another cartridge be adopted. Changes were also made in the rifling and in 1886 large orders were placed for this new rifle, known as the Enfield Martini.

The Committee had also been given a second job to do and that was to consider the adoption of a magazine rifle; like all its predecessors the Martini Henry was only a single shot weapon. Of the weapons tested one of the most successful was the magazine rifle designed by another American, James P. Lee; the magazine held five cartridges which were loaded by hand from the top. In December 1888 the first magazine rifle was officially approved for manufacture. Basically the magazine rifle was to remain unaltered, although varying in numerous details, until the adoption of an automatic rifle after World War II.

Emphasis has been placed here on military long arms and only their main line of development has been sketched in, but there were innumerable variations on a basic theme. Carbines and special experimental models of almost every variety of long arm used by the British Army were produced and these are so numerous as to preclude any mention; but reference can be made to appropriate text books for details. Although they were always considered a secondary arm of limited value, the story of military pistols is one of great interest and they are in considerable demand by collectors. The basic pattern of most of the pistols is very similar and it is largely in the length of barrel that variations may be found; as, for example, the long sea service pistol with its 12 inch barrel and belt hook, whereas the majority of issue pistols had a nine inch barrel. Essentially, the military pistol changed but little during the 18th century, although the swivel ramrod and sliding safety catch were introduced at the end of the century or early in the 19th century. A board of officers was set up to consider the question of standardisation of bore and the problems involved in the use of pistols, and in 1828 their report proposed a standard carbine and advocated the abolition of the pistol. This proposal was not followed and many percussion pistols were made and issued, including some with a detachable shoulder stock. In 1838 the pistol, after being described in a report as being "useless", was withdrawn from all units with the exception of the Lancers who were allowed to keep one for each man. In 1842 a new pattern was introduced fitted with a swivel ramrod and with very simple, almost stark, lines; but it was, unbeknown to Lovell, already obsolete. In America Samuel Colt had produced in quantity, some seven years before, a very practical and workmanlike revolver. Prompted by the interest displayed in his produce in London during the Great Exhibition of 1851, Colt set up a London factory to produce his revolver; and three years later, as the result of first class workmanship, shrewd business ability and superb public relations, Sam Colt was selling the British Admiralty some 4,000 revolvers. In 1855 the Ordnance ordered 5,000 Colt revolvers for the Army and a further 9,000 in August of the same year. From then on the single shot pistol was completely outmoded; and the next step was the change over to breech loading cartridge weapons. In 1868 some of the muzzle loading revolvers were already being converted to breech loading action. Although Colt revolvers were never general issue a large number found their way into the hands of officers and men of certain units; they were followed by Adams revolvers and later still those made by Webley. This latter model was to continue in service for many years, seeing action in both World Wars.

THE story of military weapons in the United States up to the outbreak of the American War of Independence is the same as for the British Army, since the militia and regular forces were, of course, equipped with official ordnance arms. Immediately upon the outbreak of war in 1776 Committees of Public Safety were set up in the Colonies, and one of their tasks was to encourage the production of weapons; for obviously the main source of supply had been cut off by the outbreak of hostilities between the colonies and England. The Congress of the United States passed, in 1777,

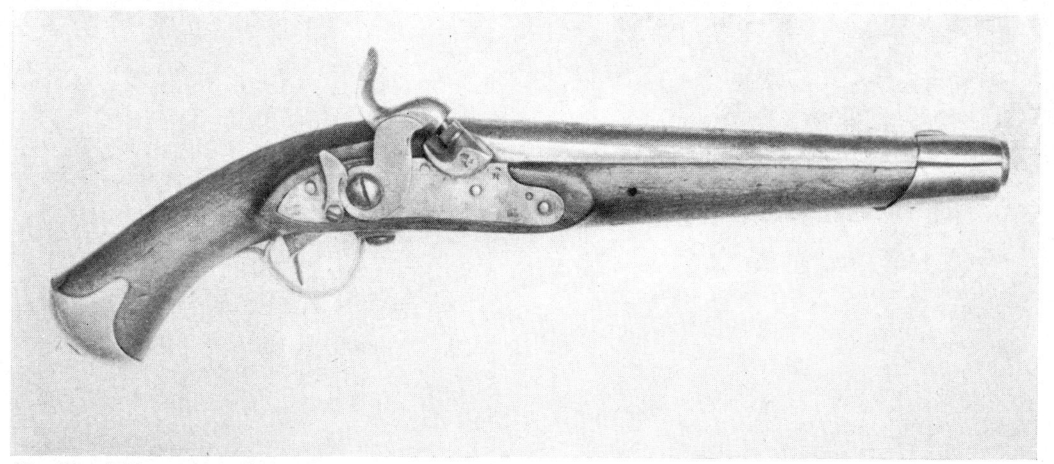

Fig. 69: A Norwegian rifled pistol with several unusual features. It has a "dog" catch, a feature abandoned in England in the 17th century. This piece was originally a flintlock, 1831 model, but was converted to percussion in 1846. (Perry Collection.)

a resolution stating that all government arms would be stamped with the words UNITED STATES. The influence of the French was strong during the War of Independence and the subsequent period, and many arms supplied to the States were French in origin. It is therefore not surprising that many of the American pistols and muskets produced at their newly founded arsenals at Springfield in Massachusetts (established by the United States in 1794) and Harpers Ferry, Virginia, exhibit every indication of strong French influence. Probably the difference easiest to spot between British, and European or American military arms lies in the method of barrel attachment. The British Ordnance required the use of pins piercing the stock and connecting with lugs brazed beneath the barrel, this practice continuing until the 1850's. During the same period the majority of European and American barrels were held in place by a series of bands encircling the barrel and stock. This system was adopted by the British for the first time on the Enfield rifle. The majority of European muskets also had a brass nose band, a feature lacking on almost all British military weapons.

Many of the European countries have issued military weapons whose history is fairly well documented and the majority of such weapons may be identified by reference to the appropriate books.

Military firearms, especially pistols, have a strong attraction for collectors of antique weapons; but the growing interest and increasing demand have already raised the prices considerably—a trend which shows no sign of abating. Despite this they are unquestionably a most interesting and fascinating field of study.

6

Duelling Pistols

DUELLING is as old as man himself, and one might argue that war is merely a magnified form of duel with groups replacing individuals. Violence has always been part of man's make up and his final resort in any sort of conflict of interests. To ancient man violence was part of everyday life, and skill in arms was a highly rated virtue in society. To question a man's courage or honour had always been the ultimate insult, and the only way to prove the falseness of such charges was to display courage and skill by fighting. The idea that right would triumph was as implicit in the duel as it was in "trial by ordeal", which was a recognised feature of early legal practice. It was felt that the Divine Being, be he Zeus, Allah or Jehovah, would not permit an innocent person to suffer and would therefore protect his disciple, or in some way intervene in his favour.

A further probable contributory factor in the development of the duel was the great importance attached to a man's given word during the Middle Ages. In return for land a pledge was given to the tenant-in-chief, and thus to the king, that under certain circumstances military aid would be offered to the sovereign. The importance of such an oath was therefore obvious to all and it was considered blackest treachery to go back on such a promise. In other words a man's honour, his ability to carry out his pledges and the respect accorded to him were of great importance, and any slur upon his good name or honour demanded a reaction from him—hence the duel.

Semi-ritual individual combat is as old as mankind, but in its strictest Western European sense it first appeared in England in the 11th century, with the Norman invaders. William the Conqueror introduced trial by ordeal to this country and trial by combat was also accepted as having a place in the legal code. From these simple and sincere beginnings an elaborate and circumspect ritual gradually evolved over the years. During the Middle Ages the duel was usually referred to as the *joust à outrance*, or the fight to the death, which might well be fought with every weapon in the armoury —lance, axe, sword, mace, spear. For "sporting" combats, blunted weapons were used and this type was known as *joust à plaisance*. Gradually the duel became more formalised, with set conditions covering every aspect, and during the 16th, 17th and 18th centuries the principal weapon became the sword. At the same period a style of fighting using the point of the sword grew up and this fencing, as it was called, became the rage. Schools of fence were set up in Italy, Spain, in fact all over Europe, to teach the novice the art of defence and attack. Many variations of fencing were evolved such as fighting with sword and dagger, sword and cloak, and even, in one style of fighting, sword and

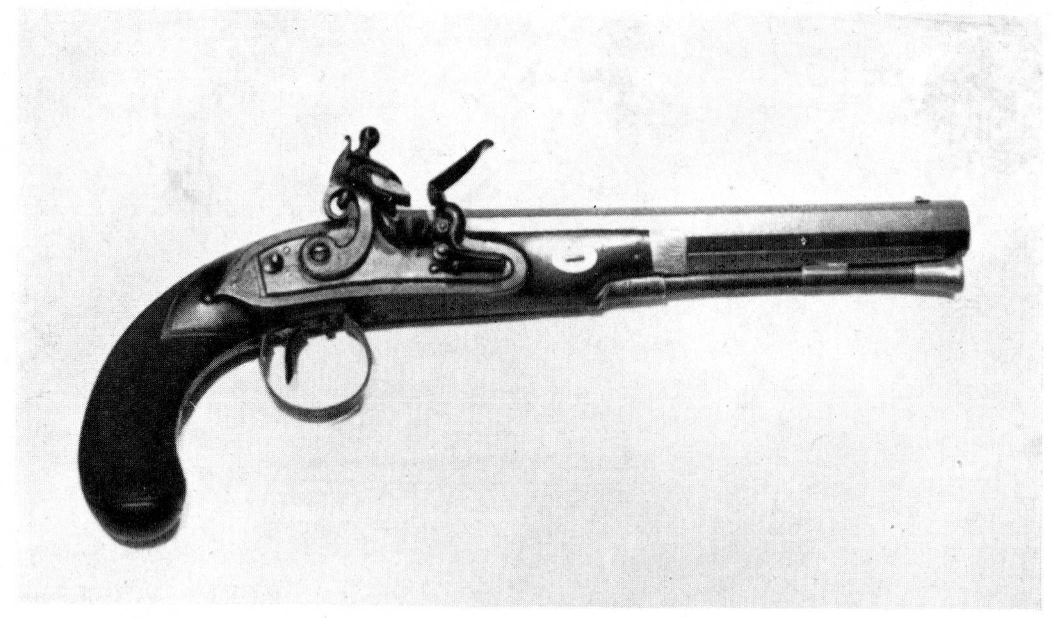

Fig. 70: A half stocked pistol by A. Key of St. Andrews, Scotland, circa *1800. On this weapon the maker's name is inset in gold on the top of the barrel. Overall length, 14 inches; barrel, 8 inches; bore, ·6 inch. (Bennett Collection.)*

lantern! Elaborate codes of conduct for the duels were drawn up and by the 19th century there were set sequences of events, common all over Europe which must invariably be followed. France and Italy were particularly noted for the zeal of their inhabitants in the matter of duelling, and were rather looked upon as the arbiters of duelling fashions.

With the advent of firearms a new factor entered into the code of the duel; success with the sword depended on a high degree of skill which necessitated long training and practice, but skill with the pistol could be more easily acquired. The pistol itself could also be made to contribute towards the successful outcome of a duel, and a number of famous gunmakers devoted their skills and energies to producing accurate, easy to aim pistols specifically for the duel.

DUELLING was not simply a matter of standing up and blazing away at one's opponent, and codes prescribed the exact procedure to be followed. A code of duelling established in France in the early part of the 19th century and given in detail by J. G. Millingen in his book "*The History of Duelling*" (1841) lists some 84 different points of conduct. He states that the rules were founded on long experience and had been sanctioned by "25 general officers, 11 peers of France and 50 officers of other rank . . . The Minister of War, who could not consistently with his public duties affix his signature to the document, gave his approbation in an official letter and, the majority of the prefects equally sanctioned the regulation." Many of the points were of course concerned with the rights and privileges of the principals and their seconds. It was stressed that the offended party had the right to choose the weapon although there are certain qualifications made about this choice. Only three legal arms were accepted:

the sword, the sabre and the pistol. It is interesting to note that the sabre could be refused even by the aggressor especially if he was a retired officer, but it could always be rejected by a civilian if he wished. Some of the nuances are rather intriguing, as for example Article 17, which stresses that two seconds are necessary to each combatant if a pistol or sabre is used, but one sufficed when the sword was to be the weapon. The qualifications and variations on a basic theme are innumerable; thus it was stated that the seconds of the aggressor could, if they thought proper, refuse to fire by signal if the aggressor had not, during the original incident, struck his antagonist! However, of more immediate interest are the stipulations set down concerning duels fought with pistols, which were never to be used at distances less than fifteen paces. Sights on the pistol were permitted but they had to be of the non-adjustable type. Although this particular code does not categorically forbid the practice it does say that the barrel should not be rifled. Both pistols should be "of a similar description" and it was to meet this requirement that so many of the duelling pistols were manufactured in pairs. Indeed Article 49 says "it is desirable that the same pair of pistols be used by both parties." As the accuracy of a pistol was seriously affected by the charge of powder the seconds were instructed to load the pistols with scrupulous care and if one pair of pistols was being used each second had to use a similar charge and was given the right to test the two charges by checking the amount with a ramrod or alternatively by loading in the presence of four witnesses. In this way it was hoped to prevent a little extra charge being given to one of the pistols; but Millingen reports how he had seen the powder measure thrown on to the grass after the first filling so that the second

Fig. 71: A pair of flintlock duelling pistols by Wheeler of Dublin, circa *1780. The maker's name is on a small gold inset in the lockplate. (Gyngell Collection.)*

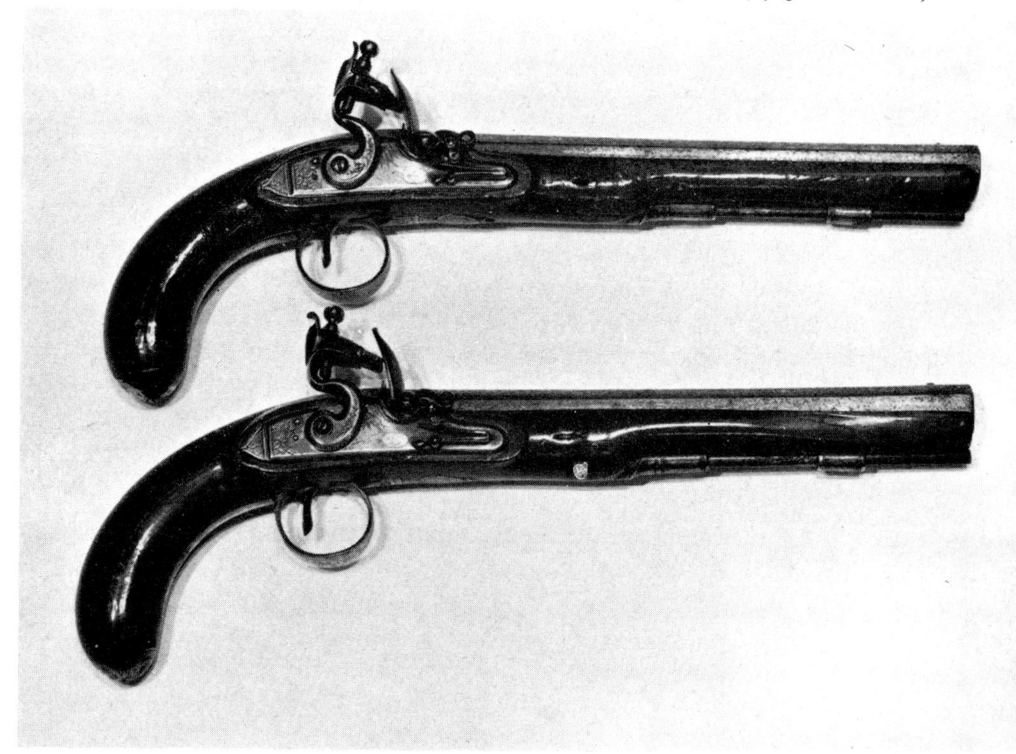

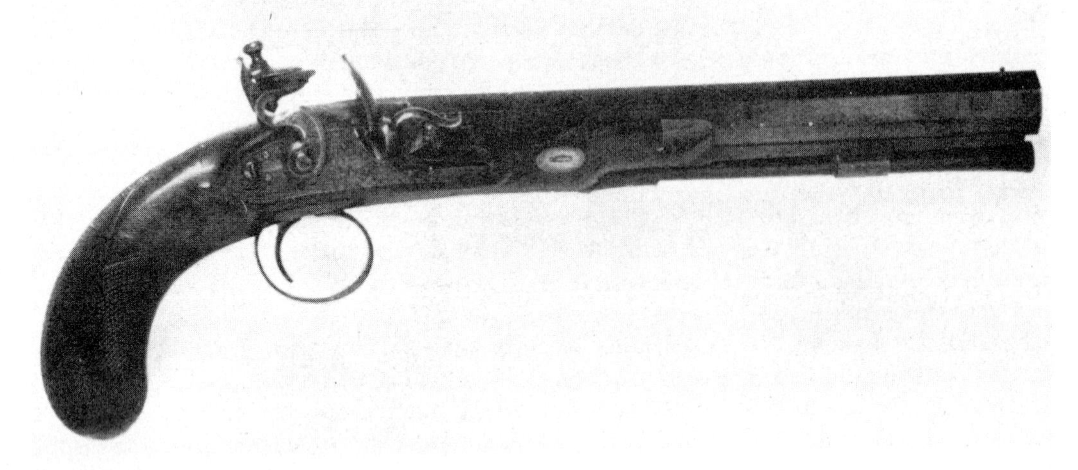

Fig. 72: One of a pair of duelling pistols by the famous London maker Joseph Manton; the weapon is half stocked, and touchhole and pan are lined with platinum. Overall length, 15 inches; barrel, 10 inches; bore, ·5 inch. (Gyngell Collection.)

filling was made with powder which was slightly damp. He says that he did not know whether the action was deliberate or not!

Quite obviously the order of firing could be of vital importance, and procedures for deciding who should fire first were emphatic but varied according to the range. If the duel was to be fought at 35 paces then the offended party had the right to the first shot. At the shorter range of 15 paces when there was a far greater chance of hitting one's opponent, the first shot was decided by drawing lots. When all was ready with the principals in position, pistols loaded, then only two commands were given: "Make ready" and the fatal order, "Fire". An unreliable pistol could well mean death for one combatant since article 54 stated that a misfire would be considered as a shot unless prior agreement to the contrary had been settled.

This, then, was the basic pattern of a pistol duel; but, as always, there were variations. In the duel *à volonté* the seconds marked out the ground at a distance of 35 to 40 paces; two lines were then traced between these two distances leaving an interval of 15 to 20 paces; each combatant could advance to this line—a maximum of 10 paces. One of the seconds gave the command "March" and both combatants could then advance, pistols held vertically, but each could aim and fire at any moment after the command. If one had not fired by the time the limit, marked by a cane or handkerchief, was reached, he was then obliged to do so. The moment one combatant had fired he had to stop where he was and stand firmly to receive the fire of his adversary who had up to one minute to advance and fire. If a principal was wounded he was given one minute's grace to fire on his antagonist from the moment he was hit. If he had fallen to the ground he was actually given two minutes to recover! If the cause of the quarrel had involved a blow then it was permissible for the combatants to be equipped with a pair of pistols each but if this course was chosen then all four pistols had to be fired before the matter was considered settled.

A variation on this form of duel was the *à marche* in which the two lines, separated by 15 or 20 paces, were drawn marking the limits of advances. The combatants were separated by 45 or 50 paces and could advance in a zig-zag fashion, two paces at a time, until either one fired or the line was reached. Again once he fired the dueller had to stop and receive fire. Perhaps most common was that form of duel known as *au signal* in which the commands were given by one of the seconds of the offended party by hand claps. The combatants, holding their pistols with muzzles to the ground, commenced walking on the first clap and on the second clap, three seconds later, raised their arm, took aim and three seconds later fired simultaneously on the third clap.

With Gallic ingenuity the French also had *Duels Exceptionnels* which might take place either on foot or horseback and with pistol, musket or carbine. They were rare, and conditions had to be set down in writing before they could take place. In the mounted form the combatants with pistols were placed at 25 paces from each other, with the carbine at 60 paces and with the musket and on foot at one hundred paces, advancing to 60 paces. The parties could fire and reload at will until they reached the agreed limits. Some duels were also fought with the combatants standing back to back; on a given signal they faced about and fired. Yet another fiendish variation of this macabre game was that in which only one pistol was loaded. Both pistols were taken away by the seconds and one was loaded normally but the other was only primed. The second now placed both pistols behind his back and the principals then advanced and chose either left or right and were given the appropriate pistol. After having stripped off their coats to show that they were not making use of any secret defence, each of the combatants grasped one end of a handkerchief. The signal to fire was

Fig. 73: A cartoon by Cruickshank, taking a satirical view of the noble art of the duel. The popularity of this murderous ritual began to decline in England in the first quarter of the 19th century.

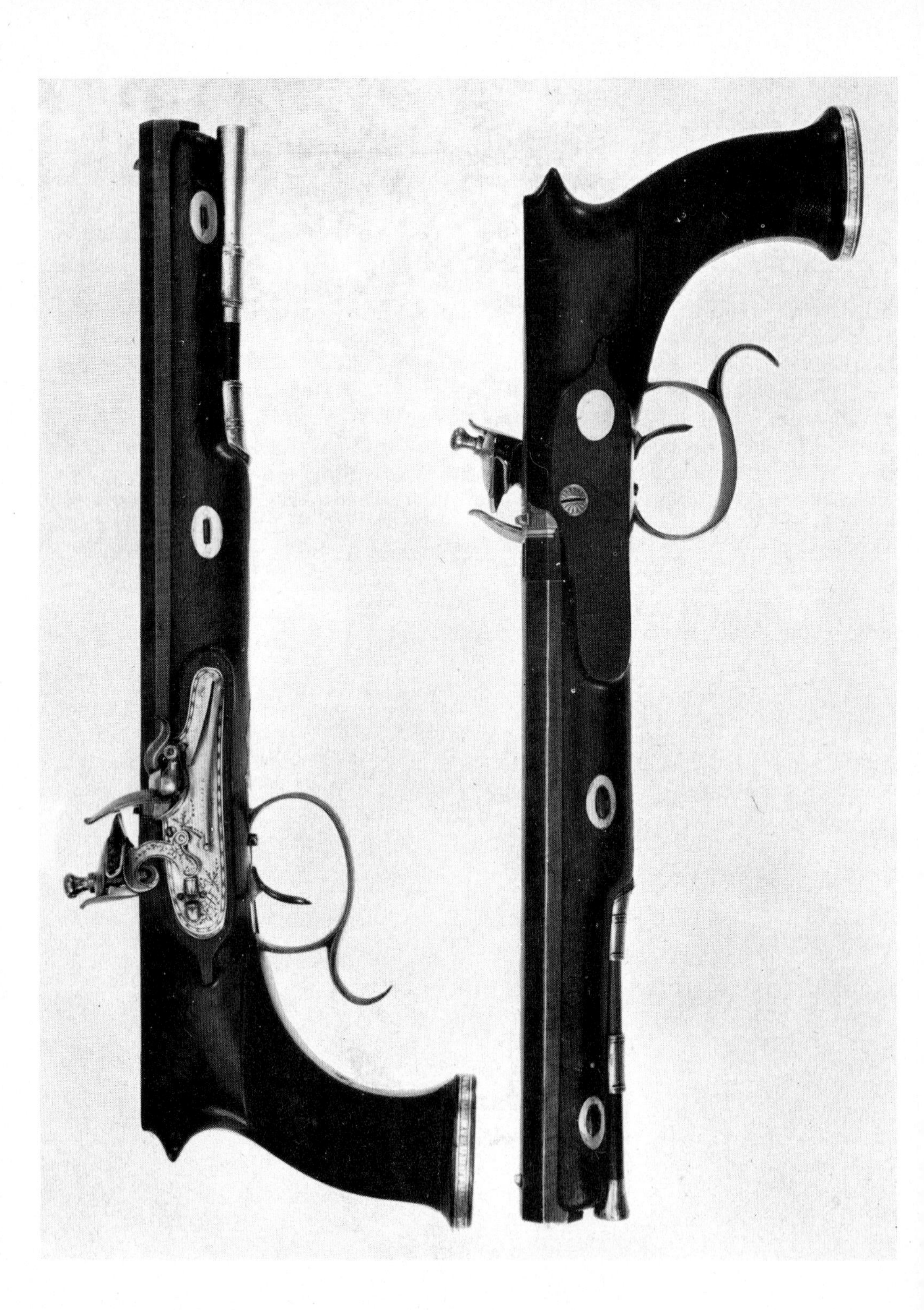

Fig. 74: A pair of saw-handle duelling pistols by Patrick, circa *1815. The trigger guards have spurs, a common feature adopted to aid the grip; and the locks are of an unusual construction, with exposed springs. The saw-handle butts are reminiscent of several types of modern competition pistols currently in use. (Tower of London.)*

given by one clap of the hand and, of course, the result was almost invariably fatal.

Similar codes to that detailed above were drawn up in England and also in Ireland, where duelling was more prevalent. A number of these codes have survived, and although there are differences of detail the majority suggest that ten paces was most frequently the distance at which duels were fought. Firing sequences were decided in a variety of ways—sometimes the toss of a coin settled matters, on other occasions lots were drawn and occasionally both fired simultaneously.

The duellist was always in a peculiar position as far as the law was concerned. Strictly speaking any case of killing was counted as murder, or at least manslaughter, and the fatal result of a duel often led to an enforced holiday abroad until the matter had cooled off. The local justice of the peace and police officers were bound to forestall any coming duels that might be brought to their attention, and this meant that the contest had to be held in a secret meeting place screened from the public gaze; parks were a favourite spot, as were heaths and commons. Preparations were made, and apart from principals and seconds the only people to attend were usually surgeons; but on occasion the news spread around and came to the ears of the local police officers. Henry Goddard, a Bow Street Runner, described in his memoirs how in 1828 he and groups of other runners or police officers heard that a duel was to be held at Wormwood Scrubs, an open patch of ground in north London. They went at once to the spot where they found eight gentlemen assembled; this was at four o'clock in the morning! They found that the party were carrying three pistol cases each containing two pistols complete with powder, bullet moulds, flasks etc.

By the 1830's the prevalence of duelling was diminishing as people were beginning to realise that it was a barbaric and meaningless method of settling an argument. The number of recorded duels decreased until the 1840's, when they were finally abolished in England. However there were always some who felt that this pathetic display of bravery proved something, and duelling lingered on, particularly in the Army. Nevertheless, public opposition was growing continually and in 1843 a particularly fruitless and stupid duel which resulted in the death of one participant and the ruin of the other, so aroused public fury that a body calling itself The Association for the Suppression of Duelling was set up. Among its members were some of the most prominent parliamentarians and high officers of the armed forces; and in 1844 a petition was placed before Queen Victoria asking that some measures should be taken to stop this malicious practice. In the same year the Articles of War which governed the conduct of all officers were amended, and the 98th article now promised serious punishment for all those who might take part in, promote or have knowledge of a duel. This restriction was generally accepted by the officers of the armed forces, probably even with a secret sigh of relief. However, as always there were one or two hotheads left; and what is generally accepted as the last duel in England was not fought until 1852,

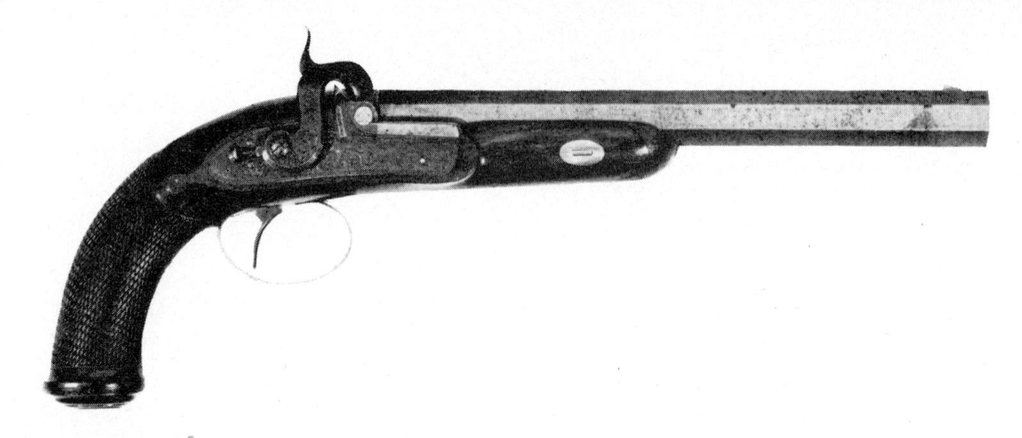

Fig. 75: An English rifled duelling pistol, by John Manton & Son of London. It is a percussion weapon, half stocked and with a separate ramrod. (*Tower of London.*)

although whether this "counts" is a matter of opinion since it was actually fought between two resident Frenchmen.

Many books on duelling were written during the latter part of the 18th century and early 19th century, and each offered advice as to the best means of getting one's man and of avoiding being "got" in return. In essence the advice consisted of one simple, obvious statement—present as small a target as possible. Among the suggestions offered were the drawing in of the stomach, holding the breath, pulling back the shoulders and turning the head to face one's opponent. The second piece of advice offered by all authorities was to know one's pistol; and here, of course, lay the essence of duelling. In any duel, no matter how cool, calm and collected the champion might be, it was his pistols that would settle the affair one way or the other. Duelling pistols intended solely for their stated purpose were obviously of immense importance to the dueller, and many gunmakers concentrated on producing top quality weapons.

WHAT is a duelling pistol? The distinction is often very vague, and the officer's holster pistol of the last quarter of the 18th century could well serve a double purpose and might be pressed into service as a duelling weapon. Even among the pistols specifically designed for the duel there were variations, but collectors would accept certain general descriptions for such weapons. The whole pistol is normally rather plain with a minimum of decoration although the butts may be hatched, that is, cut with tiny criss-crossed lines. Barrels were commonly octagonal, although a number were produced with the round barrel. Another common but by no means universal feature was an extension to the trigger guard which took the form of a downward curving half loop. Locks are normally of very high quality workmanship, but again lack almost any decoration. Every possible improving feature was added to the lock mechanism to ensure its correct, easy and swift functioning.

The duelling pistol did not evolve as a distinct variety of weapon until the period 1770-80, and it was certainly not a sudden innovation but grew gradually from the ordinary officer's or holster pistol. Its characteristics developed as each part of the weapon was improved and adapted with one specific purpose—to produce a pistol which was easy to handle, accurate, light on the trigger and which came up almost automatically into the aiming position. With this object in view almost every part of

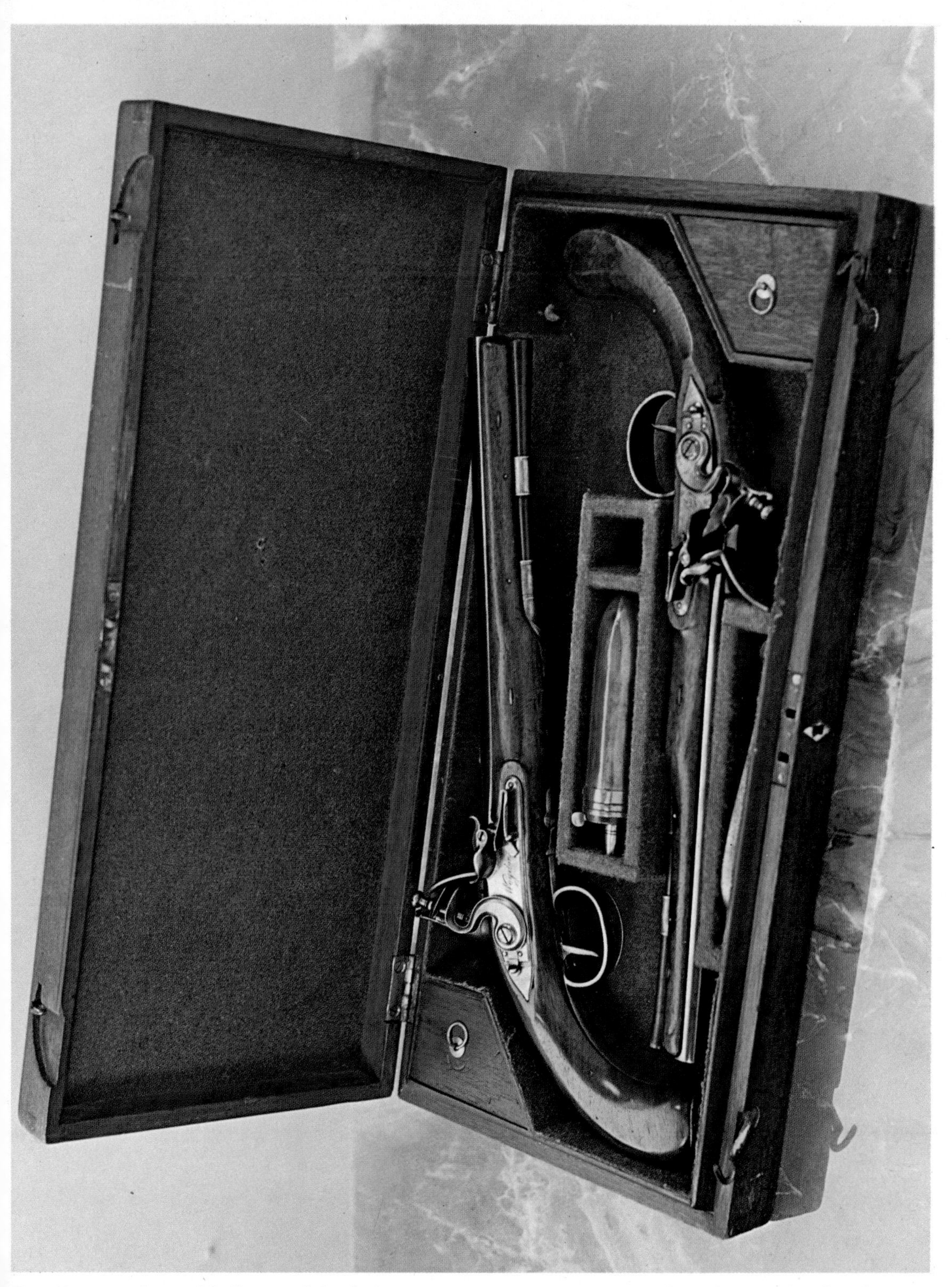

Plate 12 *A cased pair of duelling pistols by the famous London maker Wogden. Overall length, 17¼ inches; barrels, 10 inches; bore, ·575 inch. (Durrant Collection.)*

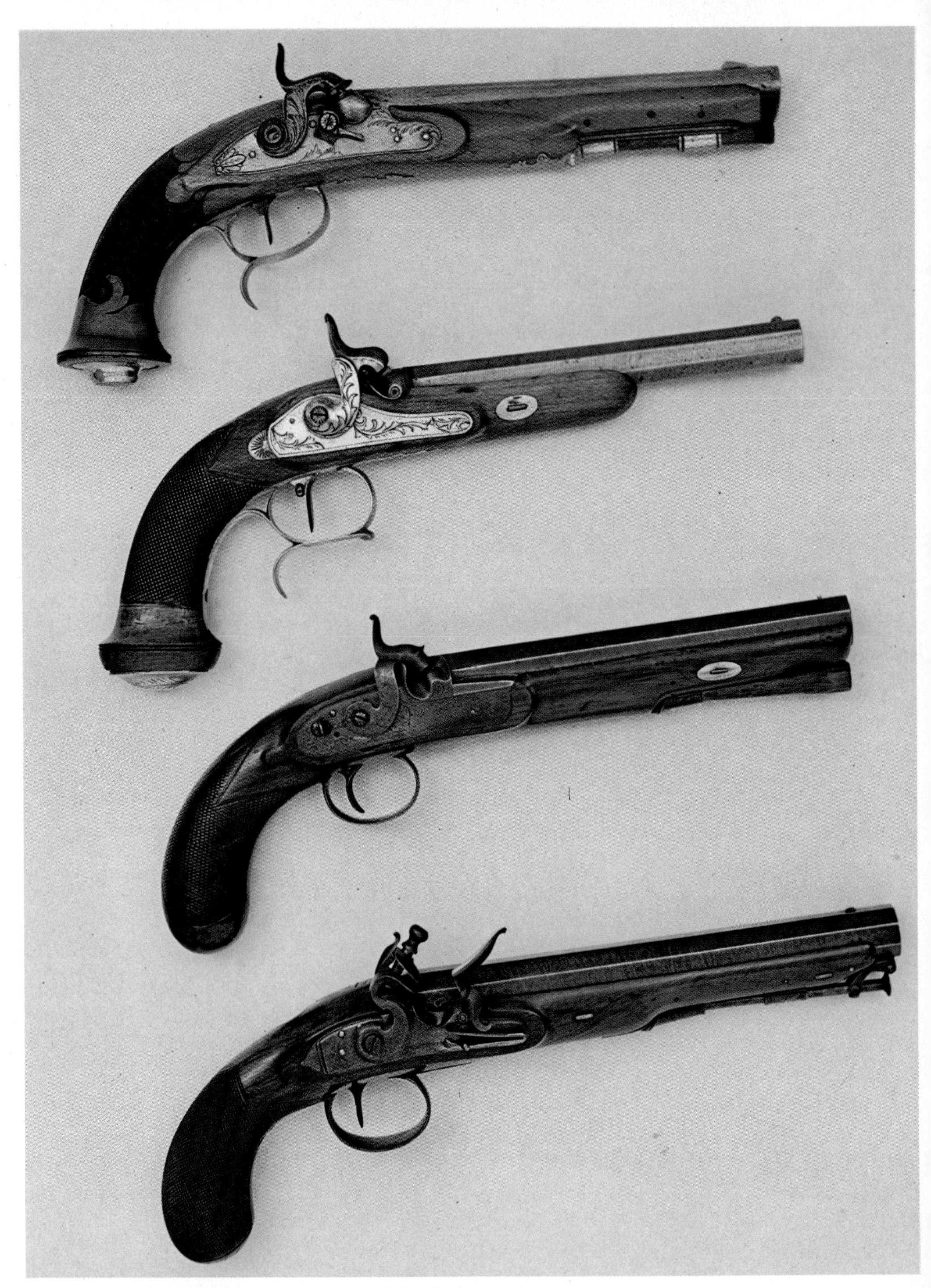

Plate 13 (Top to bottom) *French percussion duelling pistol with spur trigger*, circa *1840; overall length, 13½ inches; barrel, 8 inches; bore, ·5 inch.* (2) *is a half stocked French percussion dueller of the same period and identical specification.* (3) *is an English percussion dueller of about 1830, made by Cooper of Stockton; lengths, 13¼ and 8 inches; bore, ·62 inch.* (4) *is an early flintlock duelling pistol of* circa *1790, by Henshall; lengths, 14½ and 9 inches; bore, ·65 inch. Both the latter weapons are illustrated by courtesy of the Durrant Collection.*

the pistol was modified as each gunsmith felt best. Strangely enough, although duelling was not especially a British occupation, the duelling pistol appears to have been a British innovation. Whilst there are a number of features generally accepted as being characteristic of the pistols not all of them correspond exactly; generalisations are necessary but frequently require some qualification.

Obviously the barrel was of great importance, and the accuracy of the shot was primarily controlled by this part of the weapon. Duelling barrels were made with a fairly small bore, usually around .5 to .6 of an inch, but with very thick walls. As most duels were fought at close range the charge of powder required was small and the explosion was not, therefore, a significant feature in the design; hence the thickness was almost entirely designed to improve the aim. The weight of the thick barrel helped to reduce the recoil and the tendency for the pistol to kick up when fired. Barrels made by the top gunmakers contained only the very best quality metal; when the round tube had been formed and shaped, one end was closed with a breech plug and the outside surface was then ground as required. As a generalisation it may be accepted that the earlier duelling pistols were made with barrels which were round, or were octagonal at the breech but changed to round about a third of the way along. Later examples will be found, almost exclusively, to be fitted with octagonal barrels the thick walls of which were ground down and shaped on huge abrasive wheels.

One of the most difficult problems for the gunmaker to overcome on a duelling pistol was the tendency to shoot high, and for short range weapons it required a certain amount of skill to arrange for the bore to match the sighting in order to shoot accurately. Many schemes were introduced to overcome this problem and Robert Wogden, a great English maker, had the barrels made with a slightly crooked bore, just enough for them to compensate for the error caused by normal sighting. Manton, another famous gunmaker, thickened the barrels and made them inordinately heavy in order to overcome the slight kick, and by this means hoped to keep the shot down. However, this made the pistol a little cumbersome and tiring to hold. A firm of Irish gunmakers, William and John Rigby of Dublin, produced yet another solution by arranging for the bore to lie at a slight downward angle to the axis of the barrel and by this means they claimed that accuracy was enormously improved.

All duelling pistols were fitted with sights and in some cases these were of silver, although there was some discussion amongst the students of the duel as to whether the reflection on silver was distracting. Certainly the writer who used the pseudonym "Traveller", writing in 1836, disapproved of them, claiming that blued steel was the best material for sights. Rifling was not a common feature of all duelling pistols and in fact it was specifically forbidden under some codes; under others, it was frowned upon. Some makers, including the famous John Manton of London, produced a pistol with a so-called secret rifling, which was shallow rifling in the breech end of the barrel only, the rest being smooth. This arrangement meant it was not apparent that the weapon was rifled, but the few inches of rifling was sufficient to impart a steadying rotation to the ball before it left the pistol. The majority of barrels are usually about 9 to 10 inches long, but slightly longer ones will be found.

Early barrels were secured to the stock in exactly the same fashion as in ordinary pistols, with a pin piercing the stock and engaging with a lug brazed beneath the barrel. From about 1790 this system was improved by substituting for the pin a flat slide which was seated inside two silver ovals mounted on either side of the stock. The slide was so designed that it could not be completely withdrawn, thus eliminating

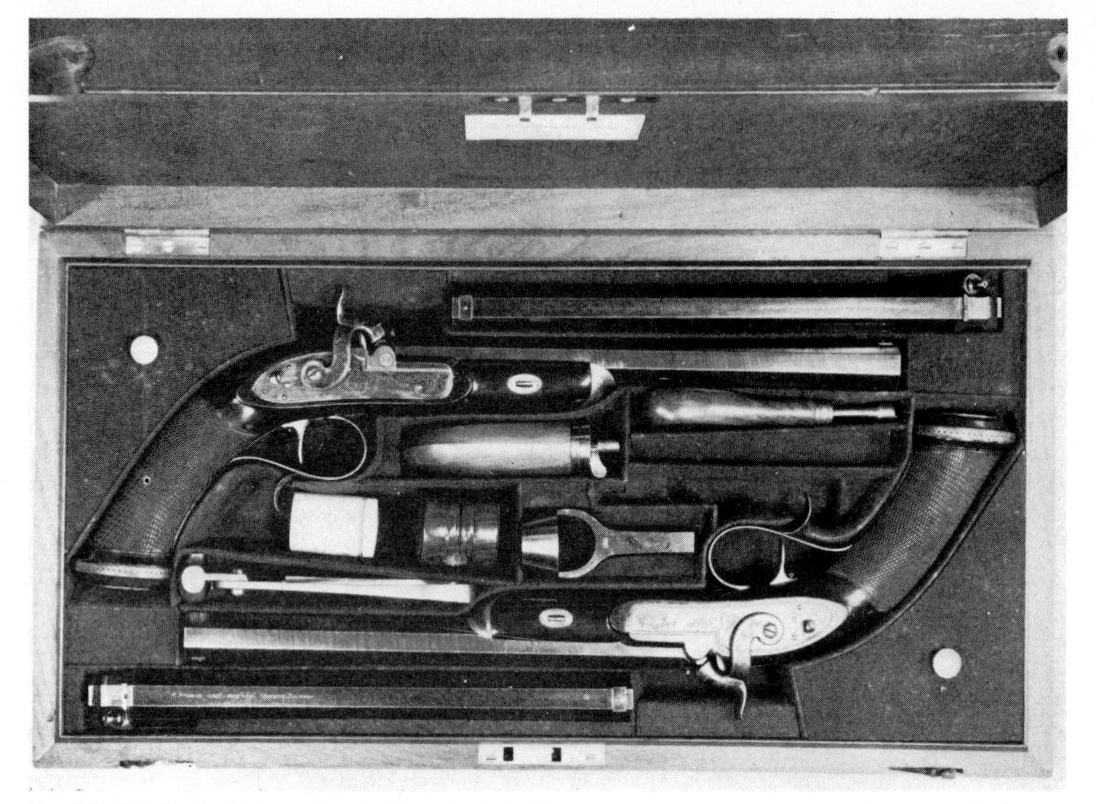

Fig. 76: Cased pair of percussion duelling pistols by J. Purdey of Oxford Street, London, once the property of Earl Canning. The set, which includes spare barrels, dates from about 1830. (Tower of London.)

the risk of loss; it passed through the stock in exactly the same way as the pin, engaging with a wide rectangular lug beneath the barrel. Improvements were also made in the breech. In the early examples the breech plug was fitted with a backward projecting bar (the tang) through which passed a screw securing the barrel to the stock. During the last decade or so of the 18th century a new system was incorporated into most pistols of good quality. The breech plug was fitted with a short, stubby hook which engaged with a metal recess mounted permanently in the stock; this method of attachment enabled quick and easy removal of the barrel for cleaning or repairs.

IDEALLY a barrel should not only be accurate but should also contribute towards the efficient combustion of the powder. Rapid burning of the powder ensured a crisp, quick explosion which would drive out the ball with maximum force, and to improve this action Henry Nock, a London gunmaker, patented a new style of breech in 1787. The essence of this innovation was a reduction in the distance travelled by the igniting spark. The connecting passage between touchhole and the main charge was widened out rapidly so that the flash quickly set fire to the powder contained therein. This produced a magnified spurt of flame which passed to the main charge producing quick and efficient burning and a consequent increase in power. The greater force ensured a flatter trajectory and so assisted in improving the pistol's accuracy. One of the hazards of the flintlock was the ease with which a small touchhole might become clogged and thus impede the firing of the main charge. The combustion of gunpowder produces a number of waste materials and these could, if not cleaned away quickly, cause corrosion and consequent blocking. However, the corrosive effect was not noticeable on the "noble" metals and it became the custom to drill a wider hole through the barrel between priming pan and main charge and into this fit a small plug of platinum or gold through the centre of which was drilled a normal size touchhole. The corrosive effects of the powder were thus controlled; thin layers of gold were also used to line the priming pan for exactly the same reason. Frequently a thin double line of gold or platinum will be found around the barrel at the breech end. When the pistols were new the barrels were almost invariably blued or browned and this delightful effect was achieved by heating or chemical treatment of the surface with the object of reducing the rusting propensity of the metal.

The wooden stock of the duelling pistol was usually of walnut and the most important feature was its shape—in particular the butt. There are two main types of butt; one is a gracefully curving, almost "hockey stick" shape in which the curve is usually fairly pronounced, and the surface of the butt is cut with a number of thin, criss-crossing lines to produce a roughened effect known as hatching. Whilst hatching is common on these pistols it is not usually found on earlier examples. Butt caps are not normally found on duelling pistols although there are, of course, exceptions. Many of the earlier pistols have flattened sides to the butt, the tip often being left plain and giving the effect of a butt cap. The other main type of butt tried by some of the gunmakers was the "saw handle" grip, in which the top of the butt was shaped off to a flattened ridge; in place of the gracefully curving top section there was a backward spur-like extension which sat comfortably on top of the hand. Many of the saw handle grips terminate in a flattened disc-like tip. Both full stock and half stock pistols were made, and as a very loose generalisation it may be said that the earlier ones were more often full stocked than half stocked. Half stock pistols are those with the wood terminating half way along the barrel, the end frequently being fitted with a horn or metal tip—the "fore-end". The majority of duelling pistols were fashioned with a ramrod which was generally of wood, although metal ones were also used. Ramrods fitted, as was common, into a recess in the stock beneath the barrel. Most are quite ordinary with a horn or metal tip but some will be found with one or two extra pieces such as the worm or jag, which is a double corkscrew-like attachment used for withdrawing a ball or charge in the event of a missfire. Less common was the ramrod fitted with a loading measure. When loading a pistol the powder was normally poured in at the muzzle, but if there was any oil or moisture on the inside some of the grains of powder might well adhere. Besides increasing fouling this loss of powder reduced the actual charge so upsetting the trajectory of the ball. A brass cup, smaller in diameter than the ball, could be screwed to the end of the ramrod. When this was filled with powder the barrel was lowered, muzzle first, down over the vertically-held ramrod until the tip of the measure actually touched the breech. If the two were now inverted the powder was deposited directly in the breech without any loss of grains on the way down. The ball and wad were then driven home with the ramrod. As the bullets cast for many duelling pistols were a very tight fit, manual pressure on the ramrod was insufficient to drive the ball home. In many cases a small wooden mallet was included to tap the ramrod and so drive home the ball.

The fittings or furniture of the pistols vary considerably; they may well be of steel, silver or brass but are usually quite plain, lacking decoration, although there is

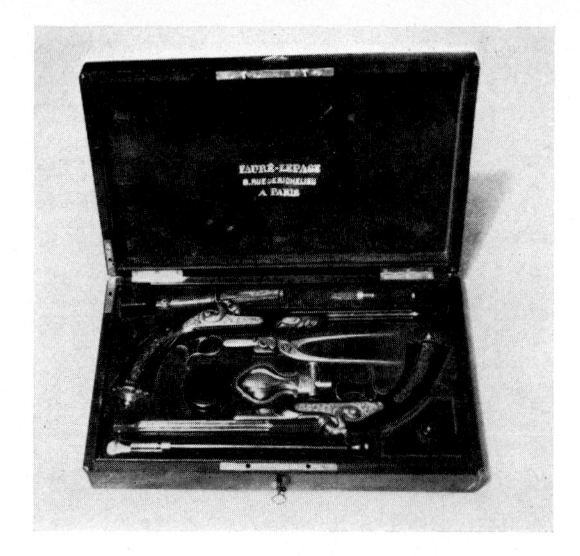

Left, *Fig. 77: Typical pair of cased percussion duellers by Fauré-Lepage of Paris; these weapons have ebony stocks and fluted barrels.*

often some engraving on the trigger guard and lockplate.

Obviously the lock was an extremely vital part and every effort was made by the gunsmith to see that it functioned as efficiently and quickly as possible. With this aim in view he sought ways in which to reduce the friction to a minimum. In the flintlock the rear arm of the frizzen pressed firmly down onto the frizzen spring and naturally there was a certain amount of drag or friction on these two surfaces. In order to reduce this as much as possible it was common practice to introduce a small roller bearing or wheel which will be found in one of two positions. Some were fitted at the end of the frizzen spring, which must have necessitated some careful and rather tricky work; but it may also be fitted to the tip of the frizzen. In both cases its sole function is to reduce friction.

Adjustments were also made to the internal mechanism with the object of reducing friction; in these locks the mainspring did not bear directly onto the tumbler, a small T-shaped link with minimal bearing surfaces being incorporated to join the spring to the tumbler. Good quality pistols were also fitted with a detent, which was a device intended to prevent the sear slipping into the notches cut into the edge of the tumbler when the trigger had been pressed to fire the weapon. It took the form of a pivoted wedge-shaped piece of metal incorporated into the tumbler in such a way that in effect the same notch was made to serve both half and full cock. Many, although by no means all duelling pistols were fitted with a safety catch of one type or another, usually a sliding bar fitted behind the cock and which could be pushed forward to engage with an appropriately cut recess in the back of the cock. The top quality duelling pistol also incorporated all the latest innovations such as the waterproof pan, which was designed to ensure that the priming would not be affected by rain running down into the pan.

Trigger action was also very important; too hard a squeeze or a jerk could so easily throw the pistol off aim. It was imperative that the trigger pull should be adjusted to the duellist's requirements and be as light as possible. A very high percentage of duelling pistols are fitted with some form of hair, or set trigger mechanism. Basically these actions consist of a compact group of levers and tiny springs which could be adjusted to set off the action with minimum pressure. Some were set by pressing the

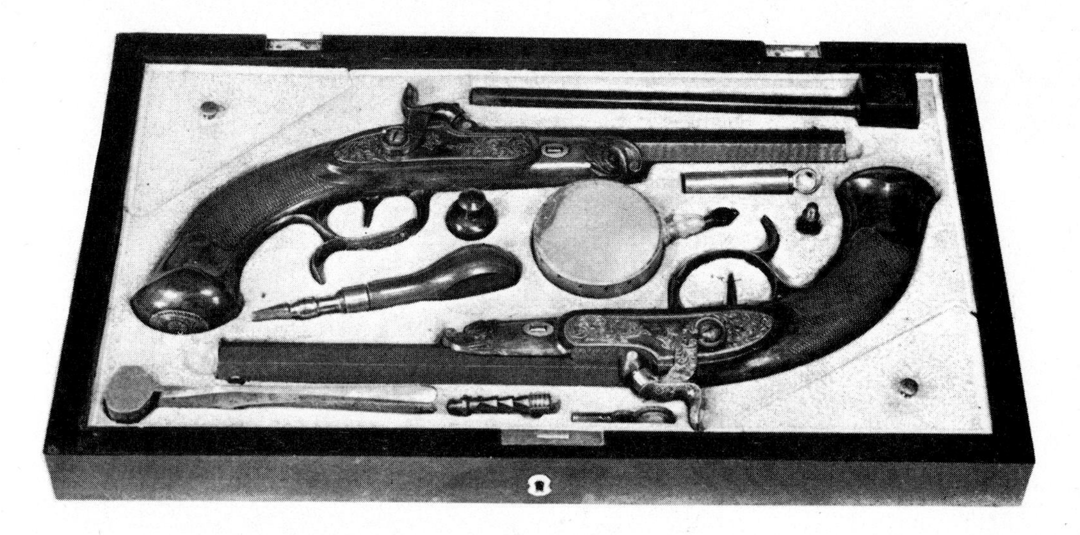

Fig. 78: Cased pair of Continental duellers, with typical recessed compartments. This set includes an unusual powder flask as well as a small mallet.

normal trigger forward, others have a second thin trigger which activates the mechanism. The setting could be adjusted and this was done by a small screw or nut head set just behind the trigger—see Fig. 70. As previously mentioned many of the trigger guards were made with an extending spur to afford a comfortable and steadying grip for the second finger of the hand.

DUELLING pistols were normally sold in pairs and were supplied in a wooden box or case together with the requisite accessories. Cases were frequently of oak or mahogany; occasionally they had brass bound corners and a carrying handle set into the top of the lid. The inside is covered with green baize and is divided by a series of partitions into compartments to hold the various accessories. In addition to the two pistols there might be any combination of a powder flask, oil bottle, screwdriver, cleaning rod, bullet mould, and, particularly in the later percussion models, a small wooden mallet. The normal style of fitting for the British weapons was that which used straight partitions, but with French duelling pistols the inside of the case was made with recessed shaped compartments so that each item fitted neatly into position. Inside the lid will be found the maker's trade card, and in the case of British produced pistols the majority of these will bear such names as Egg, Manton, Rigby, Nock and Wogden. Richard Wogden in particular acquired a special reputation for the quality and accuracy of his duelling pistols, and he is honoured by a poem composed in his honour which starts with the deathly poesy, "Hail Wogden, patron of the leaden death!"

In the case of French pistols, the best-known name is probably Lepage, and his percussion sets are highly rated by collectors. The butts tend to be somewhat florid in comparison with the stark British style, being frequently of ebony, fluted and with steel mounts.

Grace, balance and an impression of deadly efficiency have invested the duelling pistol with a special attraction in the eye of the collector. Single pistols are expensive enough, but the cased sets realise extremely high prices and few collectors can afford them. Flintlocks are the most prized but percussion examples are fast catching up.

7

The Blunderbuss and Multibarrel Weapons

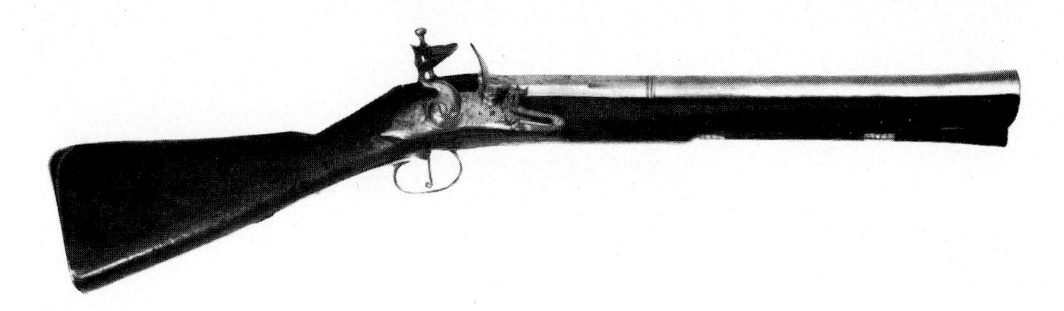

Fig. 79: Blunderbuss of the late 17th century, with octagonal breech and circular barrel. This particular weapon was used in the assassination attempt on King William III in 1696. (Tower of London.)

THE trouble with the majority of early muzzle loading weapons was that they afforded the owner no second chance. Either the first shot was decisive or the gunner might well forfeit his life. Multi-shot weapons had been produced using both wheellock and flintlock but they were invariably expensive, complex in action and a little unreliable. How then could the gunmaker offer his client an increased chance of hitting the target? One method was to produce a weapon which would fire not one bullet but twenty bullets with each shot. Certainly one of the earliest and unquestionably the best known weapon to offer this advantage was the blunderbuss.

There is one old wives tale connected with blunderbusses which seems virtually indestructible; it is repeated time and time again despite the fact that it has been shown to be without foundation. So often one reads a description of how the blunderbuss was loaded with half-bricks, stones, broken glass, bits of chain, in fact any rubbish that came to hand. This may well have happened in one or two cases but it was without doubt the exception rather than the rule but then, the whole idea of the blunderbuss is based on a misconception! It was thought that if the barrel expanded then the shot leaving the muzzle must spread in the same way. In theory, an attractive idea; aim at the target and provided you are pointing in roughly the right direction at least one of the balls should strike home. This was firmly believed for many many years, but modern research carried out with both shot guns and actual blunderbusses has shown that the expanding sides of the wide muzzle have very little, if any, effect upon the spread of the shot. The most obvious feature of the blunderbuss was, of course, the belling or swamping of the barrel. This is often illustrated in a very exaggerated manner, but in fact the spread was quite small, although one or two examples from the East are certainly a little overpowering. The degree of belling had only a very limited effect on the spread of the shot and the amount of spread was far more directly effected by the

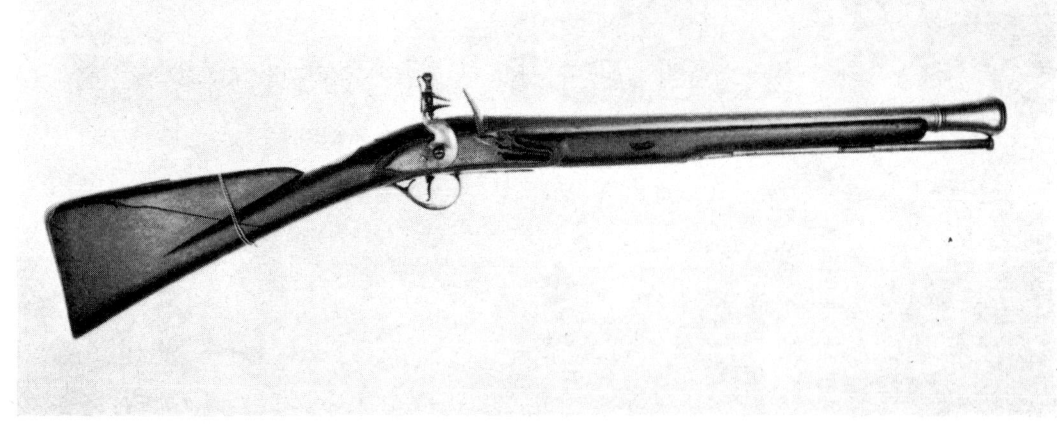

Fig. 80: A brass barrelled, full stocked blunderbuss of the mid-18th century. (Tower of London.)

bore of the firearm. This was the limiting factor; and although the wider bore did allow a greater spread, if the belling became too great it ceased to have any effect at all. Thus the best results were, in fact, obtained by a fairly short barrel with a wide bore rather than a long barrel with a widely swamped muzzle. Most of the blunderbuss barrels actually bell concentrically, but a number will be found with a vertical or horizontal oval bore, the theory being that this would spread the shot in a wedge-shaped pattern. However, this is not to say that blunderbusses were totally ineffective, for a wide barrel unquestionably made them simpler to load—a not inconsiderable advantage when the job had to be done on a pitching coach or on the deck of a rolling ship. Sheer size must have had a deterrent effect, especially if the threatened party believed the theory of the shot spread. There was also a magnifying effect on the sound of the shot, for the wide mouth acted as a megaphone; this effect was remarked on from the inception of the blunderbuss, and its very name is believed to have developed from the Dutch or German—*Donnerbüchse*—literally a thunder gun. Certainly the name *Donnerbüchse* had been converted to "blunderbuss" as early as the first part of the 17th century, although here the name is sometimes split into two sections—"blunder" and "buss".

As the origin of the name suggests, the blunderbuss apparently originated in Holland or Germany during the later part of the 16th century. Although a few examples fitted with wheellocks are known, it was with the introduction of the flintlock that blunderbusses acquired their great popularity. They seem to have been popular for use on board ships and there is some evidence to suggest that they were issued, at least in the 17th century, in proportion to the total number of cannon carried by the ships. Certainly many large sized blunderbusses were produced for defending fortified places or for shipboard use, and these may be recognised by a large swivel fitted to the stock, which would have been dropped into an appropriately placed hole on the wall or deck rail. Not a great number of blunderbusses were put into general military use although a few troops were issued with them. Among the list of stores returned from New York after the American War of Independence blunderbusses figure amongst the artillery stock. It was in the civilian market that the blunderbuss reached its height of popularity; it may be that the sheer size impressed the customer, but they were certainly in great demand for house defence and by travellers. A large number were used on

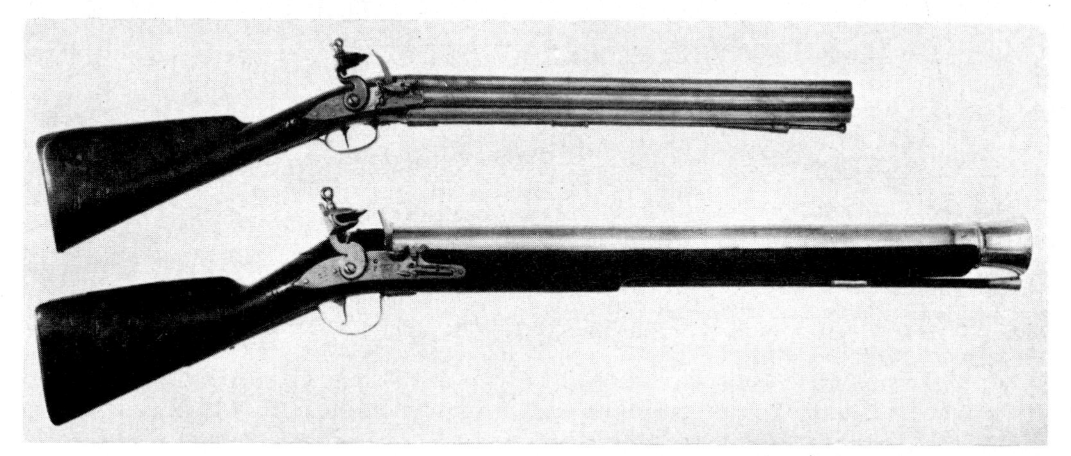

Fig. 81: (Top) *A seven-barrelled gun by Henry Nock.* Circa *1780. The barrels are rifled and the lockplate engraved* G. R. TOWER. *Barrel length, 20½ inches; bore, ·53 inch.* (Bottom) *A long brass barrelled blunderbuss of the early 18th century, the lockplate engraved* G. R. *and* COLE 21. (*Both Tower of London.*)

stage coaches or tucked on a shelf or beneath the bed of many an 18th century household.

The heyday of the blunderbuss lasted from roughly the last quarter of the 17th century to the first quarter of the 19th century, and their basic design changed only very slightly. They were finally ousted from their supreme position when the percussion cap made possible the production of simple, reliable and effective revolvers. Here now was a weapon which offered not one "all or nothing" shot but a choice of half a dozen. A number of percussion blunderbusses were produced and some flintlock ones were converted to the new system, but apart from some late examples such as those made with pinfire detonation they were largely obsolete by the 1830's.

If the life of the blunderbuss was so long and the changes of design so small, is it possible to date them? Fortunately the blunderbuss was not unique in its development; it followed the same broad lines as most long arms so that there are certain features which will give a reasonable indication as to origin. The 17th century examples tend to be rather thick-set and stubby in appearance; the stocks lack the grace that was such a feature of those produced by such fine makers as Mortimer at the end of the 18th and beginning of the 19th century. The butt is almost invariably cut straight at the back and may well be fitted with a plate of brass or iron held in position not by a screw as on later examples, but by small wood nails. This feature is almost invariably an indication of early origin, for after the turn of the century this style of attachment was replaced by a more curved and shaped butt plate with a large screw passing through the plate and into the heel of the butt. The furniture (ramrod pipes, trigger guard etc.) on the 17th century and early 18th century examples is plain and again may well be nailed into position. The shape of the trigger can be a guide, for early examples frequently have a backward curving tip, a fashion which seems to have gone out of vogue during the first half of the 18th century. However it is not invariably found on blunderbusses of the period for many of them have broad flat triggers.

When the Royal Mail Coaches were organised by John Palmer in 1784, among the innovations was the institution of a uniformed guard to travel with each coach.

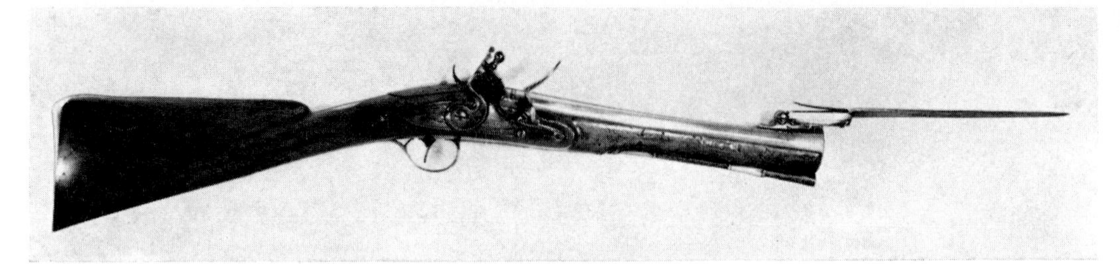

Fig. 82: Brass barrelled blunderbuss, with spring bayonet shown extended. The lockplate is marked WIGGIN & CO. *Overall length of blunderbuss, 27 inches; bayonet, 10 inches. (Gyngell Collection.)*

He was ordered to carry a blunderbuss and a pair of pistols. Both pistols and blunderbuss were brass barrelled, and the blunderbuss was carried in a holster affixed to the side of the guard's seat. Post Office records contain many references to the supply and use of these weapons; the majority of them were supplied by the London gunmaker R. Harding, whose shop was in the Borough in the South of London. Most of the blunderbusses carry the designation "His (or Her) Majesty's Coach", which is normally to be found engraved around the muzzle. Sometimes a number will also be found engraved on the weapon. It is most interesting to read among the archives of the Post Office the official instructions regarding the loading and use of these weapons. A Hand Bill of 1816 states that the weapons were to be loaded once a week and that if they had not been fired the charge was to be drawn and a fresh one inserted. Judging by some of the occurrence books a number of them *were* fired during the week, because there are several reprimands to guards for discharging their blunderbusses at stray animals as the coach passed along the road, or in a happy and inebriated state simply firing off a *feu de joie*. The load is also specified; a similar Hand Bill for 1816 states that the charge will be one measure of powder contained in the cap of the powder horn and ten or twelve balls. It is very likely that this would have been the average sort of charge for this type of weapon. The inscription round the barrel of "His (or Her) Majesty's Coach" was limited of course to those belonging to the Royal Mail, but civilian examples will also be found to be engraved with such bellicose statements as "Happy is he that escapes me!"

Some of the finest blunderbusses were made by the London gunmaker Mortimer, and his products are generally of very high quality with attractive lines and restrained decoration. Mortimer supplied both full and half-stocked blunderbusses including those with attached bayonets.

Barrels were produced in a variety of forms but there are two main groups. Early blunderbusses tend to have parallel sided barrels with an internally expanding bore, whilst those from the 18th century onwards have a barrel which bells visibly and externally. A large percentage of them were of brass but there are a number of steel-barrelled blunderbusses surviving, although naturally their less decorative appearance tends to reduce the price realised.

A few makers, feeling that if one barrel was good, two were even better, produced double-barrelled blunderbusses; but these are rather unusual and seldom appear on the antique market.

Some pistols were made with flaring barrels but they were somewhat of an oddity although they were produced in a variety of sizes. Some were small, little more than pocket pistols, but some were much larger and approached holster pistol size. One of the strangest and latest examples of a blunderbuss pistol was that patented by Henry Wilkinson in 1831; in this percussion pistol he used a paper cartridge which contained cap, powder and a cylinder of shot composed of 12 quarter segments of lead. A horizontally flared barrel was intended to scatter the shots into "a wide lateral field" according to the patent. The segmented bullets were cast in a special bullet mould and a separate shoulder stock was supplied to convert the pistol into a carbine-like weapon.

The blunderbuss was one attempt to increase the firepower of the individual, but although it may have increased the chances of a hit it was still a single shot weapon. As such it was still liable to miss, leaving the firer with an empty and useless weapon. What the gunmaker sought to do was to supply his customer with a weapon which was capable of firing several shots at will. One of the earliest and indeed one of the longest lasting solutions was the so-called superimposed load firearm. In this type of weapon two or more charges were placed in the barrel, one in front of the other, and in theory each charge could be fired in sequence. Methods of igniting these separate charges were numerous and ingenious, including such things as sliding locks. A variant of this form was the repeating type usually described as a "Roman Candle" in which a series of shots were discharged one after the other; but the firer had no control over them once the action was initiated by pressing the trigger. These weapons could fire anything up to fifteen shots but they were, of course, still liable to leave one with an empty pistol and no chance to take a second aimed shot. Moreover such weapons were

Fig. 83: Typical inscription engraved around the muzzle of a Royal Mail guard's weapon— * FOR HER MAJESTY'S MAIL COACHES *. *This particular example is taken from a pistol, not a blunderbuss.* (*Tower of London.*)

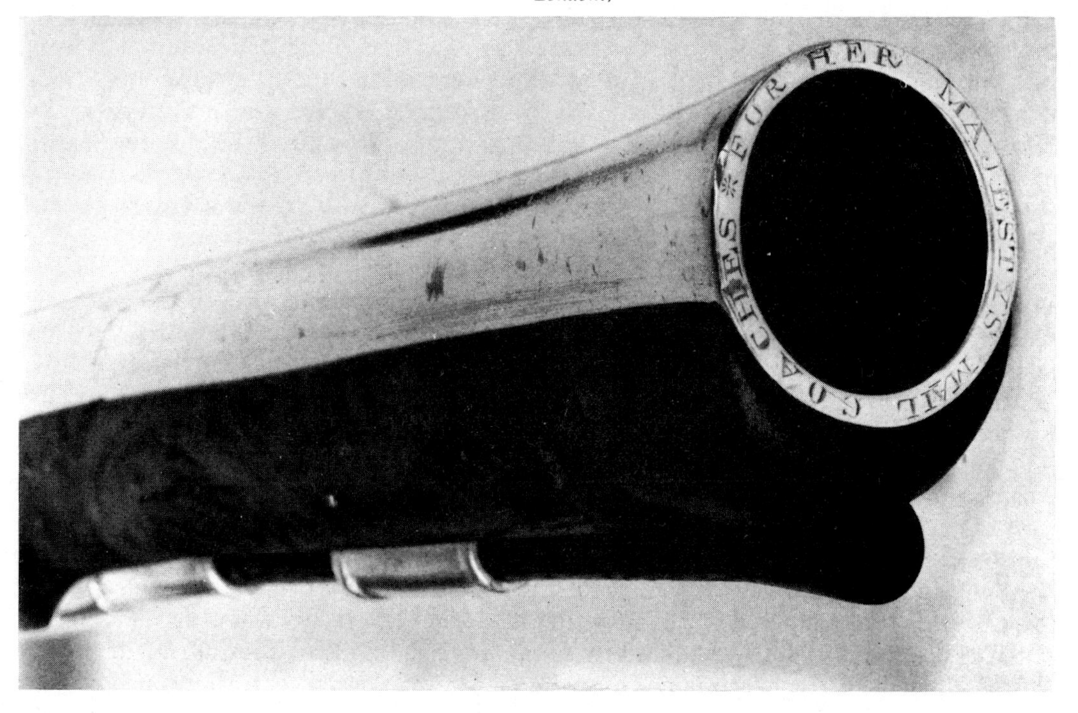

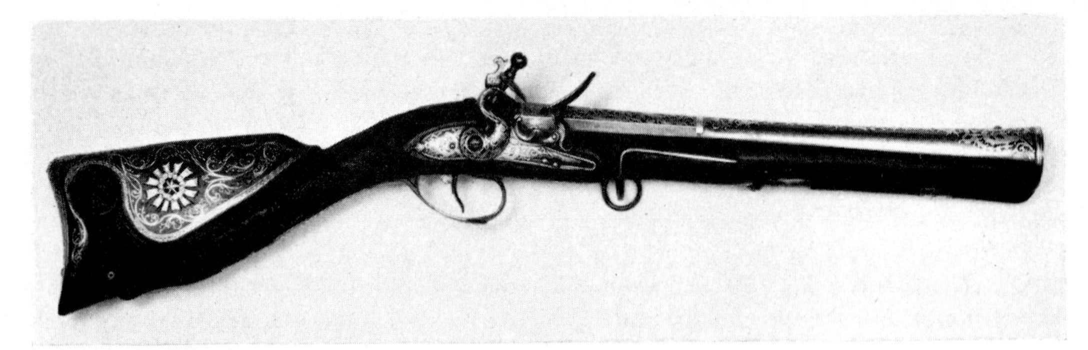

Fig. 84: Attractive Turkish blunderbuss dating from early in the 19th century, fitted with a ring and bar for attachment to a sling. The rosewood stock is beautifully inlaid with silver. (Reproduced by permission of the Trustees of the Wallace Collection.)

tricky to construct and frequently unreliable; in fact they were frequently downright dangerous. Another safer alternative was that of using several barrels, one for each shot; and multibarrel weapons were produced in every shape, form and size and using every means of ignition. The number of barrels range from two to seven; a few weapons with a larger number of barrels were made but generally seven is the highest number fitted to any weapon. Multibarrel matchlock weapons were produced in Europe and in Asia, but with the advent of mechanical means of ignition the production of such weapons became a simpler matter.

Most common of all are two-barrelled pistols, and examples will be found fitted with wheellock, flintlock or percussion actions. Obviously the wheellock examples are scarce and seldom seen outside museums, but percussion and flintlock are quite common. Basically all twin-barrel weapons are made using one of three systems. The first type is that which utilises a separate lock for each barrel. Although more expensive this system obviates the problems of rotating barrels and locking them in position. A second type uses a single lock for both barrels whilst a third uses a single cock but fits each barrel with a separate priming pan and frizzen. Further variations are possible in the way in which the two barrels are mounted; those fitted one above the other are described as "over and under", whilst those with the two barrels set next to each other are known as "side by side".

Without doubt pistols using the "over and under" arrangement are the type most frequently encountered, and there are three variations on this basic style. By far and away the most common is the so-called "tap action, over and under, box lock pistol". Although this long title might suggest a highly complex weapon the mechanism is basically very simple. The cock was set centrally instead of at the side as in most flintlock actions. The upper barrel was connected directly by a small hole to a more or less conventional priming pan. The floor of the pan was made up of a block of metal which could be rotated. Into this block was cut a small recess which in one position formed the floor of the priming pan. This recess was connected, via a small hole, to the lower barrel. To prepare the weapon for firing the two barrels were unscrewed, powder was placed directly into the breech, a ball seated on top and the barrels screwed back home. The tap or block was now turned so that the recess was uppermost, and a pinch of priming powder was placed therein, thus priming the lower barrel. If the tap was now rotated through a quarter turn the recess and powder were disconnected from the lower barrel and safely out of the way of any sparks since it was seated inside the solid block of metal of the frame. Another section of the block now formed the base of the priming pan and a second pinch of priming powder was placed therein and the frizzen closed, leaving the top barrel primed and ready for action. When the cock was pulled back to the firing position and the trigger pressed, the cock flew forward and struck the frizzen. Sparks fell into the priming which flashed and so ignited the upper barrel through the small touchhole, but the second barrel was unaffected until the tap was turned to bring the powder filled recess into position at the bottom of the priming pan. If the frizzen was now closed and the action cocked, the lower barrel was ready for firing. Tap action pistols were popular during the last decades of the 18th century and early part of the 19th century, and the idea was adapted for use in three-barrelled pistols, although this type was never very common.

Earlier double-barrelled pistols did not have tap action but operated on the basis of a rotating pair of barrels. Each of the barrels, mounted one above the other, was fitted to a central block which was locked in place by a spring clip; they were loaded and primed separately. The action comprising mainspring, cock and trigger was fitted to the butt section and when the top barrel was in position it functioned as a normal flintlock pistol; when it had been fired a second trigger was pressed to release the block which was then rotated by hand to bring the lower barrel up into the firing position ready for the second shot.

A third and far less common variety of pistol was the side by side action which utilised a single frizzen and single cock for both barrels. The action was of the box lock type, with the cock mounted centrally behind the two barrels and the frizzen pivoted in front of the pans. Each barrel had a separate touchhole and recessed

Fig. 85: Tap action over-and-under box lock pocket pistol by Nicholson of Cornhill, London. Circa *1800. The tap can be distinguished; the small projection at the top is a safety catch. Overall length, $8\frac{3}{4}$ inches; barrels, 3 inches. (Gyngell Collection.)*

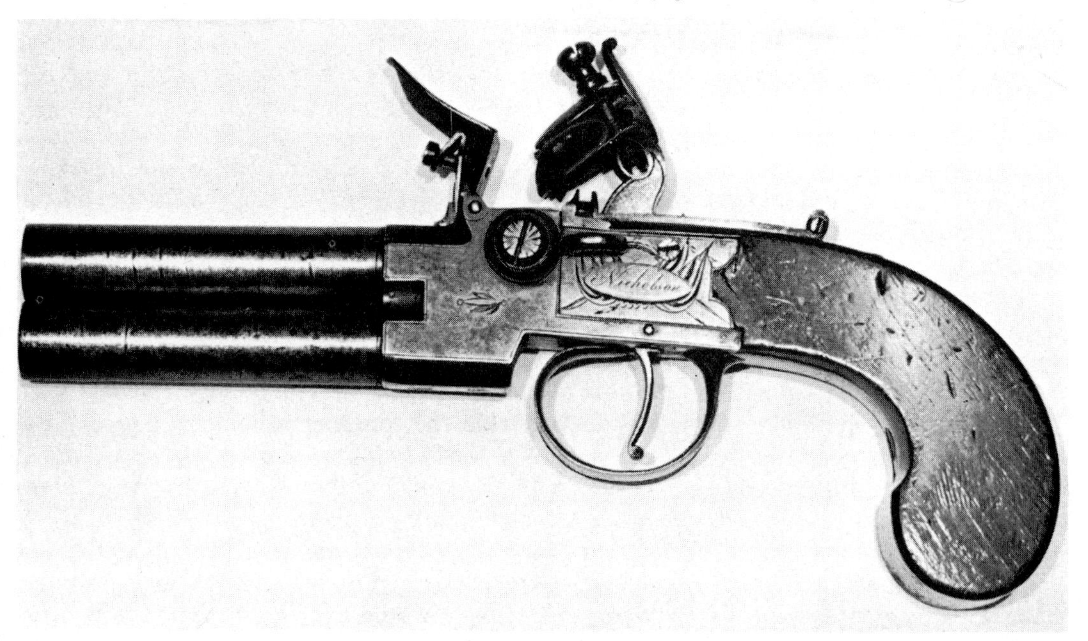

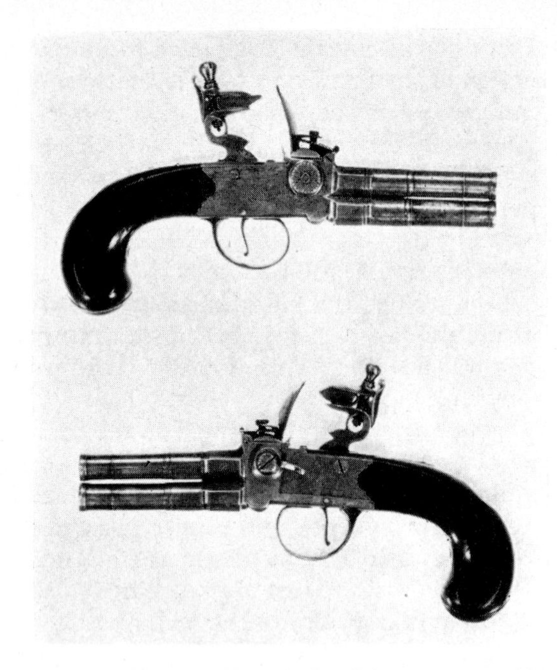

Left, *Fig. 86: A pair of tap action flintlocks by Rea of London. Late 18th century. It is unusual to find such weapons in pairs, especially pieces of such fine quality as these.* **Foot of opposite page,** *Fig. 87: A pair of side-by-side pocket pistols with double triggers, cocks, and frizzens; a comparatively unusual arrangement for such pistols. The lockplates are marked* GRIFFIN & TOW *and* LONDON. (*Both Tower of London.*)

priming "saucer" and the frizzen was wide enough to serve both pans. The left hand pan was sealed off by a sliding cover leaving the right hand barrel free to fire. By removing the sliding cover the left hand pan was open to receive the sparks from the frizzen which of course had to be closed before the second shot could be fired—the lock also had to be cocked again.

When the percussion system was adopted life became easier for the gunmaker since the simple action meant that double-barrelled weapons could be produced cheaply and efficiently. Both over and under and side by side percussion pistols were produced, but tap action and sliding pan covers were no longer required and almost every double barrelled pistol had two locks fitted to a single barrel block drilled with both bores. It was normal for twin triggers to be fitted, one for each lock, one fairly straight and the other set back and with a pronounced curve to accommodate the finger. Although percussion pistols were normally fitted with double triggers a few flintlock and wheel-lock pistols were operated by a single trigger, the first pressure firing one lock and continuing pressure firing the second.

Double-barrelled pistols were fairly common but double-barrelled long arms were a far less frequent occurrence. Certainly a few sporting wheellock weapons with double barrels are known, and there are one or two flintlocks fitted with twin barrels, but the weight required for a double barrel rendered it difficult to produce a weapon which could be handled easily. It was not until the middle of the 18th century that improved technical skill on the part of the gunmakers was sufficient to enable them to produce two light but strong barrels suitable for sporting weapons. Since these double-barrelled sporting guns were normally for wealthy patrons they were almost invariably beautifully decorated. Stocks were frequently inlaid with silver wire, often in the prevailing fashion of the time, and butt cap and furniture may also be in silver. Continental sporting guns tended to go in for slightly more decoration in the form of carving on the stock than was fashionable in Britain, where decoration was normally limited to inlay and some hatching on the grip. These double-barrelled guns will be found with full and half stocks, and a number of them were sold cased with powder flasks, wad cutters, cleaning rods and, with best quality weapons, a spare set of barrels.

With the adoption of the percussion system and its much simpler construction double-barrelled shot guns were produced in quantity by Birmingham and London gunmakers. Some were of good quality but many were fitted with barrels of inferior quality, and were only marginally safe. Hunting books of the period contain frequent admonitions to the reader to ensure that their barrels were of top quality because of the prevalence of accidents resulting from bursting barrels. The double-barrelled percussion shot gun is not in very great demand by collectors although many of them are quite pleasing. Differing methods of barrel construction produced some very attractive patterns in the metal, although on the cheaper examples the effect was produced by chemical means rather than construction. Contemporary prices for double-barrelled shot guns in 1859 ranged from £4 to 50 or 60 guineas. The writer "Stonehenge" in 1859 stated that any gun costing less than £20 could not be considered safe. He also thought that the top price paid for a cased gun of good quality should not exceed 35 to 40 guineas—a not inconsiderable sum at that period. Many of them may be found with full or half stocks, though in general half stocking was the more common and cheaper style of construction.

Military long arms were seldom double barrelled although Major John Jacob, commander of the Scinde Irregular Horse in India and a pioneer in the use of rifled

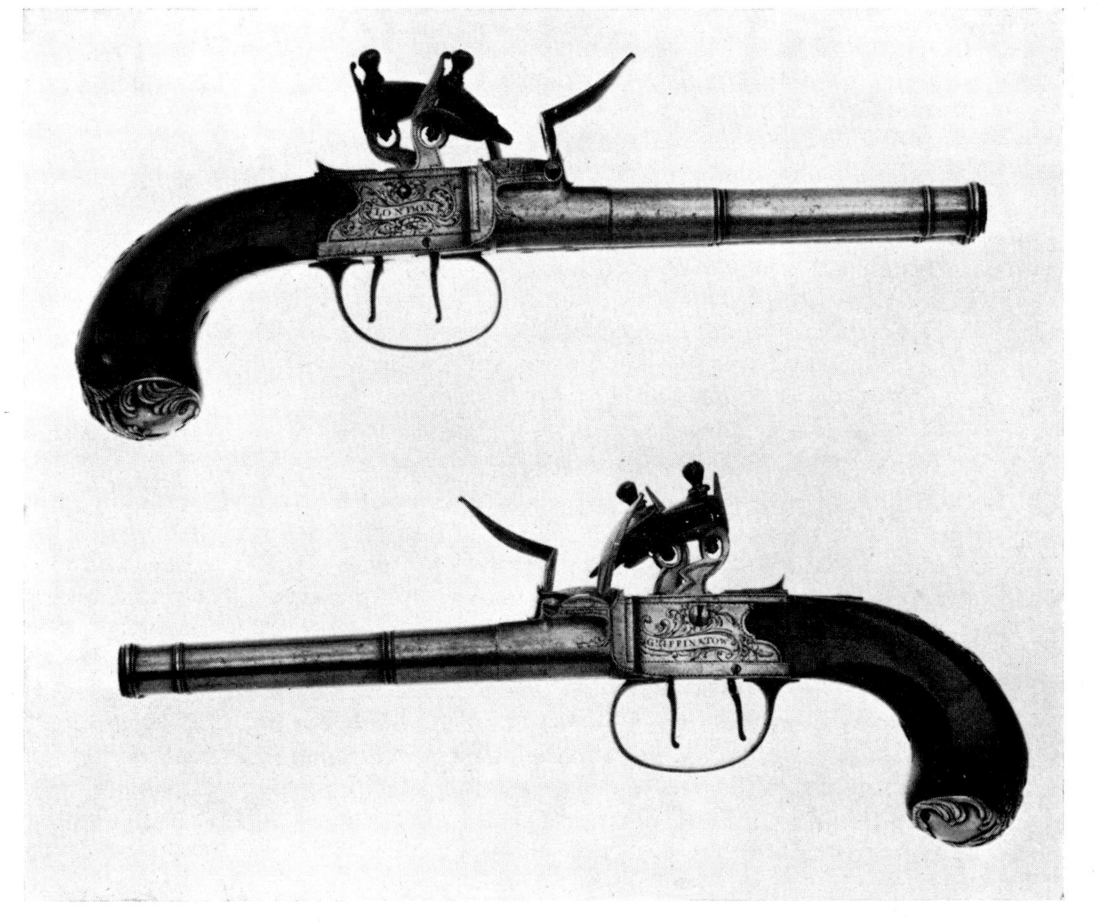

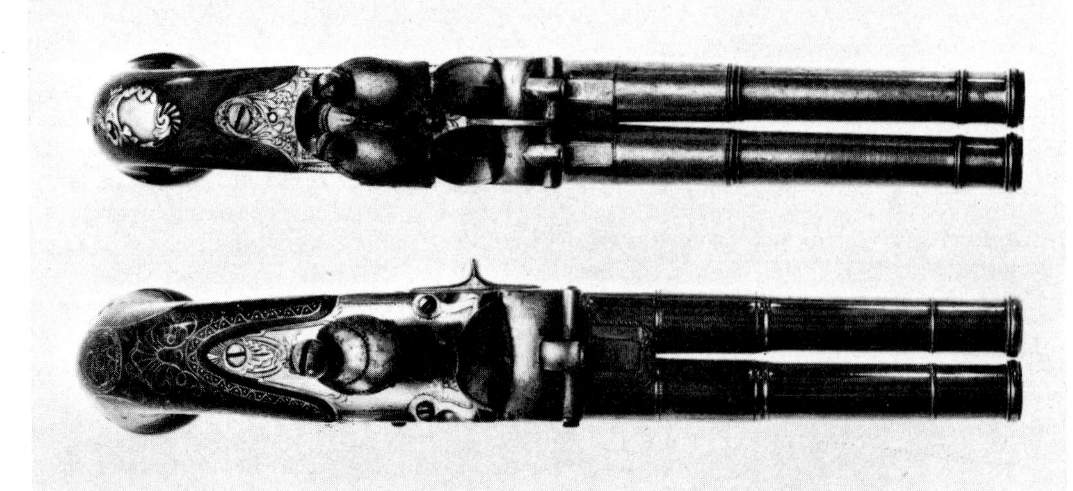

Fig. 88: Top views of (above) *a side-by-side pistol with twin cocks and frizzens; and* (below) *a side-by-side pistol fitted with a single cock and frizzen and a sliding pan cover. The catch for operating the slide may be seen projecting from the left side of the pistol.* (*Tower of London.*)

weapons and explosive bullets, became convinced in 1856 that double-barrelled rifles were the ideal weapon for troops. A number of these rifles were made privately for his troops in India, but the Jacob's rifle was never a general issue although later double-barrelled rifles were ordered for Cape of Good Hope forces.

Far rarer than double-barrelled rifles are those long arms fitted with one smooth-bored barrel and one rifled, but a number of such weapons were made. Very few double-barrelled revolvers were produced, probably the most famous being that patented by Jean Alexandre Le Mat, a French born physician who served on the staff of the Governor of Louisiana. He was granted an American patent in 1856 for a two-barrelled pistol which comprised a nine shot cylinder revolver with a central barrel which fired a charge of shot. The choice of barrels was effected by a movable hammer nose so that the weapon might be used either as a revolver or as a "small shot" pistol. A number of the Le Mat revolvers were produced in France and England and many of them were used by the Southern States in the American Civil War.

So far all the multi-barrelled weapons discussed have been those in which each barrel was fired at will; but there was another group, usually described as volley guns, in which all the shots were discharged automatically once the trigger had been pressed. The system differed from those of the "Roman Candle" principle in that each charge was in a separate barrel. One of the rarest forms was the so-called "duck foot" gun which made its appearance during the last quarter of the 18th century. It comprised a small box lock flintlock pistol with four barrels fitted to a single breech block. The barrels were splayed out from the breech so that the angle covered was something in the region of 45 degrees. A single touchhole and priming pan was incorporated and from the touchhole four connecting passages fanned out to the four barrels. The theory behind this weapon was that in certain circumstances such as riots, mutiny on board ship or attacks by a crowd, the threat of four balls fanning out would have a far greater effect.

Plate 14 (Left) *A brass barrelled blunderbuss, complete with a spring bayonet, by H. W. Mortimer. Mid-18th century. Overall length, 30 inches; barrel, 14½ inches.* (Right) *A brass barrelled blunderbuss by Smart. Mid-18th century. Overall length, 29 inches; barrel, 14 inches.* (*Durrant Collection.*)

Plate 15 *Blunderbuss pistol with spring operated bayonet fitted beneath the brass barrel. Engraved on one side of the boxlock is Waters and on the other Patent. Circa 1780.*

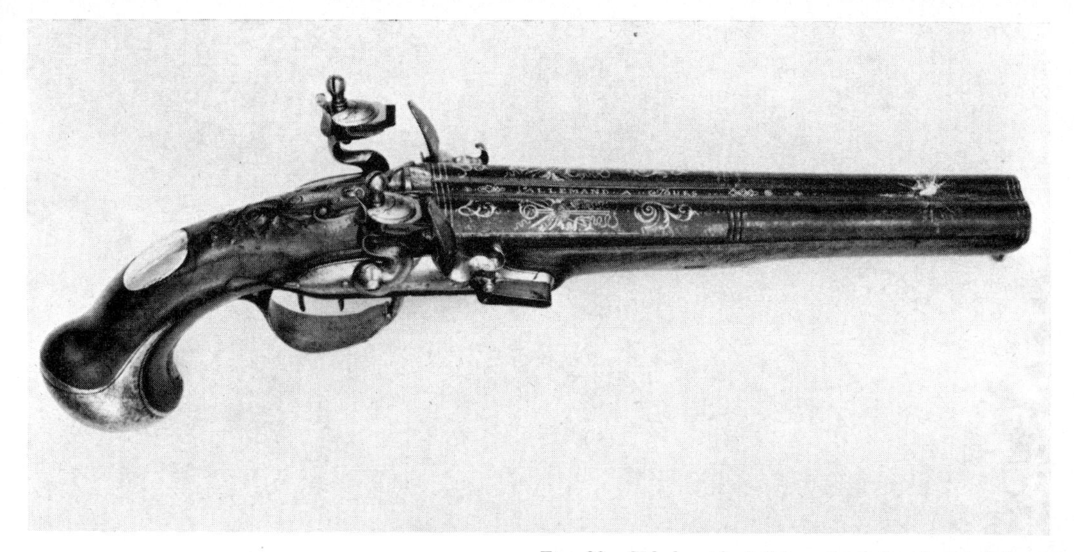

Fig. 89: Side-by-side holster pistol fitted with left and right hand locks; the barrels are decorated and bear the inscription L'ALLEMAND A TOURS. *French; mid-18th century. (Tower of London.)*

Far more popular, although still very rare, was the seven barrelled volley gun. Despite all the efforts of firearms historians the old story of their origin still persists. It is to the effect that after the death of Nelson, shot by a marksman on the mast of a French warship, at Trafalgar in 1805, the British Navy sought some means to clear marksmen and marines from the fighting tops of enemy ships. To fill this need the seven-barrelled volley gun was produced, a weapon which sent a shower of seven balls whistling through the rigging raking out any snipers. This very credible story is marred by the fact that the seven barrel volley gun was in use by the British Navy some 20 years before the battle of Trafalgar! The idea of the volley gun is very old and examples dating back to the late 16th and early 17th centuries are in existence; in some weapons the number of barrels rises to as many as twelve. Credit for the resurrection of the idea in 1779 should be given to Capt. James Wilson, who sought to interest the British Board of Ordnance in such a weapon. Two prototypes were made, with each of the seven barrels rifled, and tests suggested that they might indeed be useful for naval warfare. A payment of £400 was made to Wilson, and the famous London gunmaker Henry Nock was given the contract for producing these weapons. Construction was not easy, for the plan was to have six barrels forming an outer circle with the seventh at the centre. Each of the seven rifled barrels were made separately and then brazed together to form a solid block. The centre barrel was threaded so that it could be screwed to a plug and this chamber was connected to the touchhole. When the trigger was pressed and sparks were made it was the centre barrel which was actually ignited by the priming. The six outer barrels were connected by means of small holes to the centre barrel so that as this was fired the flash travelled immediately to the six outer barrels and so discharged all barrels together. Basically this idea was sound but in practice it proved to be a little difficult since the connecting channels between the centre and outer barrels tended to become very fouled, and the only means of cleaning them was to strip down the entire assembly. Not only did these channels become blocked, but the rifling made the whole weapon extremely difficult to load and

Fig. 90: Four-barrelled percussion pistol with separate cocks. The barrel block was rotated to bring the lower pair of barrels into the firing position when required. Circa *1850.* (*Blackmore Collection.*)

the cumulative recoil from seven barrels amounted to a very considerable kick. These problems were tackled and eventually the charge of powder was reduced and in place of rifled barrels smooth bores were substituted. It is difficult to assess how effective such weapons were but some indication is probably given by the fact that only 655 of them are recorded as being produced; one feels that if their value had been substantial the Napoleonic wars would certainly have created a much higher demand. They were extremely heavy, and one cannot but sympathise with the unfortunate marine or sailor who was faced with the job of handling this weapon on board one of His Majesty's pitching ships. Weighing twelve pounds each, these weapons were too heavy for sporting use; but the idea was adapted and modified and the construction lightened by such makers as Henry Nock. Sporting versions incorporating twelve and and even fourteen barrels were produced, and there is one beautiful example in Her Majesty's collection at Windsor. It was made by Henry Nock in 1792/3; it has seven rifled barrels and is beautifully decorated with silver mounts.

The idea of using several barrels to give greatly increased firepower was one which appealed to the early gunmakers, and the so-called "organ guns" which date from at least the 15th century were simply rows of musket barrels mounted on some form of wheeled carriage. It was not until the mid-19th century that the idea was improved on, resulting in the first really practical machine guns. An English inventor, James Puckle, had patented in 1718 a revolver-type machine gun incorporating a bizarre feature. He suggested that round balls be used against Christian enemies, and square ones against Turks, who apparently excited his intense hostility; and his design provided for separate magazines for the two types of ammunition!

However, it was to be the famous Gatling gun that became the first practical mass-produced machine gun. Richard Jordan Gatling seems to have had the idea first in 1861; the gun was intended as a defence weapon to hold bridges and fortified positions. In the same year Dr. Gatling had a prototype made which was demonstrated in 1862, and a patent was duly granted for a "Revolving Battery-Gun". Essentially the Gatling gun consisted of six parallel barrels mounted around a common axis.

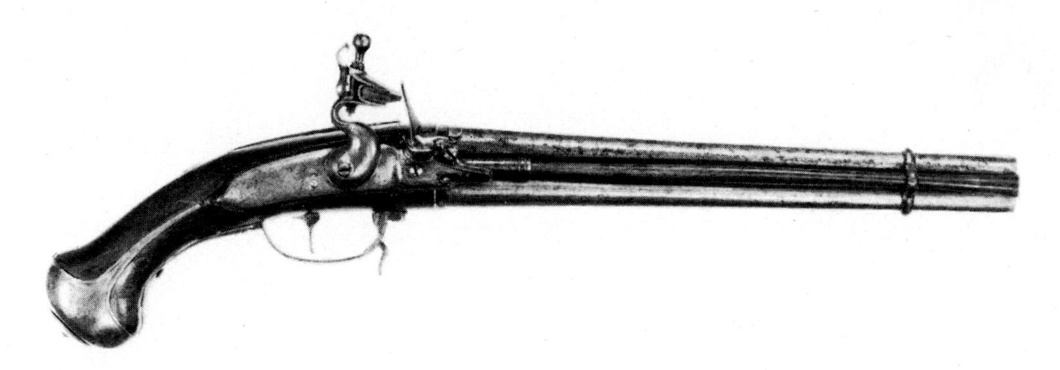

Fig. 91: A flintlock holster pistol with hand-rotated barrels. As the top barrel was fired the catch visible at the front of the trigger guard was pressed, freeing the lower barrel and allowing it to be brought up into the firing position. Late 17th or early 18th century. (Tower of London.)

Behind each barrel was a small self-contained metal chamber into which fitted a paper cartridge and a bullet of .58 diameter. The chamber was primed with a cap and dropped into position. When the handle was turned at the side the barrels rotated, and as the barrels passed a fixed point, six separate strikers hammered, one after the other, on to the percussion caps and so discharged the load. The first Gatling gun achieved a rate of 200 rounds a minute but suffered from certain inherent technical disadvantages. Another model was produced in 1862 which fired a metal rim-fire cartridge, but again there were problems involved in feeding the cartridges into the barrels. A number of these guns were used during the American Civil War but they did not gain general acceptance by the military. Development was continued and as a result the Gatling was soon proving a very reliable and fast-firing weapon and was adopted by a large number of the world's armed forces. Ironically enough the same principle is now being used to produce a gun which can fire something like 6,000 rounds a minute—the Vulcan aerial cannon employed by the United States forces.

Blunderbusses and multi-barrel weapons are undeniably fascinating, and are in great demand; and as supply is limited prices have risen enormously. Reasonable quality examples of brass barrelled blunderbusses now command prices well in excess of three hundred pounds. Of the multi-barrel weapons only the over and under tap action flintlocks are likely to turn up in the market, with perhaps an occasional specimen of a three-barrelled pistol, and these too are climbing in value. Percussion examples of multi-barrel weapons are fairly common and excite some interest.

8

Combination Weapons and Curiosa

"IN matters of life and death it is better to be safe than sorry!" This was probably one of the gunmakers' best sales lines, and no doubt one of his main arguments when trying to convince a client that he should purchase a far more complicated and expensive weapon than he actually needed. One may be sure that this was one of the main points that he tried to put across when selling a so-called "combination weapon". One can imagine the gunmaker putting forward to a military man the argument that if his pistol was empty he could still rely on a good sword; and many of the combination weapons comprise a firearm of some description and an edged weapon.

Combination weapons were produced in a profusion of shapes, sizes and varieties. Some were intended to supply a second means of ignition for a firearm, and in the early days of the wheellock it was not uncommon to find a long arm fitted with both matchlock and wheellock mechanisms. Later, when the change over from flintlock to percussion lock was in fashion, some weapons were supplied with fittings to provide alternative actions. Nevertheless the term is usually understood to apply to those examples which are formed from two different weapon systems, rather than two different mechanisms.

Some of the earliest firearms were, in fact, combination weapons comprising

Below, *Fig. 92: Box lock flintlock pocket pistol with under-barrel spring bayonet. This example is unusual in having an octagonal barrel; most were round. Note that the trigger guard doubles as a sliding catch to hold the bayonet in the retracted position.* (*Gyngell Collection.*)

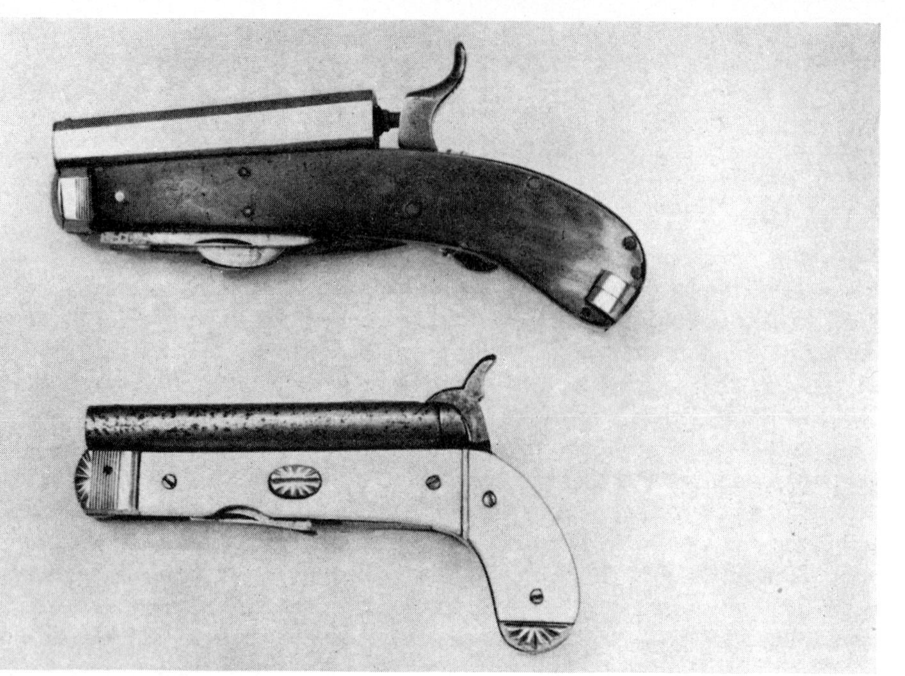

Fig. 93: Two pocket knife-pistols in the closed position; the top one is a percussion device while the lower takes a rim-fire cartridge. (Vokes Collection.)

pistols married to clubs or missile weapons. In an inventory of the Tower of London in 1547 there appears an entry recording "holy water sprinklers" with "gonnes in the topp". These holy water sprinklers have only a very tenuous ecclesiastical connection and were, in fact, spiked clubs mounted at the end of a long pole. Examples of such weapons have survived; they comprise a spiked block in which are incorporated three barrels, about nine inches long, fitted with touchholes; the muzzles may be covered by metal plates. Whether this was a serious weapon or not is uncertain, but clearly it could have served as a hand gun, for basically it resembles the early type of firearm in which the small barrel was mounted at the end of a long pole. Once the three barrels had been discharged by a glowing match, the spiked head would certainly have served as a reserve means of defence or attack.

A little later, around 1570/80, there appears to have been a vogue for pole arms such as axes and halberds fitted with wheellock pistols. The triggers were often set well back along the shaft and might take the form of a button or a wire rod. Incredibly enough some of these awkward weapons were equipped with sights, although it seems unlikely that they could have been seriously considered as anything other than a last resort weapon. Maces were also fitted with wheellock pistols, and one or two examples are known which are fitted with a small compartment to hold the charges of powder. Far rarer was the sword-stick pistol, which combined a wheellock with a long thin blade which fitted into a slim sheath, giving the appearance of a long walking stick typical of the type used during the 17th and 18th centuries. The wheellock pistol was situated just below the grip and was fired by a small projection underneath the handle.

Possibly the most unusual of all these combination weapons was the shield and matchlock pistol issued to certain of Henry VIII's bodyguards. A circular metal-plated shield was fitted with a breech-loading matchlock pistol, the barrel of which formed the boss of the shield. Just above the pistol was a small barred opening through which the guard could sight on his target. A number of these have survived; they are extremely interesting to the historian, being among the earliest known examples of breech-loading hand guns.

One of the very earliest examples of a wheellock known to students is fitted to a crossbow, and closely resembles the lock designed and recorded by Leonardo da Vinci in the very early 16th century.

The combination weapon which has probably had the longest life is the pistol-sword. These weapons occur at all periods between the 16th and 19th centuries, and all forms of ignition have been used for the firearm portion of the weapon. There is an interesting difference of emphasis in surviving examples; some are clearly intended to be primarily swords with the pistol added as an "extra"; but in a few cases, and these are rarer, the designs suggest that the pistol is the prime weapon with the blade serving as a form of bayonet. Early examples comprise a fairly long bladed sword or dagger with a wheellock pistol attached to the top of the blade just beneath the quillons; but the majority of these weapons which survive today date from the late 17th and 18th centuries, and are small "hangers" with a flintlock pistol attached. The hanger was the travelling sword of the period, and was made with both straight and curved

Fig. 94: The same pistols opened; the top example is the Unwin and Rodgers model, complete with bullet mould and tweezers. A cartridge can be seen under the raised barrel of the lower piece. (Vokes Collection.)

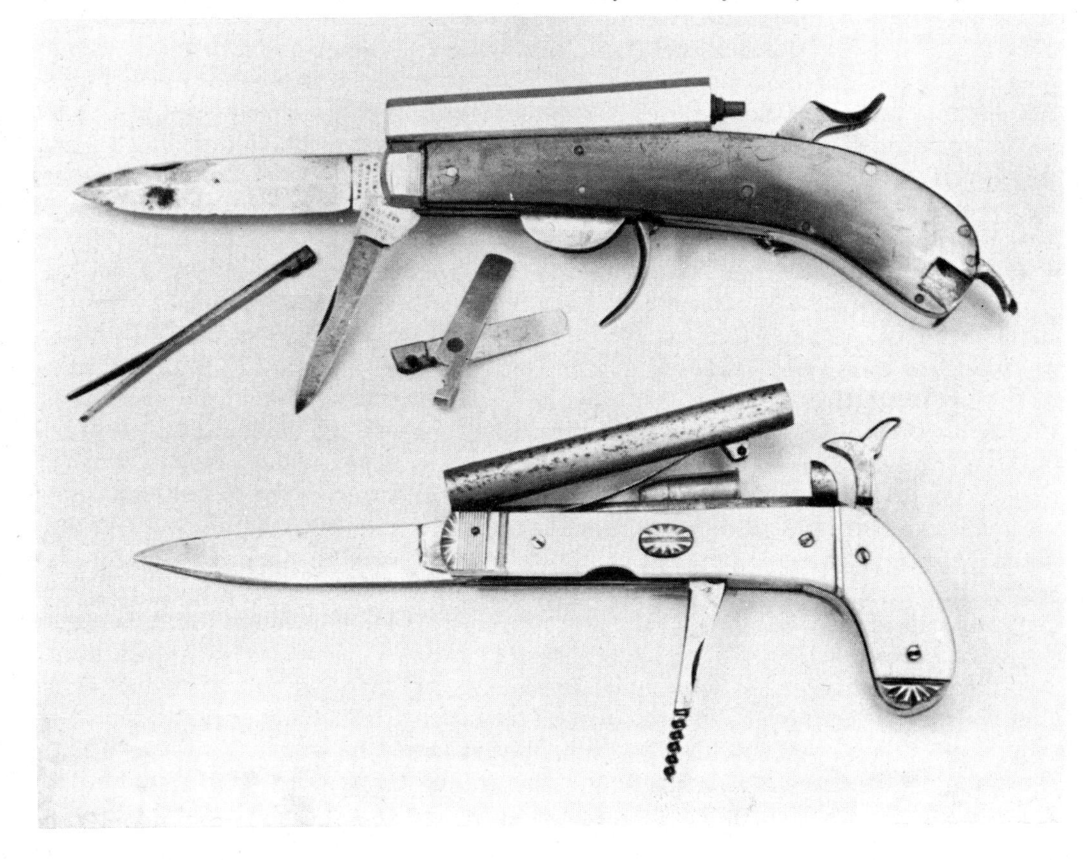

Fig. 95: An English spring gun, showing the method of mounting with trip-cords. The pivot is driven into the ground immediately below the lock, and the device is free to rotate to the limit of the rear chain, in the direction of the cord pull. (Vokes Collection.)

blades. Many were obviously intended primarily as hunting weapons, and the pistol may well have been used to dispatch wounded beasts rather than as a serious defensive weapon. A typical example of this weapon comprises a short blade on one side of which is mounted the barrel and on the other the frizzen and spring, with the touchhole piercing the blade. The cock is situated at the back of the grip and in arrangement is very similar to a box lock pistol. In the grip (often of horn) is set the trigger, usually an inch or so back from the quillons. The great majority of these weapons have a single shell, typical of hunting swords, projecting down over one side of the blade. Pistols are normally of fairly small calibre, seldom more than half an inch. Very rarely is more than one barrel fitted, although there are examples of weapons with two or even four barrels. Sheaths, where they have survived, are carefully shaped at the top so that the pistol section fits in comfortably and is guarded from rain and wind.

A second style, which is far rarer, comprises a Queen Anne type pistol with a butt longer than was usual, this forming the hilt of the sword. This principle of using a pistol butt as a hilt was employed by one George Elgin; in 1837 he acquired a patent for the device which he called a "Pistol Knife" or a "Pistol Cutlass". This was basically a fairly conventional percussion pistol, but fitted beneath the barrel and uniting with the trigger guard was a large bowie-like blade with a curved edge. These Elgin pistols vary in detail but by and large they all display a basic pattern. They must have made a very effective cutting weapon, for the blade is substantial, but whether the pistol was of any value is uncertain. The Secretary of the U.S. Navy authorised the purchase of 150 of these weapons for issue to an expedition sent out to explore the South Seas. They were apparently fairly expensive, for they cost 20 dollars each in 1833. There is in existence a letter of 1837 which gives the specification of the weapon; it states that the barrel was to be five inches long, and "the blade shall be of best sheer steel 11 inches long, forming a guard over the hand of good temper". Blade and barrel were combined by a tongue and groove, and the leather scabbard was fitted with a metal tip or chape. The price appears to have dropped; by then the cost was quoted as 17 dollars and 60 cents each.

Fig. 96: The lock of a four-shot flintlock gun made by H. W. Mortimer & Son in about 1815. Each charge was fired by sliding the lock into position by the appropriate touchhole; this is an unusual weapon in that it also incorporates a self-priming magazine. (*Winchester Gun Museum, Newhaven, U.S.A.*)

The concept of the sword-pistol or dagger-pistol lingered on, and there are even one or two examples of pinfire revolvers fitted with a blade. As late as 1862 an American patent was granted to R. J. Colvin of Pennsylvania for a pistol sword which was a conventional type of cavalry sabre to the back of which was fitted a double-action percussion revolver, the trigger being mounted inside the knuckle bow. In 1864 the same gentleman also acquired a patent for a quite incredible revolver-bayonet. This was intended to be attached to the muzzle of a normal long arm, so providing a triple weapon; the long arm, the bayonet, and the revolver attached to the rear of the bayonet. This extra cylinder was fired by a second trigger set in front of the normal trigger of the long arm—a highly bizarre and potentially hazardous weapon. In 1863 yet another patent was granted for a 16-barrelled revolver attachment which was designed to fit on to the shaft of a lance. Possibly the pinnacle of pistol-sword design was reached in 1877 when a British patent granted to Walter Davis permitted him to offer for production a regulation sword which combined a cartridge revolver mounted just below the grip. What distinguished this weapon was the scabbard, which was made in sections so that it could be folded in three and then be clipped to the hilt of the sword to form a crude and, one would have thought, very uncomfortable shoulder stock, so converting the entire imaginative invention into a carbine!

THE most common form of combination weapon is, of course, the bayonet. This weapon has a long history, and appears first during the 17th century, apparently deriving its name from the town of Bayonne in France. The name itself seems to have applied first of all to a long dagger; tradition has it that the inhabitants of this area pushed the hilts of their knives into the muzzles of their empty musket barrels to convert them into pikes; thus the bayonet was born. At first bayonets were little more than broad, triangular-bladed knives with small cross-quillons and a tapering wooden handle which was pushed into the muzzle of the musket. Obviously with the bayonet in position the musket could not, under any circumstances, be loaded or fired; so every effort was made to produce a bayonet which could be attached to the barrel in some way

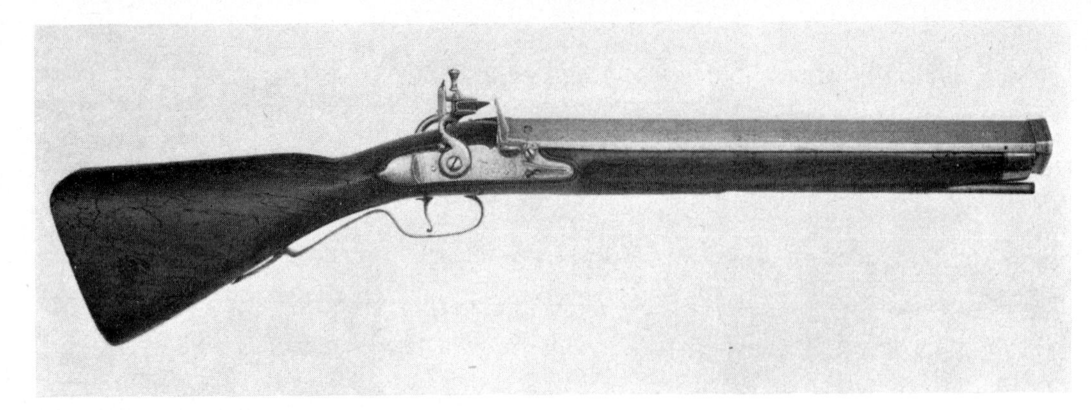

Fig. 97: Four-barrelled German flintlock carbine working on the Roman Candle principle. The piece dates from the middle of the 17th century and is signed by the maker, Francisco Mambach. (Tower of London.)

that left the user free to fire if necessary. The final solution was the introduction of a socket bayonet, in which the blade was fitted to a short tubular section which slipped over the outside of the muzzle and locked in position. This form of attachment, with variations in the way of locking rings and spring clips, lasted well into the 19th century. The middle of the 19th century saw the introduction of the lug beneath the barrel which engaged with a slot cut into the handle of the bayonet, which was then locked into position beneath or beside the barrel.

Of more immediate interest is the folding or spring bayonet, which ensured that there was little or no danger of losing the bayonet by having it permanently attached to the muzzle of the pistol or musket. Certainly such an idea was in use as early as 1680, the date of a gun by Duringer which had a long knife-bayonet hinged to the barrel. There are references to these weapons during the early part of the 18th century, but it was not until 1781 that one John Waters actually patented the idea. During the last quarter of the 18th and the first quarter of the 19th century these spring bayonets were common attachments to both pistols and blunderbusses. Basically they consisted of a hollow-ground triangular section bayonet of varying lengths secured at the muzzle of the weapon and fitted with a spring which was under compression when the bayonet was folded backwards along the barrel. The point of the bayonet was secured by a spring clip which took the form of a sliding bar or, on some pistols, a sliding trigger guard which then served both functions. When the catch was released the tension of the spring caused the bayonet to fly forward and snap down and lock on to a pierced lug fitted at the muzzle. The bayonet was now firmly locked into position and would remain so until a small release catch at the side was pressed; the bayonet could then be folded back along the length of the barrel. Whether any of these fearsome flick-knife devices ever proved of practical value is not clear; certainly very few, if any, references to their use have been traced. They were fitted in a variety of positions on the barrel, sometimes above, sometimes below and sometimes to one side. They are frequently to be found on blunderbusses and will also be seen on both flintlock and percussion pocket pistols of varying sizes. Indeed there are even examples of the device fitted to transition-type revolvers. One cannot help but feel that if the enemy retained his health and vigour after five shots with the revolver, the bayonet was indeed the last hope!

THE tradition of combining edged weapons and pistols never really died out, and one type which gained a certain popularity around the middle of the 19th century was the knife-pistol. A great variety of these were produced, but basically they comprised a fairly sturdy penknife fitted with two to four blades, and sometimes a corkscrew as well. The grip curved down slightly, and situated on top of the grip was a short but substantial barrel with a simple but effective hammer at the rear. Normally the trigger was hinged and only came down when the weapon was cocked. Early examples were made using percussion caps, but it was with the advent of the rim fire cartridge that they gained their greatest popularity. Most of the specimens likely to be seen by collectors are those marked with the name of two Sheffield firms: Rodgers, and Unwin and Rodgers. These knife-pistols frequently have a horn grip and most have only two blades. Although the article is marked "Sheffield" the firearm section normally carries Birmingham proof marks. The great majority of these weapons are single-barrelled, but a few rather clumsy double-barrelled examples do exist. There is little likelihood of their being mistaken for an ordinary penknife for they are fairly bulky and clumsy; but

Fig. 98: Detail of the barrel of the carbine shown in Fig. 97; the lines of brazing by which the four barrels were joined can be clearly seen. (*Tower of London.*)

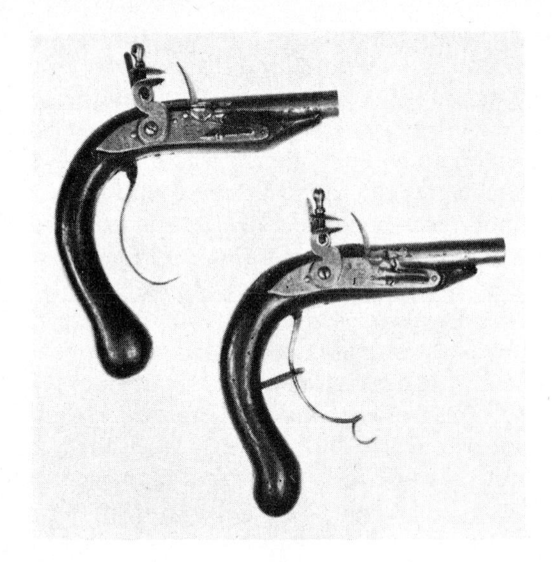

Fig. 99: Two most unusual pistols; the mechanisms are conventional flintlocks, but the strangely extended butts and triggers defy obvious explanation. They both carry the Royal Cypher; the upper piece is additionally marked TOWER 1736, *and the lower* SMITH 1747. (*Tower of London.*)

there are some, like that patented in 1916 by L. L. Rodgers, which look like an ordinary small pocket knife but which fire a .22 cartridge. Other examples had no external trigger but were fired by pressing one of the screw heads on the grip of the knife. A few of these knife-pistols were of all metal construction, but again these are quite unusual.

One particular type patented in 1865 by A. J. Peavey served a double purpose; it was claimed that not only could it be used as a hand gun but could also serve as an alarm gun. A cord secured to the trigger passed through a hole in the butt end of the handle; if the penknife were secured to the floor or the side of a window, the cord could be tied to the knob or latch in such a way that anybody opening the door or window would operate the trigger and fire the weapon.

Alarm guns firing only a blank cartridge or a charge of powder are fairly common and were only intended to give a warning, but there were some very special devices which were fired by the rays of the sun concentrated by a lens. These were essentially "alarms" in the clock sense, and could be adjusted on a sun dial to be fired at any given hour.

Perhaps one of the most unusual and effective forms of alarm gun was the so called door-lock alarm, in which the key would operate the lock only if turned in a certain sequence. If this sequence was not correctly followed a flintlock mounted inside the lock was discharged, and the explosion naturally raised the alarm. Many alarm "guns" were basic in the extreme, comprising little more than a spring arm and a nipple at the end of a barrel; they were designed to be tripped in a number of ways. One of the most substantial (and fairly common) varieties comprised a solid wedge-shaped body which could be secured to the floor by sharp projections on the base. The short barrel was loaded with powder, a cap placed on the nipple and the hammer was cocked. The rear of the body was ramp-shaped and the trigger was simply a small projection in the centre of the ramp. This door-stop pistol was placed near the door; if it were opened, the edge of the door rode up the ramp, pressed the trigger and so fired the pistol. It had a second purpose; as it was wedge-shaped it would jam the door and prevent it opening further.

Most of the alarm pistols did no more than make a noise and give warning of an unauthorised presence, but "spring guns" were actually designed to shoot the intruder. They could be set up at any point on an estate, in a churchyard or in a garden, indeed anywhere that required defence. Typical examples are fairly crude; the large wooden box-like structure has a flintlock mechanism mounted to one side and a short, bell-shaped barrel. They were usually fixed to a swivel and were free to rotate. The trigger was operated by means of lines, a number of which were spread out to cover a large area, all being attached to the trigger. An unwary intruder stepping on one of these lines not only fired the gun but also caused it to swing in his general direction before blasting off a charge of shot. They were not officially forbidden by law in England until the 1820's. Spring guns were not a new idea and examples fitted with wheellocks are known. The French produced a much later version which comprised a pistol with an adjustable vice mounted on the butt. These were usually known as "chicken thief guns" and could be secured, by means of the clamp, to any convenient spot. The trigger, again, was operated by some form of trip line.

SPRING guns were intended to guard and protect property and land; but the firearms inventor frequently turned his mind to the problem of more personal protection. One of the more ingenious ideas was the purse pistol. At first glance it was an ordinary, straightforward metal and leather purse—indeed one half of it was exactly that, with pockets for small change. However, the other half concealed a small revolver with a short barrel which fired a 5 mm. pin-fire cartridge. The idea presumably was that when stopped by a thief one withdrew the purse from the pocket and in the process of handing it over slipped down the concealed trigger and fired, to the surprise and discomfort of the would-be robber. This faintly bizarre invention was granted a British and American patent in 1877. Purses were not the only objects which concealed a pistol: other examples, admittedly rare but fully authenticated, are flashlights; a

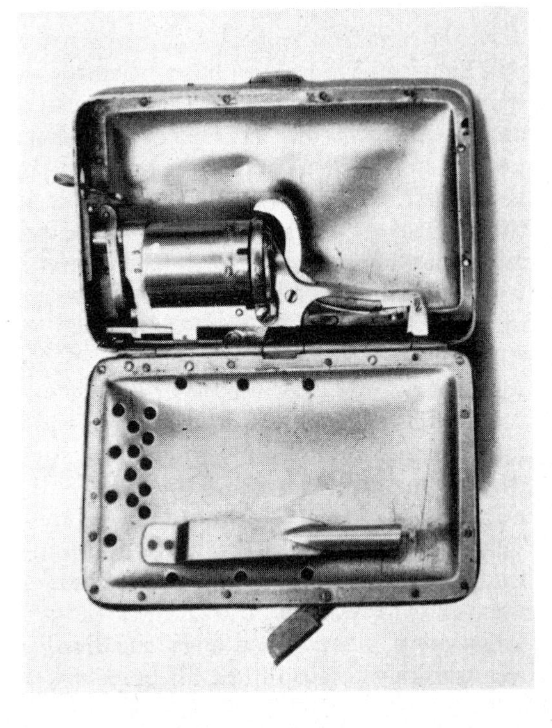

Fig. 100: A Frankenau purse pistol opened at the pistol side; the other side was a perfectly normal purse. This weapon fired a small 5 mm. pin-fire cartridge. (Vokes Collection.)

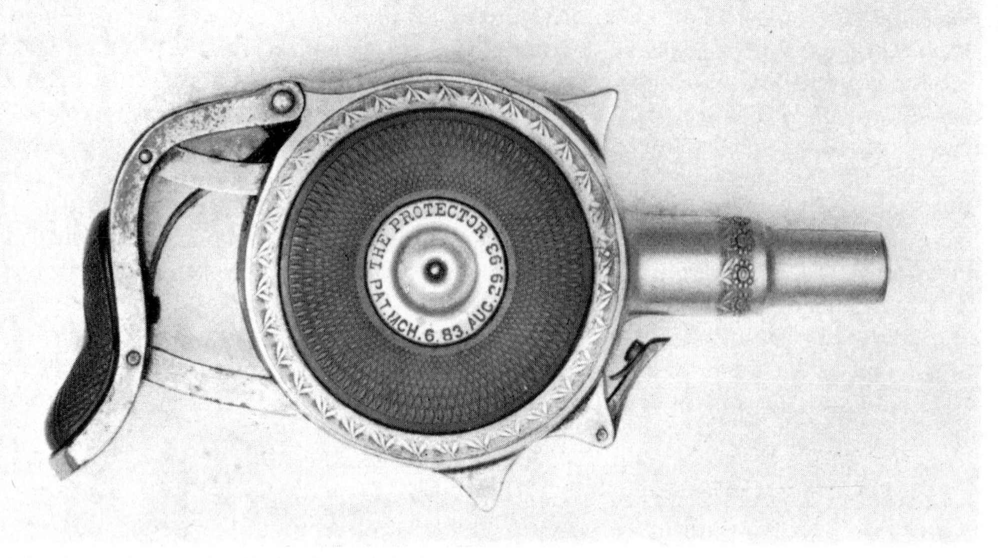

Fig. 101: A good example of the famous Protector *"squeezer", a revolver fired by squeezing between the palm and the fingers. This model fired a small ·32 cartridge. "Squeezers" were popular personal defence weapons in the 1880's.* (*Vokes Collection.*)

Japanese fan which concealed a percussion pistol; and, perhaps the most paradoxical of all, an apparent Japanese dagger which housed a Japanese percussion pistol.

As already suggested in *Chapter* 7, another problem to which the inventor turned his attention was that of finding a weapon which would fire several shots with one loading. One of the most hazardous and complex devices was the "superimposed load". The theory behind the idea was that the barrel could be loaded with several charges of balls, one in front of the other. If they were adequately separated the one nearest the muzzle could be fired, then the next, and so on until the "magazine" had been emptied. This was indeed possible in theory but in practice it was not so easy, these weapons having an unfortunate tendency to blow up as one charge was fired and ignited the others. However, a great deal of effort went into producing a worthwhile superimposed load weapon. Some of the earliest varieties were matchlocks with the charges one above the other in the barrel, each with its own separate touchhole. An extension of this principle was the "Roman Candle" gun in which a series of shots were set off one after the other once the action had been started. Wheellock weapons using this principle are well known, and the method of construction usually involves four barrels united into a single block; one of the side barrels was loaded in the normal way while one of the others was filled with powder only. The others were loaded with a number of charges, one on top of the other, and the weapon was then primed and fired. The priming set off the barrel containing one charge; as the powder flashed the flame was diverted to the powder-filled barrel, and as this burned down it ignited, via a number of tiny holes, the charges (anything from 15 to 30) in the other two barrels. This type of weapon had a serious disadvantage in that once the action had started it was unlikely to stop until all barrels were empty, the firer having no control at all.

What the gunmaker wanted was a similar arrangement but one which could be controlled; and the ingenuity expended on achieving this effect was absolutely incredible. Many of the designs were centred on a movable lock which could be slid along to fire successive charges, and this system was used with all forms of ignition, matchlock, wheellock and flintlock.

The advent of the cartridge simplified many problems for the designer of firearms; no longer was he bothered by external locks and complicated mechanisms. The metal cartridge required only a small pin driven by a spring to detonate it. This meant that it was now very easy and cheap to produce small pistols in a variety of designs. Certainly miniature weapons had been made from quite an early period, but surviving examples are rare and many of those to be seen in displays and exhibitions are of no great age. In the 1880's and 1890's there was a strong demand—which was naturally met by the gunmakers—for small personal weapons, and among these were the so-called "squeezers". One of the best known of these was the "Protector", patented in 1883 by a Frenchman named Jacques Turbiaux. This pistol consisted of a round body with the barrel projecting from one side; when the centre section was unscrewed the cylinder could be loaded with small cartridges. The weapon was held with the rear bar pressing against the palm of the hand, two fingers encircling the barrel. If the hand was now squeezed in, pushing the rear projection against the palm, the weapon was fired and the cylinder revolved bringing the next cartridge into position. A variety of designs were used, some with extra safety catches, some without; but most fired a .32 cartridge and held seven shots. Of similar design but more conventional shape was the Rouchouse pistol,

Fig. 102: A Rouchouse *pistol, another model of "squeezer" which was sometimes incorporated in a wallet or cigar case. (Vokes Collection.)*

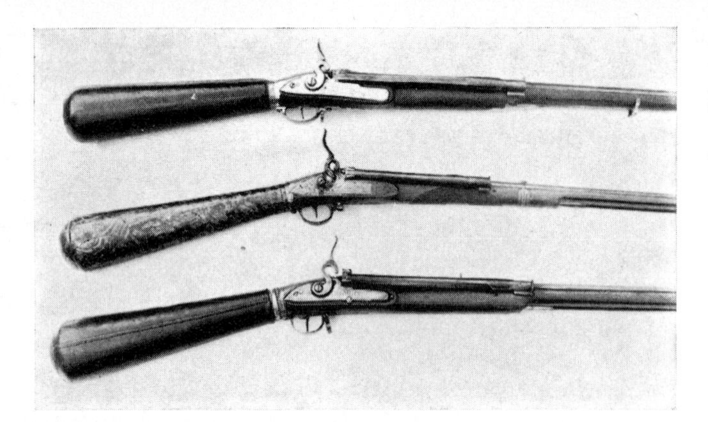

Fig. 103: (Top) *An Austrian military magazine airgun with the reservoir fitted in the butt; a similar but better quality weapon, made in Vienna; and a third, made by Ridiger. All three date from 1780/90. (Vokes Collection.)*

which was also held in the palm of the hand with the barrel pointing out between the first two fingers. Similar to this was one known as the Gaulois which was often fitted inside a leather cigar case. This small type of weapon was the cartridge equivalent of the old pocket pistol and was intended solely as a self defence weapon.

Apart from pointing in the general direction of the target the user had no facility (and little need) to aim such a weapon; but larger pistols and long arms obviously required aiming. This was not always easy; certainly with box locks it was impossible, and even with side locks and percussion it was sometimes difficult. One of the methods adopted to overcome this cluttering of the barrel was the underhammer principle; in this type of weapon the hammer or the cock was placed beneath the barrel so that the top was left clear for the fixing of sights of any description. Even more important from the gunmaker's point of view was the extreme mechanical simplicity of such locks, for the moving parts were reduced to an absolute minimum. They also offered an additional safety factor in that priming flashes and exploding caps were beneath the gun and well away from the face of the firer. In the case of pistols they also offered a clean and simplified line, in much the same way as the box lock flintlock had offered an improved line over the old side lock. For these reasons they were particularly popular in America; the majority of them date from the 1830's and 1840's. A number of patents covering this particular form of weapon were taken out both in England and in the United States. Underhammer systems were frequently used for target weapons but did not gain general acceptance among the military and civilian users of firearms.

ANOTHER type of weapon which never gained general acceptance was the airgun. The principle of the airgun was certainly known at the time of Leonardo da Vinci, for his writings mention how to make one, although unfortunately he only describes in detail the methods of barrel construction and gives no indication as to how the propulsive forces were to be supplied. There are increasingly common references to them during the 16th and 17th centuries; and Marin le Bourgeoys produced one which was capable, so it was said, of firing a ball or dart for 400 yards. It is also reported that the English Royalists planned to assassinate Cromwell with an airgun! The earliest form of airgun worked by the principle of a piston forcing the projectile out. Pistons operated against a spring which was compressed by a crank fitted into the side or by some form of lever attached to the stock. A second type used bellows which were fitted in the butt and which were compressed suddenly by a strong spring, and the powerful

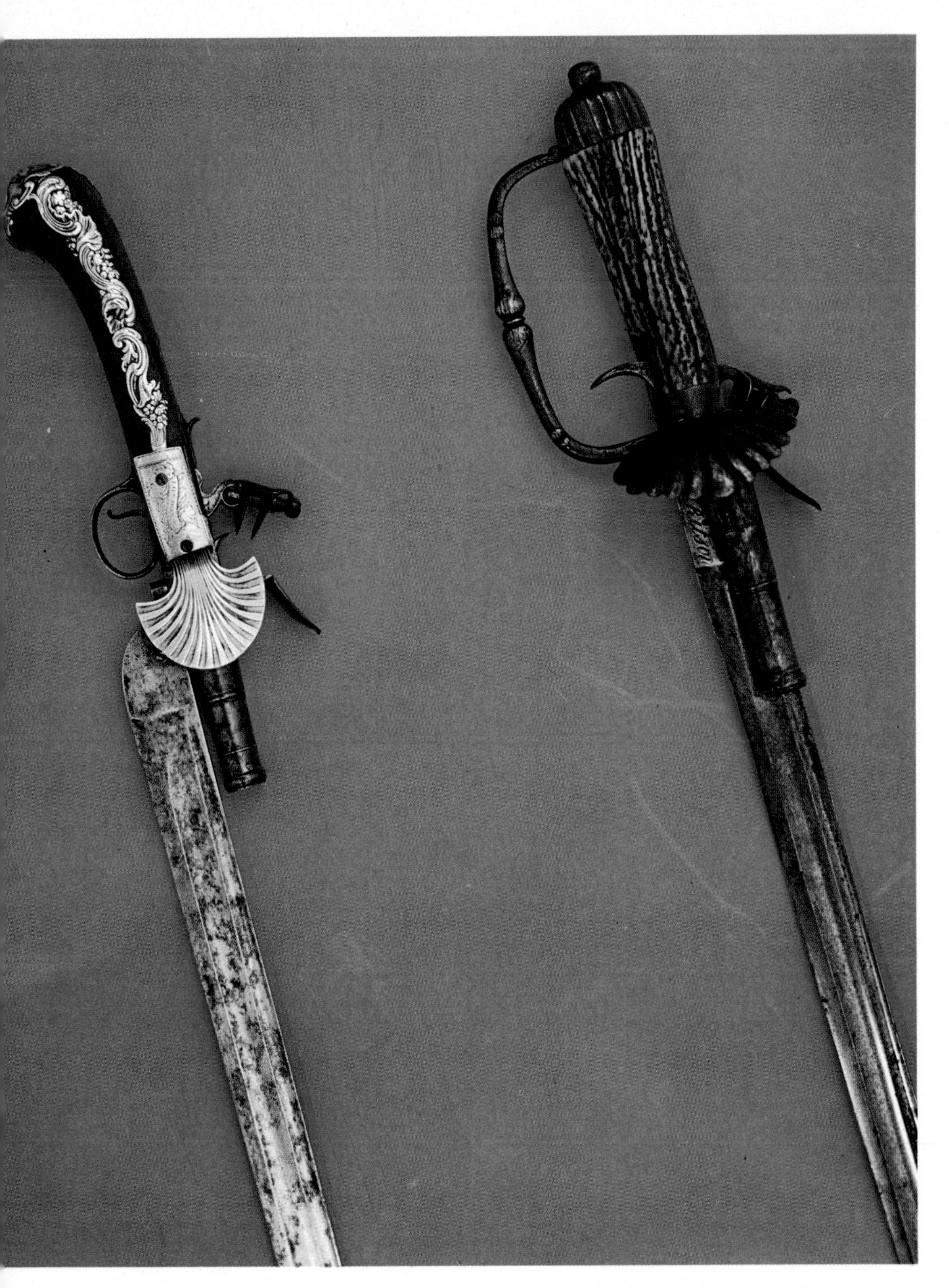

Plate 16 *Silver-mounted pistol-sword by George Jones of London. Late 18th century. Overall length of pistol, $9\frac{1}{2}$ inches; barrel, $3\frac{1}{2}$ inches; bore, ·48 inch. (Durrant Collection).* (Right) *A mid-18th century sword-pistol with a horn grip, the blade bearing the name* Ritson. *Overall length, 30 inches; pistol barrel, 4 inches. (Miller Collection.)*

Plate 17 *Combined double barrelled flintlock pistol and sword, an unusual combination. The butt/hilt is inlaid with silver wire and has a silver butt cap; the lock is engraved Edmund Pendley. The blade is 29½ inches long and slightly curved; barrels 5 inches long, bore ·54 inch* (*Peter Finer.*)

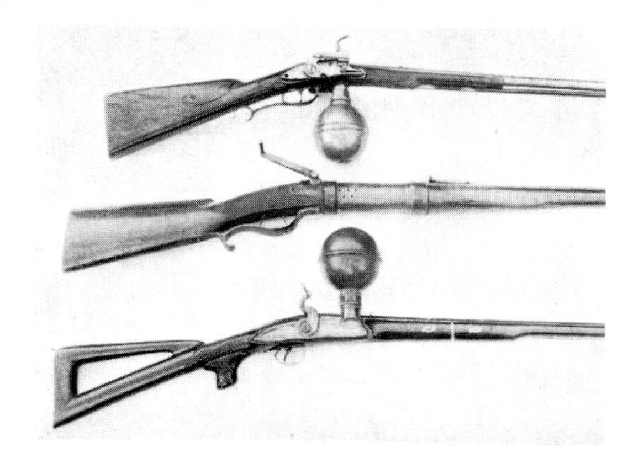

Fig. 104: (Top) *A German air rifle of about 1800, with brass ball reservoir.* (Centre) *A German spring gun of about 1850, with loading crank in position.* (Bottom) *A London-made airgun with ball reservoir, the silver mountings hall-marked for 1778.* (*Vokes Collection.*)

jet of air expelled the bullet. A third type utilised a reservoir of compressed air which had to be pumped up prior to firing. The reservoir most commonly seen is a copper ball fitted beneath the stock, but there were earlier examples which fitted around the barrel or into the butt. The compressed air was obtained by pumping, and these reservoirs could supply the power for a large number of shots. In the normal manner of firing the trigger operated a small valve which released a sharp "puff" of compressed air. During the 17th century the barrel reservoir was the most popular form; the ball reservoir seems to be of Austrian origin, appearing during the middle of the 18th century. Some airguns were produced with rifled barrels and were extremely accurate; and a special corps of Tyrolese sharpshooters, mustering over 1,300 men, was formed in 1790 and fought gallantly in many actions over the next few years. Although the weapon was shown to be very accurate it was especially hated by the French—in fact any Austrian air gunner unfortunate enough to be captured was hanged out of hand, for the French refused to consider them as true soldiers. The weapon itself proved to be difficult to maintain and was withdrawn from service in 1815. Naturally airguns were far quieter than conventional firearms and for this reason were popular among hunters—even more so among poachers—and a variety of poaching guns using air power were produced. Of course, it is recorded that Sherlock Holmes feared the airgun more than anything else!

The airgun was at least a practical proposition and proved itself in many circumstances. The same cannot be said for some of the other curiosities produced by the firearms designers; for instance it is difficult to visualise the purpose of a knife and fork fitted with a small flintlock pistol in the handle! Admittedly they might be useful for the assassin or as a means of self protection, but as the mechanism is not concealed in any way it is difficult to imagine any practical use for them. Similarly one might argue that a whip-pistol combination has some obscure value, and examples of these are known. However, the prize for the most ambitious of firearms curiosa must surely go to the breastplate which was found in Bordeaux in 1917. It weighed 30 lbs. and was fitted on the front with 19 cartridge revolvers, which normally hung barrel down for loading but were then raised to the horizontal position ready for firing. They were fired in groups of 4 or 5 by pressing certain studs and levers. As if this were not enough, the cache also included a pair of stirrups each of which contained two pistols which could be fired by pulling on the straps. One cannot help but speculate upon the fate of the unfortunate horse should his owner at any time forget that his feet were loaded!

9

Pocket Pistols and Decoration

FOR the gunmaker there were three main fields of demand. There was the military man who demanded a substantial, rugged pistol which would serve him well in battle and yet be reasonably accurate. He needed a pair of fairly long-barrelled pistols as well as some method of carrying them. This type was known as holster or horse pistols and they were carried in a pair of holsters which hung just in front of the saddle. The second area of demand was for a traveller's pistol which was not quite as long as a holster pistol but was still moderately substantial, and might be carried when travelling by coach. It could be simply tucked in behind a belt, or might be fitted with a belt hook—a shaped bar attached to one side of the stock, which could slip over the sash or belt. Lastly there was need for a "personal" pistol—a smaller version of the coaching pistol which could be slipped into a pocket or pouch and was intended only to be used as a last resort or a personal defence weapon by the pedestrian or the casual town

Fig. 105: "Queen Anne" pistol by Govers of Dublin, of intermediate size but of the pattern later used for many pocket pistols. Note the silver escutcheon plate and butt cap. Overall length, 12 inches; barrel, $5\frac{1}{4}$ inches; bore, ·6 inch. (Gyngell Collection.)

traveller. In this class of weapon the customer wanted a pistol which was reasonably powerful and safe but, above all, was small enough to be carried with ease.

Pocket pistols were produced from the 16th century right through to the 20th century, and utilised every form of ignition: snaphaunce, flintlock, percussion and cartridge. They are a popular collectors' item, for they are still fairly common, since the contemporary demand for them was heavy and their size made them cheap to produce in a great variety of types. Pocket pistols were fitted with single barrels, doubles and, more rarely, three barrels; the majority of them were made with a "turn off" barrel, this arrangement offering a number of advantages. Firstly, the loading was easy; in order to load, the barrel was unscrewed by means of a key which could take the form of a spanner-shaped bar which slipped over the barrel and engaged with a raised lug beneath the breech. Another key consisted of a tapered bar which slipped into the muzzle to engage with a number of indentations and was then rotated to unscrew the barrel. When the barrel had been removed the breech was revealed; this was normally fairly small so that only a minimum charge of powder was required.

Fig. 106: Pair of double-barrelled side-by-side flintlock pistols by Griffin and Tow of London, circa *1775. Each barrel has a separate lock operated by an individual trigger. Barrels, 4½ inches; bore, ·46 inch. (Tower of London.)*

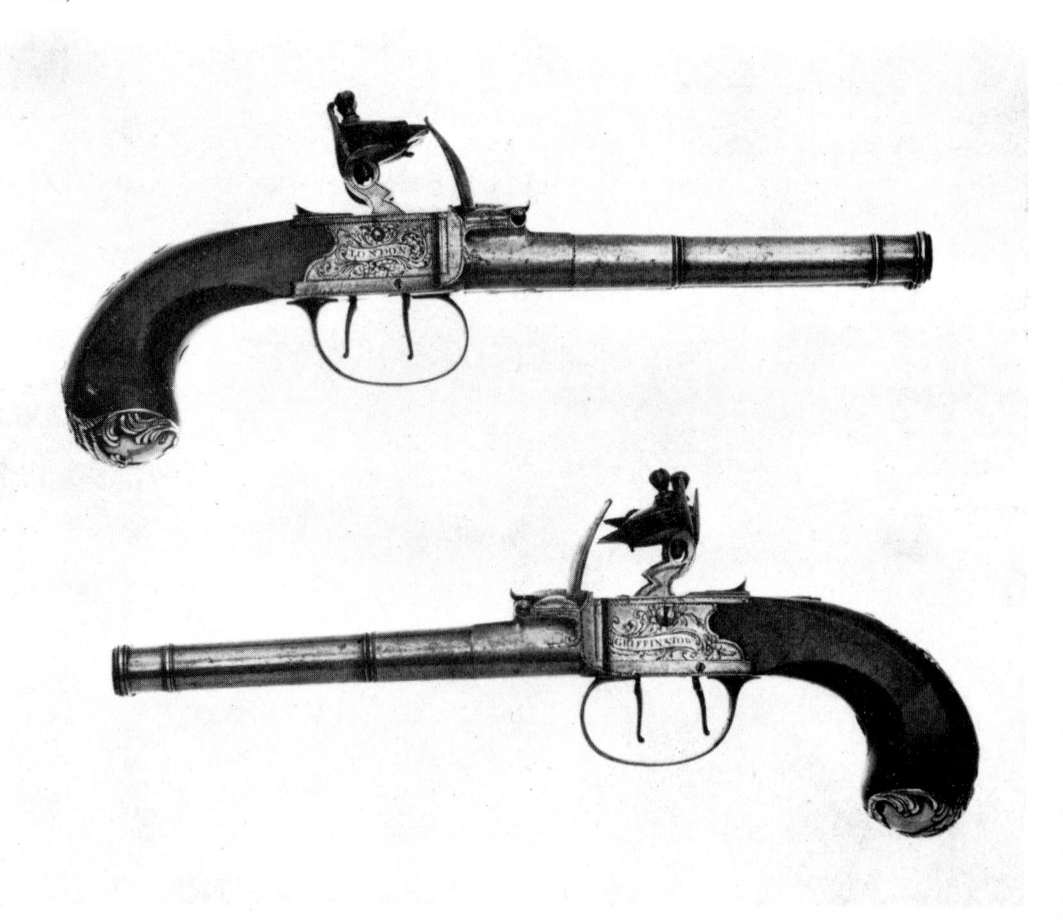

Fig. 107: Flintlock pocket pistol made by T. Ketland in the last quarter of the 18th century. On this weapon, the barrel unscrews for loading; and the trigger guard doubles as a safety catch, locking the mechanism when it is slid forward. Overall length, 8 inches; barrel, 3½ inches; bore, ·43 inch.

The breech was set at the centre of a saucer-like depression, and once the charge of powder had been placed in position the bullet was seated in the recess and the barrel screwed back on and tightened with the barrel key. This method of loading obviated any ramrod and therefore simplified the construction of the pistol while at the same time ensuring that there was a correct charge and a firm-fitting ball, both factors which help produce the best results from a small pistol.

Since these pocket pistols were intended primarily as a self defence weapon the necessity to aim was negligible, and therefore very few, if any, of these pistols will be found to have sights. Since it was highly likely that the circumstances in which such a pistol had to be used would hardly allow time to reload, many of them were fitted with double barrels, either side by side or "over and under". Tap action, over and under, boxlocks were very popular indeed and as a result these are still fairly common items on the antique market. If the single or double barrel were not enough to achieve the purpose then the gunmaker offered an extra in the form of a bayonet, and a high percentage of these pocket pistols were fitted with a spring-operated bayonet. These were frequently mounted on the underneath of the barrel and were locked back by engaging with a small recess cut in the front of the trigger guard which was designed to permit a slight backward and forward movement. In the forward position the notch in the trigger guard engaged with the tip of the bayonet holding it firmly in position. If the finger was now slipped in behind the trigger and the guard pulled backwards the bayonet was released to be propelled forward by the spring and given sufficient impetus to lock itself on to the lug at the end of the barrel. In other types the bayonet was mounted above the barrel and was held back by a small sliding bar which was seated above the breech and again engaged with the tip of the bayonet to hold it down. Withdrawing this bar released the bayonet and allowed it to fly forward. This second arrangement was probably most common on the percussion pistols, although it will be found on many of the flintlock pistols as well. Round or octagonal barrels were fitted to such pistols, although the octagonal type seems to have been more common on the percussion pistols.

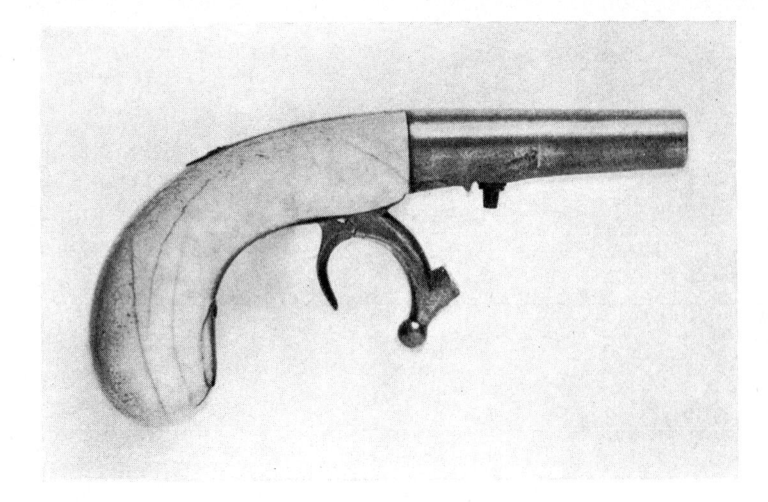

Fig. 108: Ivory-butted under-hammer percussion pocket pistol, one of a pair. The mechanism in these weapons was very simple, but despite this advantage they never became very popular. (*See also* Signature 4, *Fig. 52* and Signature 8, *Plate 17.*)

The flintlock and the percussion pistol could both be carried in reasonable safety if they were fitted with a half-cock position, and it will be remembered that in this position the trigger could not activate the mechanism. However this safety device was not considered sufficient for pocket pistols—after all, they were being carried in a coat or jacket pocket which could easily snag or be accidently knocked, and the danger of an accidental shot was always present. This danger was clearly recognised and to overcome it safety catches were a common feature on pocket pistols. One of the commonest forms which appeared around the middle of the 18th century was the sliding bar type, and this is commonly found on boxlock pistols. A bar terminating at the butt end with a slight upward curve sat along the top of the lock mechanism and was cut with a rectangular hole allowing it to encircle the cock; at the lock end a small pin projected forward. In the "fire" position the catch was pulled back and the steel and cock were free to move. When the pistol was taken to the half cock position the bar was pushed forward and brought into action two safety devices. First, the forward projecting pin engaged a small hole drilled in the base of the steel and so locked this firmly down; even if the face of the steel were struck by the flint it could not open and so could not spark or expose the priming. At the same time the slot through which the cock passed was so designed that in the forward position the rear end of the recess engaged with the back of the cock and locked this firmly into position.

Another type of safety mechanism usually found on the earlier 18th century pistols consists of a sliding trigger guard which could be moved forward to lock the cock firmly in the half cock position. Less common were other forms of safety device such as the dog lock, and the small sliding bolt situated just to the rear of the cock which could be pushed forward to engage with a small recess cut on its inside face. A number of much rarer self-operating safety devices are known, but these are discussed in appropriate books and are sufficiently rare to exclude them from such a brief outline.

Yet another form of safety device was the so-called concealed trigger. Obviously there was a great danger that when the pistol was being drawn from the pocket it might snag on clothing or be accidentally discharged in some other way. Around 1790 a new idea was introduced, whereby the trigger was concealed in a small recess beneath the breech. In the half cock position the trigger was hidden but if the cock was pulled back to the full cock position the internal mechanism pressed down the trigger, which clicked into the firing position. Thus in the half cock carrying position, with the trigger

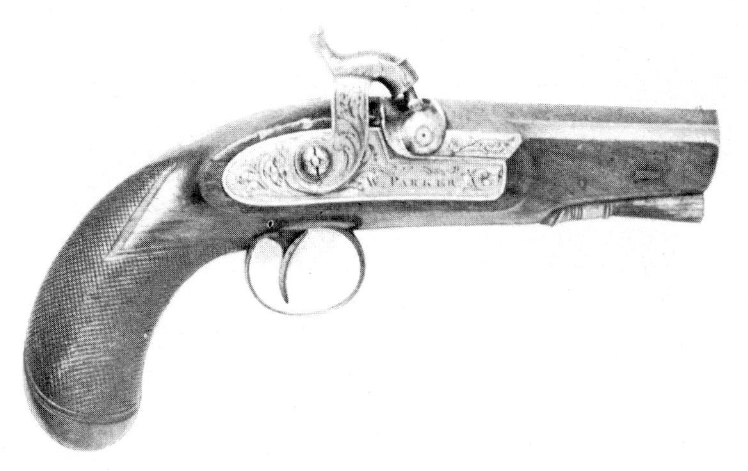

Fig. 109: Percussion pistol by W. Parker of London, circa *1830. This type of weapon is frequently described as an "overcoat pistol". Overall length, 8 inches; barrel, 4 inches; bore, ·5 inch.*

safely recessed into the breech, there was little danger of an accidental discharge from mishandling the weapon, and should the need arise for the weapon to be cocked then the trigger was automatically brought down into position. These concealed trigger mechanisms are usually somewhat delicate and care should always be exercised when handling them.

Although a general definition of pocket pistols has been given above there were considerable variations within this broad field. As well as single, double and triple-barrelled pistols there were some very small examples which are often described as muff pistols, although it is not at all clear on what basis this term was chosen. Certainly there is little or no evidence to suggest that they were intended primarily for ladies or indeed were ever carried in the muff, for both men and women of the period used muffs. Probably many were sold purely as a novelty, but nevertheless they form a most attractive group in their own right.

The decoration of pocket pistols is normally rather limited, although some are of very high quality with silver wire inlay. The wooden butts were of two main types and many of those made during the third quarter of the 18th century have rounded butts very similar to the larger holster pistols of the period, although they were only fitted with a butt cap and perhaps an escutcheon plate. It may not be out of place here to say something of the escutcheon plate, which is a feature to be found both on pocket pistols and on larger holster pistols. It was a small plaque of material—silver, steel, even mother of pearl—usually set at the top of the centre curve of the butt, on which were engraved the owner's initials or arms. Unfortunately their value is limited, for it is recorded by Henry Mayhew, writing in the 1850's, that many of the street traders increased the apparent value of their goods by having fictitious or quite unauthorised coats of arms engraved on these escutcheon plates. However a number of perfectly genuine arms will be found on them and Fairburn's *Book of Crests* will some times offer a useful guide in identifying these.

Pistols of the fourth quarter of the 18th century tend to be slab sided—that is, the butt is cut from a plank of wood and is rectangular in cross section. This style continued through the early part of the percussion period although some weapons were fitted with rounded "hockey stick"-shaped butts. Many are plain, but a number will be found with a cross-hatching of thin lines cut diagonally one across the other to offer a firmer grip.

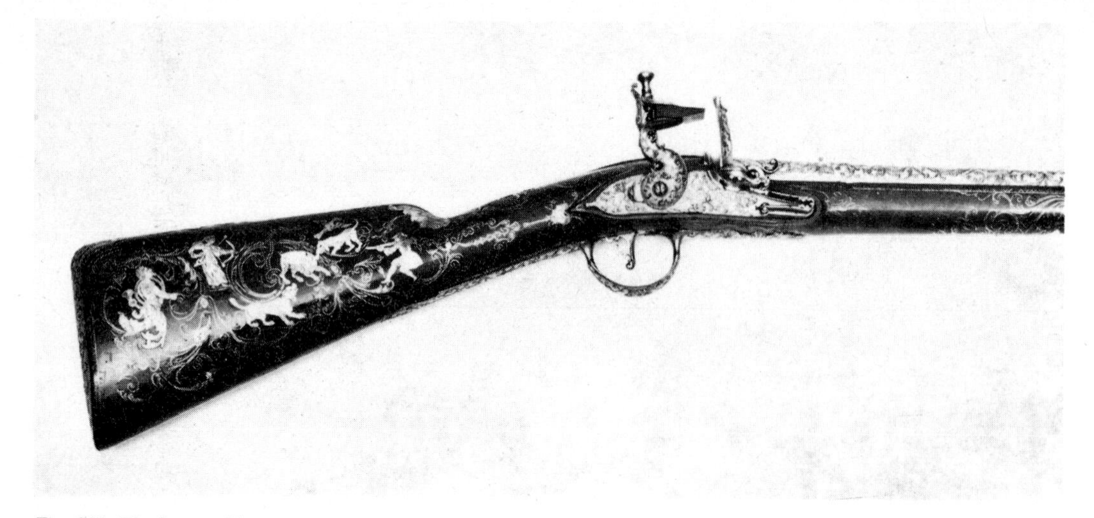

Fig. 110: The butt and lock of a Russian flintlock gun made at the Tula Arsenal in 1752. Barrel, lock and trigger guard are chiselled and the stock is inlaid with silver. (Tower of London.)

The majority of pocket pistols are equipped with a boxlock in which the mainspring, cock, trigger and frizzen are set centrally on the breech instead of being mounted on one side as was the normal practice with most flintlocks. This arrangement made for a clearer line and a simpler construction, and somewhat increased the safety factor. The same practice was adopted by percussion pistol makers when the new system was well established. As remarked above many of these pocket pistols are fitted with two barrels and in the case of flintlock the most common arrangement was the "over and under" system; barrel selection was made by means of a tap set to one side of the breech. The method of operation of this system has been discussed in *Chapter* 7. A few triple-barrelled pistols were produced using the same system of tap selection, but with four-barrelled pistols this would have proved too complicated an arrangement. With four barrels the simplest method was to arrange them as two pairs of "side by side"; when the top two had been fired, the whole assembly was rotated by releasing the barrel block, so that the fresh pair moved up into position ready for firing. In the case of percussion pistols the tap action was seldom if ever used; the simpler means of ignition favoured the use of two locks with separate hammers and nipples. Examples of four-barrelled flintlock pistols are quite uncommon for they were obviously complicated in construction; but the simpler percussion system resulted in wider production of multi-barrel weapons.

As already stated, pocket pistols date back to the 16th century and a number of wheellock pocket pistols have survived. Matchlock pistols were seldom made and European pocket matchlock pistols are unknown, although examples of Japanese matchlock pistols do occur (see *Chapter* 10). Although of pocket pistol size they are in fact miniature weapons intended either as models or for boys' festivals, and do not, strictly speaking, come within the category of serious weapons. The small pocket pistol introduced a new and serious threat to the safety of the public figure. Since they were so easily concealed about the person, the threat of assassination by shooting suddenly became a very real risk. The danger was recognised early in the 16th century, and there were injunctions as early as 1517 forbidding the carrying of wheellock pistols in the

Plate 18 (Top to bottom) *Silver-mounted flintlock pocket pistol by Ketland, late 18th century. Double-barrelled over-and-under percussion pocket pistol*, circa *1840. Concealed trigger flintlock pocket pistol*, circa *1800. Percussion pocket pistol of* circa *1830; overall length, 8 inches; barrel, 4 inches; bore, ·5 inch.* (*Gyngell Collection.*)

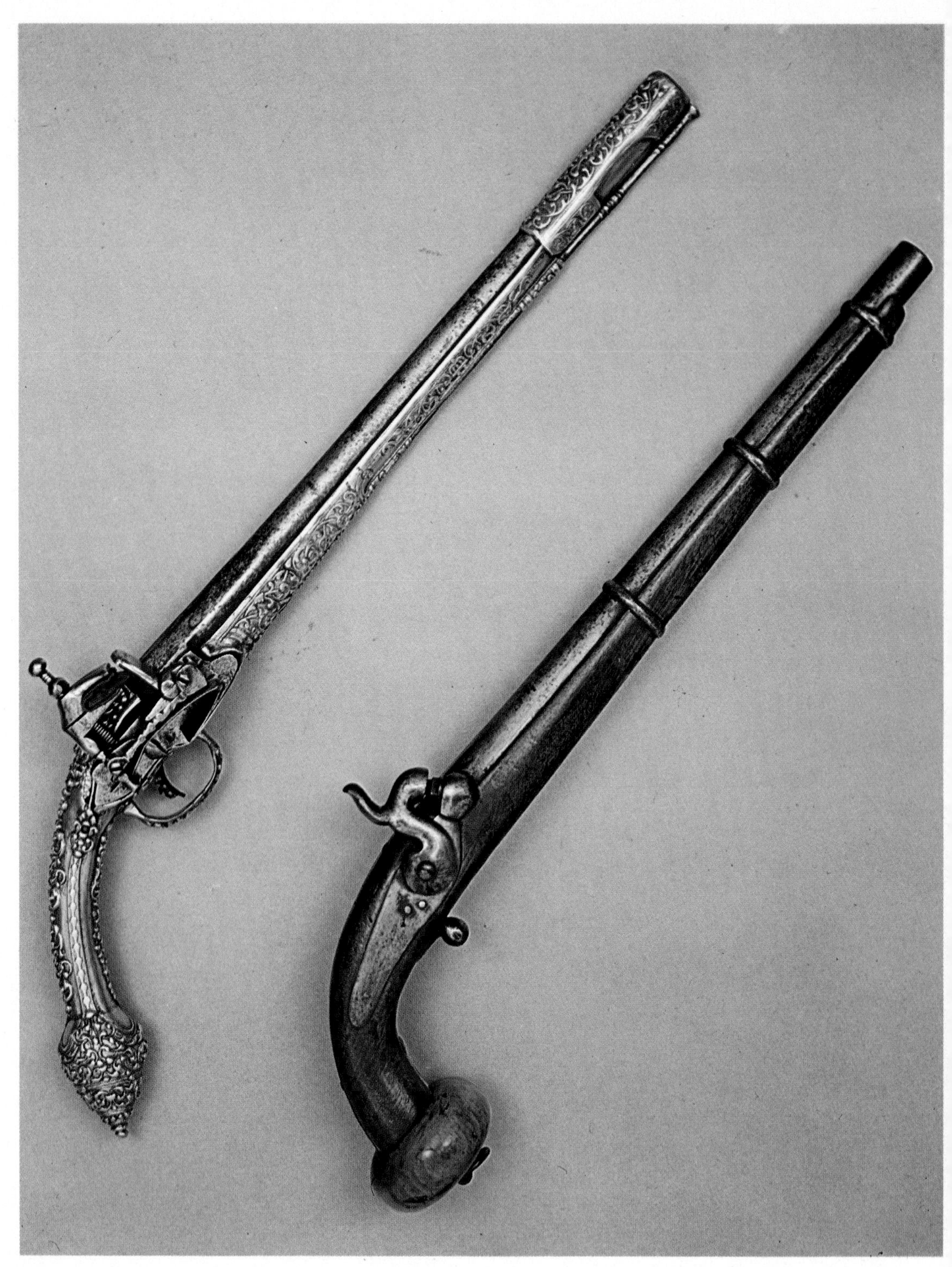

Plate 19 (Top) *A Balkan pistol, the stock covered with embossed silver plate.* (Bottom) *One of a pair of rifled Russian percussian pistols, brought back to England after the Crimean War. The ball pommel was a very common feature of Russian pistols.* (*Winsbury Collection.*)

Hapsburg lands. In 1594 Queen Elizabeth I forbade the carrying of these small wheellock pistols, known as "pocket dags". In 1612 or 1613 an injunction was placed on the manufacture or importation of pocket dags, and the order also demanded the surrender of these pistols. The pistols themselves were simply small scale wheellock pistols and had no special feature apart from their size. The same applies during the 17th century when the pocket flintlock pistol was, in essence, a miniature of the ordinary holster pistol. During the early part of the 18th century the so-called "Queen Anne" pistols were produced in a variety of sizes including some small ones. They were made complete with silver butt caps and with silver wire inlay on the butt and stock. By the middle of the century the pocket pistol had emerged as a distinct and separate type of weapon.

FLINTLOCK pocket pistols were usually of reasonable quality, but the percussion system initiated a flood of cheap-jack weapons. A large number of these were made in Birmingham, and many others in Belgium; the majority were single-barrelled boxlock percussion pieces of a low quality and offer little attraction to the average collector. A few were made with two barrels, while others were fitted with a spring bayonet.

The Deringer, however, was one notable exception to the generally poor standard of pocket percussion pistol; this type is particularly interesting because its name came to be used as a generic term for a whole series of weapons. It was in essence, a pocket percussion pistol but it differed in many respects from the normal pattern. The stock of walnut was short with a very characteristic "bird beak" shape, and the pistol featured a back action lock. The short, rifled barrel ranged in length from less than one inch to four inches, and the calibre was almost as varied—anything from .3 to .5 inch. The

Fig. 111: Typical silver wire inlay work on the butt of a Queen Anne pistol. Channels were cut in the wood and flattened wire was then gently hammered into the depression until a flush surface was achieved. (Gyngell Collection.)

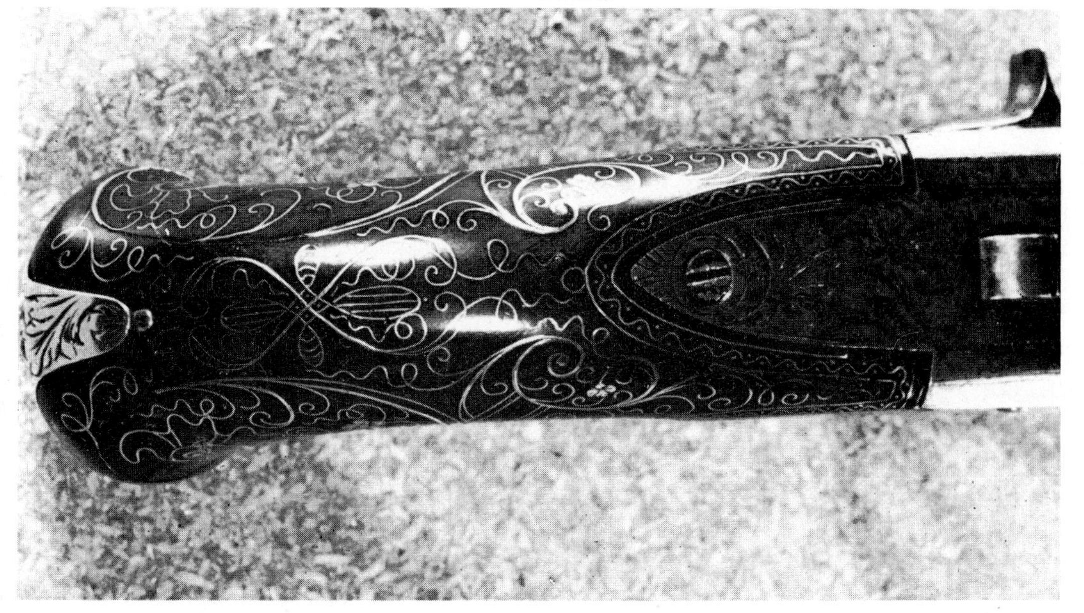

Fig. 112: The browned barrel of a mid-18th century French holster pistol. A trophy of arms and a sunburst of gold inlay decorate the barrel and the inlaid word TORDU *indicates that the barrel was made by a special method using twisted metal. (Gyngell Collection.)*

fittings (trigger guard, side plates, escutcheon, butt plate, etc.) are normally of German silver. Originally the Deringer pistols were sold cased in pairs with accessories, but apparently less than a thousand pairs came from the Philadelphia workshop of Henry Deringer during his lifetime (1786-1868). The type first appeared during the 1830's and quickly gained popularity, since its short barrel and heavy calibre made it a good "stopping" pistol. So well did it sell that soon other makers were openly copying it, and despite legal action Deringer was unable to prevent this pirating of his design. One scheme intended to circumvent the legal rights of the owner was to mark the pistols DERRINGER. The name "Derringer" is now used by many collectors to describe small pocket pistols irrespective of the method of ignition. When metal cartridges were introduced the Derringer retained its popularity, and the first cartridge model was patented in 1861 using a .41 rimfire cartridge. Soon Colts had taken up the invention, and the firm produced a number of them with single and double barrels pivoting sideways or tipping up and down for easy loading.

Derringers were rather a special case, for the introduction of the pepperbox and the revolver spelled the end for other pocket pistols; a single-shot weapon was of little value in comparison with a small revolver which could fire up to six shots. Thus from the 1840's onwards the output of pocket pistols began to decline, until by the late 1870's even the demand for Derringers had begun to diminish. It is of interest to note that facsimiles of the Deringer pistols are still made today.

Muff pistols were the smallest "operational" firearms made in quantity, but there are in existence a number of miniature weapons which are too small for serious use and are obviously models. A few appear to be of some age but the majority are of fairly recent manufacture dating from the late 19th and early 20th centuries.

While the pocket pistol itself is primarily an English development, numbers were produced on the Continent, especially in Belgium at the large arms manufacturing centre of Liège. Some of the Belgian manufacturers felt that an English name would help sell their wares, and they produced a whole series of all-metal pistols bearing spurious London marks. They also copied the name of a London gunmaker—Israel

Fig. 113: This over-and-under flintlock pistol, with separate locks, displays the gold-inlaid name of the renowned London maker Durs Egg together with a double line of gold at the breech. (Bennett Collection.)

Segallas—although they spelt it Segalas. Multibarrel examples bearing this name were also produced. Obviously an all-steel pistol has something to offer in the way of increased strength and durability, but the majority of these weapons are plain and serviceable with little aesthetic appeal.

THIS is not so with many other pistols, for early in the history of firearms gunners began to demand something other than just a plain weapon. Early handguns were, by any standards, crude and functional; but with the appearance of the matchlock some form of decoration was introduced—often it was no more than some simple lines inscribed on the serpentine to suggest a snake. Later, when the wheellock mechanism was introduced, it became possible to produce a smaller, more sophisticated weapon which naturally appealed to the monied classes. They were often men of learning and culture who wanted the weapon to be beautiful as well as practical. Naturally decoration tended to be more profuse on what one might describe as civilian or hunting weapons and, as a broad generalisation, military weapons tended to be much plainer and devoid of "frills". The same is true of duelling pistols, in which an emphasis was placed on the clean functional line. There are exceptions, and revolvers and long arms intended as presentation pieces will often be found decorated in many styles.

Early wheellocks, as a group, were most decorative, displaying all available techniques. The manufacture of weapons was a complicated process and in the case of an order for a decorated weapon outside experts were called in. The gunsmiths did little themselves in the way of decoration but did not hesitate to call upon artists and craftsmen outside the industry to embellish their products. Artists were employed to draw up designs and sketches, and some of the great masters of the 16th century did not consider it beneath their dignity to undertake such work. This practice of commissioning experts may well have produced attractive weapons, but it raises problems in identification; it was quite possible for an Italian to be called upon to decorate a French pistol or for a Spanish gunmaker to supply an Englishman with a barrel decorated to the Englishman's taste. Research into the question of decoration of firearms has shown that many of the designs and patterns found on certain styles of pistol can be traced with certainty to original paintings and etchings.

Both the barrel and the stock came in for their share of decoration, and the style varied over the centuries. Barrels of wheellock weapons were frequently left quite plain but some were chiselled—a technique used as far back as the 13th century on some sword hilts. Later the lockplates and cocks were also chiselled or carved with intricate patterns, as was the steel furniture of the weapon. The craftsmen of Northern Italy, and of Brescia in particular, acquired a reputation for the excellence of their work. It is of interest to note that in this same area the production of snaphaunce pistols continued long after it had ceased elsewhere. Many of these snaphaunce and flintlock weapons are covered with chiselling of superb quality showing patterns of intertwining leaves, branches, and bunches of fruit, or raised patterns on lockplates, barrels, frizzens, and, in the case of the snaphaunce, on the steel and its arm. Italy did not hold the monopoly of first class chiselled decoration, and some extremely fine quality work was also done in Germany and France.

Besides the chiselling on the barrel and the dogshead, there was frequently engraving on the lockplates. In the late 16th and early 17th century wheellocks were big and offered a fine flat surface on which to inscribe appropriate hunting or military

Fig. 114: The carved ebony butt (here reversed for clarity) of an extremely elaborate French shotgun; the central scroll bears the name of the maker, Le Page Moutier, and the date 1860. (Harolds Club, Reno.)

scenes. Engraving was carried out by incising a line into the steel with a sharp pointed tool known as the burrin. It was skilled and difficult work, and some of the engraved scenes on these early wheellocks are little masterpieces of technical artistry. With the advent of the flintlock the available flat surfaces were reduced, but even so many of the flintlocks have some simple engraving on the lockplate. Sometimes it is no more than a border or a simple pattern, but more often it is a small military motif. Frequently the only decoration to be found on such lockplates may be the maker's name and possibly an address which may also be repeated on the top of the barrel. In the case of mass produced weapons the apparent engraving was, in fact, done by dies, and the majority of Samuel Colt's early revolvers had engraved cylinders which were produced by this process. Engraving also played its part in the inlaying or damascening of metal. Some of the top quality makers had their name inlaid in gold along the top rib of the barrel. The name was deeply engraved, and then a strip of gold or silver wire was placed in the cut and gently hammered in to fill the channel; the top surface was then polished. Gold, silver, platinum and brass were all used in this fashion.

Another method of decorating flat surfaces popular in the 16th and 17th centuries was etching, although this process was never as widely used as engraving. Here the effect was produced by attacking the surface, not with a sharp point but with acid.

Fig. 115: Detail of the lock of the same weapon, showing the hammer chiselled as a dog. This piece was presented by the President of France to the President of Mexico sometime during the period 1880-84. (*Harolds Club, Reno.*)

The metal surface was covered with wax or paint and the pattern to be etched was then scratched into the coating leaving the bare metal open to the action of the acid. When the required depth of penetration had been achieved the acid was washed away and the action halted.

Although etching and engraving declined in popularity during the 18th century other forms of decoration became more fashionable. Barrels were often gilded and this process, combined with blueing, produced a most attractive and very colourful finish. The barrel to be blued was heated to a high temperature and then quenched, that is plunged into oil or water; and the result was a blue-coloured finish to the surface of the metal—the shade of blue depending upon the temperature to which the metal was heated prior to quenching. Gilding was essentially a technique of depositing a film of gold on the metal, and was achieved by one of two methods. An amalgam of mercury and gold was prepared and painted onto the surface of the metal. If the metal were now heated to the correct temperature the mercury was volatised but the gold was left behind in the form of a very thin deposit. The second method, more common in the Orient but occasionally used in Europe, was to mark out the desired pattern and then to roughen the area with a file or punch. A thin sheet of gold foil was then placed over the pattern and pressed and burnished until it adhered firmly to the roughened surface. Not only barrels but lockplates, cocks, and indeed any steel furniture of the pistol might be either blued or gilded or both. Another method of treating the barrels was to brown them, using a chemical treatment which left a very pleasing light brown coating which was not only attractive but also helped to resist rusting.

Decoration was applied not only to the metal surfaces but to the stock as well, and frequently the stock decoration remains in better condition than that on the barrel, for the blueing, gilding and browning may well become rubbed. Wheellock stocks were possibly the most decorated items of all, and one of the most commonly used techniques was that of inlay. A great variety of materials were used including mother-of-pearl, staghorn, tortoiseshell, copper, brass, ivory, coloured bone and sections of wood of different texture from that of the stock. This style of decoration remained popular and was used occasionally on later flintlock weapons. The plaques of inlay were themselves often engraved with small scenes and motifs. Silver wire was particularly popular during the 18th century and the technique of application was the same as for damascening. A small line was chiselled into the stock and a piece of soft silver wire was laid into the channel and gently tapped so that it expanded and was held firmly in place. Some stocks were carved, usually around the tang and the butt cap, with some simple volutes which were also continued along the sides of the stock. Such carving was normally restrained and tended to be used less as the 18th century progressed.

Butt caps were a common feature of pistols until the end of the 18th century. They were of brass, silver and steel and were sometimes decorated with chiselling or moulding. During the early part of the 18th century they tended to be rather large and florid but became more restrained as the century progressed and were largely abandoned during the early part of the 19th century.

As a conscious generalisation it may be said that Continental weapons were more elaborately decorated than British examples, often incorporating many styles on one piece. British gunmakers tended to limit their choice of techniques to one or two for each weapon, silver wire inlay being the most popular. For obvious reasons military weapons were almost invariably plainer than their civilian counterparts, although some

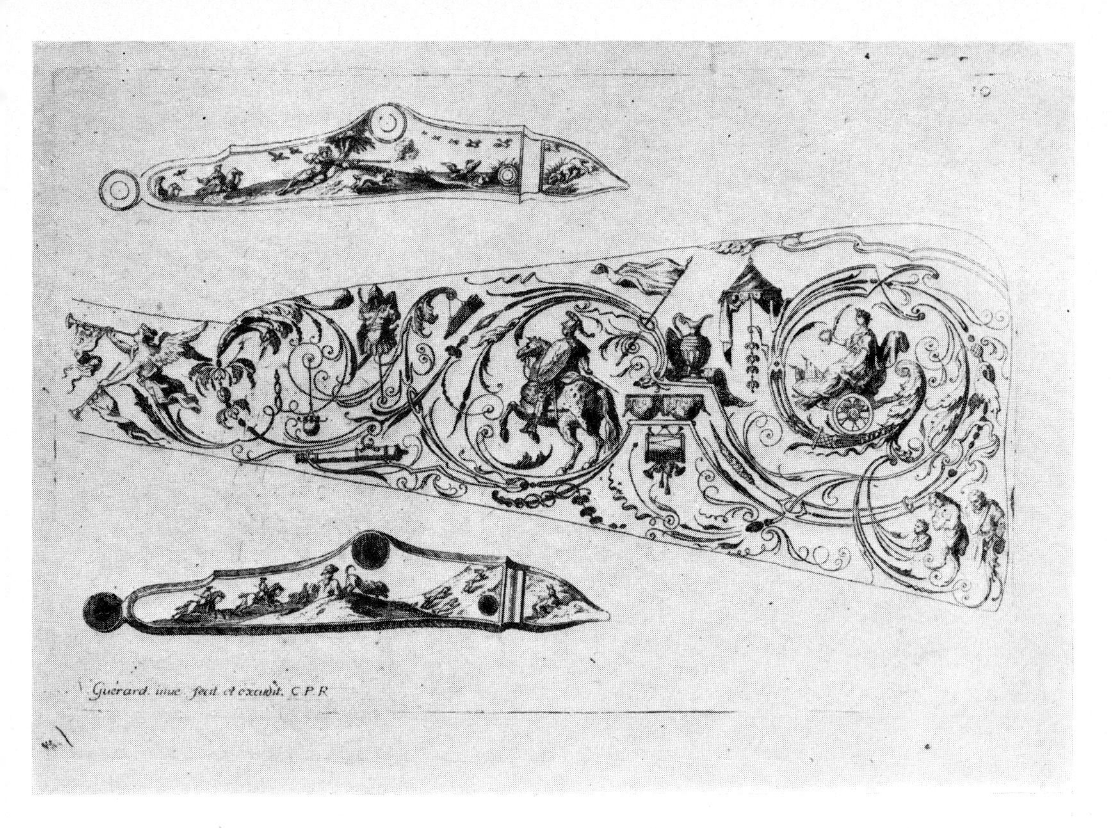

Fig. 116: Many gunsmiths issued books of designs from which customers could select the patterns which they preferred. This is a page from a book issued by the Parisian maker Nicholas Guerard in about 1700. (*Victoria and Albert Museum.*)

of the earlier examples were often well decorated, as were presentation pieces.

All the styles and methods of decoration listed above have been, at one time or another, used to embellish pocket pistols. Many of the later examples were rather cheap and unattractive, but as a group these small pistols offer an interesting field of collecting and, excepting the elaborate examples, they are far less expensive than larger holster pistols.

10

Asian Weapons

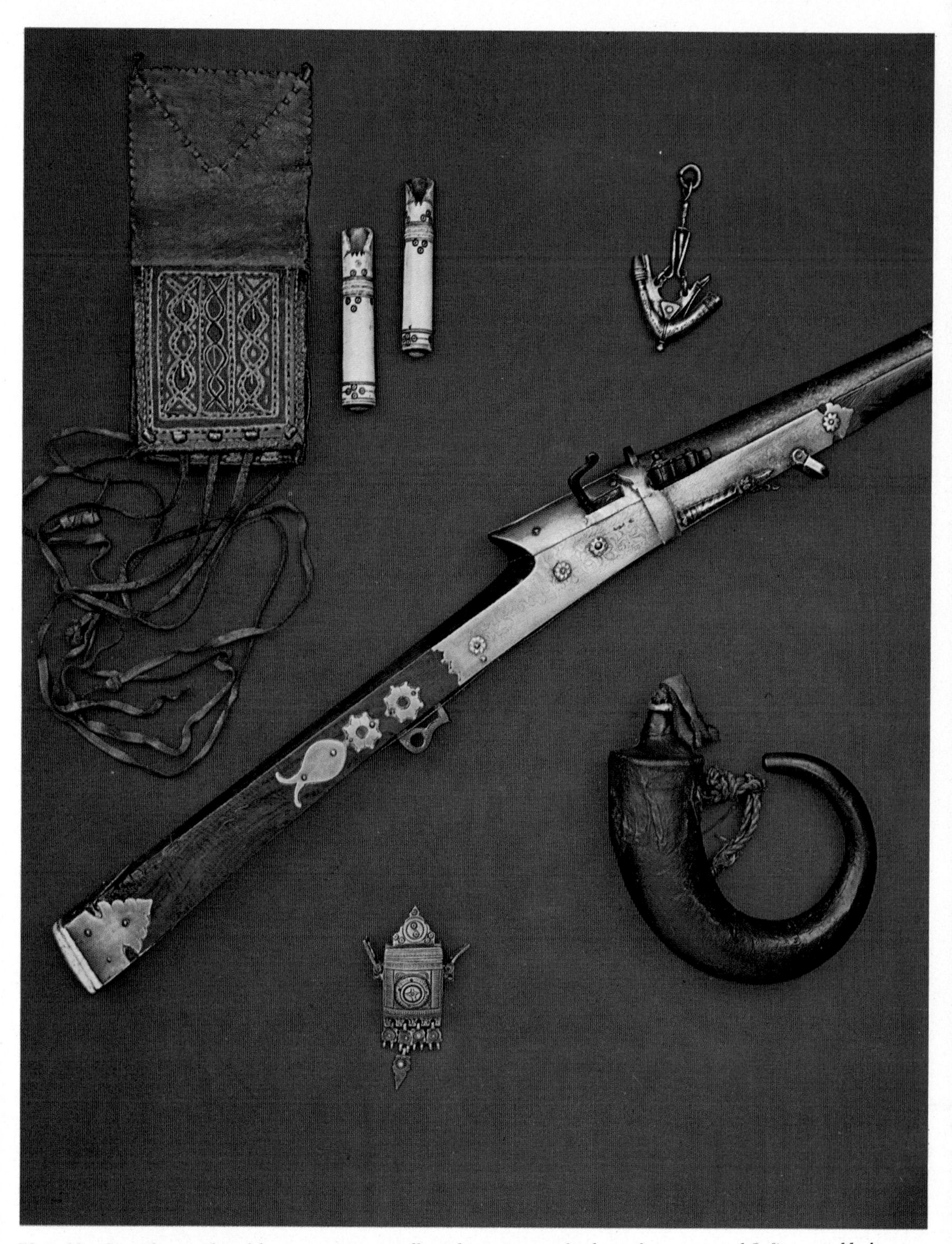

Plate 20 *Cartridge pouch and bone measures; small steel priming-powder horn; brass-mounted Indian matchlock musket; powder horn; and brass bullet box. Overall length of musket, 5 feet 2½ inches; barrel, 3 feet 8 inches; bore, ·6 inch.* (*Durrant Collection.*)

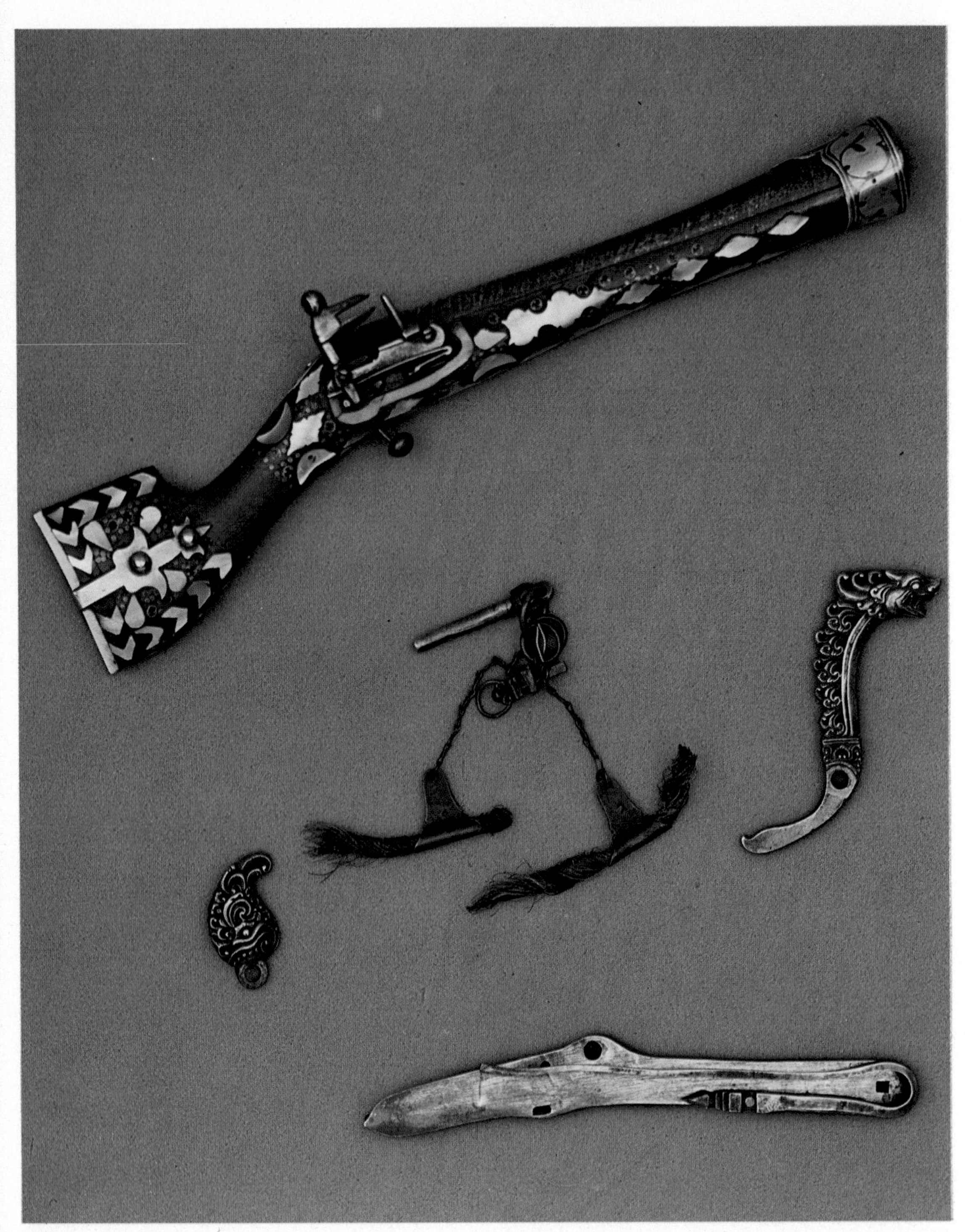

Plate 21 (Top) *A fine quality Turkish blunderbuss, the stock inlaid with mother of pearl and decorated with silver. Overall length, 14½ inches; barrel, 8¾ inches.* (*Winsbury Collection.*) (Bottom) *A dismounted Japanese matchlock with cast brass match holder. The brass lockplate has the characteristic long U-shaped brass spring.* (*Blackmore Collection.*)

INTEREST in antique firearms has increased consistently over the last decade, and from being the taste of a knowledgeable few it has grown into a very important part of the antique trade. Prices have appreciated enormously although the ratio of increase has varied from section to section of the antique market. Obviously elaborate and rarer items such as wheellocks have shown an enormous rise in price, as have military weapons, but even within each group there are variations; thus pistols have appreciated more than long arms, and top quality specimens in any category will always realise top prices.

However, there are certain groups of weapons which have not shown such startling increases. With the exception of Japanese swords, which have always had a large following among enthusiasts, Asian weapons have not increased in price to the same extent as many others. As a group such weapons have always been less popular than European firearms and generally less regarded by collectors. There are some grounds for the undoubted prejudice which exists against these weapons; many of them are crude, others are garish and rather too ostentatious for many conservative collectors. However, in addition to the large number of rather poor quality weapons there are some which are deserving of much greater appreciation than they receive at the moment.

Owing to the considerable language difficulties involved there has been far less comprehensive research in this field than in that of European firearms history. It is far more difficult to locate reliable information about Asian firearms than about European ones of a similar period. The development of style and decoration did not change in the same fairly clearly defined sequence as in the West and it is consequently very difficult to date these weapons.

Fig. 117: Top view of a large Japanese wall piece, the beautifully decorated barrel bearing an inscription which identifies it as dating from 1685. The barrel was restocked in 1852. Length, 40 inches; bore, 1·4 inches. (*British Museum.*)

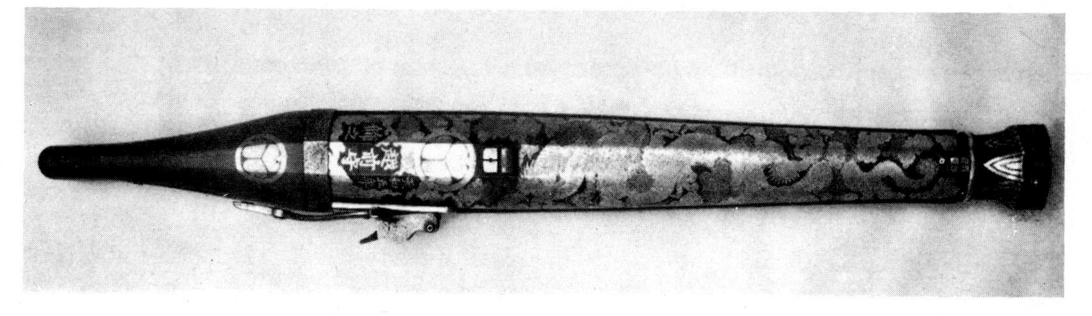

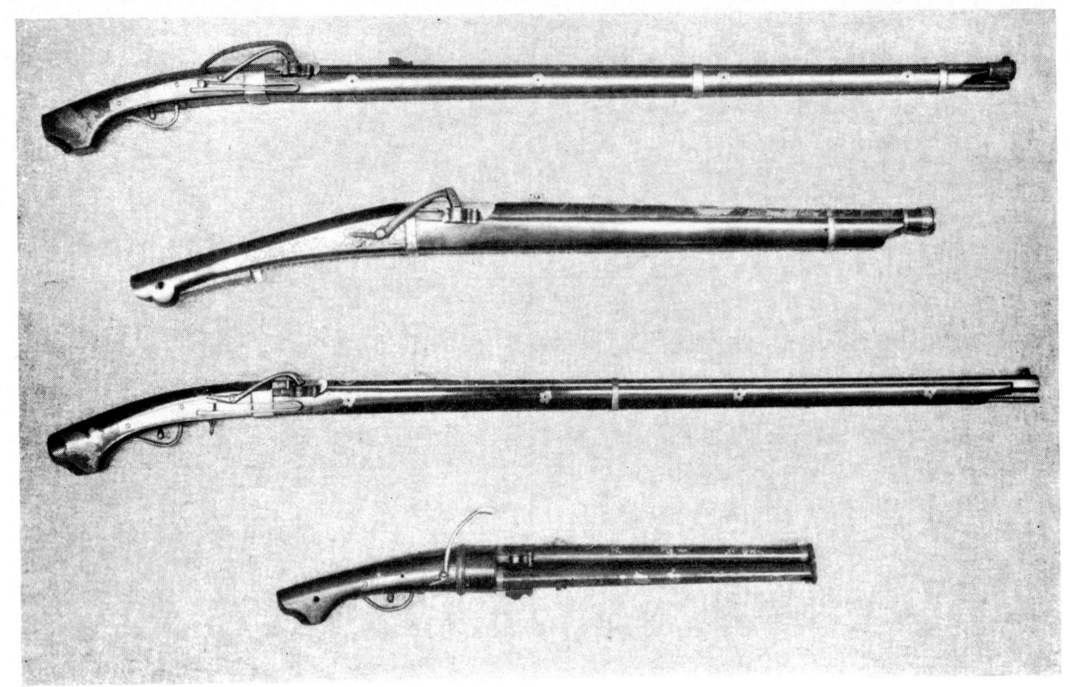

Fig. 118: Japanese matchlocks, with their characteristic short butts and long brass lockplates; in all cases the cock movement is forward, towards the muzzle. The bottom weapon has hand-rotated barrels. (Victoria and Albert Museum.)

How long this lack of interest will continue is uncertain but there are signs—unfortunately indicated by a rise in price—that these weapons are beginning to receive more attention and are in greater demand from collectors. It would seem likely that in the foreseeable future they will soon be accorded the interest that they deserve.

Gunpowder was almost certainly a Chinese discovery, but beyond producing some rather crude handguns the Chinese seem to have developed the idea not at all. In fact the appearance of firearms in the Far East may be traced to contact with the West in the form of Portuguese explorers. Prompted by the discoveries of Columbus the Portuguese sought to find routes to the east that would increase their trade and augment their empire. Under the aegis of Prince Henry the Navigator their small ships nosed down the coast of Africa and in 1488 the Portuguese navigator Bartholomew Diaz rounded the Cape of Good Hope. Soon they made their way up the eastern coast of Africa and then crossed the Indian Ocean. They reached the Indian coast first in 1498 and by 1505 they were in Ceylon; some nine years later one of their number had made the hazardous journey to Peking. Apart from the visit of Marco Polo and one or two Franciscan missionaries few Europeans had penetrated this far East. Three Portuguese traders landed on one of the small Japanese islands in 1545 and were received by the inhabitants with interest and curiosity. Naturally the Portuguese were armed and carried with them a number of matchlocks. To the Japanese and the Indians these seemed incredible, almost magical weapons which they soon learned to fear, for the Portuguese came more as conquerors than peaceful traders and did not hesitate to use force when they were threatened. Soon the local princes, chiefs and war lords were demanding similar weapons for their own troops. Craftsmen of the country were perfectly competent to copy these weapons and were soon constructing their own version of the matchlock. Although they attempted to copy the European pattern there gradually evolved forms which became more or less peculiar to certain areas.

Asian smiths were well used to decorating metal, having used damascening and inlay on their edged weapons, and they quickly applied their skills to decorating this new weapon; it is safe to say that the weapons of Asia are far more brightly decorated than their European counterparts. The finished products varied enormously in quality ranging between superb technical and decorative masterpieces to extremely crude, rough and amateur weapons which were probably as dangerous to the user as to his enemy. Considering their limited technical resources the craftsmen produced some incredibly fine work. They continued to use the matchlock which remained essentially unaltered throughout the centuries and comparatively few flintlock or percussion weapons were produced in Japan. In India a large number of flintlocks and a few percussion weapons were made, but the overwhelming majority of native weapons were matchlocks. Many of the flintlock weapons were made with locks imported from Europe, and Indian and Turkish weapons will be found with English-made locks.

Fig. 119: This small Japanese matchlock pistol is a miniature version of the typical Japanese long arm, complete with inlaid stock, sights and ramrod. The pan cover is open, and the cock in the fired position. (Dominion Museum, New Zealand.)

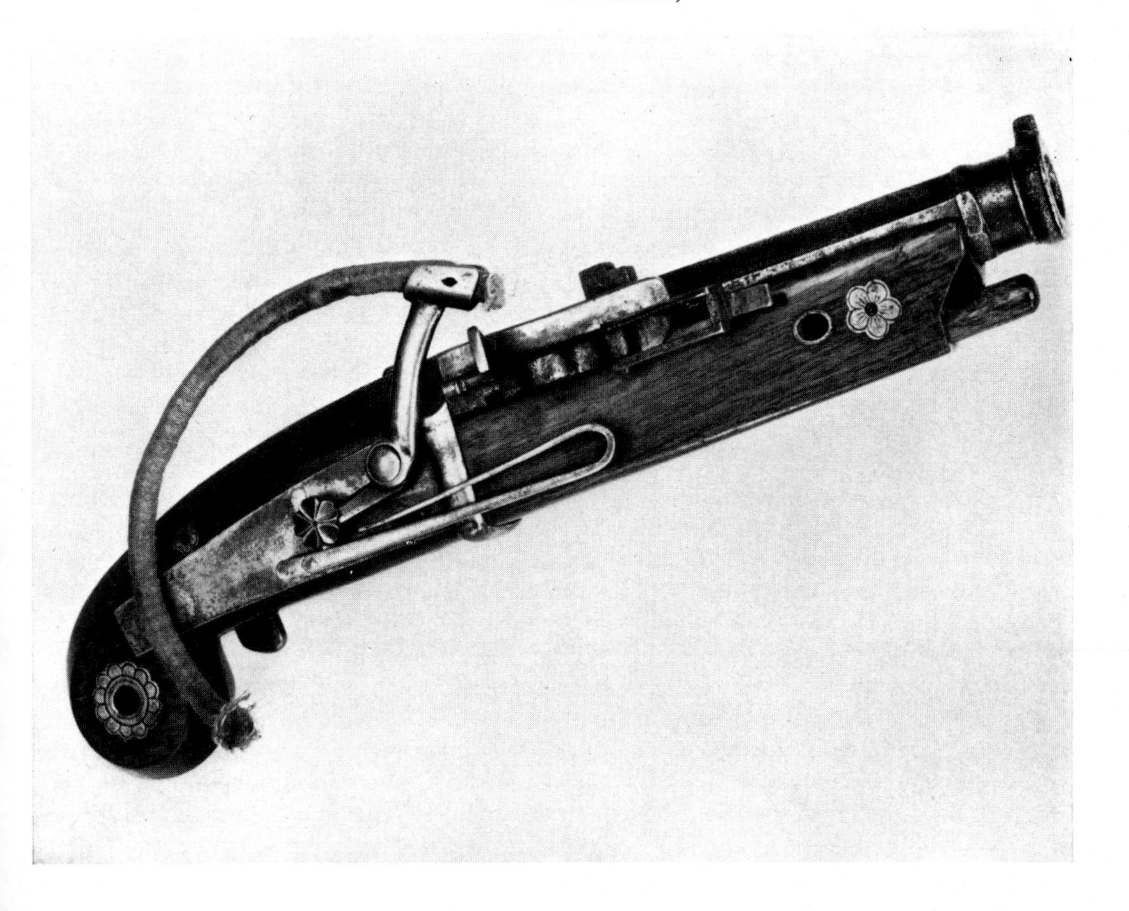

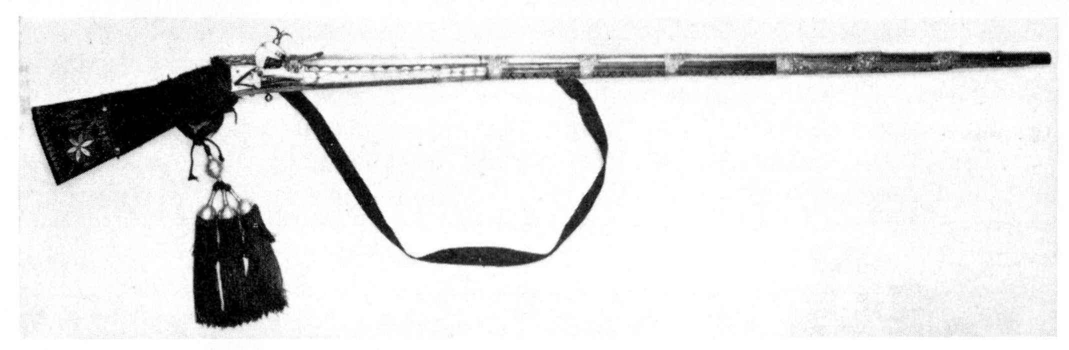

Fig. 120: An 18th century Turkish gun, the rosewood stock inlaid with brass and ivory, and with brocade tassels attached. The barrel is European, probably from Vienna. (Reproduced by permission of the Trustees of the Wallace Collection.)

In particular some Indian flintlock weapons will be found to carry locks imported by the East India Company, bearing a date as well as the Lion mark of the Company.

During the 17th and 18th centuries the export of barrels and locks was a profitable trade, and in the West Indies Belgian-made muskets formed a generally accepted currency used in the barter of slaves. During the early 17th century Dutch and English makers exported to North Africa large numbers of the snaphaunce lock. Local craftsmen soon mastered the techniques involved in the manufacture and began copying and selling their own version of the lock. This tradition of European style locks, begun in the 17th century, was to continue until quite recently when the traditional long-barrelled musket was ousted by modern weapons.

This conservative attitude of the East is particularly noticeable in the case of weapons, and for the Western student is a serious stumbling block, making it almost impossible to date with any certainty any form of Asiatic weapon on stylistic grounds. The shape and style of the matchlock changed very little and dated examples of the 17th, 18th and 19th centuries exhibit remarkably little variation. Some indication as to age may be given by inscriptions but even these can be unreliable evidence for in many cases, with shrewed thriftiness, the Asiatic gunsmith restocked an old barrel or lock long after it was made. Thus it is difficult to be dogmatic in the matter of dates and it may safely be assumed that all dates ascribed to Asiatic weapons can only be approximate.

THE metal workers of Japan were among the foremost in the world and their technical skill in the handling of all kinds of metal was outstanding. Their sword blades have long been regarded by connoisseurs as the most perfect form of cutting weapon ever produced. A soft iron centre was sheathed in a hard shell with an even harder cutting edge so that the sword combined the ideal qualities essential for a good cutting sword. This skill the craftsmen soon applied to the matchlocks, and since most of their patrons were persons of rank their products were decorative and usually of top quality.

Although the Portuguese landed there in 1545 the Japanese did not for long leave the door open to European visitors, and from 1638 until the middle of the 19th century Japan was isolated from the rest of the world. It was only when Commodore Perry of the U.S. Navy literally forced open the door that contact was again established. The Japanese gunsmith knew little or nothing of the development of firearms in the

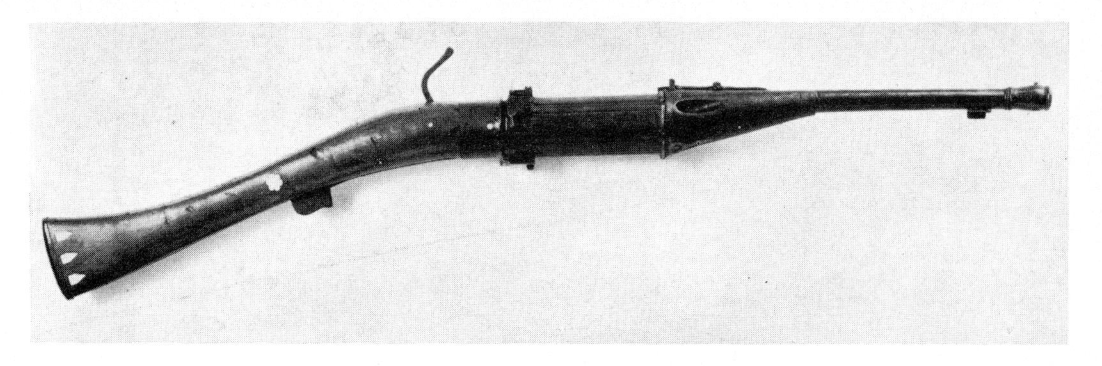

Fig. 121: A 17th century Indian revolving matchlock gun, with inlaid redwood stock. The six chambers are rotated by hand and locked in place by a spring clip. (Wallace Collection.)

West until Perry arrived with the latest 19th century weapons, and the wheellock and flintlock figures hardly at all in Japanese firearm production. Modern researchers have failed to unearth more than one example of a Japanese flintlock; this weapon is remarkable, for it is a simple three-barrelled revolver and seems to date from the 17th century. There is some slight evidence of the existence of Japanese flintlocks since a few early Japanese prints show flintlock weapons amongst the arms carried by some of the soldiers. After the arrival of Perry in 1854 the Japanese gunsmith dabbled with percussion, and some Japanese percussion pistols are known. Some were made in the form of concealed weapons—a Japanese dagger drawn from the sheath proves to be a percussion pistol, or an apparent writing case holds a concealed percussion pistol. A number of conventional boxlock percussion pistols were also produced. However, by and large, the flintlock and percussion systems were to by-pass Japan and the subsequent step was from the matchlock to cartridge weapons.

Although Japanese firearms naturally enough vary in detail there are a number of features which are common to the majority. Despite the Japanese mastery of metalwork they seem to have experienced difficulties in the production of springs, for one of the remarkable features of Japanese matchlocks is the poor quality of the spring. They are almost invariably made of brass and steel seems never to have figured in spring production. Many of the Japanese matchlocks are operated by a large U-shaped brass spring fitted to the outside of the lock, but some rare examples incorporate spiral springs rather like those found in clocks. Coiled springs are, however, usually fitted on the inside, one operating the cock while a smaller one operates the seer. Most frequently the Japanese fitted a snaplock in which the cock was at rest pressing down on the pan. The lock was prepared by raising the arm, and this engaged with a sear which projected through the lockplate and which was withdrawn by pressing the button trigger. Obviously such a system was very liable to accidental discharge. It is also remarkable that Japanese, Indian and indeed most Asiatic matchlocks operated in the reverse direction to those from Eurpe. Eastern matchlocks have the arm pivoted at the butt end with the head swinging forward and down; in almost every European example the reverse is the case, with the cock pivoted at the front of the lockplate and swinging down and backwards. There seems no logical reason for the prevalence of either system but each seems to have continued unchanged in its own area.

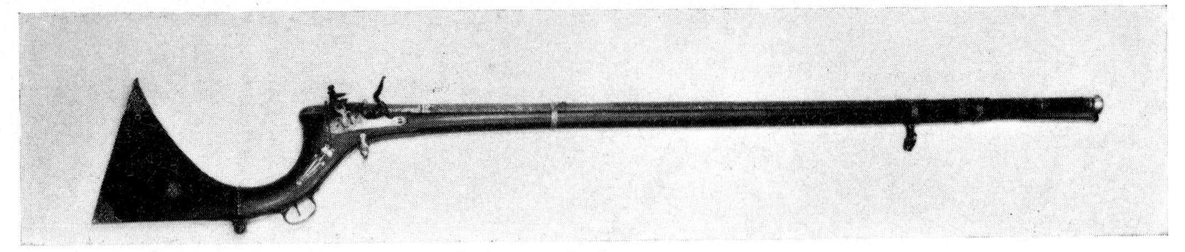

Fig. 122: A long-barrelled 43-inch gun with the so-called "Afghan stock". The stock is of ebony and the whole weapon is decorated with gold, silver and enamel. (Wallace Collection.)

Not only were the Japanese troubled by the matter of spring manufacture, but they also apparently found difficulty in producing screws; Japanese matchlocks are almost invariably secured by pins rather than screws. A common feature of most matchlocks is the pan cover, and this was made to fit both below and above the pan so that instead of a screw a pin could be passed through the top plate and the pan to engage with the lower plate of the pan cover. Cocks and springs are also secured by pins. This strange reluctance to produce screws also had its effect on the method of securing the barrel to the stock. Barrels had no tang or rear projection such as that

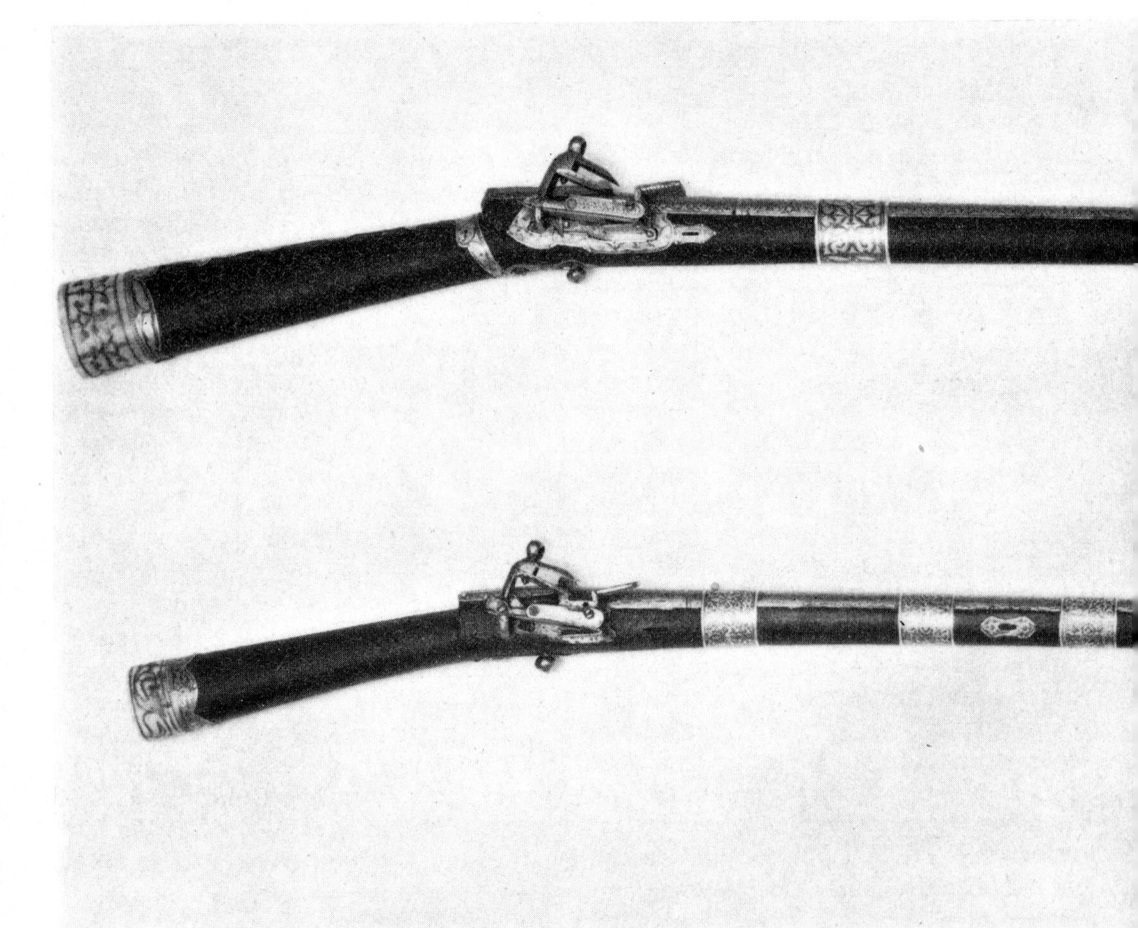

found on European barrels; they terminated at the breech and were pegged to the stock in the way commonly used on British weapons, but without the tang screw. Barrels were normally substantial, with very thick walls of fine quality, and were produced by a system of folding and welding metal strips in a rather complicated technique. The most popular shape was octagonal but there were many which were round, and these latter were frequently fitted with a flat rib at the top to hold the rear sight. These rear sights were seldom more than a large block with two cuts in it, while the foresight was usually a leaf style tapering to a fairly sharp point. Barrels were seldom left plain but were damascened with gold or silver scrolls, or, less frequently, representations of animals, dragons and birds. It was the fashion of the large and important Japanese families to have a badge very similar in intention to the coat of arms of the West. This small badge known as the *Mon* was frequently damascened on the barrel and occasionally inlaid in the stock, and in many cases these *mons* can be identified. Unlike the barrels the stocks were left fairly plain except for a small brass lined hole through

Fig. 123: (Top) *Long Turkish flintlock gun of the 18th century, the round-section butt covered with leather and fitted with docorated silver bands.* (Bottom) *Short Turkish flintlock gun with an 18½-inch barrel, probably made for a youth.* (Right) *19th century Greek cartridge case made of ebony tubes mounted in silver.* (*Wallace Collection.*)

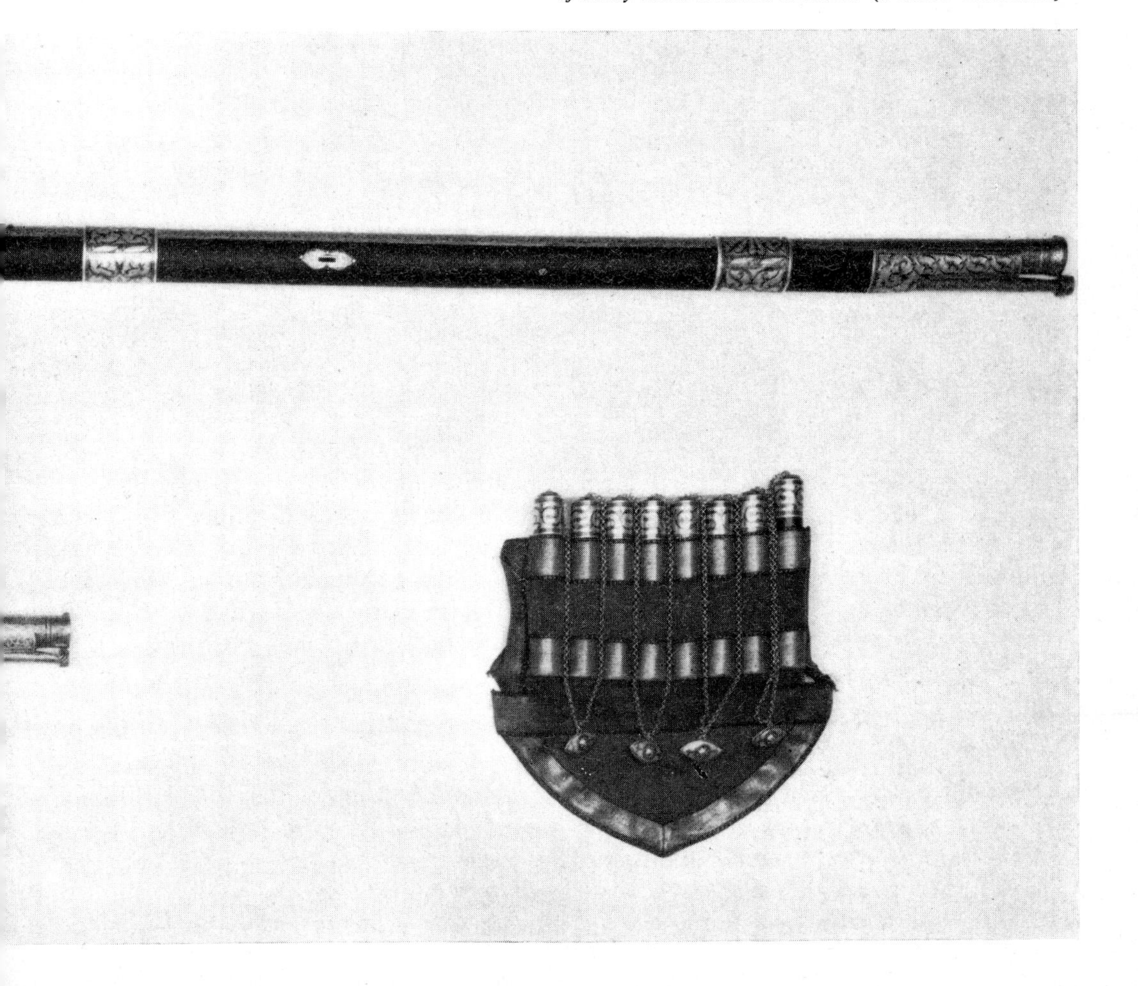

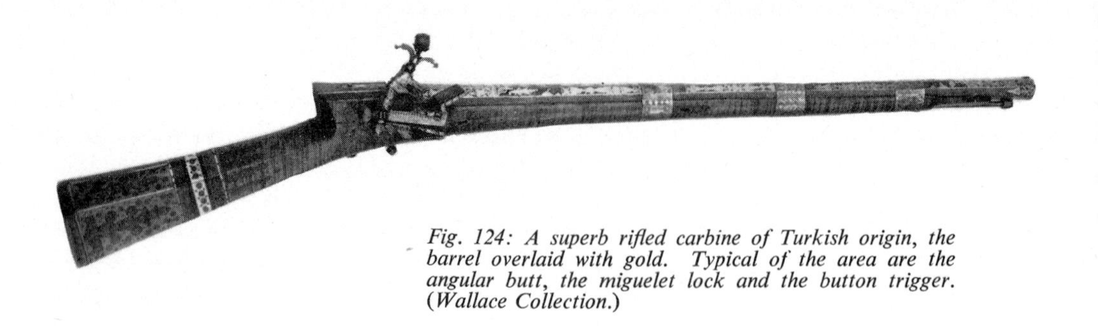

Fig. 124: A superb rifled carbine of Turkish origin, the barrel overlaid with gold. Typical of the area are the angular butt, the miguelet lock and the button trigger. (Wallace Collection.)

which the end of the match passed before being wrapped around the stock. Some have simple brass inlay, while the richer examples may be lacquered or embellished in some other manner, but carving was very seldom used. They are usually fitted with a short curved butt.

Japan was one of the very few countries which produced matchlock pistols; these are essentially miniature matchlock muskets ranging from two or three inches to a foot or so in length. Design and construction is identical with that of the larger models. In some cases they are not strictly speaking pistols but boy's matchlocks; there was an important festival held in Japan for which ceremony it was not uncommon for armour, swords and matchlocks to be made in appropriate sizes to be carried by boys taking part. At the other extreme some very large wall pieces were also produced, but again these are merely larger versions of the same basic design of weapon. The Japanese also produced a number of repeating matchlocks in the form of a group of barrels, each with its priming pan, which rotated by hand to bring a fresh unfired barrel into position.

The Chinese seem to have acquired the matchlock at a later date than the Japanese and although the Japanese weapons are almost invariably of very good quality it is remarkable that China, the home of firearms and in so many ways closely associated with Japan, should have produced such crude matchlocks. Few pistols were made by the Chinese but their long arms had as characteristics a very long thin barrel and a hook-type butt reminiscent of a pistol. Triggers were usually of the button type. A few long arms were fitted with percussion locks but the great majority were matchlocks. The barrels were occasionally damascened, but apart from this decoration, construction and quality were generally poor. Korean matchlocks are also known and these are very similar to those of Japan but normally bear Chinese inscriptions along the length of the barrel.

THE other main centre for the production of matchlock weapons was the sub-continent of India; here the basic pattern was very different from that of Japan. The matchlock mechanism used by the majority of Indian gunmakers was European in style, with the cock at rest away from the priming pan. Pressure on the trigger operated levers and springs inside the stock and so caused the cock to swing forward and press the glowing end of the match into the priming pan; when the trigger was released the cock swung up again. Unlike the Japanese weapons there was no lockplate, and the lock mechanism was normally housed inside the stock while the trigger was set some distance back along the butt and was frequently chiselled into the shape of an animal or bird. Barrels were usually long and often chiselled for their entire length. Gold inlay was used and sights, when fitted, were likely to be elaborately chiselled. Indian matchlocks are seldom fitted with trigger guards but some Japanese guns are so equipped. Indian stocks vary in size, shape and quality but generally those made in the north had a large curved butt which swung round in a very pronounced upward curve which was occasionally bifurcated at the end to produce a fishtail appearance. This northern shape was also used for flintlock weapons and is usually referred to as the Afghan stock although, in fact, it is more typical of the Sind. Afghan guns are also known as "jezails" and have a butt which is oval and only slightly curved. Most characteristic was the long, slim, angular "Torador", with its straight-sided butt sloping gently down from the breech. Barrels were usually round and were generally swamped slightly at the muzzle, and the sights were often elaborately fashioned into animal shapes. Indian smiths delighted in decorating the barrel with chiselling and inlay of gold and silver. Many had a pricker secured to the stock by a short length of chain and housed in a small container fastened to the stock. These prickers seem to be popular in the East; although the necessity of keeping the touchhole clear was obviously not peculiar to India, the Western musketeer seems to have coped with the problem by less sophisticated methods.

Construction of Indian barrels was complex and in many ways paralleled that used by European gunsmiths to produce the best quality barrels. Even more remarkable were the outstandingly good results that they obtained with the most basic of equipment. The boring of barrels was a long and complicated process and it would take up to three days to bore out a single barrel, for the entire job was done using bamboo and iron borers. The barrel was actually made up of sections about 18 inches long which were then welded together on a straight iron former. Ramrods are normally fitted beneath the barrel and housed in the stock in the same way as in European weapons.

Indian weapons invariably had the barrel secured to the stock by means of six or seven bands and these "capucines" took the form of metal bands or, quite frequently, rawhide thongs. The stocks too were often inlaid or embellished with tassels or velvet and material coverings, although this is a more typically Turkish practice.

Unlike the Japanese, the Indians produced both flintlocks and percussion firearms and the general remarks given above apply equally well to these later types of weapons

Fig. 125: Butt and lock of a North African snaphaunce musket; the weapon dates from the 19th century, but the lock is an obvious copy of the 17th century Dutch mechanism. It is shown here in the firing position. The butt is modestly decorated with inlay work. (*Bennett Collection.*)

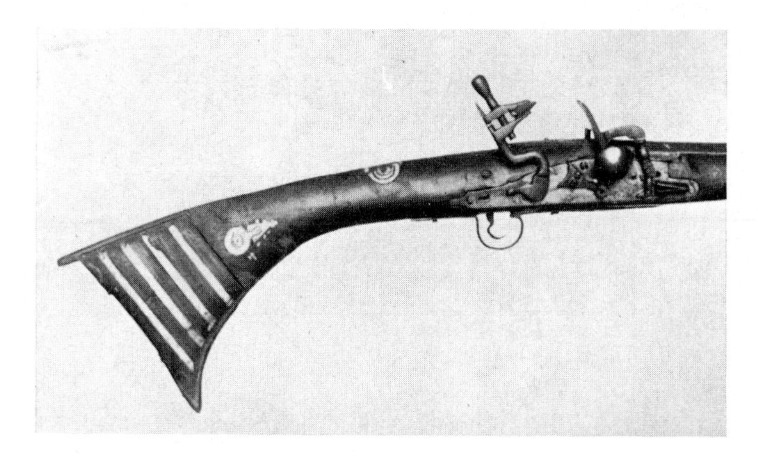

except for the different methods of ignition. Afghan stocks and "jezails" were frequently fitted with flintlocks and less commonly with percussion locks. The Indian smith also seems to have been fascinated by the unusual, and produced some very complicated combination weapons. Examples include an arm guard which had a pair of flintlock pistols fastened above the hand, the triggers projecting inside the glove section, as well as a spring-operated fluted dagger, normally folded back along the arm guard and held in place by a clip. When the spring was released the dagger flew forward to lock into position and formed, in effect, an Indian "katar" or punching dagger. Similarly shields were made with four small percussion pistols fitted in a style somewhat reminiscent of Henry VIII's matchlock shields mentioned previously.

India also produced a few matchlock pistols, but like the Japanese their use seems to have been limited and they are frequently merely miniature versions of the standard long arm. It is quite remarkable that the very long Indian matchlock was used on horseback but there are authenticated reports and illustrations in existence showing that this was quite certainly the case.

Turkish and Persian long arms were most often flintlocks with a lock basically the same as the Spanish "miguelet" and operated by a sear which pierced the lockplate. The stocks were typical in having a section with sharp angular edges and a very marked and distinct step behind the breech. Decoration was often profuse, with silver wire inlay, or insets of ivory, ebony or coral; and they were frequently covered with material

Fig. 126: Two pairs of Caucasian pistols of the late 18th or early 19th century; most of the pistols from this area have ball pommels, miguelet locks and ball triggers. Decoration is in silver, silver gilt, ivory and gold. (*Wallace Collection.*)

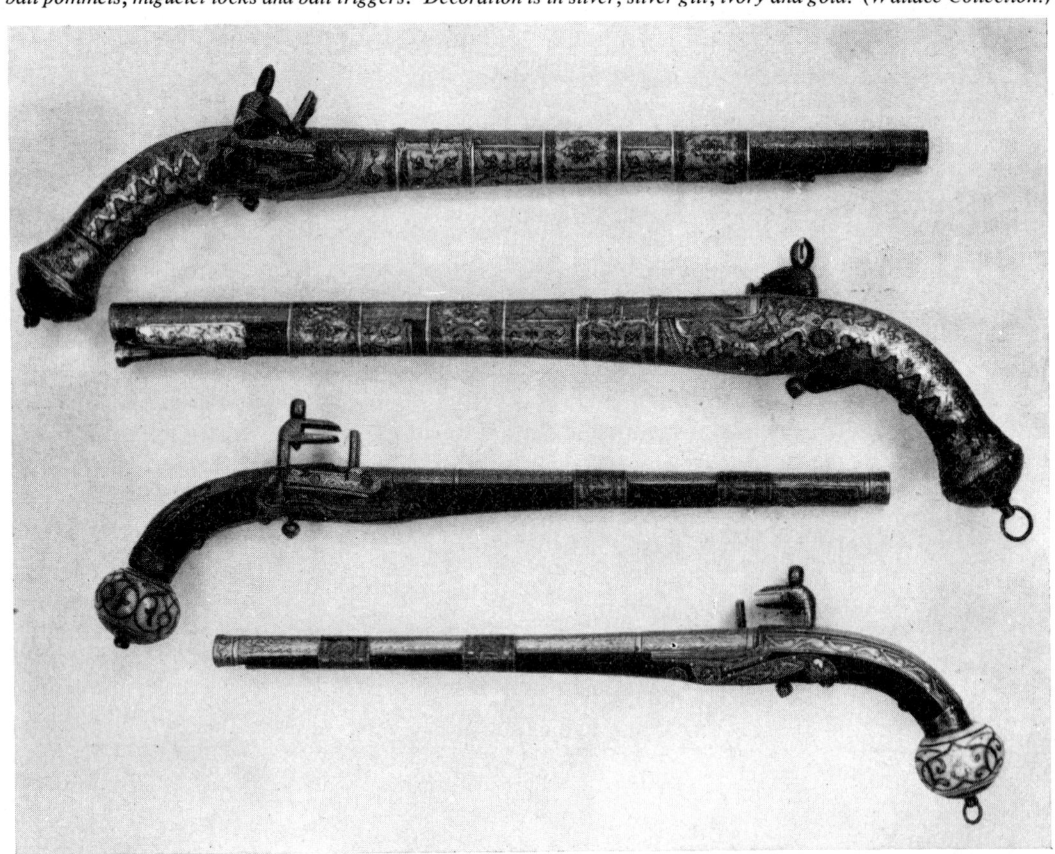

and dangling tassels. One weapon peculiar to Turkey and Persia is the miniature blunderbuss, although this type of weapon was also found in the neighbouring Caucasus region and was fitted with both flint and percussion locks. The weapon was only about 18 inches or so long but it was literally a miniature blunderbuss. Its small size precluded its being fired from the shoulder and it is not at all clear how it was intended to be used. One theory that has been advanced is that they were fired from the hip when on horseback, and this may well be the case. They are often profusely decorated with the same materials used on the longer matchlocks. Not all Turkish pistols are of the miguelet style; a large number of locks were imported from the West and many of the Turkish gunsmiths copied these, so that it is not unusual to find a European-style pistol with a lock bearing most peculiar translations of European gunsmiths' names. These are often attempts by the local makers at copying names and addresses but the gunsmith has been unable to understand them and the results are often rather peculiar. Until the 20th century the Turkish empire embraced large areas of Europe and Turkish fashions were often imposed on European tradition; the so-called Balkan pistol is typical of this combination.

Different areas of the Balkans appear to have produced local variations but it is not easy to be precise as to their place of origin. There has been little research into these weapons and much of the evidence is derived from accounts given by travellers in the past, and from illustrations. Pistols popular in Albania and neighbouring countries were made with an all-metal stock which was very straight and terminated in a small pommel. The stocks were often embossed with raised patterns and the barrel was fitted with a very long muzzle band holding it in place on the stock. They are frequently referred to as "rat tail pistols" because of this long thin shape. The flintlocks are of the usual European pattern although the quality of workmanship is likely to be slightly inferior. Albanian long arms also have this long thin appearance with the butt drooping gracefully and terminating in a rounded fish-tail shape. Stocks may be overlaid with mother-of-pearl or other decorative materials and the trigger is usually ornate; the overall quality of these weapons is quite reasonable.

Another very common type of Balkan pistol closely resembles the European flintlock pistol in shape and construction, with its butt cap, long spurs and lockplate, all reminiscent of an early 18th century European pistol. Indeed many of them were made in England, France or Italy and exported to Turkey. Some of these pistols while retaining an apparently Western style were made with all-metal stocks, frequently of silver or silver gilt, and have slightly rounded pommels. This type is often classed as Greek, but they were also used in adjoining countries. Niello silver was a very popular form of decoration, produced by engraving the surface of the metal and filling in the lines with a black metal amalgam. After heating the result was a hard black enamel-like coating which strongly contrasted with the silver. Silver gilt, silver wire, metal foil and metal plates were all used to give these weapons a rather garish appearance. Frequently the furniture (trigger guard, ramrod pipes and side plates) were of silver, and barrels might be blued and gilt. One characteristic feature of many of these pistols is the simulated ramrod; the stock is carved to resemble a ramrod housed in pipes but the real ramrod, a "suma", was carried separately suspended on a cord around the neck. Suma were often quite elaborately carved and were sometimes combined with powder measures or edged weapons. Most of these Balkan pistols were elaborately decorated, sometimes with the entire stock covered with embossed silver plate bound in place with silver wire and fitted with semi-precious stones or pieces of coral, but beneath this

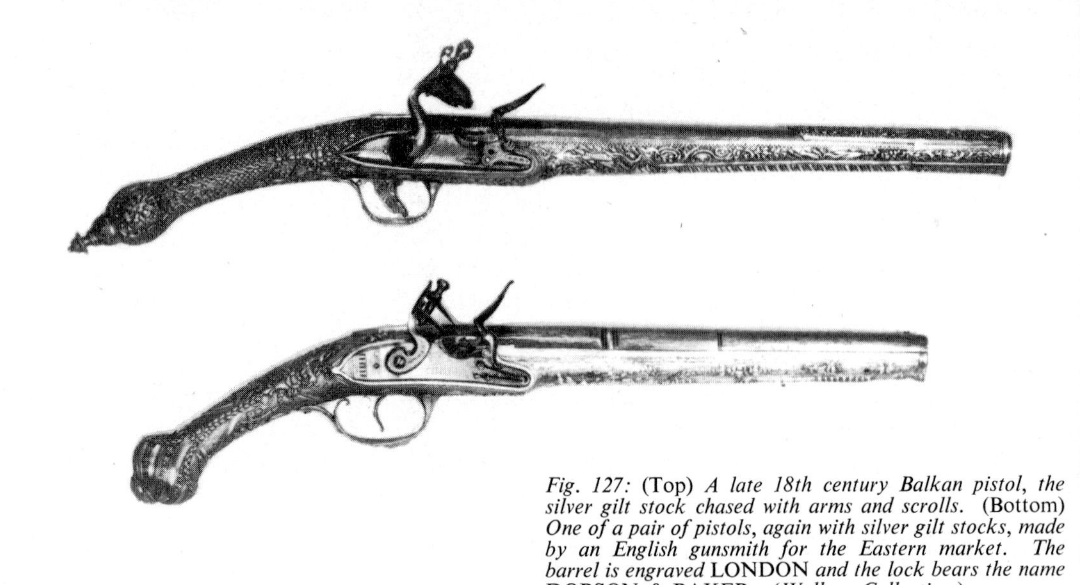

Fig. 127: (Top) *A late 18th century Balkan pistol, the silver gilt stock chased with arms and scrolls.* (Bottom) *One of a pair of pistols, again with silver gilt stocks, made by an English gunsmith for the Eastern market. The barrel is engraved* LONDON *and the lock bears the name* DOBSON & BAKER. (*Wallace Collection.*)

ostentatiously high quality surface the general standard of workmanship was often poor. Locks and springs were sometimes below standard and stocks were often of poor wood; many of the Turkish weapons, on the other hand, were of a very high standard.

To the north of the Balkans, in the Caucasus region, there evolved the so-called Cossack pistol. Like many of the Turkish long arms the Cossack pistol was fitted with a miguelet-style lock with typical square jaws, grooved face to the steel and external mainspring. The thin stock had an acutely down-curving butt, but the most obvious characteristic was a ball pommel to the butt. This was often of ivory and in some cases had the appearance of a billiard ball; others were of metal, and all were frequently carved and decorated with incised lines and simple inlay. Entire stocks were often covered with leather and then overlaid with bands of niello work or silver gilt. Many of them have the barrels secured to the stock by a series of capucines or bands and again these are frequently of niello silver. A majority of these pistols were fitted with ball triggers and lack any trigger guard.

Turkish influence was also very strong in North Africa where many Turkish firearms were used, but most African firearms show signs of strong European influence. There appears to have developed in North Africa during the 16th century a special type of mechanism known as the Kabyl lock, which may well have originated in Spain since it closely resembled the miguelet lock. The most noticeable feature is the small cock, fitted with very large rectangular jaws, while the top jaw screw usually has a bar or ring fitted to offer a good grip, since the mainspring was very powerful. Full cock was held by a sear which engaged with a slot in the cock, while half cock was held by a dog catch. Many African guns were fitted with European barrels but they were usually of very inferior quality and frequently bore indecipherable pseudo gunmakers' marks.

Stock shapes offer a reasonable guide to the place of origin, and from the north

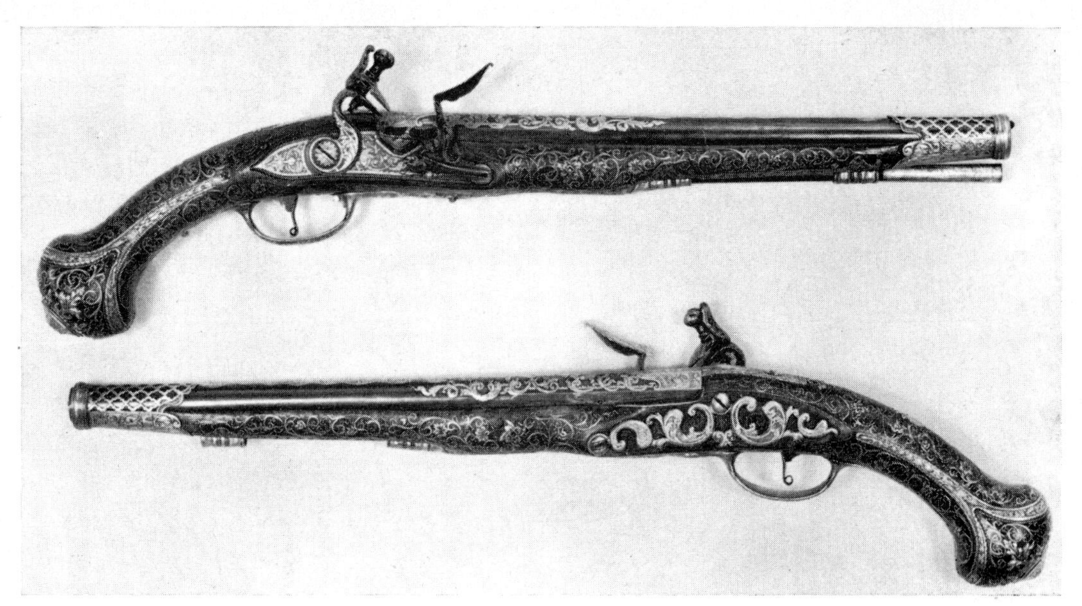

Fig. 128: A magnificent pair of 19th century Turkish flintlock pistols, richly decorated with gold and silver gilt. The barrels are blued and the stocks are covered with exquisite silver wire inlay work. (Wallace Collection.)

came a gun with a very large triangular butt fitted with a thick plate of ivory or alternating layers of ivory and wood. The furniture was rather crude, and these guns retain one or two features once common on earlier firearms; the tang screw is inserted from the bottom of the stock, passing upwards to engage with the barrel tang, and the trigger is also reminiscent of those of the early matchlocks. Guns from Morocco were basically similar but had a marked cut-away concavity at the end of the butt. In common with Indian guns the barrel was secured to the stock by means of bands of many metals; brass, iron or copper were the most common.

Associated with these Asiatic firearms are a number of interesting accessories—powder flasks, priming flasks and cartridge pouches or boxes. Admittedly many are crude and lack any grace but some are interesting and frequently extremely attractive, being fashioned from horn, brass and steel. It is an interesting fact that the bayonet was apparently never developed in the East, presumably because the knife and sword remained a central part of the warrior's arsenal until so much later.

For the collector who is just venturing into arms and armour, these Asiatic and African weapons offer one of the very few fields in which he may hope to acquire weapons of quality at prices which are within the range of the average pocket—for how much longer is uncertain.

11

Continental Weapons

It has already been pointed out that gunpowder and firearms had their origins in the Far East and that knowledge of the discovery spread slowly across Europe, probably arriving first by way of the followers of Islam. It was natural that those countries which had most contact with the East were the first to learn of the new weapons, and it is not surprising that so many of the earliest references to firearms occur in Italian records. However, knowledge is of little value unless it can be used and it was inevitable that many of the well established arms-producing countries should quickly apply their skill to firearm production. Both Italy and Germany were known for the quality of their arms and armour—Turin, Milan, Augsburg and Nuremburg had long been established centres and Solingen and Passau were famous for their edged weapons. The nobility of Europe ordered their personal armour and weapons and supplied their armies with "munition" armours from such centres. Certainly weapons and armour were produced in England, but the native industry did not develop on any scale until much later.

Fig. 129: A pair of flintlock holster pistols made in Paris; the butts are typically French, but the barrels are in the Spanish style. They are blued, with the name JUAN PEDRO ESTEVA *inlaid in gold. Barrel length,* $8\frac{1}{2}$ *inches; bore, ·6 inch.* (*Tower of London.*)

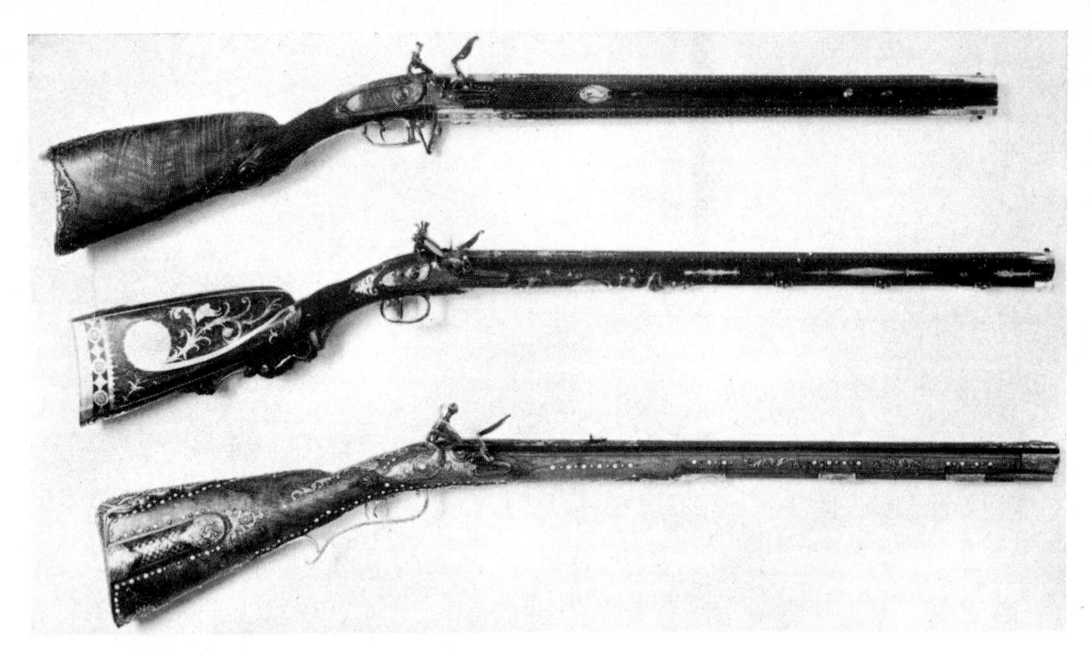

Fig. 130: (Top to bottom) *A superb double-barrelled flintlock rifle made at Versailles in about 1805; it bears the name of the famous maker Boutet and is profusely decorated with precious metals. Another flintlock rifle made by Boutet at Versailles, the walnut stock carved beneath the butt and inlaid with red gold. A German flintlock rifle by Johann Christoph Stockmar*, circa *1750; the lock is chiselled and the barrel blued.* (*Reproduced by permission of the Trustees of the Wallace Collection.*)

Towns such as those mentioned above were well equipped to deal with the production of the new weapon when it became established, for the great armourers had the necessary skilled craftsmen and machinery available. Although it might be thought that the sword and the gun had little in common, the techniques involved in their production were not vastly different. For these reasons it is not surprising that most of the earliest surviving examples of matchlocks and wheellocks apparently originated in Italy or Germany.

Although travel was on a very limited scale during the Middle Ages there was a degree of communication, direct and indirect, between craftsmen in all trades. Many were related by family or marriage and the medieval fairs offered opportunities for personal contact. It is not an unreasonable assumption that gossip, news and details of technical processes passed either by word of mouth or by letter between the suppliers, manufacturers and users of firearms. For these and other reasons it is never profitable to be dogmatic as to the country of origin of many firearms unless they bear certain identifying marks. The examination of numerous specimens will often suggest common points which can be accepted as useful guides, but in general it is a very foolhardy student who will dogmatise. That there was a considerable interchange is shown by many records of foreign craftsmen settling in strange lands to take up their trade; and it was not unknown for princes and kings to encourage visits by, or immigration of, certain master craftsmen to set up arms centres in their own country. Sometimes the products of the foreign craftsmen were limited to the King's use, but even so the new fashion would percolate through much of the native trade. Certain countries gained a

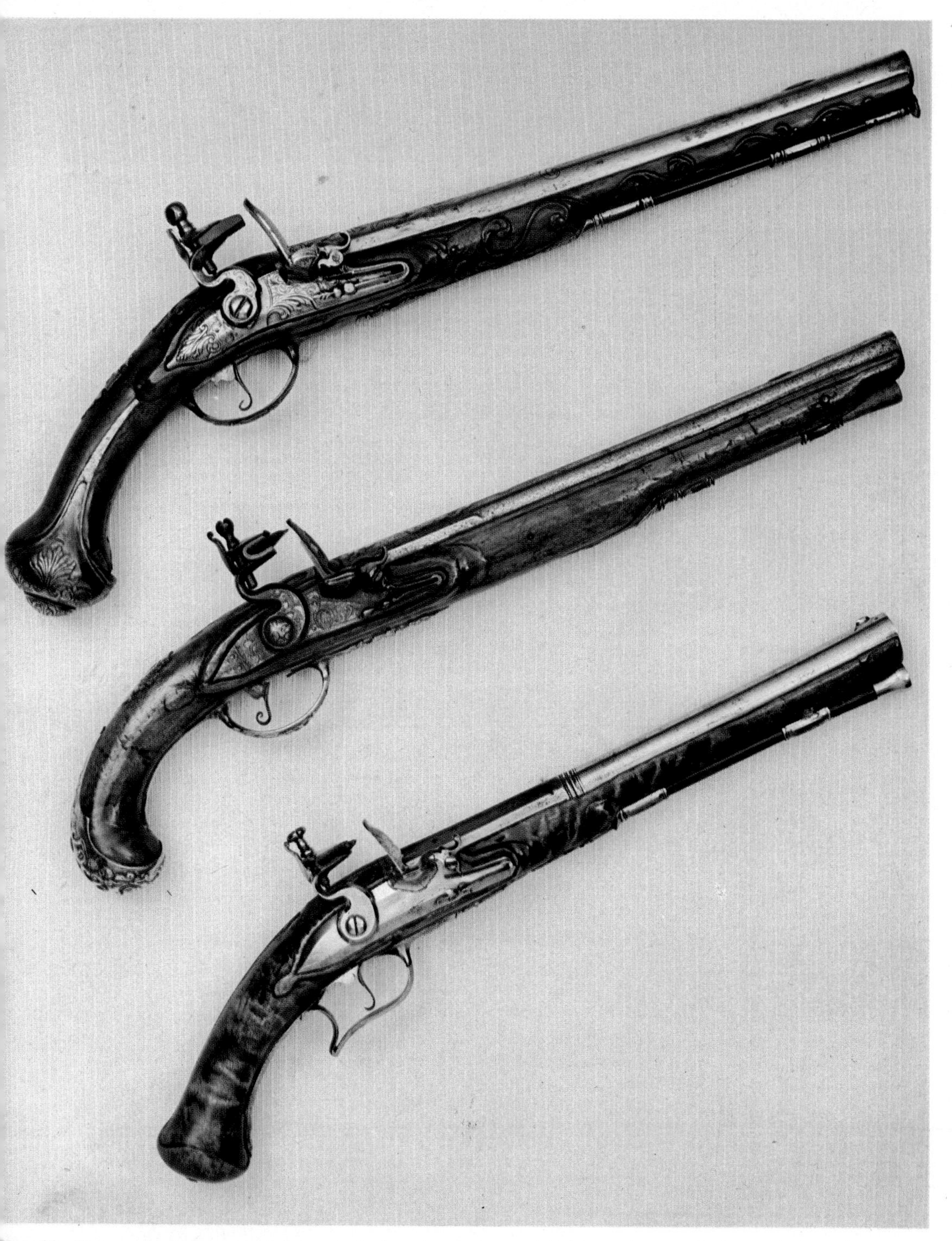

'late 22 *Three early 18th century holster pistols from* (top to bottom) *Belgium, Austria and Spain; the latter has a ger-wood stock*. (*Gyngell Collection.*)

Plate 23 *Algerian flintlock bound with silver wire and applied silver and coral decoration. The ramrod is only simulated and there is an Arabic inscription inlaid in silver wire. Overall length 17 inches, barrel 10¾ inches, bore ·57 inch. (Michael German.)*

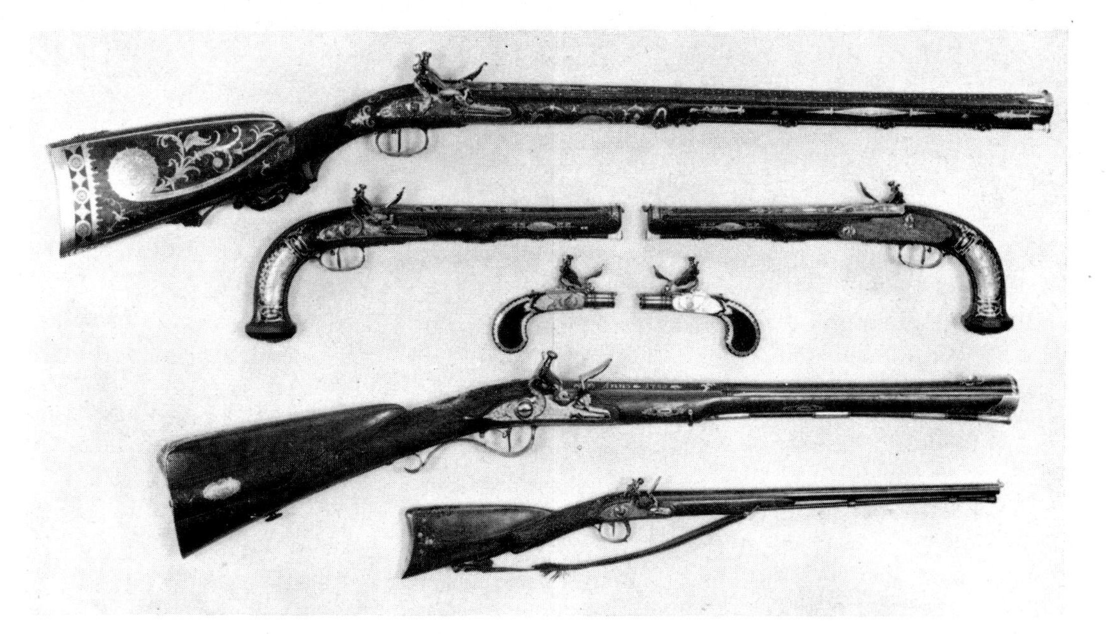

Fig. 131: (Top to bottom) *Another view of the Boutet rifle illustrated in the centre of Fig. 130. A pair of flintlock pistols by Boutet*, circa *1810; the butts are inlaid with ebony and gold and the mounts are of chiselled silver. A pair of ebony-stocked pocket pistols by Boutet*, circa *1810. A blunderbuss made in St. Petersburg (Leningrad) by the Swedish gunsmith Johan Crecke, the blued and damascened barrel dated 1780. An unusual miniature flintlock gun; overall length, 25¾ inches; barrel, 15⅜ inches. (Wallace Collection.)*

reputation for the high quality of a special product—thus the Spaniards were highly regarded for the strength and quality of their barrels and in many cases these were imported by sportsmen and then fitted to a stock of their own choice. The appearance of a Spanish barrel on a firearm does not necessarily mean that the weapon as a whole is Spanish in origin.

In a few cases it is possible to be specific, for some weapons were produced only in certain areas. Unfortunately such weapons are almost invariably rare and quite beyond the wildest dreams of the average collector. The *Tschinke*, a very light sporting wheellock gun, was produced only in a limited area of Bohemia; therefore one is quite justified in attributing examples of these guns to that particular area. However, the number of *Tschinke* that appear in the antique shops at reasonable prices is, to put it mildly, very limited indeed.

Fortunately, many of the towns which became centres for arms production proved and marked their wares; this had been common practice with armour and swords and the marks have always been most useful for purposes of identification. May those bearing the Liège mark be designated with confidence as Belgian? Alas no! Centres such as Liège manufactured barrels and components to order, and although a barrel may bear the Liège mark it could well be that it was fitted to a British military musket—it is known that numbers of barrels were ordered from Liège during the late 18th century. Further confusion is compounded during this period by the distribution of captured material, and the British records include many references to the allocation of French,

Dutch and Russian weapons to certain groups of volunteers during the Napoleonic Wars.

Despite these cautionary remarks it should not be thought that antique firearms cannot be identified with any degree of certainty. With a knowledge of the history of firearms and of some of the main centres of production it is possible to make a reasoned assumption as to the place or origin.

Although it does not appear that France was one of the first countries to undertake the bulk manufacture of firearms her gunmakers can be described as having dominated, to a great degree, trends in the firearms world from the second half of the 17th century until the end of the 18th century. French firearms production began during the 17th century at places such as Charleville and St. Etienne and especially in Paris. Certainly the gunmakers received every encouragement from the Monarchy, and Louis XIII (1610-42) acquired a superb collection of firearms known as the *Cabinet d'Armes*. The collection remained intact until the Revolution, but during this disturbed period some items were lost; and after Waterloo the English and Prussians extracted some of the weapons, claiming them as legitimate booty of war, and these may still be seen in some of the national museums. It is possible to identify these items, for an inventory of the collection was made at an early date. In the Palace of the Louvre a row, or Grand Gallery, was set up and rooms in this were allocated to various craftsmen; some of the well known names in the history of French firearms had their *logement* here. This meant that they were, in fact, under the care and protection of the king and were supplied with free lodgings. This centre was no doubt reponsible for many of the fashions current in French firearms at one time or another.

One peculiarity found in the construction of French wheellocks was in the method

Fig. 132: (Top) *Ornate flintlock holster pistol made in Paris in about 1720; the round barrel is chiselled at the breech and the walnut stock is inlaid with silver wire. The lock is inscribed* CHASTEAU Á PARIS. (Bottom) *Flintlock pistol probably made for Louis, Dauphin of France (1729-65) by La Roche of Paris,* circa *1740/1745. The lock is chiselled and the stock inlaid.* (*Wallace Collection.*)

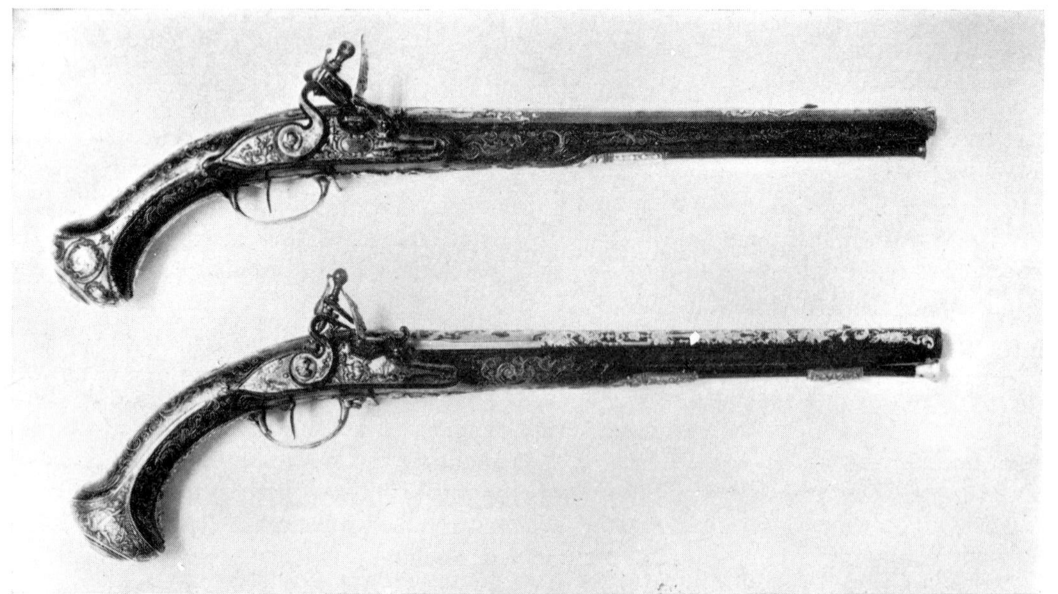

Figs. 133 and **(foot of page)** *134: Barrel and lock details of a Spanish 12-bore gun made in Madrid by Gaspar Fernandez and dated 1699. The maker's* poinçon *in gold is set at the breech and the touchhole is gold lined. The intriguing legend on the barrel reads:* GASPAR FER.-ZNANDz - PARA EL SENOR DONIVAN - EN MADRID 1699. (*Dominion Museum, New Zealand.*)

of securing the mainspring; unlike those made elsewhere it was separate, being housed with the wheel spindle in the stock. The French stock of the 16th and 17th centuries was very sharply curved and swept down in a fashion reminiscent of a hockey stick; weapons fitted with this stock were fired not from the shoulder but from the chest. In view of the inconvenience that would have been caused by a heavy recoil in this situation, most early French weapons fitted with this type of stock were quite light weapons. French wheellock pistols tended to be rather long and slim with heart-shaped pommels, usually ornamented with metal inlay—iron, brass and pewter wire was commonly used, while the wood was usually walnut.

French firearms were far more lavishly decorated than their British equivalents which tended to be very restrained. The French were frankly flamboyant—gold, silver, inlay, blueing, gilding and chiselling were all used freely. They also made

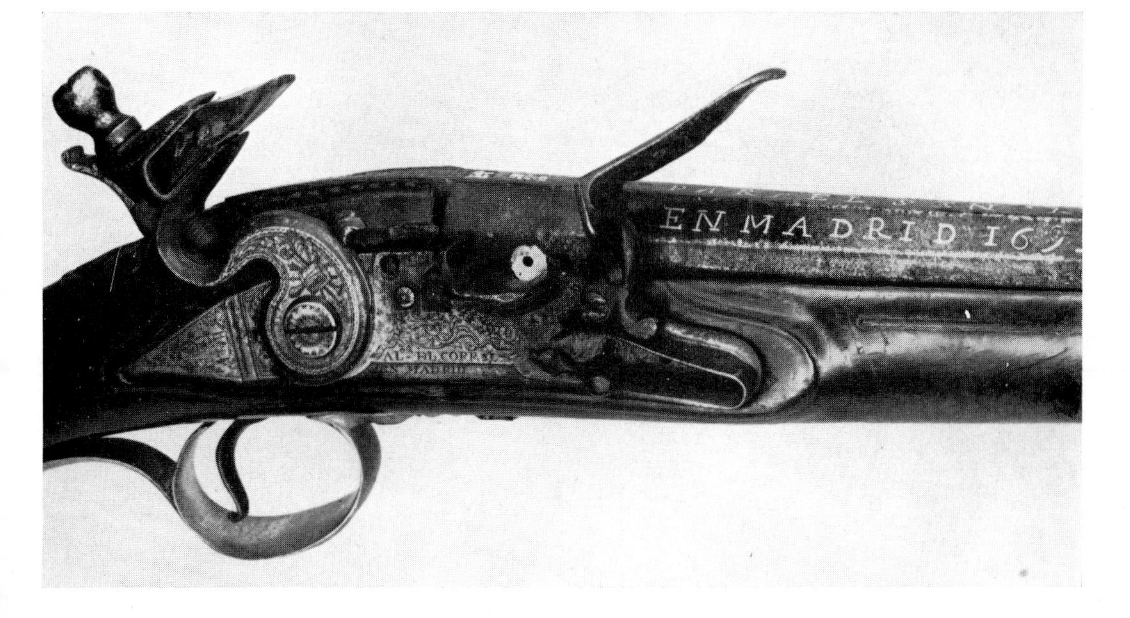

frequent use of carving, and one feature which so often marks the French long arm is the carving on the lower part of the stock just behind the trigger guard. The carving is frequently fashioned into an animal's head and the form is designed to afford a pistol grip as an aid to careful aiming. This is a feature seldom found on British arms.

French styles began to exert a stronger influence in English decoration after 1685, for in this year the Edict of Nantes, which granted religious freedom to the Huguenots, was revoked and large numbers of these French Protestants left France and settled in London. Many were skilled craftsmen, particularly in the art of silver decoration, and many English firearms of this period exhibit strong French influence suggesting that they were indeed made by Huguenot silversmiths. This is a classic example of the way in which extraneous events affected national characteristics in firearms.

A feature which often marked the French barrel was the division into three

Fig. 135: (Top to bottom) *One of a pair of Italian flintlock pistols made in Brescia late in the 17th century and inscribed* Lippus Spinodus Fecit; *the brass butt is chased with intricate scrollwork. A three-barrelled flintlock pistol, the lock signed* LORENZONI*; it bears the arms of Cosimo de Medici, Grand Duke of Tuscany 1670-1723. A mid-18th century Italian fowling piece, the lock signed* GALVARINO*; the whole weapon is decorated with silver and gilt.* (*Victoria and Albert Museum.*)

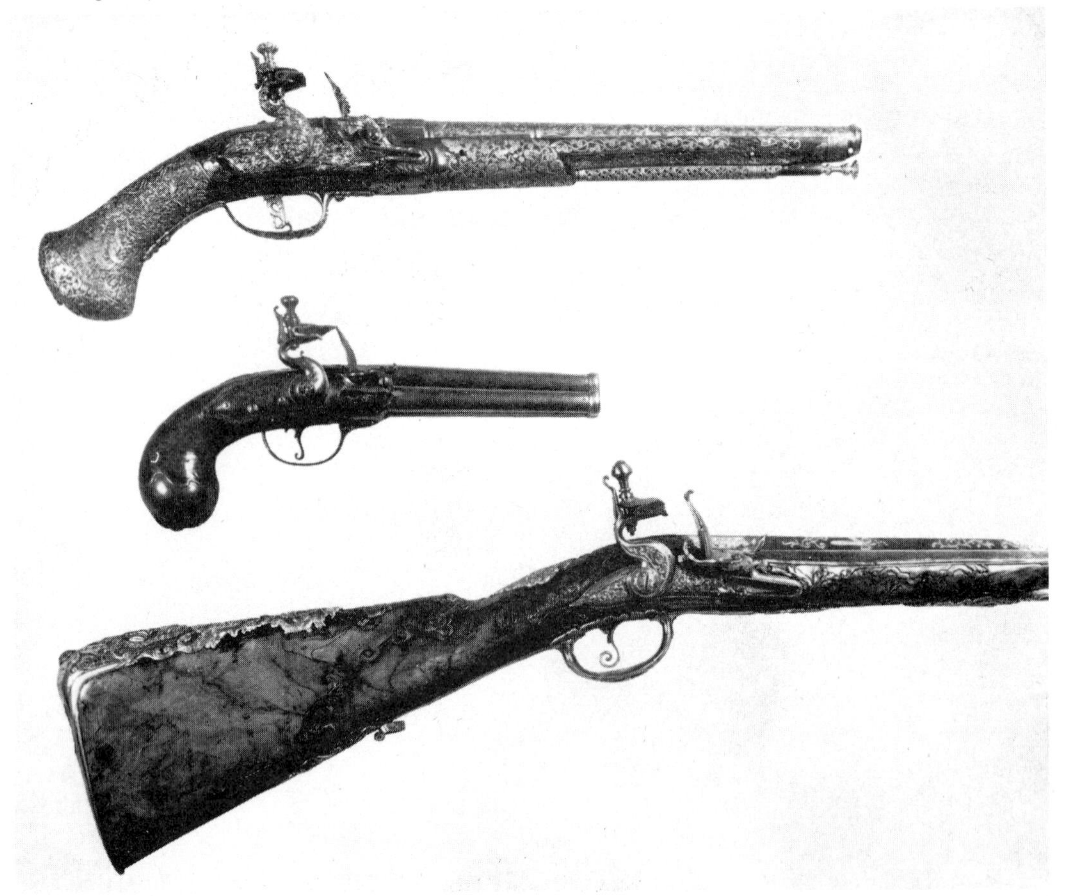

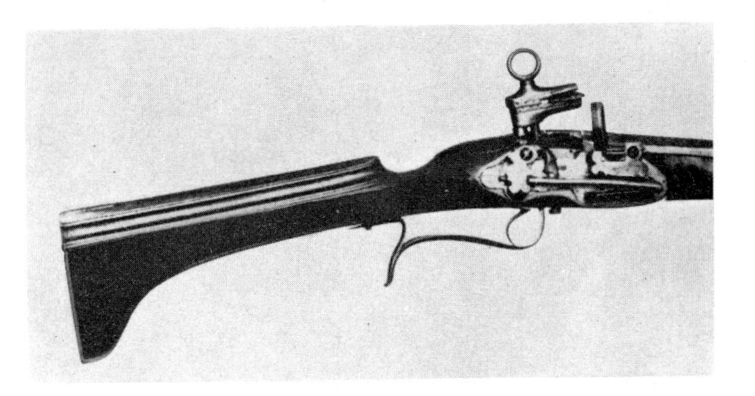

Fig. 136: Butt of a Spanish gun showing the typical down-projecting toe; the lock is of the miguelet type, with the top jaw screw terminating in a ring. Circa *1750. (Bennett Collection.)*

clear sections—at the breech it was normally octagonal; then came a small rounded baluster, with the next section frequently fashioned with sixteen sides; and the rest of the barrel was usually rounded. French barrels were frequently much thinner than those on English pistols and in order to give a little extra strength at the muzzle there was often a small round baluster or ridge. As the 18th century progressed gunmakers tended to reduce barrel length and by the second quarter of the 18th century they are usually fairly short—six to twelve inches was usual. One of the reasons for this change was the improvement in the quality of gunpowder. Early gunpowder was generally rather impure and the ingredients were of poor quality, making it slow burning. In order to obtain the maximum force from the explosion it was important for the ball to remain in the barrel for the maximum possible time—hence the long, smallbore barrels of the 16th and 17th centuries. Improved methods of manufacture in the 18th century made the gunpowder much quicker burning; greater force was built up in a shorter time and the length of barrel could be reduced without affecting the total energy from the explosion.

French barrel makers differed from the English in that although they made barrels using the twisted metal technique they did not treat the surface in such a way as to make this twist apparent. In order to indicate that the barrel was of good quality (for this twisting and folding gave the metal greater strength) they were frequently marked with the words "*Canon Tordu*" in gold along the top of the barrel. French barrels were often decorated by blueing and gilding and frequently the name and address of the maker is also damascened along the top of the barrel.

During the Napoleonic wars it was a custom of the French authorities to present "*Fusils d'Honneur*" to members of the army for outstanding deeds of bravery. These were military muskets; even for enlisted soldiers they were specially decorated and the officers' presentation weapons were even more elaborate. Such weapons were made at the Royal Manufactory of Versailles and were frequently the work of Nicolas—Noel Boutet, who was appointed as the Technical Director of Versailles in 1792. In 1800 he was given an 18-year concession at Versailles and one of the conditions of service was that he should train artists. After Waterloo, the manufactory at Versailles, like Louis' *Cabinet d'Armes*, was ransacked by the Prussians and many of the contents were sent to Berlin. Boutet set up a private business in Paris, where he died in 1833. Boutet's work was of a very high standard and his items are particularly decorative and pleasing and his teaching was to have great influence on the French style. Boutet is also credited with the re-introduction of rifling to France, although he favoured what is known as a micro-rifling. In this system instead of a small number of fairly broad

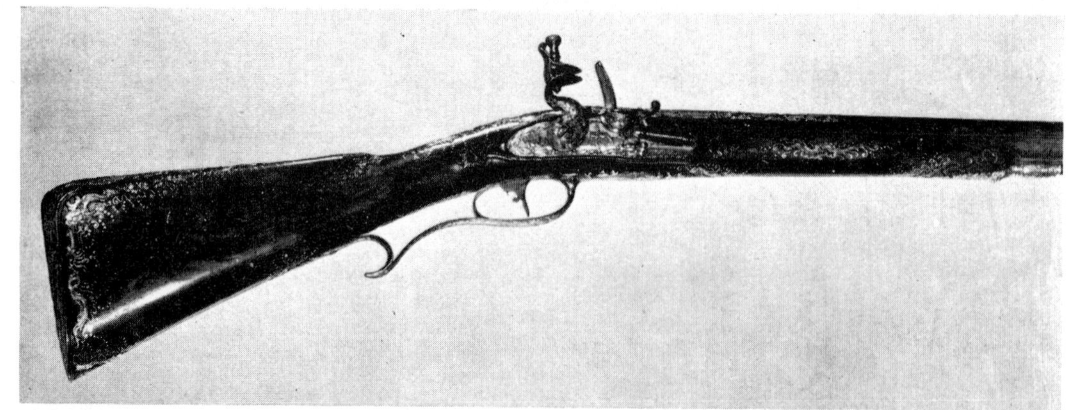

Fig. 137: A fowling piece, the barrel and mounts decorated with gilt and chiselling; this weapon is the work of J. N. Stockmar, for many years Court Gunmaker to the Electors of Saxony. (Victoria and Albert Museum.)

grooves he used a large number of very fine grooves.

Another famous name in the French gunmaking world was that of Le-Page of Paris—possibly best known for his duelling sets and high quality pistols. He also has the unusual claim to fame of being responsible for what must be the latest known pair of wheellocks, for he produced a pair which are dated 1829. Quite apart from a name on the inside of a lid, it is possible to distinguish French cased sets by the style used. Casing in Britain was usually done simply by dividing the inside into a series of compartments by straight wooden fences. Continental makers favoured contoured compartments to hold the various accessories and in contrast to the green baize favoured by the British they used a silky material to line the cases.

Another big centre of arms production besides Paris and Versailles was Charleville on the River Meuse. Workers from Liège founded armouries there as far back as the 17th century. Like Charleville, Saint Etienne was an arsenal producing military firearms in quantity from the 17th century and both centres supplied large numbers of weapons during the Napoleonic Wars.

Obviously there were variations of detail in French firearms, but there were some features which are common enough to be taken as characteristics. Most non-military firearms of the late 18th century and early 19th century had the end of the butt cut square and slightly flared to give a disc-like termination—a fashion found on some British duelling pistols and percussion revolvers but seldom on conventional flintlock pistols. French military pistols had a curved, round-ended butt fitted with a cap which lacked any side spurs but had an upwards extension which joined with a metal strip extending the full length of the butt. Another feature found on many French firearms was the style of trigger guard in which that portion situated in front of the trigger was pillar-like and round in section, while the rest was flat and much wider.

The French, in common with many Continental countries, adopted quite early in the 18th century the system of securing the barrel to the stock by using bands—a trend which the British did not follow until the mid-19th century. The bands slipped over the barrel and stock and were held in place by spring-operated plates set in the stock; and there was often a larger nose band at the muzzle. This system was far simpler than that favoured by British makers, which required lugs to be brazed beneath the barrel and the stock to be pierced by pins which engaged with the lugs. Most

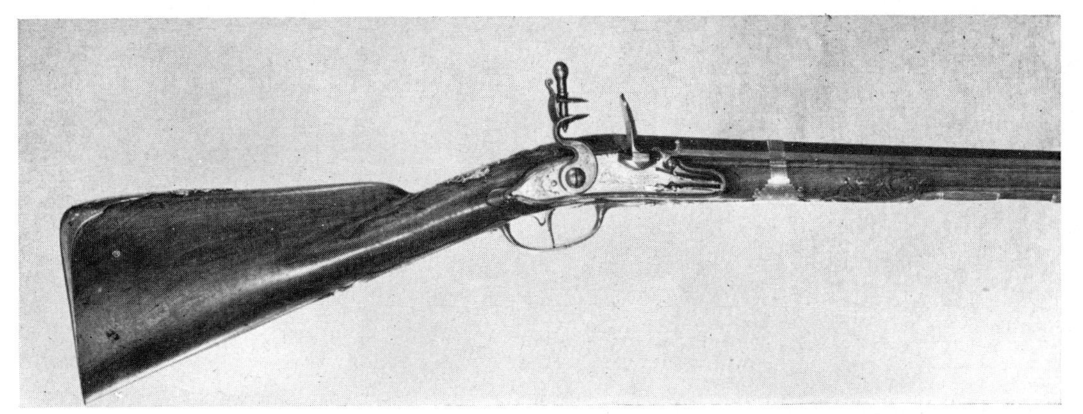

Fig. 138: A Saxon fowling piece, plainer than that illustrated in Fig. 137; it bears the Arms of Saxony and the inscription TANNER A GOTHA 1724. *(Victoria and Albert Museum.)*

French flintlock firearms of the 18th and 19th centuries were fitted with ring neck cocks, a design which was much stronger although less graceful than the swan neck type; again, this style was taken up later by the British.

French military firearms usually had the place of manufacture inscribed on the lockplate or barrel and many also bore the date. The year of introduction is used to designate the type of firearm—thus the Model 1763 pistol or the Fusil Model 1777.

France was, from the beginning, a very progressive and adventurous nation in the field of firearms production, frequently changing styles and introducing new ideas. Her influence was felt in many other countries including the U.S.A. and Spain.

MADRID was made the capital of Spain in 1561 and it soon became one of the main centres of Spanish firearms production. In contrast to the later fashion, the earliest wheellocks produced in Madrid were extremely simple with restrained decoration. Barrels became a feature of the Spanish makers, and were usually octagonal at the breech, becoming round for the rest of their length. Stocks were generally of cherry, pear or walnut.

Another great centre of production was at Ripoll in Catalonia; the pistols made here were all very similar in character remaining basically unchanged throughout the centuries. Normally they had a small ball pommel on the end of the butt and the stocks were frequently covered with steel or brass plates. Barrels, locks, furniture and stock were often carved with volutes. The short, rather stocky barrel was pinned to the stock and the barrel tang was secured by a screw which was an integral part of the trigger guard. A small spur was formed by an S-shaped sweep of the guard. The majority of the Ripoll pistols, indeed most Spanish pistols, were fitted with belt hooks.

Spanish gunmakers were using gold to line their touchholes as early as the 1640's, a fashion not taken up by most gunmakers until much later. Gold was naturally a popular decorative material with the makers; in the early 18th century there was an increase in French styling among the Madrid gunmakers, and many copied the French fashion of producing blued barrels embellished with gold inlay. Madrid makers claimed to do what few others could compass—to produce a complete weapon, making their own stock, lock and barrel without calling on outside help. From the end of the 17th century it became the usual thing for the maker to impress his mark, or *poinçon*, into

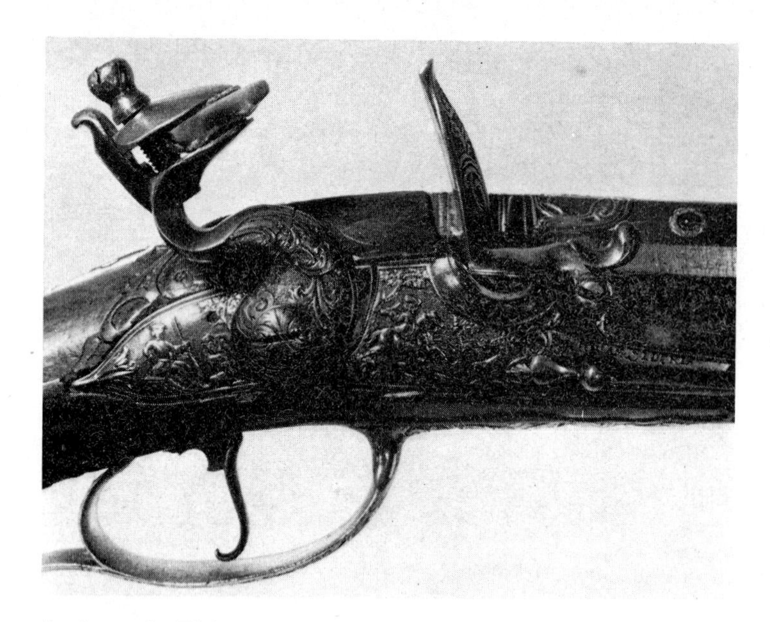

Left and right, *Figs. 139 and 140: A superb fowling piece of about 1730, the chiselled lock* (left) *signed by the Neustat maker Johan Stockl; the Turkish barrel* (right) *is also decorated with chiselling.* (*Bubear Collection.*)

the barrel. This was usually in the form of a crown surmounting a rectangle enclosing his name, the whole inlaid in gold. Occasionally this mark was also placed on the steel.

For the collector the most noticeable feature of the Spanish pistol is the miguelet lock, which remained in use for two centuries, largely unchanged in detail. Its jaws were oblong and the cock had a rather squat appearance, but its most characteristic feature is the external mainspring bearing directly on the cock. There was, however, a lock which was more or less peculiar to Madrid and its environs and which was superficially very like the usual French flintlock but was, in fact, a variety of the miguelet with sears which operated through the lockplate engaging with projections on the cock.

Spanish long arms were usually fitted with a relatively simple stock which was either fluted or had a long downward toe to the butt, giving it an L-shape.

At various times Spain ruled parts of Italy and Spanish influence is apparent in some Italian firearms, although the earlier history of gunmaking in Italy shows the distinctive native qualities of the region. Italian wheellocks of the 16th century all had a fairly short butt curved downwards acutely and with a very high comb. With muskets the lockplate was usually extremely large, while the dog was very angular and gave a square look to the lock. The Germans preferred to inlay their wheellock stocks with horn but the Italians much preferred metal, using silver gilt, bronze, or more commonly, iron. It is interesting to note that while the Germans maintained the wheellock long after the rest of Europe had abandoned it, the Italians tended to extend the life of the snaphaunce. In the north, especially around Brescia, there developed a group of steel chisellers whose work was of outstandingly high quality. Cut steel inlay was used on the stock and the lock and all the mounts on the pistol were often chiselled overall with designs of scroll work, animals, birds and monsters. This style flourished particularly at the end of the 17th century and it was in this same area that the production of the snaphaunce lock was continued until well into the 18th century.

Brescia, like Spain, was also noted for the quality of its barrels, especially those from Gardone; and best quality examples carried the name Lazarino Cominazzo. These barrels soon achieved a very high reputation for quality and other barrelsmiths began

stamping the Cominazzo signature on their own barrels; many of these spurious Cominazzo barrels were produced and fitted to pistols. The true Cominazzo barrel had a very small bore, only about half an inch, and the barrel had three distinct surfaces. The breech was octagonal and filed with longitudinal grooves while that section nearest the muzzle was circular or polygonal. The authentic pieces also had little shamrock or trefoil punch marks, arranged in groups of three. One group was applied at the beginning of the signature and another at the end, with two more separating the Christian and surname. Almost invariably the Cominazzo barrel is smooth bored. The Cominazzo family had a long association with Gardone and it is reported that the family was still represented there in 1843—an unbroken tradition of three centuries.

Despite the very high standards of the Brescian craftsmen their work was limited and they seemed disinclined to progress or develop their techniques and consequently, during the early part of the 18th century, the area declined in importance.

GERMANY was another country which pioneered the firearms industry only to suffer later eclipse. Augsburg, with its long tradition of high quality arms and armour, became one of the prime centres of arms production in Germany. Wheellocks made there had lockplates which were narrow and rather long and the arm of the dog's head tended to be rather straight. Early German wheellocks had very little ornamentation, but from the middle of the 16th century there was an increase in its use, barrel and lockplates being etched or gilded or sometimes damascened with precious metals. The stocks of German wheellock long arms were usually rather straight, with a cheek stock. During the early part of the 16th century the top and bottom edges of the German cheek stock are parallel, but at the end of the century the lower end of the cheek piece was extended below the angle of the butt.

German wheellock pistols of the mid-16th century were of two main types—one with a more or less straight butt and a small pommel, the other with a large ball butt which sloped down abrubtly from the breech; this latter type was primarily a horseman's weapon. German firearms were frequently decorated with inlay or marquetry of wood and ivory and the gunmakers also produced numbers of all-metal wheellock pistols. Cutting away the stock to accommodate the lock tended to weaken it considerably and an all-metal construction was one way of avoiding this problem. Augsburg also became noted for its use of ebony in stocks, while the workshop at Munich became famous for chiselled and gilded barrels and lockplates. A feature in which these smiths differed from others in this field was that they gilded the ground and left the chiselled section plain, whereas most gilders decorated the chiselling and left the background plain.

Left, *Fig. 141: The chiselled lock of a late 17th century flintlock pistol; the lock is signed* Diomede Barent, *the barrel* Lazarino Cominazzo. (*Gyngell Collection.*)

Although the wheellock mechanism in pistol and fowling pieces was largely abandoned by the middle of the 17th century, its use was continued in hunting rifles and target rifles for another 50 years and this type of weapon was still being made in Germany during the last half of the 18th century. Production continued even longer in Austria and Bohemia. When the wheellock was finally abandoned Germany and Austria ceased to play such an important part in the development of firearms. Their gunmakers seem to have been so preoccupied with the wheellock that they rather lost touch with the latest developments in the technical fields and as demand for the wheellock diminished so did their influence.

There were a few makers who were less conservative and who continued to flourish; among these, members of the Kuchenreuter family maintained their reputation for quality pieces—their barrels were particularly valued. The family worked in the small town of Regensburg and produced pistols which were the result of a combined effort by several members of the family. Fittings were normally of gilt brass and most stocks were quite plain, although some of the grips were chequered; the barrels were blued, with the name inlaid in silver letters along the top. Butts tended to be flat-sided and many of the pistols will be found to be rifled.

Traditionally it was an Austrian, Gaspard Kollner of Vienna, who invented rifling. The Emperor Maximilian was one of the first of Europe's monarchs to show a keen interest in firearms and his Imperial Armoury held racks of weapons, some of which have survived. Vienna seems to have been the main centre of arms production in Austria and there was a gunmakers' guild in existence there in the 17th century. Some of the Austrian gunmakers were equal to any in Europe. La Marre of Vienna was one of the leading exponents of the art of steel chiselling in the late 17th century; and examples of Viennese breech loading flintlocks of the middle of the 17th century still exist.

One feature of 17th century Austrian weapons was the use of some of the Turkish barrels captured after the siege of Vienna in 1683. It is said that the demand in Europe for barrels using the "twist" method of construction can be traced back to the fact that this effect was noticed on some of the Turkish barrels used by the Austrians.

One of the most unusual types of firearm to come from Austria was the range of

Fig. 142: One of a pair of flintlock holster pistols by Hans Keiner of Eger, Bohemia. The rifled barrel is covered with chiselled scrolls and the lock is engraved. (Victoria and Albert Museum.)

cutlery produced in the early part of the 18th century—knives, forks and spoons fitted with small flintlock pistols. Most of the few surviving examples were made by a certain Franz Richter, and one or two bear the name of Reichenberg in Bavaria.

The Austrian army have a very good record for initiative in trying new types of firearms and in the 1770's the army was experimenting with a breech-loading system. This was designed by Giuseppe Crespi of Milan; the rear portion of the barrel was pivoted and tipped up to allow a paper cartridge to be loaded directly into the breech. The Austrian army used them between 1770 and 1779 but seems to have abandoned them largely because of the very severe gas leakage that occurred. They were also active in the use of airguns and late in the 18th century a unit of airgun marksmen fought in the Low Countries; but difficulties in servicing the airguns caused their withdrawal in 1815 (see *Chapter* 8).

Further to the East the chief centre of arms production was the town of Tula in central Russia; in 1705 a factory was set up there by Peter the Great, who was most anxious to bring Western ideas and mechanical techniques into his backward country. He persuaded or bullied craftsmen from Germany, Sweden and Denmark to settle in Tula and a large number of weapons made there are dated from 1720 onwards. Prior to the setting up of the Tula factories the Russians had largely followed the current French type of flintlock; but when Tula flourished under Catherine the Great it followed closely the designs of the early 18th century Parisian maker Nicholas Guérard, and tended to use rather lavish ornamentation. One of the fashions that was perpetuated in Tula was the encrusting of guns with gold decoration—a technique that differed from damascening in that the gold ornamentation was made in relief and was then keyed to the metal of the lock or barrel.

Armouries in the Kremlin at Moscow produced many weapons and again the tendency was for rather lavish ornamentation. Although it is by no means a standard feature, many Russian pistols are fitted with bird's head butts which curve round and terminate in a rather sharp point.

Apart from the so-called Cossack pistols Russian weapons are quite scarce. The Cossack pistol was usually fitted with a small miguelet type lock and may be recognised by the large ball terminal to the butt. Later Russian firearms were often based on Western types, and the government ordered a number of Beaumont Adams percussion revolvers from England. (See also *Chapter* 10).

Outside Europe continental firearms are rather neglected by collectors, emphasis not unnaturally being placed on the products of British and American makers. However, they are generally very decorative and of a very high standard of workmanship—features which recommend them to the discerning collector.

12

Revolvers

THE most significant limitation of early firearms was, obviously, the fact that once fired they ceased to be a useful weapon, and became a positive encumbrance for the length of time required to reload them. This was an entirely new problem in the history of weapons, practically speaking, with the single exception of the cross-bow. All other projectile weapons were quick and easy to reload; indeed, the English long bow in the hands of an experienced archer was capable of a rate of accurate fire which put all early firearms to shame. All the innumerable varieties of edged weapons used by mankind since the dawn of history could be wielded continuously until they actually broke in pieces.

Once the basic principles of the firearm had been mastered, it may fairly be said that the technical efforts of the designer broke down into just two parallel endeavours; the need to improve the speed and reliability of the firing mechanism, and the need to

Fig. 143: (Top) *A Collier flintlock revolver with side cock and hatched wooden butt.* (Bottom) *Collier five-chamber flintlock revolver with variant butt. Both models date from about 1820 and have automatic priming pans.* (*Tower of London.*)

eliminate or circumvent that period of time after its use when the firearm was of no more value to its owner than a rather clumsy club. It was this second need which produced such partial solutions as multibarrel weapons, uncontrolled multi-shot weapons such as the "Roman Candle" gun, and all the many examples of combination of a firearm and an edged weapon. The first genuinely practical answer to the problem was provided by the revolver.

The value of multibarrel weapons was severely restricted; four barrels were the highest practical number, and the construction of these weapons during the days of the wheellock and flintlock systems involved serious mechanical difficulties. Some of these weapons, which were usually pistols, provide the earliest examples of "revolvers" in the strictest sense of the term; they comprised a number of barrels which could be rotated by hand around a central axis. Within this strict definition there were even matchlock revolvers—the "holy water sprinklers" of Henry VIII's day (see *Chapter* 8) comprised four matchlock barrels mounted inside a club; after each shot the shaft was turned to bring the next barrel into position. However, the earliest surviving revolver in the more generally accepted meaning of the term is preserved in the Ducal Palace at Venice, and dates from about 1540. It is a matchlock with a short, unadorned wooden butt and three barrels which are secured to a hand-

Fig. 144: Percussion pepperbox of the Allen type, six-chambered and with a bar hammer; note the nipple guard. There is a small recess in the base of the butt to hold caps. (Dominion Museum of New Zealand.)

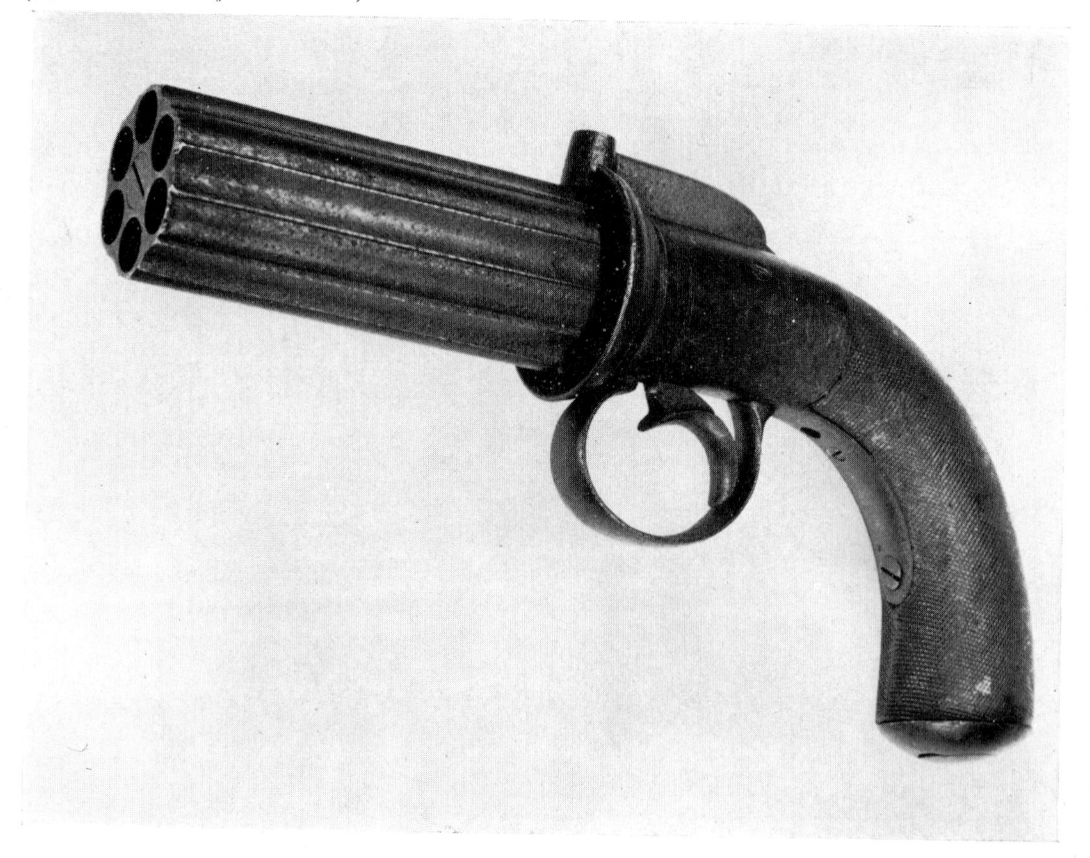

rotatable plate. Each barrel is fitted with its own priming pan and cover, and the barrel assembly is held in position by a spring catch which may be released by a small trigger. A three-barrelled German wheellock which once belonged to the Emperor Charles V dates from about the same period. Of all-steel construction and covered with gilding, it is unusual in a number of respects; not only does it have a safety catch and a double dog's head, but the hand-rotated barrels are designed to fire steel darts instead of the more conventional balls.

There do not appear to be any surviving examples of pistols with rotating barrels made between the mid-16th and mid-17th centuries. Since it does not seem likely that every single example has been lost, it may be assumed that they were not regarded very highly and were presumably thought unworthy of widespread development.

In the middle years of the 17th century the French, who were at that time among the foremost pioneers of firearm design, began producing a number of "over and under" pistols, each of the two barrels being fitted with its own separate pan and steel. The cock and lock were fitted into the butt section, and, obviously, the weapon had to be recocked after each shot. Curiously enough the idea does not seem to have been developed to include more than two barrels except in one or two rare cases. The principle was taken up in Holland and Germany, and a number of the pistols made in these countries still survive.

There were always a few gunmakers who were prepared to experiment, and one such man was a German, Johan Gottfried Kolbe. A pair of pistols in H.M. The Queen's collection at Windsor Castle, made by Kolbe in about 1730, have five turn-off barrels fitted to each breech block; the outstanding feature, however, is that as the cock is pulled back the barrel block is automatically rotated to bring the next barrel into the firing position—one of the most significant characteristics of percussion revolvers of the 19th century.

It was not until the late 18th and early 19th centuries that flintlock revolvers were produced in Britain in any quantity. They usually had seven barrels, each primed and loaded separately, although a few were fitted with self-priming devices. The barrel assembly was rotated by hand. To observers of the period the end view of the cluster of barrels suggested a large pepper pot or pepper box—and these popular names have been applied to this type of pistol ever since.

With the appearance of the percussion cap and the important simplification of construction which resulted from this advance, the pepperbox became quite common; and one big difference in the construction of flintlock and percussion pepperboxes lay in the method of making the barrel blocks. Almost invariably the flintlock examples had each of the barrels made separately and then screwed to a central breech block; but in percussion weapons the barrels were drilled into a single block of metal. The usual number of barrels, or chambers as they might now be called, was six, and less commonly five. The percussion pepperbox apparently made its debut during the 1830's; although examples vary widely in details of construction, the majority of early pieces are hand-rotated and have the nipples facing outwards from the axis. The first recorded patent taken out with the United States Government for such weapons appears to be that of Benjamin and Barton Darling, granted in 1836.

The Darling pepperbox consisted of a group of four or six barrels around a central pivot; the nipples projected laterally from each barrel, each being struck in turn by a large conventional percussion hammer mounted centrally in the style of a box lock. The special importance of the Darling patent lies in the fact that it was for a self-rotating

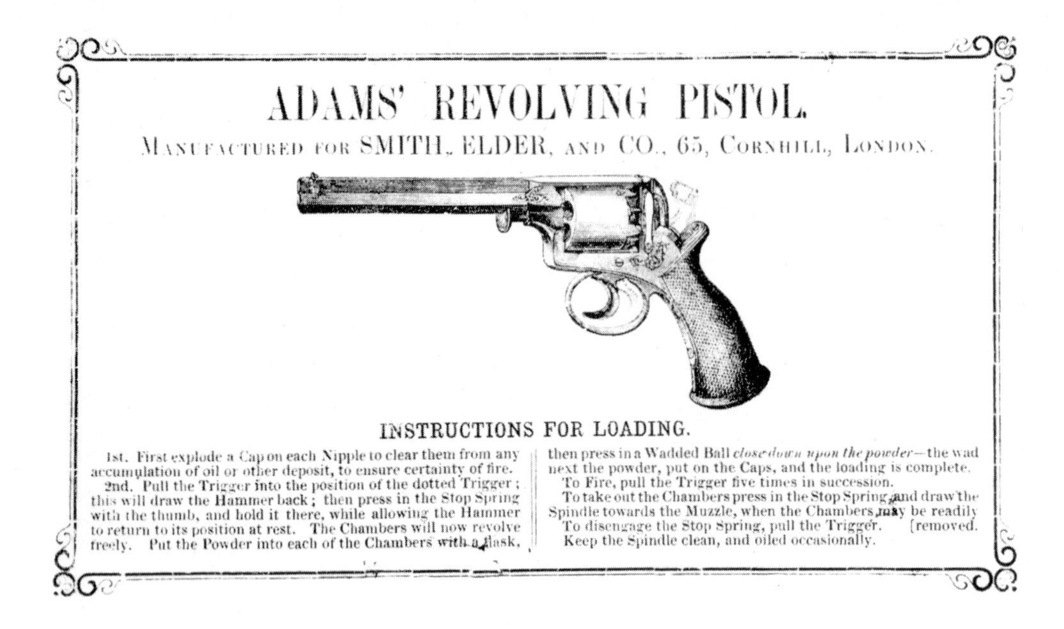

Fig. 145: Trade label from the lid of an Adams revolver case. Sometimes these labels merely carried an advertisement for the maker, but others, like the example illustrated, included instructions on the care and use of the weapon.

device; as the hammer was cocked, so the cylinder was rotated to bring the next chamber into the firing position. Some of the early Darlings have no nipple shield; this was a fold-over rim at the front of the breech block which covered the nipples except for a small gap where the hammer could strike through. This simple device prevented the caps shattering or splintering on detonation, and possibly injuring the user. The butts were of plain wood, and were usually round in section. Apart from a few Swedish examples most of the Darling pepperboxes were made in the United States.

Mention must be made here of a unique type of English pepperbox made by a small manufacturer named Budding; a weapon far in advance of its time. There was no external hammer; the mechanism was completely enclosed and firing was achieved by a hammer which moved backwards and forwards. Very few examples of the Budding pepperbox have been recorded.

An interesting variation on the pepperbox principle was that in which the barrels were fixed and the nose of the hammer was rotated. The nipples of the barrels, either four or six, were arranged in a small circular group on top of the breech block. The tip of the hammer was fitted with a plate which had one downwards projecting nose, as fitted to a conventional percussion hammer. This plate could be turned until the hammer section was in the appropriate position to fire any one of the chambers. The idea was practical, but one cannot help but feel that in the heat of action it must have been fatally easy to misjudge the degree of turn.

The American and English pepperbox market continued to employ the box lock type of hammer mounted centrally in the breech, although a few were made with the hammer fitted at the side. Convenient though the pepperbox was, the hammer sitting high on the breech was a hindrance; in the pocket or holster it was awkward and

Plate 24 (Top to bottom) *Double action five-chamber percussion revolver by G. R. Daws*, circa *1855; barrel length, 5½ inches. A Webley-Bentley percussion revolver with Kerr rammer. A five-chamber English transition revolver with bar hammer.*

Plate 25 (Top to bottom) *Deane Adams double action percussion revolver with Kerr rammer*, circa *1851. Tranter double trigger percussion revolver* (*third model*), circa *1860. Adams self-cocking percussion revolver; this example has had the barrel shortened and is fitted with the so-called Rigby rammer.*

clumsy, and all too liable to catch at the worst possible moment. It is to Mr. Ethan Allen, a Massachussets gunmaker, that the credit for a solution must be given; for in 1837 this maker took out an American patent for a self-cocking pepperbox. In fact, both the principles incorporated in this patent had been in use before, but Allen combined them and produced a weapon which in time became the norm. The barrels or chambers were drilled from a solid block of metal and arranged concentrically around the axis. In place of the large hammer which had to be cocked each time the weapon was fired, Allen substituted a flat bar which terminated in a small, thick disc. This bar lay flat along the top of the weapon, and pressure on the trigger caused it to rise, simultaneously rotating the barrels. Continued trigger pressure allowed the bar hammer to fall and strike the nipple, discharging one chamber. When the trigger was released to its original position and pressed again, the action was repeated. In fact, this weapon was what we would now understand as a true self-cocking revolver. Barrel blocks were usually fairly substantial, firing a .4 or .5 inch ball, and the butts were gently curved with a rounded end. Allen went into partnership with a man named Thurber, and later with a certain Mr. Wheelock; and he continued to produce pepperboxes until the mid-1860's.

Although the pepperbox remained basically unchanged from the 1840's to the 1860's there were some minor variations. Some were supplied with a dagger which fitted to the centre of the cylinder block. Many pepperboxes were carried in holsters, and they were one of the first types of firearm to be carried in a personal holster as opposed to a saddle holster. In general, the later British models all have butts which are cut square at the bottom. The wood is normally cross-hatched, and the screw securing the two side grips is set in a diamond-shaped metal retainer. A few will be found to have butt caps, and these seem to have been made mostly by Samuel Nock, of London. Early examples of British-made pepperboxes retain the American style of butt, gracefully rounded and usually plain. On the Continent large numbers were

Fig. 146: Adams self-cocking revolver, with the full length $7\frac{5}{8}$ inch barrel. The lack of an attached ramrod identifies it as an early model, circa *1851. (Bedford Collection.)*

produced, nearly all of them with ring triggers; the majority are marked *Mariette Brevete*. One J. R. Cooper of England also produced pepperboxes with ring triggers. Although the great majority of pepperboxes have five or six barrels, a few were manufactured with more—sometimes up to 24. Many were sold cased, with a powder flask, bullet mould and separate ramrod; there were obvious difficulties involved in fitting a ramrod to these unconventionally shaped weapons.

The pepperbox was simple, efficient, inaccurate, and extremely heavy. Its strength and its weakness both lay in the cylinder block. It was comparatively simple to drill out the five or six chambers, but it was a very different matter to rifle them for increased accuracy. The sheer mass of metal made the pepperbox very top heavy, and consequently awkward to carry and difficult to aim. Nevertheless, it was an important step in the line of development which was to lead from the early hand-rotated revolvers to the efficient self-cocking, self-rotating revolvers which were to become such a feature of the late 19th century.

There was nothing startlingly new in the actual principle of the revolver, for, as we have seen, numbers of wheellock, snaphaunce, and flintlock models had been produced. All, however, presented considerable construction problems. Many of the

Fig. 147: Tranter double trigger revolver retailed by Stephen Grant of London, cased with a bullet mould, wad cutter, powder flask and tins of lubricating grease. (Perry Collection.)

early flintlock revolvers have a slightly bizarre appearance, with their numerous barrels each with its separate steel and priming pan. However, there had in the past been successful attempts to produce revolvers comprising a single barrel with several chambers. Some had been hand-rotated, but towards the end of the 17th century a Swiss gunmaker working in Britain, Jaques Gorgo, had made a pistol which at first glance seemed a perfectly ordinary flintlock but which in fact had three chambers concealed in the thickened breech. John Dafte, another London maker, had produced in about 1680 a practical flintlock revolver with six chambers, each with its own pan and sliding cover. When this weapon was cocked the cylinder, like those of the much later pepperboxes, was turned through 60° to bring a fresh chamber into line with the barrel. Although it was a perfectly sound, workable system it made for a very heavy pistol—6¼ pounds before loading. It was also a very complex item to make in those days before the advent of power or precision tools; and although the idea had been clearly demonstrated to be feasible it fell into disuse, and the hand-rotation system continued to occupy the main sources of production until the early 19th century.

In 1818 an American named Elisha Collier obtained a British patent for a flintlock revolver in which the cylinder was rotated automatically; it was unique in that it had to be wound up first. Rotation was achieved by a spiral spring which was put under pressure by rotating the cylinder by hand in the reverse direction. A second advantage of the Collier revolver was that one steel operated for all cylinders, and also doubled as a self-priming device; as the pan was closed a small amount of powder was discharged into it. A third feature was the efficient way in which Collier fitted chamber to barrel to reduce, as far as possible, the gas leakage which normally occurred with this type of weapon. The mouth of each chamber was slightly countersunk, and the end of the barrel was ridged; when pressed together by a spring they made a very secure union. The spring method of rotation was apparently not very successful, for Collier omitted it from his later weapons; the only surviving examples are hand-rotated. The British Government examined the revolvers but rejected them for the Army and Navy, probably quite rightly; they were rather too mechanically complicated for use in the field. However, surviving correspondence from private customers suggests that they were extremely efficient. Although the early examples are flintlock pieces, Collier did make some percussion weapons at a later date.

As discussed in previous *Chapters*, the percussion cap simplified many of the gunsmith's problems; and this was particularly so in the case of revolving pistols. It obviated the need for any attachment to the cylinder other than the nipples, and these could be countersunk or fitted in such a way that they did not hinder the rotary action of the cylinder. There were several attempts, like Collier's, to produce an efficient percussion revolver; but it took an astute Yankee to design a really satisfactory weapon.

More words of print have probably been devoted to Samuel Colt and his products than to any other gunmaker in history. His revolvers have achieved a standing and glamour in the eyes of the collector and the layman alike unequalled by any other single firearm; and it is interesting to speculate on why this should be so.

The Colt revolvers were pleasant in design and efficient in operation; but from the 1850's onwards there were others on the market which matched them, and yet as far as many collectors are concerned the name of Colt has an almost mystical ring to it. Part of the answer lies in the circumstances of their use, and in the publicity which

Fig. 148: (Top to bottom) *Adams self-cocking revolver of 1851. Deane, Adams and Deane revolver, fitted with Adams-type side rammer. Colt London Navy Model, 1851. London Armoury Company revolver fitted with Kerr rammer.* (*All J. B. Bell Collection.*)

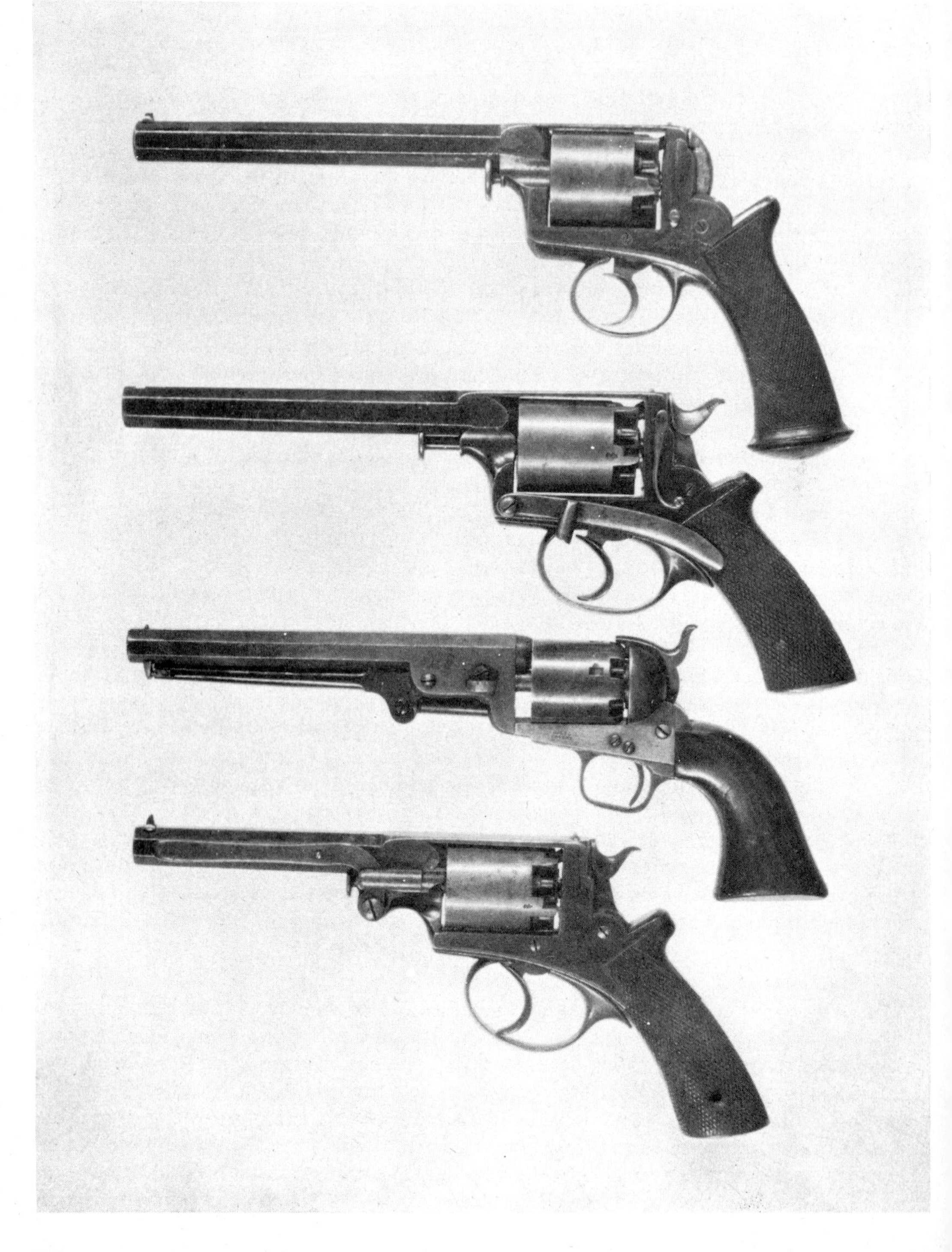

Fig. 149: Tranter double action revolver with side rammer. Apart from the characteristic projection on the rear face of the trigger, it closely resembles the Beaumont Adams revolver.

surrounded their production and sale. Sam Colt was not only a skilful engineer, he was also one of the patron saints of the public relations exercise. He knew that if he was to be financially successful his products had to be widely known; and in order to make them known, he missed no opportunity to present examples of his work to persons of note, to exhibit them at trade and industry fairs (including the Great Exhibition held in London in 1851) or to arouse interest by writing to journals, lecturing, and indulging in tests which attracted considerable publicity. The revolvers certainly played a valuable part in the opening of the American West; indeed, if one judges solely by the fictional efforts of today's mass entertainment media, one could be forgiven for thinking that the Colt was the only revolver to see service in the American Civil War and during the stirring decades which followed it. In fact, a close examination of such contemporary photographs as have survived suggests that a multitude of other models saw equally wide use on the Frontier. It is certainly true that in England, Colt revolvers had a market lead over all British products, and this combines with other factors to make Colt's name a household word. Despite the fact that thousands of models were manufactured, they are still one of the most highly priced percussion revolvers on the antique market.

Colt produced many patterns, including some which he manufactured in a factory set up in London, which naturally aroused fierce opposition from British gunmakers. The leading manufacturer of English percussion revolvers at that time was Robert Adams; and in 1851 he patented a five chambered self-cocking pistol. Colt's revolvers were all single action, the hammers being fitted with a large spur. As the hammer was pulled back (most conveniently, by hooking the thumb over this spur) the cylinder rotated. If the hammer was pulled back further, it locked in the fully cocked position. Pressure on the trigger now allowed the hammer to fall forward and fire the first chamber. Before the revolver could be fired a second time the hammer had to be cocked again, and this process was repeated for each shot. With a self-cocking revolver there

Fig. 150: (Top) *Colt "Army Model" percussion revolver of 1860.* (Bottom) *Double action five-chambered percussion revolver by Webley.* (*Tower of London.*)

was no need for a spur on the hammer; pressure on the trigger cocked the hammer, rotated the cylinder, and then fired the shot. Each system had its advocates and there were constant debates among officers and civilians on their respective merits. Single action was said to be better for aiming and made for more economical and careful shooting, while supporters of the self-cocking system argued that the ability to maintain the higher rate of fire was of paramount importance in practice. It is true that the heavy trigger pull characteristic of all double action revolvers made it far more difficult to fire carefully aimed shots.

There were other differences between the products of Adams and Colt, mainly in the design and method of construction. Adams' revolvers were solid framed, with the barrel and cylinder housing united in a single piece. Colt's weapons had the barrel attached to the central cylinder spindle by means of a metal wedge. Adams' self-cocking revolvers were extremely rugged and attractive and, arguably, were of higher quality workmanship than Colt's. On the other hand the American gun had an advantage in its attached ramrod, whereas Adams' early models had a separate ramrod which, as may be imagined, was easy to mislay. In 1854 Adams was granted a patent for a simple rammer permanently attached to the weapon; it is usually described as a Rigby rammer, although Rigby's patent was for a different design. Later models used a Kerr rammer which was fitted at the side of the barrel. The single action self-cocking controversy was less easy to resolve; but eventually Adams produced a revolver which incorporated both actions. Pressure on the trigger enabled it to be used as a self-cocking weapon, but the hammer was fitted with a spur, and if so desired it could be cocked and fired in exactly the same way as a Colt.

This simple double action system was patented by a Lieutenant F. Beaumont of the Royal Engineers in 1855, and thenceforward it became a standard feature of most English percussion revolvers, although mechanical variations were produced by other designers. The Beaumont Adams revolver was manufactured mainly by the firm of Deane, Adams and Deane and the London Armoury Company. Some 2,000 were ordered by the British Ordnance, and others found their way over to the United States during

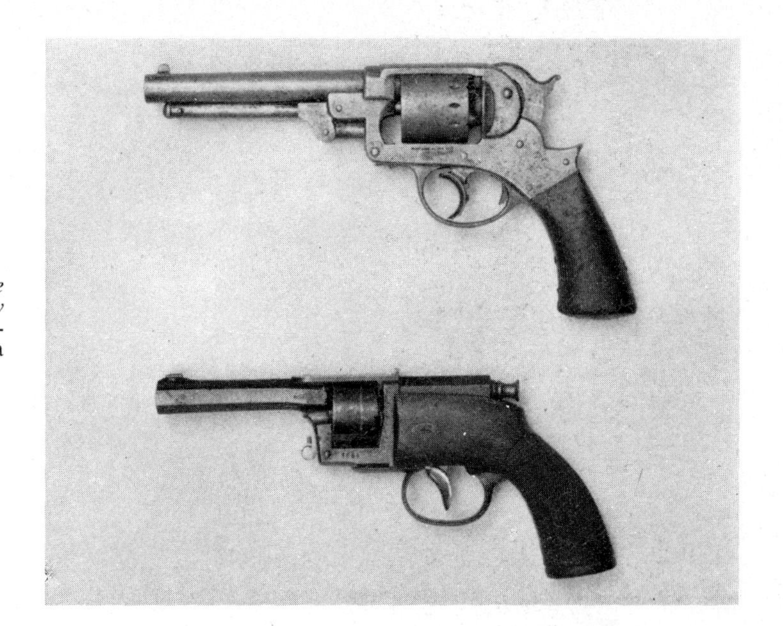

Fig. 151: (Top) *American double action percussion revolver by Starr.* (Bottom) *Needle-fire revolver by G. L. L. Kufahl,* circa *1852.* (*Tower of London.*)

the American Civil War. Some were also made in Birmingham, but these are a little less common. Adams revolvers were sold cased, usually in oak boxes complete with all the usual accessories; such revolvers frequently bear the name of the retailer.

Possibly the other British gunsmith whose name became as well known for his revolvers was the Birmingham maker William Tranter. He was a Birmingham Company Gunmaker who had already filed a number of patents for pepperbox revolvers, but he is best known in the collecting world for his double trigger revolver. This was built on the Adams frame but differed in one important aspect; a long, double-curved trigger projected through the trigger guard. The lower section which extended beneath the guard was pressed with the second finger, causing the cylinder to rotate and also cocking the hammer, which would remain cocked as long as the lower trigger was depressed. Pressure by the first finger on the top trigger, inside the guard, released the hammer and fired the weapon. The great advantage was that the weapon could be cocked, held thus, and then fired in exactly the same way as a single action revolver. This double trigger was patented in 1853 and William Tranter produced a number of different revolvers using this system. Many collectors distinguish between three models of the double trigger Tranter, differentiated by the method of attaching the ramrod. The most common is the third model, which has a ramrod permanently attached to the frame of the revolver. Tranter's double trigger weapons also carry a very ingenious spring operated safety catch which was quite automatic in action; as soon as the cocking trigger was pressed a spring arm automatically imposed itself between hammer and nipples, and remained in position until the weapon was fully cocked. These revolvers were of excellent quality and seem to have been extremely satisfactory and reliable. Tranter also produced a single trigger, double action revolver which bears a superficial resemblance to an Adams, but a point of difference will be found on the rear of the trigger, where there is a short rearward projecting arm; it is this extension which actually disengages the hammer and allows the weapon to fire.

One of the English revolvers which most closely approximates many of the features associated with Samuel Colt's weapons was the so-called Daws revolver

Above, *Fig. 152: A Le Mat revolver; produced in the United States in about 1860, this was basically a nine-chamber percussion revolver, with a central barrel for firing a charge of shot. (Dominion Museum, New Zealand.)*

patented in 1855. It incorporated an under-barrel ramrod such as was fitted to most of Colt's revolvers, and had the barrel secured to the central spigot of the cylinder in exactly the same fashion as on a Colt. One common feature to be found on revolvers by Adams, Daws and Tranter is the spur at the top of the wooden butt, in some ways resembling an attenuated saw handle grip as fitted to some duelling pistols.

It is interesting to note that although Colonel Colt had so clearly pointed the way to the manufacture of efficient and accurate revolvers, many British manufacturers continued to turn out what can only be described as thoroughly second rate weapons. Usually termed "transition revolvers", they had the general appearance of late-model pepperboxes, with a very truncated cylinder barrel block fitted with a single barrel. Some had the traditional bar hammer but others had the typical upward spur of the percussion hammer and were cocked manually. The majority are rifled and fitted with a foresight, although the practical value of the latter is highly questionable; the sights were usually obscured by the rising hammer as the trigger was pressed. Some weapons of slightly higher quality had the trigger mechanism offset, to allow sighting. The barrels of these transition revolvers were usually secured by screwing to the central spigot. They were produced in some quantity, for a number have survived, and bear the names of many of the better-known gunmakers.

There is some difference of opinion among students as to the date of these weapons, but a recently published book puts forward a strong case for dating them around 1850. The authors suggest that they were indeed a cheap answer to the more expensive revolver produced by Colt, and pointed the way to better revolvers produced later by the British gunmaker.

Another name which was to became famous in the world of weapons was that of Webley. The brothers John and Philip Webley established a firm which was to produce a number of famous revolvers. The Webley percussion revolver differed in shape from that of Adams and retained a butt reminiscent of the pepperbox; judging from the numbers surviving, the total production was far lower than that of rival weapons.

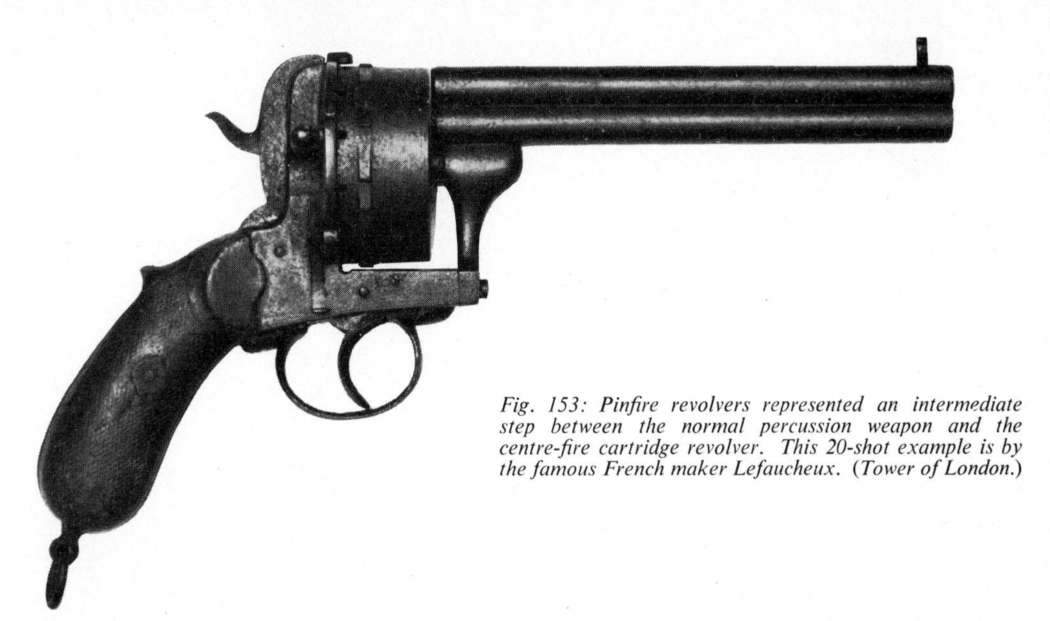

Fig. 153: Pinfire revolvers represented an intermediate step between the normal percussion weapon and the centre-fire cartridge revolver. This 20-shot example is by the famous French maker Lefaucheux. (Tower of London.)

Later, a Webley cartridge revolver was adopted as a standard issue weapon by the British Army.

Although the rotating cylinder was now firmly established as the standard revolver system, this did not mean that it was the only system in use. As early as 1837 patents were granted for the use of flat, disc-like cylinders with the chambers placed radially and the nipples set near the centre of the disc. These "turret guns" were made with the turrets rotating in both the horizontal and the vertical plane, and both hand guns and long arms were produced incorporating this system. Colt and Adams were just two of the revolver manufacturers who also produced long arm versions of their revolvers, but these are far less common.

By the middle of the 19th century firearm production had been thoroughly mechanised, and for many collectors this lack of individual craftsmanship detracts from the interest of the weapons. To them, one Adams is exactly the same as another, one Colt model 1851 is identical to any other. Enthusiasts will deny this and point out that even within one apparently identical run there are numerous minor variations. While it is only the dedicated collector who will concentrate on one particular model, there is still plenty of scope for the more general collector in the field of percussion revolvers. It will be noted that the term *percussion* revolvers is used, for, alas, flintlock revolvers are scarce and extremely expensive. However, the collector who specialises in percussion revolvers has a tremendous field open to him; in Britain alone there were numerous variations of the weapon produced by half a dozen makers and a host of lesser known firms. Until recently the English percussion revolver has been sadly neglected in favour of the Colt; and there was a great disparity in the prices realised by a Colt and an Adams, especially if the weapon was cased complete with accessories. There is still some disparity today, but the gap has been closed to some extent and the demand for quality English percussion revolvers is increasing. Prices have, as always, risen but it is some consolation to see these well made, usually very well designed items receiving at last some of the interest and care which they truly deserve.

13

American Firearms

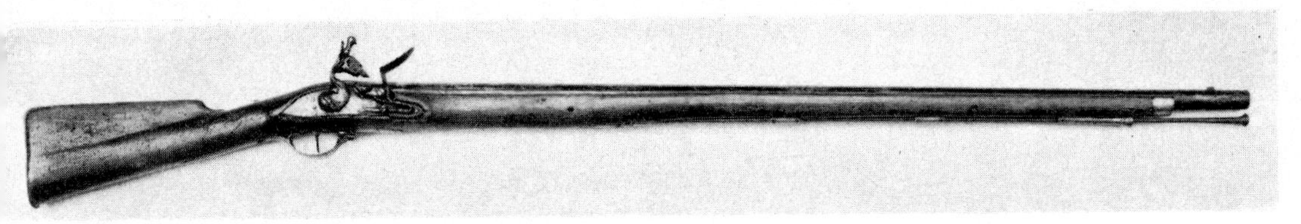

Fig. 154: Committee of Public Safety musket produced according to a specification laid down by the Colonists, but essentially a copy of the British "Brown Bess", with a 42-inch barrel and ·75 inch bore; this example has Maryland proof marks. (*H. L. Peterson Collection.*)

No casual observer of modern entertainment media could be blamed for forming the impression that the only two firearms produced in America during the last century were the Colt revolver and the Winchester rifle. Directors of cinema and television dramas spanning the whole period between the fall of the Alamo and the outbreak of the First World War have armed their casts with little else. Needless to say, this is a gross distortion of fact; the profusion and variety of firearms produced in the United States almost beggars belief. The citizens of that nation have long cherished their constitutional right "to keep and bear arms", and consequently the production of firearms in the United States has always been enormous. Many of the most famous names in the industry—Colt, Smith and Wesson, Winchester and Remington—are American.

During the earliest Colonial days there were, of course, no such things as American firearms, for Canada and the Colonies imported their weapons from England, France and the Low Countries. Excavations carried out on the sites of the early colonies have unearthed a number of relics all of which are apparently European in origin. Naturally there developed a native gunmaking industry but it was, at first, on a very small scale—probably more concerned with repair than manufacture.

During the 17th century this native industry developed and expanded, often due to the presence of immigrant craftsmen who were experienced metal workers. Certainly there is every indication that the first peculiarly American firearm was influenced by German styles; the Kentucky rifle has a close kinship with German hunting rifles. Although it has long been associated with the Blue Grass State, this is a false connection, for Kentucky has no great reputation as a gun producing state. The first recorded use of this title is believed to be in a song written about 1815 describing the Battle of New Orleans in 1812, but the "Kentucky" tag stuck and its use has continued ever since. In fact this weapon belongs more to the state of Pennsylvania, but its first beginnings have been ascribed to a variety of sources.

It is now generally agreed that its most probable origin lies in the German and Austrian Jaeger or hunting rifle. This weapon was derived originally from the earlier wheellock with its octagonal rifled barrel, firing a small calibre ball. As the traditional

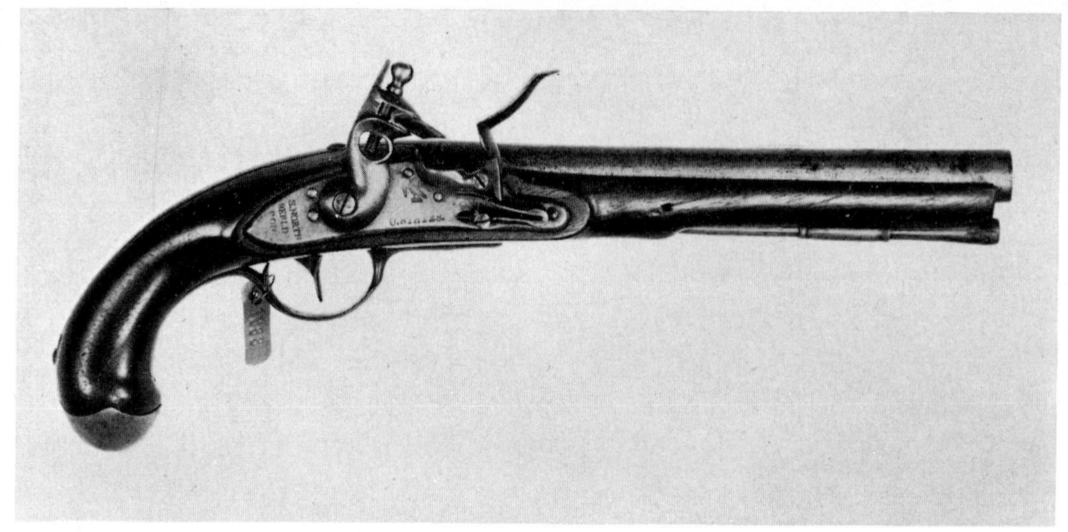

Fig. 155: Model 1808 flintlock pistol by Simeon North; this weapon, designed for use by United States Navy boarding parties, was fitted with an iron belt hook. Overall length, 16¼ inches. (Winchester Gun Museum.)

predominance of wheellock rifles continued in Germany long after they had been abandoned elsewhere in Europe, it would seem natural that the Pennsylvanian rifle should evolve in those Colonies where the German influence was strong; and such rifles were certainly produced in Kentucky, Ohio, Pennsylvania, New York and Massachusetts.

This arm evolved gradually and one may assume that in the beginning the new immigrants sought merely to reproduce the weapons they knew at home. There were certain difficulties; in the first place walnut, the wood most commonly used for Continental stocks, was scarce in the New World. The immigrant gunsmiths sought a substitute and settled for maple, which answered the purpose extremely well; and the use of this wood is one of the features of these rifles. As it was a rifle it was essential that the ball should fit as tightly as possible, and in order to do this it was common practice to wrap the ball with a patch of linen or similar material. Obviously it was important to have a supply of these patches to hand, and patch boxes were fitted on many wheellock rifles—a fashion continued on the Jaeger rifle. The covers of these patch boxes were usually sliding lids held in place by spring catches, but around the middle of the 18th century some German craftsmen modified this style with a hinged lid. These lids were sometimes of solid brass, or if of wood were decorated with brass, and this feature is common to almost all the rifles.

Barrels were very similar to those used on the earlier wheellock rifles and were almost invariably octagonal with a thick wall. Lengths varied from 42 to 46 inches and the ball fired was only about ·4 inches in diameter; these features together with the effect of carefully designed rifling made them extremely accurate weapons. Pennsylvanian rifle barrels were secured to the stock by the pin-and-lug system favoured by the British gunmakers. Many contemporary accounts from the American War of Independence speak with admiration of the accurate shooting of some of the colonists. This, coupled with their skilful use of the terrain, were factors which contributed to their victory.

The makers of these rifles liked to decorate their pieces and brass was a favourite material, often inlaid along the stock and usually including two fretted pieces on each side of the brass patch box cover. Other shapes and designs were scattered along the stock and butt, which latter was carved with a cheek rest—again a feature of the earlier wheellocks. Further restrained carving was often used along the stock. It was the graceful, gently down-sloping, almost drooping butt which gave the rifle its distinctive appearance; and many have a fairly pronounced curve at the end.

Locks were often of European origin and are frequently engraved with the name of the maker. To afford a firmer grip the trigger guard was often extended along the lower side of the butt with a graceful scroll-like turn.

Pennsylvanian rifles were produced using both flintlock and percussion, and it was during the latter period that the weapons tended to become rather elaborate with, perhaps, an excess of inlay. However, improved powder manufacture and the improvements in design and construction of other firearms tended to reduce the demand for these fine weapons and they lost favour, gradually becoming less and less popular until by the middle of the 19th century they were more or less discarded. Despite their general similarities the rifles produced in various Colonies did acquire certain local characteristics, sufficiently strong to permit reasonably certain allocation to an area of origin.

Many of the famous makers who produced the Kentucky rifles also made a number of pistols which very closely resembled the rifles. Surprisingly enough many of the makers did not mark their products, presumably because they made so few and were content to take orders as they came rather than soliciting for a wider market. Barrels were octagonal, rifled and with a fairly small bore like that of the rifle.

Although these Kentucky rifles and pistols were superbly accurate and well-fashioned weapons they were hand made, produced by small gunmakers who laboured long and hard to produce each weapon. Their number was never sufficient to meet the

Fig. 156: Another contract pistol by Simeon North, dated 1828; the contract was originally issued in 1826. This model has a swivel ramrod, a belt hook, and a securing band round the barrel and stock. Overall length, 13¼ inches. (Winchester Gun Museum.)

demands of an emergent nation and a high proportion of the firearms used in 18th century America were European in origin. Large numbers were imported from England, while other stocks were captured from the French during the many skirmishes and wars. Although the British, seeing the temper of the colonists, had banned the export of arms to America, some had trickled in; but when the final break came at Concord and Lexington the main source of supply was cut off. The Royal Navy was effectively in control of the coast, and although some supplies from France did get through the blockade, the quantity was small. Groups of colonists set up Committees of Safety to run the affairs of each district, which granted contracts to local gunmakers to produce firearms to specification; and these, broadly speaking, were copies of the British 42-inch barrel Brown Bess fitted with brass furniture.

After the confusion following the outbreak of hostilities had dissipated, Congress began to organise and legislate. In time of war arms production was vital, and Congress devoted some of their attention to this matter; and in 1777 it was decreed that in future all firearms belonging to the State should be marked with the words "United States"—a practice generally followed although abbreviations and variations of style were used.

Below, *Fig. 157:* (Top) *Over-and-under flintlock pistol; the release catch which allows barrel rotation is on the left side.* (Bottom) *A percussion pistol of similar design. Both weapons are of the Kentucky type, and date from* circa *1820-30.* (*Winchester Gun Museum.*)

Opposite, *Fig. 158: Silver-mounted ·44 calibre flintlock pistol of 1790-1810; the brass barrel is 8¼ inches long and marked* COLCHESTER, *and the lock bears the name* BIELBY & CO. (*Winchester Gun Museum.*)

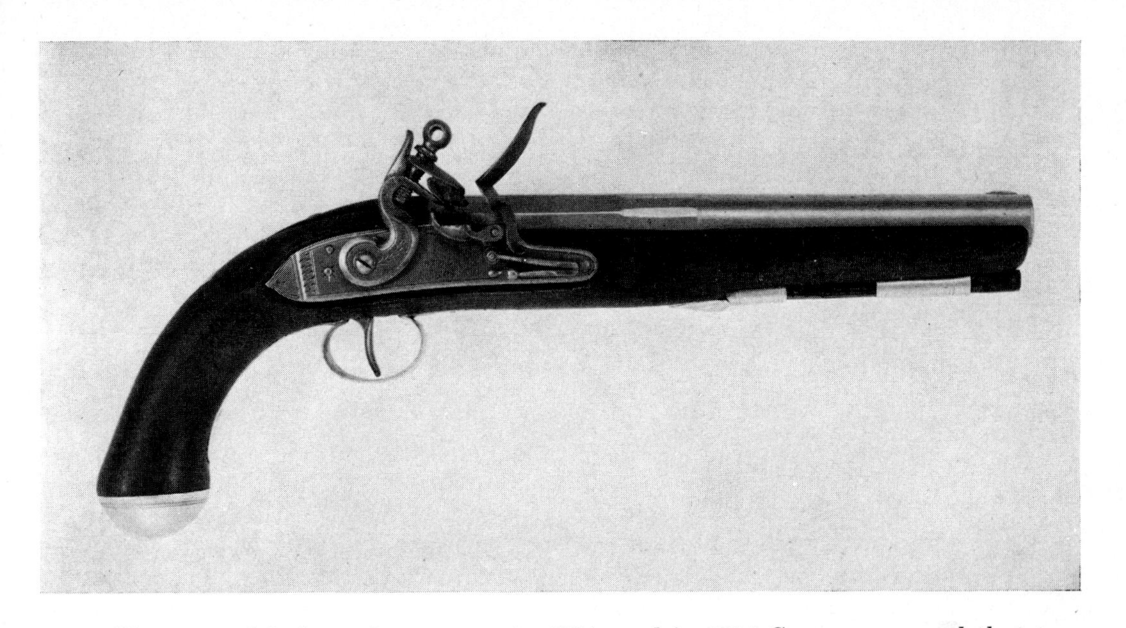

Victory and independence came in 1781, and in 1794 Congress agreed that two national armouries should be established. In 1796 George Washington set one up in the State of Virginia on the site of an old river ferry started by one Robert Harper. It took several years to acquire machinery, build accommodation and hire workers, and consequently it was not until 1801 that the first muskets, a batch of some 250, began to trickle off the production line. Harper's Ferry was remarkable in many respects, not least in that it later supplied arms to both North and South during the American Civil War. In April 1861 Confederate forces were advancing, and the armoury was evacuated by Union forces who tried to destroy the stock and machines. Confederate troopers occupied the site and were able to salvage some of the machinery and spares, which were promptly pressed into service. The second arsenal was set up at Springfield, Massachusetts—there had been a magazine on the site during the War of Independence—and began producing in the following year.

The standard musket produced at both factories was a copy of the French Model of 1763. Basically this flintlock did not differ greatly from the Brown Bess except for the usual French features of a ring cock and barrel bands. It continued in production at Springfield until 1844 when the percussion system was introduced, and a new model was manufactured until 1858. In that year there was a change to a rifled musket which was later converted to breech loading by means of a trapdoor conversion. In 1892 a magazine rifle was adopted; and further development and production has continued at Springfield until the present day.

The American system of arms supply did not differ greatly from that adopted in Britain, and Congress granted contracts to civilian manufacturers since neither arsenal was able to supply the full demands of the armed forces. Strict specifications were laid down, and contractors were expected to adhere to them in all details. Some of the weapons made after the War of Independence incorporated locks imported from England—particularly those made by the firm of Ketland & Co. of Birmingham and London.

Some of the earliest contract pistols were made by the well-known American maker Simeon North, either on his own or in conjunction with Elisha Cheney. Both

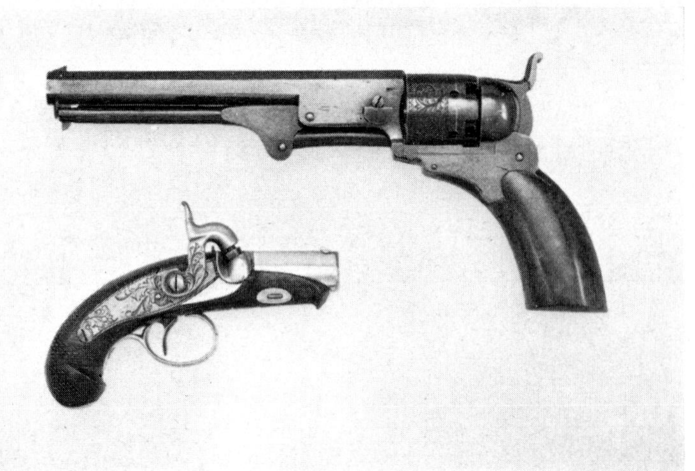

Fig. 159: (Top) *Paterson Colt with attached ramrod and engraved cylinder.* (Bottom) *Deringer pocket pistol with typical back action lock and shaped butt.* (*Tower of London.*)

men hailed from Berlin in Connecticut; North appears to have been the more important and energetic of the two, and Cheney's name was omitted from the pistols after 1802. North's factory employed some 50 to 70 workers using three trip hammers as well as numerous lathes and grinders. North lived to the ripe old age of 87. Another contractor to the government was the father of Henry Deringer, who later produced the famous pocket pistol (see *Chapter* 9).

Like the muskets produced at Harper's Ferry and Springfield, the pistols were very largely based on the French models. Many were later converted to percussion by the usual method of removing frizzen and pan, plugging the touchhole and screwing a nipple into the top of the barrel.

All the pistols produced at these armouries and by the private contractors were single shot, and it was not until the advent of the remarkable Colonel Colt that the use of revolvers became widespread (see also *Chapter* 12). Samuel Colt was not the inventor of the revolver but he was certainly the man most responsible for making it a practical and reliable weapon. He was born in Hartford, Connecticut on July 19th 1814, and even as a boy showed an interest in explosives. At the age of 15 he advertised that he would blow up a raft floating on a pond. Apparently he misjudged the charge required in his electrically operated mine, and succeeded in drenching the spectators. Driven by an enquiring nature Colt signed on as a trainee midshipman in the brig *Corco*, and sailed for Calcutta in August 1830. It was during this voyage that he carved from wood the working model of what was to be his patented revolver. On his return to the States he sought professional help to produce official drawings and models, and later visited London and Paris. He was granted an English patent for his "repeating pistol" in December 1835, and received his American patent in February 1836.

Colt's revolver incorporated a number of novel features, but one of its greatest virtues was its simplicity, for all preceding models had been quite complex. It was a single action weapon; as the hammer was pulled back with the thumb the cylinder was automatically rotated and locked into position. For loading purposes there was a half cock position allowing the cylinder to be turned freely while powder and ball were loaded and the nipples capped. A shielding partition was positioned between the nipples to ensure that the flash did not accidentally discharge adjacent chambers.

Colt soon persuaded a number of merchants and others to advance a large working capital, and forming the Patent Arms Manufacturing Company with a factory at Pater-

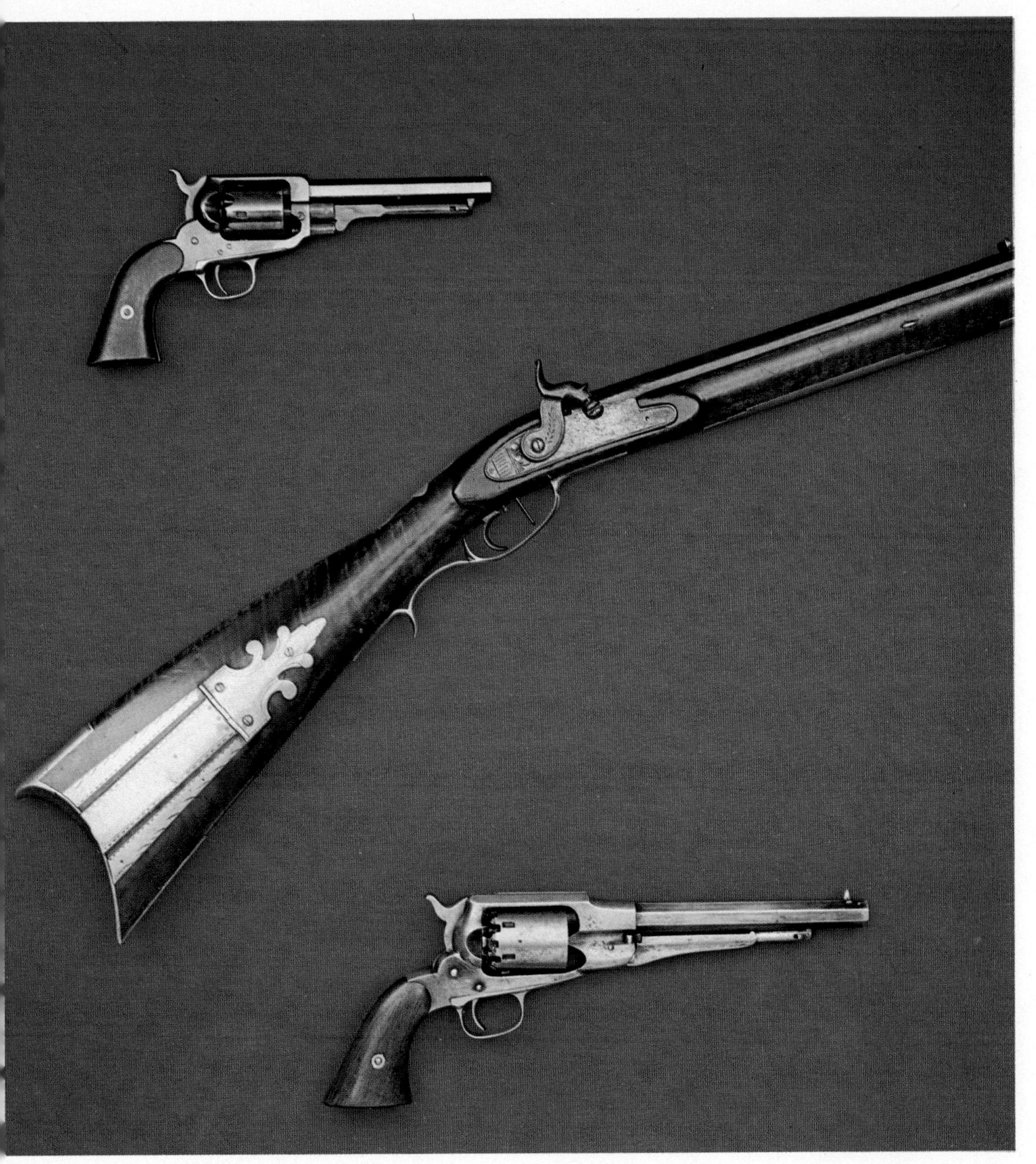

Plate 26 (Top to bottom) *Whitney revolver; overall length, 10 inches; barrel, 4½ inches; bore, ·31 inch. Percussion Kentucky Rifle by W. Golcher; overall length, 49 inches; barrel, 37½ inches, bore, ·36 inch. Remington revolver; overall length, 15 inches; barrel, 7½ inches, bore, ·36 inch.* (*Durrant Collection.*)

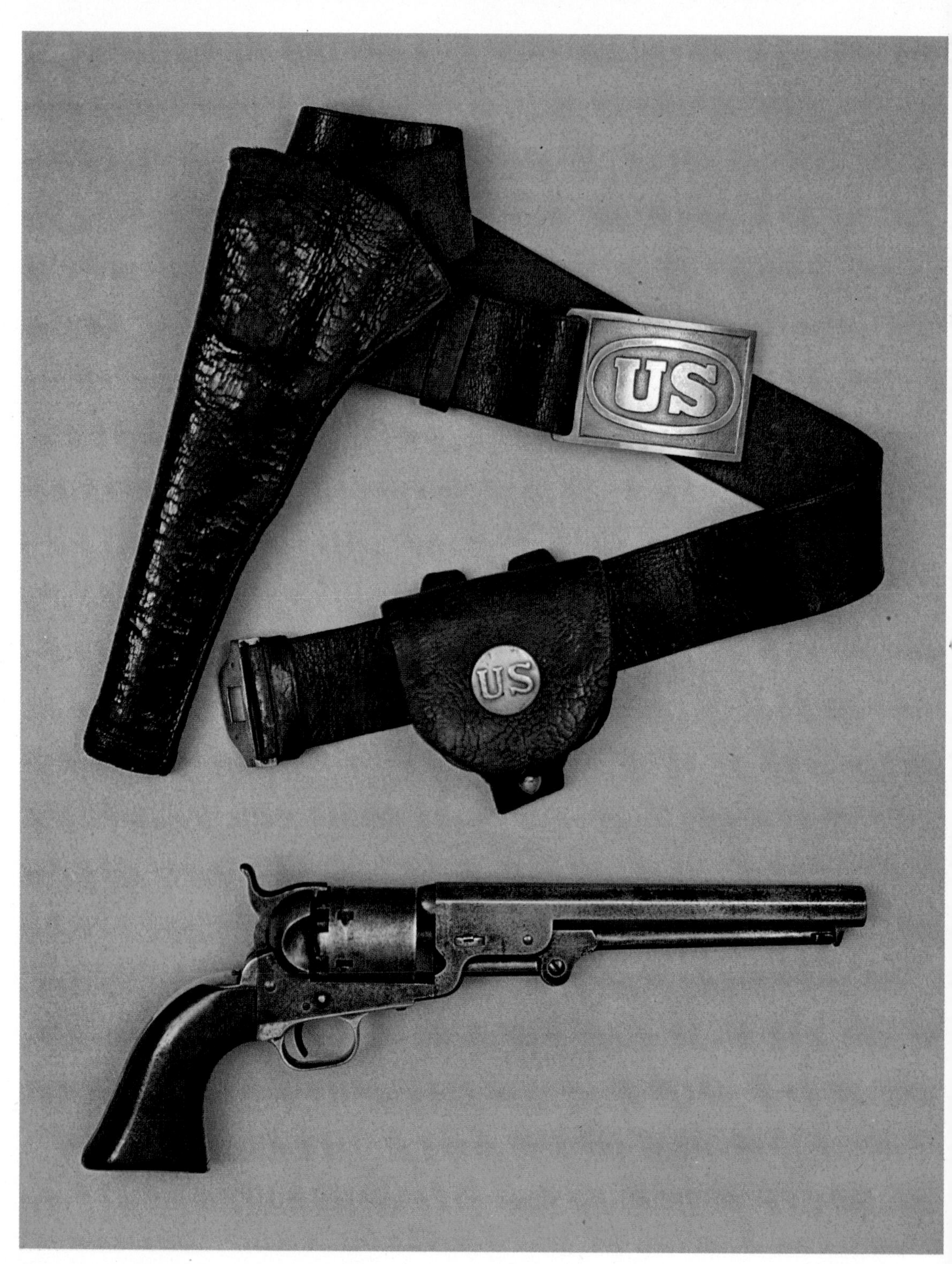

Plate 27 *Navy Model Colt with holster and belt*, circa *1851. The black leather belt is stamped* Rock Island Arsenal, *and the fold-over flap has been cut from the holster, presumably in the interest of speed.*

son, New Jersey, he set about making revolvers and revolving carbines and rifles.

Paterson Colts, now highly prized and priced, were made in various calibres between ·28 and ·36, and with differing lengths; unlike his later models these weapons had concealed triggers. In 1839 some modifications were made; an attached loading lever was introduced, and one model incorporated a conventional trigger and guard. Examples of the revolver were submitted to a Committee at West Point in 1837 for consideration by the U.S. Army, but it was rejected as being too expensive, wasteful of ammunition and difficult to maintain. Other orders were small although some were purchased by the Texas Navy, and Colt took samples to troops engaged in the Seminole Indian War and managed to sell a few. However, business was poor, and despite a great deal of effort the company went into liquidation in 1842/43.

In 1846 Colt was approached by an old acquaintance, Captain Walker, a one-time Texas Ranger and now in the U.S. Army. The Mexican War (1846-48) had created a new market for firearms and Colt was asked to supply 1,000 revolvers in January 1847. He contracted with Eli Whitney of Whitneyville, another established gunmaker, to produce the model known as the Dragoon or Holster Pistol. It was a heavy weapon, 4½ pounds, firing a ·44 bullet; and with this model Colt's weapons acquired what might be termed their characteristic shape. Another order for 1,000 followed, enabling Colt

Fig. 160: Third model Dragoon Colt, the cylinder engraved with the "Indian fight" scene. Barrel length, 7½ inches; ·44 calibre; weight, 4 lbs. 2 oz. (Dominion Museum, New Zealand.)

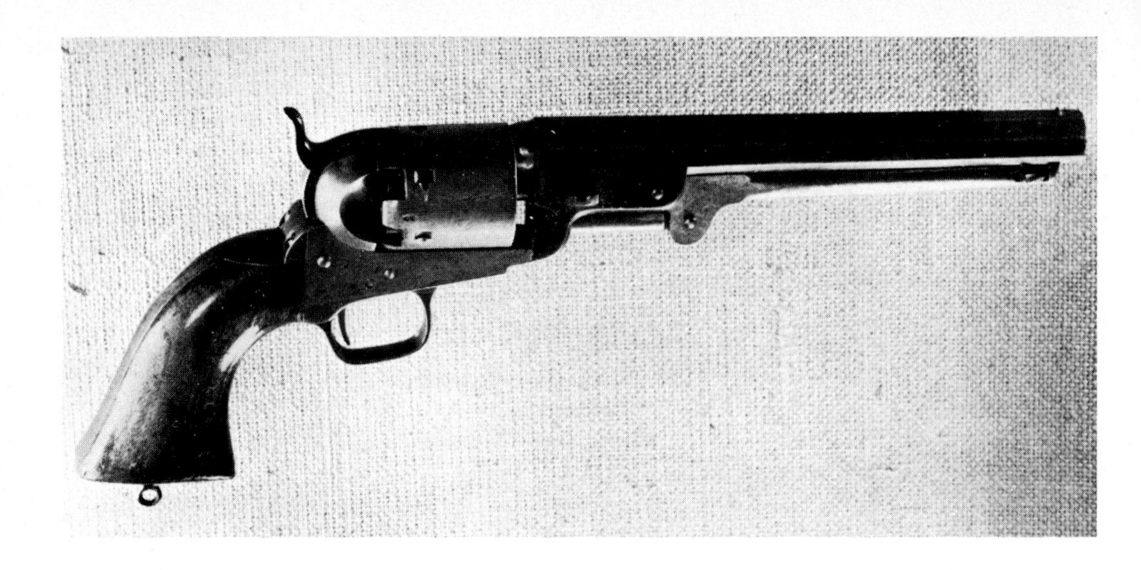

to set up his own factory at Hartford; and henceforward he prospered and his business flourished.

Prosperity enabled him to extend his range of products, and the first of the small pocket pistols in ·31 calibre was produced in 1847, followed by another version in 1849. In 1851 he introduced possibly his most popular revolver, the six-shot Navy Colt in ·36 calibre with a $7\frac{1}{4}$-inch octagonal barrel. An Army revolver of ·44 calibre with an eight inch barrel followed in 1861, as well as a new model Navy. In 1862 came the New Model Police Pistol in ·36 calibre, and it was on January 10th of this same year that Colonel Samuel Colt (he was commissioned in the Connecticut Militia) died.

Colt served a good apprenticeship in the field of public relations, for at one time he did a spell of public lecturing, and acquired a genius for bringing his revolvers before the public by every means possible. Public trials, lectures, interviews and presentations were all grist to his mill, and so well did he succeed that his name has become more or less synonymous with revolvers. He exhibited his revolvers at the Great Exhibition held in London in 1851, and deciding that Britain represented a tremendous potential market he acquired a factory by the Thames in Pimlico, near Westminster. From 1852-57 this factory turned out Colt's revolvers; the main production model was the 1851 Navy, but some Dragoons and pocket pistols may also be found to be inscribed *LONDON*. In 1854 the Royal Navy placed an order for 4,000, followed soon afterwards by a further order for 5,500, but much to his disappointment his revolvers were not adopted as the official weapon.

In 1854 a Parliamentary Committee was set up to consider the cheapest form of providing "small arms for Her Majesty's Service" and among evidence which it considered was that provided by Colt on the method of producing revolvers in quantity and with interchangeable parts. In theory this system meant that any part of any revolver would fit any other revolver of the same pattern. Some of the witnesses examined by the committee were questioned about the quality of Colt's revolvers and the facts of interchangeability. Many of the expert witnesses gave adverse reports but as Colt was obviously a potential rival to the established British gunmakers it may be assumed that much of this evidence was tinged—consciously or unconsciously—with malice and envy. Some of the other evidence on reliability and accuracy was very

Left, *Fig. 161: 1851 Navy Model ·36 calibre Colt, with 7½ inch barrel. This example is London-made, and is unusual in having a lanyard ring fitted at the bottom of the butt.* **Right,** *Fig. 162: Smith and Wesson rimfire cartridge revolvers, with the typical sheath trigger and up-swinging barrel. (Tower of London.)*

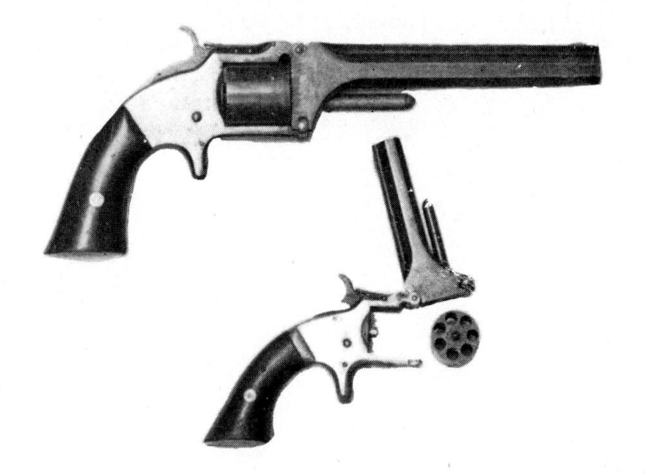

flattering, but despite all his efforts the orders were insufficient to maintain the factory as an economic proposition and Colt closed it in 1856, although a smaller factory continued in London for a year or so longer.

The American Civil War (1861-65) created a terrific demand for firearms and over 146,000 Colts were purchased by the U.S. Government. In addition, Southern makers such as the Dance Brothers of Texas produced large numbers of copies of Colt's revolvers—apparently identical in shape, size and style. It is also worth remembering that Colt revolvers were produced in quantity in Belgium, and these are usually described as Colt Brevetes. They are stamped *COLT PATENT* or *COLT BREVETE*, and bear Liège proof marks. These Belgian Colts also have a variety of scenes engraved on the cylinders, ranging from copies of the Indian scene found on Dragoons, to presentations of birds and flowers.

COLT revolvers were used all over the world and were sold either singly or in sets of two of a kind, or a combination of different calibre weapons. Cases of the recessed type and the division type were both used. In the divided style of case the American layout for single Colts tends to differ from that used by British makers. American divisions were usually more angular, with the powder flask placed next to the revolver and the mould further out, whereas in the British case the mould is usually adjacent to the pistol and the powder flask furthest away. The L-shaped nipple key was also designed to serve as a screwdriver and in British cases was usually set into a recess in one of the divisions, whereas the Americans tended to leave it loose in one of the compartments. Some models were designed to take a detachable shoulder stock which converted the revolver into a carbine, and there was a special section for this large item.

Although presentation models had the surface engraved and blued the ordinary commercial weapon was only blued. The cylinders on most of Colt's percussion arms were engraved—not by hand but by machine—with set scenes; on the heavy Dragoon cylinder was depicted a running fight with Indians; Pocket pistols had a stage-coach hold up, and the Navy Model showed sailing ships in battle.

Most of Colt's models were in production for quite long periods, but there were

COLT'S BREECH-LOADING ARMS.

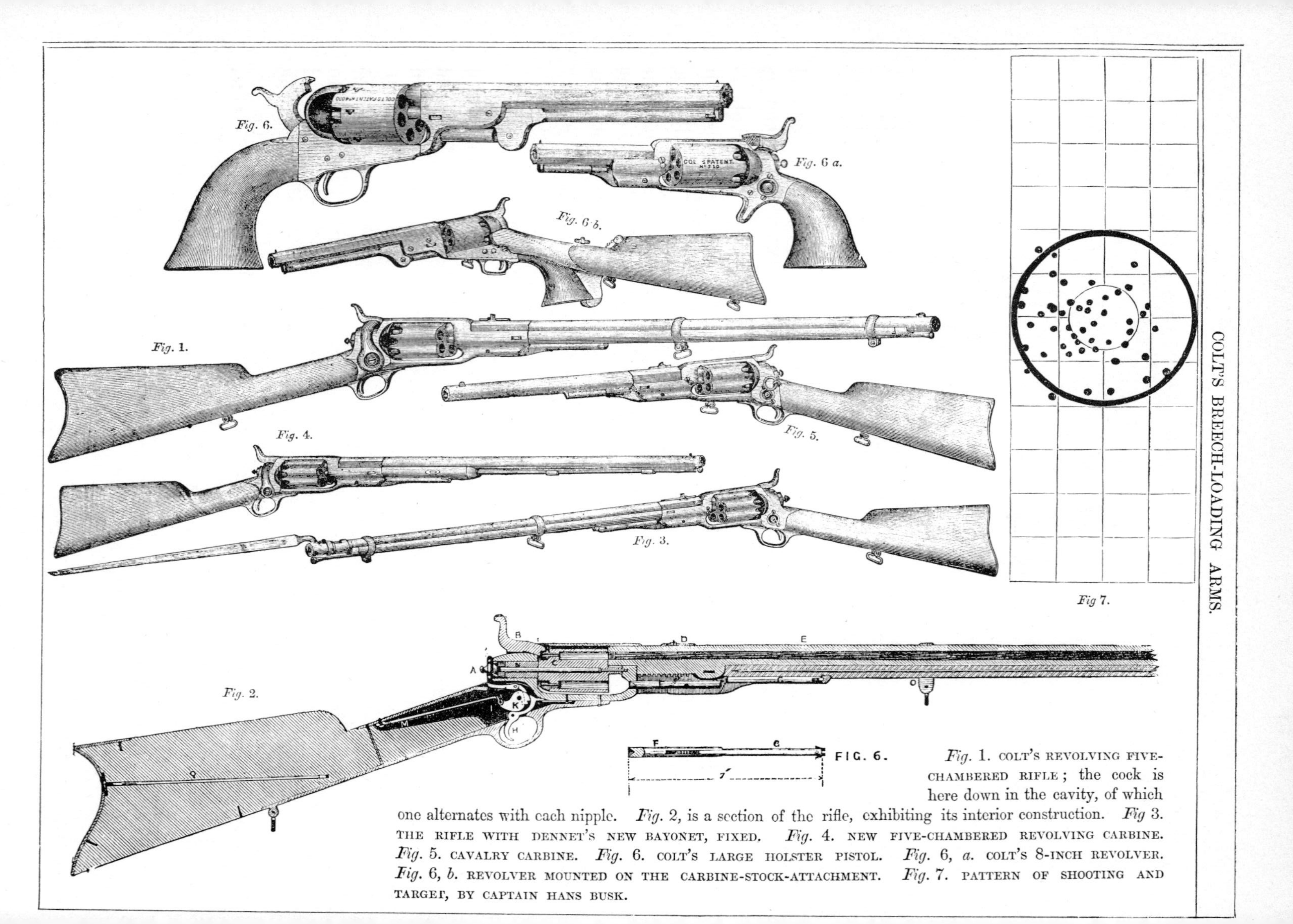

Fig. 1. COLT'S REVOLVING FIVE-CHAMBERED RIFLE; the cock is here down in the cavity, of which one alternates with each nipple. *Fig.* 2, is a section of the rifle, exhibiting its interior construction. *Fig* 3. THE RIFLE WITH DENNET'S NEW BAYONET, FIXED. *Fig.* 4. NEW FIVE-CHAMBERED REVOLVING CARBINE. *Fig.* 5. CAVALRY CARBINE. *Fig.* 6. COLT'S LARGE HOLSTER PISTOL. *Fig.* 6, *a*. COLT'S 8-INCH REVOLVER. *Fig.* 6, *b*. REVOLVER MOUNTED ON THE CARBINE-STOCK-ATTACHMENT. *Fig.* 7. PATTERN OF SHOOTING AND TARGET, BY CAPTAIN HANS BUSK.

Opposite, *Fig. 163: A page from the* "Book of Field Sports" *by H. Miles (1860) showing some of Colt's products available at that time, including his Navy and side-hammer revolvers. The target pattern is that produced by the renowned Captain Hans Busk, firing 48 rounds at 400 yards range with a Colt rifle; the target diameter is two feet, the bullseye, 8 inches.* **Above,** *Fig. 164: Examples of the famous single-action Army revolver of 1873. Cartridges were fed into the cylinder on the right after opening a loading gate; and empty cases could be ejected by a spring-loaded rod beneath the barrel. (Tower of London.)*

many minor modifications and changes in detail. True Colt enthusiasts will point out distinctions not obvious to the casual observer, such as the variation in the style of the address engraved along the top of the barrel, the differing styles of screws, and numerous other fine details.

Colt dispensed with a fixed back sight, using instead a notch cut into the nose of the hammer; at the full cock the nose of the hammer was correctly positioned. It might be thought that this was not very satisfactory, but it was retained until the 1870s, and the accuracy of the long-barrelled Navy and Army models was particularly good.

A number was stamped on the cylinder, ramrod and frame of each Colt revolver, and a specimen with matching numbers on all parts is more highly regarded than one in which the numbers differ. This difference in number suggests that the weapon has been altered, repaired or cannibalised.

From the earliest weapons produced—excepting the first Patersons—all Samuel Colt's revolvers have the same basic shape with the characteristic butt and open frame, that is, lacking a bar across the top of the cylinder. There is one exception to this sequence, since from 1856 until 1873 a new model pocket pistol was produced which had several distinctive features. Most obvious was the hammer, which was mounted on the outside of the solid frame; this model also had a trigger which lacked a guard but was protected by two ears extending down from the frame.

With the introduction of the metal cartridge under a patent held by the firm of Smith and Wesson, the Colt Company was placed at something of a disadvantage; but 1873 saw the appearance of what was to become one of the best known of all handguns. The single action Army Colt, known also as the Frontier or Peacemaker, was produced in a variety of sizes with barrel lengths ranging from three to 16 inches. It had a tremendous popular success, and was manufactured until 1940; so great was the demand that production was recommenced in 1955 and continues today. Models of the single action Army Colt with very long barrels are known as Buntline Specials, and take their name from the pseudonym—Ned Buntline—of a writer of "dime" novels named Edward

Judson. He was one of the first to realise the potential market for "Westerns", and his lurid accounts of adventures among the rustlers, outlaws and Indians brought him fame and fortune, as well as giving him the opportunity of meeting many of the famous figures of the West. He presented Wyatt Earp, Wild Bill Hickock and others with specially made Army Colts with 12-inch barrels and detachable shoulder stocks.

Despite the phenomenally large number of revolvers produced by the Colt factory—not to mention the long arms, rifles, carbines and shotguns—collectors still prize all the earlier models. Values continue to rise, and collecting Colt percussion revolvers is becoming—if indeed it is not already—a rich man's hobby.

Almost, if not equally, as well known as the Colt is the name of Winchester—almost synonymous with rifles. The name comes from the Winchester Repeating Arms Company of Connecticut, founded in 1866. The firm was started by an Oliver F. Winchester who was, in fact, a manufacturer of shirts. In 1855 this very shrewd man became interested in the Volcanic Repeating Arms Company, which had been created to market the Volcanic pistol; this was a repeating magazine pistol produced in a variety of calibres from ·31 to ·41 and with barrels varying between 3¼ and eight inches. It had a generally simple appearance, but the most striking feature was the trigger guard, which terminated in a ring. It was the downward movement of this ring trigger guard which operated the loading mechanism, withdrawing a cartridge from the magazine situated beneath the barrel and inserting it in the breech. This system was modified and improved, and adapted to the Henry Rifle of 1860, which in turn led to the Winchester repeater of 1866. The Company went bankrupt in 1857 and Winchester took it over and formed the New Haven Arms Company which, in 1866, became the Winchester Repeating Arms Company.

In the field of pistols and revolvers another American whose name became world famous was Eliphalet Remington, who was born in Connecticut—it is surprising how frequently this state crops up in the history of firearms—in 1793, but moved to New York State when still very young. Tradition has it that Remington built his first barrel and then took it to a blacksmith for reaming and rifling. So successful was he in the construction of this barrel and the accuracy of his shooting that other enthusiasts pressed him to make them similar barrels; and in 1816 he was more or less pushed into the arms production business.

At first his output was small and limited to rifles, but Remington persevered and gradually built up a factory and a reputation for first class workmanship. In 1842 he moved into the big business field and took over a contract for 5,000 percussion rifles which had been granted to another manufacturer who was unable to fulfil the conditions. So good were his rifles that the U.S. Ordnance were soon placing additional orders; and from then on the Remington family never looked back. With the outbreak of the Civil War in 1861 business naturally increased, and in that year he received an order for 12,500 rifles; but he was not to enjoy his success for long, dying shortly afterwards in August of the same year. His rifle, model 1862, often known as the Zouave rifle, was a conventional muzzle loading rifle with a particularly graceful line and a brass patchbox in the butt.

In 1857 the Remington factory produced its first revolver intended primarily for civilian use. It was designed by a man called Beales and was a five-shot ·31 calibre weapon supplied with bullet mould and copper powder flask in a wooden case.

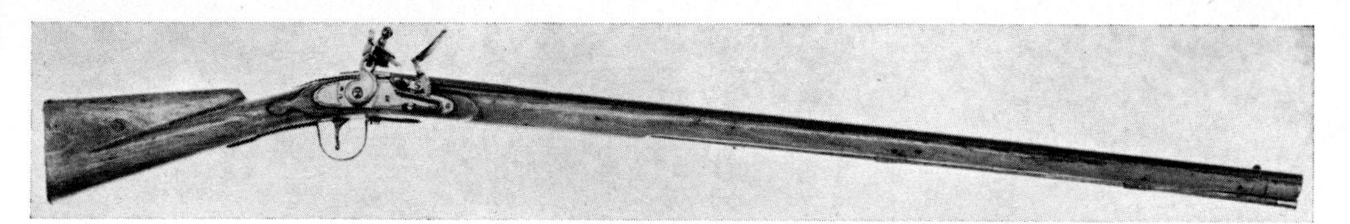

Figs. 165 and 166: Overall and detail views of a Hudson Bay trade gun, made in England and bearing Birmingham proof marks. Such weapons were used for barter by fur traders. The overall length of this example is 57½ inches. (Winchester Gun Museum.)

FROM the 1860s onward the number of patents granted and firearms produced in America was enormous; and famous names such as Smith and Wesson, Browning, Savage and Starr represent only a fraction of the revolvers, automatics and rifles which first appeared during this period. The demand for firearms was exceptional because of the Civil War, the pioneering of the West, and the Spanish-American War; and naturally the inventive powers of makers seeking to supply this market were stimulated. America had for centuries been a good market for firearms with its wars between France and England and Mexico and Texas, as well as the numerous Indian campaigns.

Trade guns for barter with the Indians had long been a profitable export from Britain; they were usually full-stocked flintlock muskets fitted with a serpentine or dragon sideplate—a feature the Indians demanded, and the absence of which would often result in an Indian refusing to accept the trade. Additional decoration took the form of designs in brass-headed tacks, and occasionally the makers supplied the musket already "tacked". Long after the introduction of the percussion system the Red Indian still demanded his familiar flintlock.

Undoubtedly films and, more recently, television have created widespread myths about American history—in particular about the West. It may well be that this publicity has contributed to the great interest in all things American, and nowhere is this interest more pronounced than in the field of antique weapons. There is, too, a heritage of interest in firearms in the United States and this, coupled with a higher spending potential, has resulted in a heavy demand for American firearms of all types.

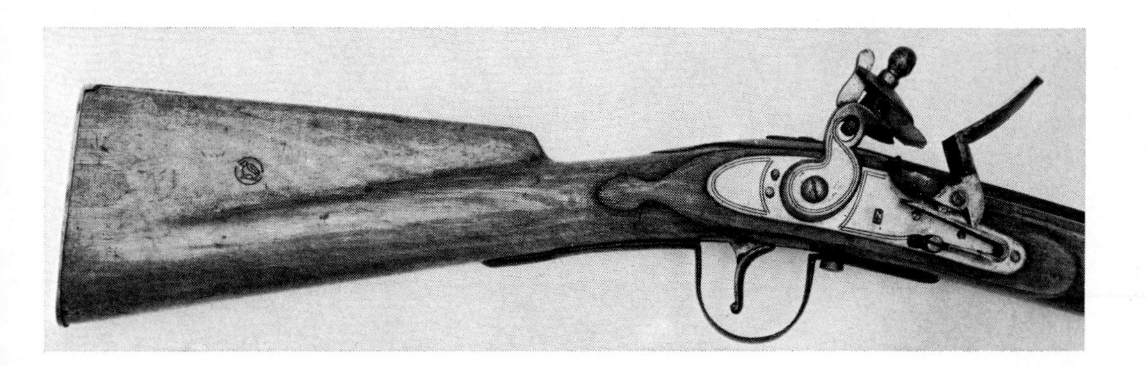

14

Rifled and Breech Loading Weapons

GUNPOWDER gave man the ability to throw objects over a distance but did not, in the beginning, give him the ability to throw them accurately. Early firearms were unreliable and erratic, for there were many uncertainties involved in the loading and firing of any shot. Consistent, absolute accuracy is, even today, extremely difficult to acquire—how much more so when ballistics were in their infancy. As a propellant gunpowder was subject to so many variables that no two charges would produce exactly the same explosion. Sighting was also susceptible to fairly wide variations, and the element of luck involved in every shot was considerable.

It was possibly in the projectile itself that there were most conflicting factors present. Despite all efforts the ball was never absolutely spherical, and these minute variations in size and shape could affect its flight through the air. Even if the discrepancy in shape was negligible there were variations in the density of the lead body—any slight unevenness in weight distribution would again affect the flight. Unless the ball fitted perfectly then there was bound to be a gas leakage through the tiny space between the inside wall of the barrel and the bullet. Apart from a loss of power there was a tendency to make the ball "bounce" along the bore touching first one side then the other. As the ball left the muzzle it was entirely a matter of chance which point last touched the bore, and that part would be subject to a drag which could throw the bullet very slightly to one side. If the ball were made to fit as tightly as possible then it became difficult to load, since friction was excessive, leading to broken ramrods, deformed bullets and, above all, a considerably lower speed in loading. Each of these tiny errors and variations contributed a minute degree of deviation; although this might be very small at the muzzle, at a range of 70-100 yards the variation had been multiplied many times and would be quite sufficient to make the bullet miss by a wide margin.

Many of the factors making for inaccuracy were not understood at the time, but observation over the years had made clear certain effects. Archers had found that if the feathers of an arrow were set at certain angles the arrow rotated in flight and was more accurate. It was not understood why this should be, although it was thought by some that the rotation made it difficult for devils to stay on the arrows when they tried to divert them ! One unknown innovator presumably reasoned that the same effect could be achieved by spinning the bullet, and the idea of rifling was introduced. The inside of the barrel was cut with a number of shallow grooves, and as the ball was pushed down the lead expanded to fill them. If the grooves were cut spirally

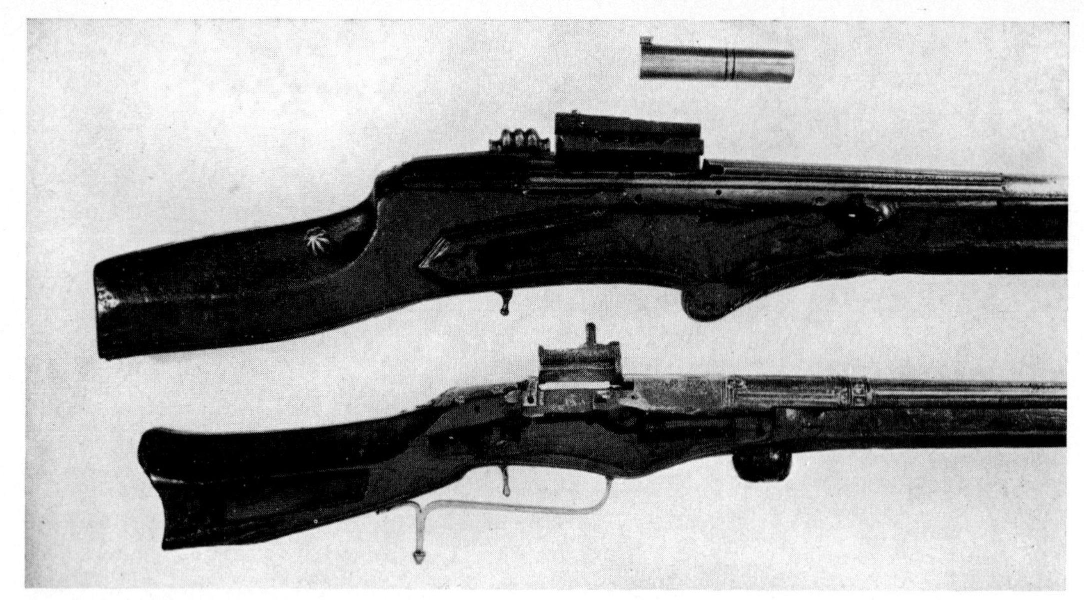

Fig. 167: (Top) *Henry VIII breech loading gun*, circa *1535, with a 43½-inch barrel.* (Bottom) *Henry VIII breech loading carbine with a 26-inch barrel. Both weapons were originally fitted with wheellock mechanisms which were later removed; both have a "trap door" which gives access to the breech, and were loaded with separate metal chambers.* (*Tower of London.*)

it meant that the ball was given a spin as it travelled along the bore, and as it left the muzzle it was spinning about its axis. To achieve the best results it was important that the grooves were evenly cut and correctly spiralled, and cutting them was a slow and complicated business—one reason why the rifle never became a common weapon prior to the Industrial Revolution and the introduction of reliable machinery.

It is ironical that the spin imparted to a ball by rifling could be both an aid to accuracy and a hindrance. As the ball spun about its axis it tended to achieve a gyroscopic effect, and the minute variations of surface and shape were generally cancelled out; at short ranges this improved accuracy. At longer ranges the ball following the normal trajectory began to drop towards the ground; as the ball was then spinning at right angles to its line of flight, the spin tended to deflect it to one side or the other.

The spin given to the ball was normally achieved by rifling, but other attempts were made to produce the same effect by fitting vanes to the bullet, or by cutting spiral holes into the bullet so that as it passed through the air they would impart a rotating motion. More ambitious inventors even sought to rotate the barrel at the moment of firing in order to give the bullet the important spin.

When and where that first genius hit upon the idea of rifling is unknown, but there are a number of traditional accounts as to the origin of the practice. The two most popular names given for the inventors are Gaspard Kollner of Vienna and August Kotter of Nuremberg; and Leipzig is also named in this connection. All that can be said with confidence is that rifling does not appear to predate the end of the 15th or the beginning of the 16th centuries, and that from the middle of the 16th century rifled weapons were not uncommon.

Fig. 168: A 17th century breech loading rifle signed H. Barne; *the barrel has eight-groove rifling and fired a ·56 ball. When the trigger guard was pressed the barrel could be swung to the left and a loaded chamber inserted in the breech.* (*A. O. Hamon Collection.*)

The amount of spin required to improve the accuracy of a projectile was never clearly understood until the latter part of the 19th century, and prior to this it was very much a matter of trial and error. Yet another factor controlling the rifling and degree of twist, which was really quite small, was the problem known by the gunmakers as "stripping". If the grooves were too sharply spiralled or were not deep enough the pressure acting directly on the ball in the chamber might well be so great as to blast the ball through the barrel. Instead of gripping the ball the grooves simply sheered a thin layer from the surface of the soft lead bullet. If the ball was stripped it did not, of course, receive any spin, and accuracy suffered. If the ball was to be gripped firmly by the rifling then size was important, and if the soft lead was to protrude into the grooves then the ball obviously had to be a tight fit. If this were so it would require an effort to force it home down the barrel and loading would be slower than with a musket, and this was one of the objections raised against the more general use of rifling in military weapons. It necessitated a strong ramrod, and many of the early rifles were fitted with metal ramrods instead of the commoner wooden ones which were more liable to break when forcing down one of the tight fitting balls. One solution produced in quite early times to overcome this problem was to cast the ball slightly smaller than it needed to be for a tight fit and to wrap it in a greased patch of material. If a supply of ready-cut patches were kept to hand, one could be placed over the muzzle, greased side down, and the ball placed centrally on top of it; patch and bullet could then be forced home with moderate ease. Greasing also helped to keep the grooves clear of fouling, which was produced by the rather poor quality powder and which might well block the grooves completely over a period of time.

Some firearms historians suggest that the first grooves were primarily cut to

Fig. 169: A magazine gun by the English maker John Cookson. The lever operates the breech block, which rotates and transfers powder and ball from the internal butt magazines to the breech. (Victoria and Albert Museum.)

reduce this problem of fouling rather than to give increased accuracy; and in support of their argument they point out that the earliest known examples of rifling are, in fact, plain straight grooves cut down the inside of the barrel. However, some of the very earliest surviving rifles have spiral grooves and it seems more likely that the theory of rotation was at least dimly understood and was the object of the exercise. A very early rifle owned by the Emperor Maximilian and dating from the turn of the 15th century has a bronze barrel rifled with twelve to 14 grooves with a slow twist.

Most early rifles were made with fairly shallow grooves, six to twelve in number, for it was probably argued that if two grooves made for greater accuracy then the more grooves the better. In fact the number of grooves is largely immaterial and of far greater importance are their depth and degree of twist.

THE improved accuracy of rifles was soon apparent to all, and as early as the 16th century special competitions were introduced for it. Target shooting was a very popular pastime in much of Europe and many of the prizes were, for their time, quite valuable. The rifle was also taken up for hunting, and the European Jaeger hunting rifle was, as we have seen in *Chapter* 13, the forerunner of the famous American Kentucky rifle. Since hunting for sport was normally a pastime of the wealthy and leisured classes the majority of wheellock rifles are of very high quality, and are outstanding items of decorative value in their own right.

A chivalrous concept lingered on after the Middle Ages, and the idea of coolly selecting one's target seemed to the combatants of the 16th, 17th and 18th centuries to be a particularly barbarous form of warfare. Many resisted the introduction of the rifle on the grounds that to choose a target and strike him down in this fashion was unsportsmanlike, ungentlemanly, and almost tantamount to murder. This feeling does not seem to have affected the Danes to quite the same extent, for King Christian IV of Denmark (1588-1648) was using rifles as early as 1611. Their use was gradually taken up by more and more monarchs, who raised small units of riflemen; although the British seem to have lagged behind in this trend.

When the American War of Independence broke out the Continental Congress, in June 1775, authorised the first steps towards creating a Colonists' Army, and the first groups formed were Corps of Riflemen; for the rifle had long since been accepted as indispensable to frontier life, both for hunting and as a defence weapon. Although the majority of the British Army engaged in the American War of Independence were equipped with smooth bore muskets, a number of rifle units were employed, being mostly of Hessian or German origin; nevertheless the authorities seem to have regarded them as expedient rather than desirable. Even the great military innovator Napoleon did not appreciate the military significance of the rifle, for he had them withdrawn from skirmishers on his own personal instructions; but ironically, at about the same time, the English made their first foray into rifle country.

When the Napoleonic Wars broke out a number of foreign troops escaping from Napoleon landed in Britain; amongst them were some using the Jaeger rifle, and interest in such weapons was stimulated. The Board of Ordnance began to consider the adoption of a British rifle, and in 1798 it is recorded that 5,000 rifled muskets were ordered from Prussia; but they proved to be generally unsatisfactory. The demand for rifles, once started, grew in volume, and from 1798 onwards there was growing pressure. The Board of Ordnance sought official comments, and in October 1800 the Corps of Riflemen was officially established. To distinguish them from the ordinary red-coated infantry their uniform colour was to be a dark green, a tradition which has persisted until the present. The question now arose as to the type of rifle to be issued; and according to a book written by Ezekiel Baker, a London gunsmith, trials of a number of weapons were held at Woolwich, just outside London, in February 1800. The rifle accepted was that designed by Baker, having a barrel 32 inches long, seven-grooved, and with the rifling

Fig. 170: (Top) *Italian magazine gun signed Bartolomeo Cotel, dating from about 1690.* (Bottom) *Another Lorenzoni-type magazine flintlock gun—possibly English,* circa *1740.* (*Tower of London.*)

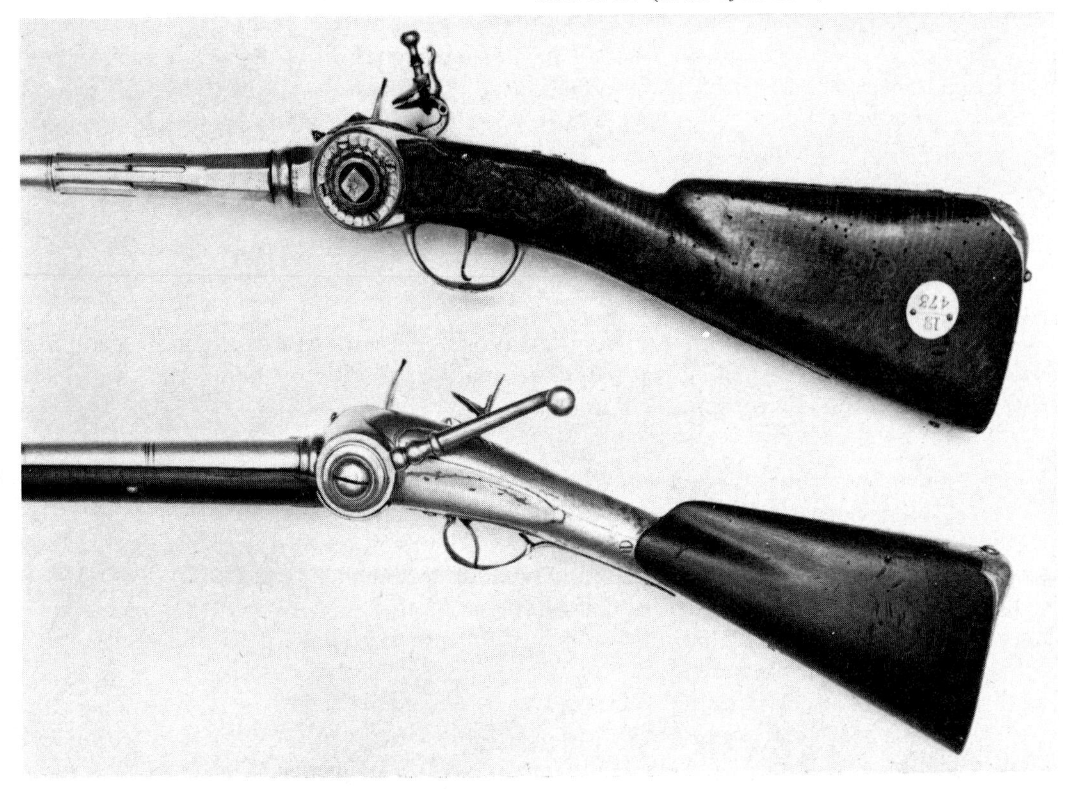

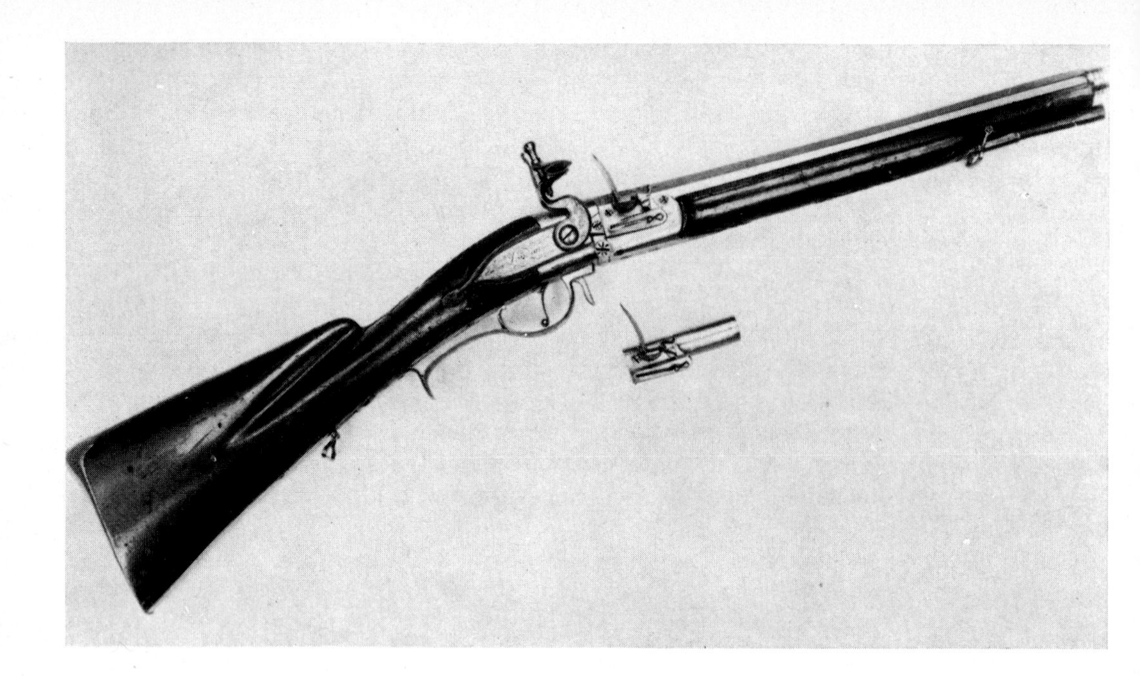

completing one quarter of a turn. The Baker rifle became the more or less standard rifle for the British Army, although slightly differing versions were produced. Large numbers of volunteer units equipped themselves, at their own expense, either with "civilian" Bakers or with rifles of very similar design.

Basically the Baker resembled a German Jaeger rifle; it was fully stocked and, an uncommon feature for British weapons, had a cheek rest on the butt. The furniture was brass and the trigger guard had a rear-curving projection to afford a better grip; but perhaps most distinctive was the large brass patchbox cover fitted to the butt. A number of variations of pattern in the Baker rifles were introduced at different times, but basically the weapon continued in production until 1838; even then it was not entirely abandoned, and there are records of Baker rifles being issued from the Tower as late as 1841. It is even reported that ten years later it was being used in the Kaffir wars in South Africa. On the whole it seems to have been a reliable weapon, although somewhat slow to load—Baker thought that one shot a minute was not unreasonable. Earlier examples were supplied with a small mallet for tapping home the ramrod to drive down the tight-fitting ball, but this was later discarded.

THERE were numerous attempts to overcome this problem of tight fit, including one by Captain Gustave Delvigne who, in 1828, designed a rifle in which the chamber holding the powder was actually smaller in diameter than the bore. The theory behind his idea was that the ball would be made slightly smaller so that it could slip easily down the barrel until it rested on the top of this chamber. A few moderately light blows with the ramrod would spread the ball just sufficiently for it to grip the rifling. Delvigne was also one of the first experimenters in the use of a cylindrical bullet to replace the ball. Another French Officer, Colonel Thouvenin, experimented with a "pillar breech"; here the breech was fitted centrally with a small pillar parallel with the axis of the barrel. The powder and ball were tipped down in the usual way, but the top of the

Left, *Fig. 171: Flintlock breech loading gun with spare chamber. The barrel unlocks and drops down to expose the breech and permit the loaded and primed chamber to be inserted. Possibly Flemish,* circa *1740. (Tower of London.)* **Right,** *Fig. 172: Lock of a fine Ferguson rifle made by Henry Nock of London; the piece is dated 1776, and was intended for the East India Company's forces. (Blackmore Collection.)*

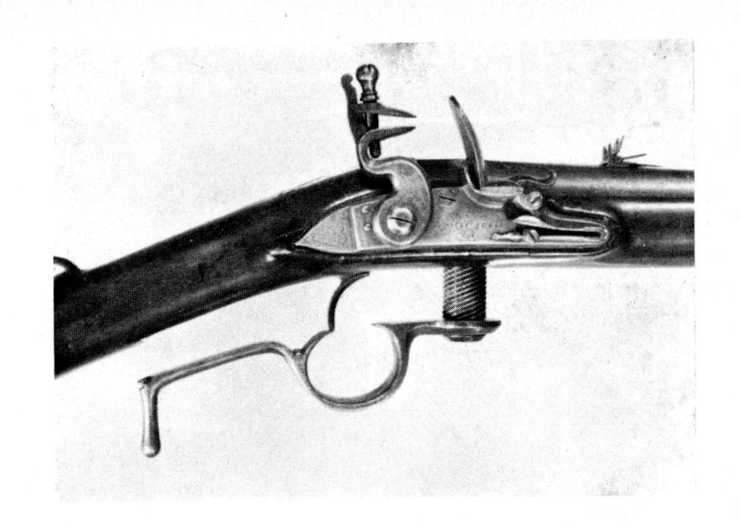

pillar acted as an anvil against which the ball might be slightly flattened to bite into the grooves.

In 1836 the British Government adopted the Brunswick rifle, and sought to overcome the problem of loading rifles by adopting a two-groove system. The ball was cast with a continuous raised belt around the circumference. However, despite the use of two grooves fouling was still considerable, and generally the Brunswick was considered to be a most inaccurate and unsatisfactory rifle. It was a percussion weapon with a 33-inch barrel, and was abandoned in 1851 in favour of the Minié rifle.

It fell to another Frenchman to produce the first generally effective muzzle-loading rifle. Claude Etienne Minié produced a bullet the base of which was hollow and fitted with a small conical plug. The cylindrical bullet passed easily down the barrel, and when the powder was fired the small plug pressed firmly into the base of the bullet causing it to expand slightly and grip the rifling. Experience soon proved that the plug was largely unnecessary and that the pressure of the gases alone was sufficient to expand the bullet. Another version of his bullet was designed to reduce fouling and increase lubrication; this had a series of grooves cut round the base which were filled with tallow.

Although conventional rifling was made up of raised ridges and sunken grooves, this was by no means the only method used to spin the bullet. Some of the finest engineering brains of the period applied their expertise to the problem; Sir Joseph Whitworth produced a hexagonal rifling, and Charles Lancaster used an oval bore which was twisted slightly. Another great engineer, William Metford, preferred a shallow seven-groove rifling which in a straightforward test proved more reliable than Whitworth's hexagonal rifling. By the end of the 19th century experience had shown that the conventional rifling was, by and large, the most satisfactory, and most modern rifles use a variety of grooves.

One specialised form of rifle was the "Schuetzen", which was specifically designed for target shooting. Most are elaborate, with deeply recurved butts, cheek pieces, elaborate finger grips projecting from the trigger guard, vertical sights, horizontal sights, wind gauges and set triggers; a great variety of combinations of these features have been observed. Some were very light, but others were made with tremendously heavy barrels and were intended to be fired from a rest.

MUZZLE loading had been used for some 250 years; it was efficient, usually reliable, but very slow. Ironically the very earliest firearms had been breech loaders, and the early cannon of about 1400 had a cylinder which was loaded with powder and ball and then secured adjacent to the barrel and wedged into place. Cannon such as this were made up to the beginning of the 18th century, while some of the great siege cannons were made with a screw breech in which the chamber was actually screwed on to the barrel prior to firing. Attempts were made to produce breech loading hand-guns, and by the early 16th century numbers of such weapons were being manufactured. There are in the Tower two surviving examples; one, dated 1557, belonged to Henry VIII. These weapons have a hinged "door" at the breech. When this was opened a small

Fig. 173: A selection of breech loading carbines: (Left to right) *Terry's carbine, marked* TOWER 1857; *sealed pattern Terry's carbine, marked* TOWER 1860; *Barton's carbine, marked* ENFIELD *1858*; *Restell's carbine of* 1858; *Manceaux's carbine, marked* ENFIELD 1858. (*Tower of London*).

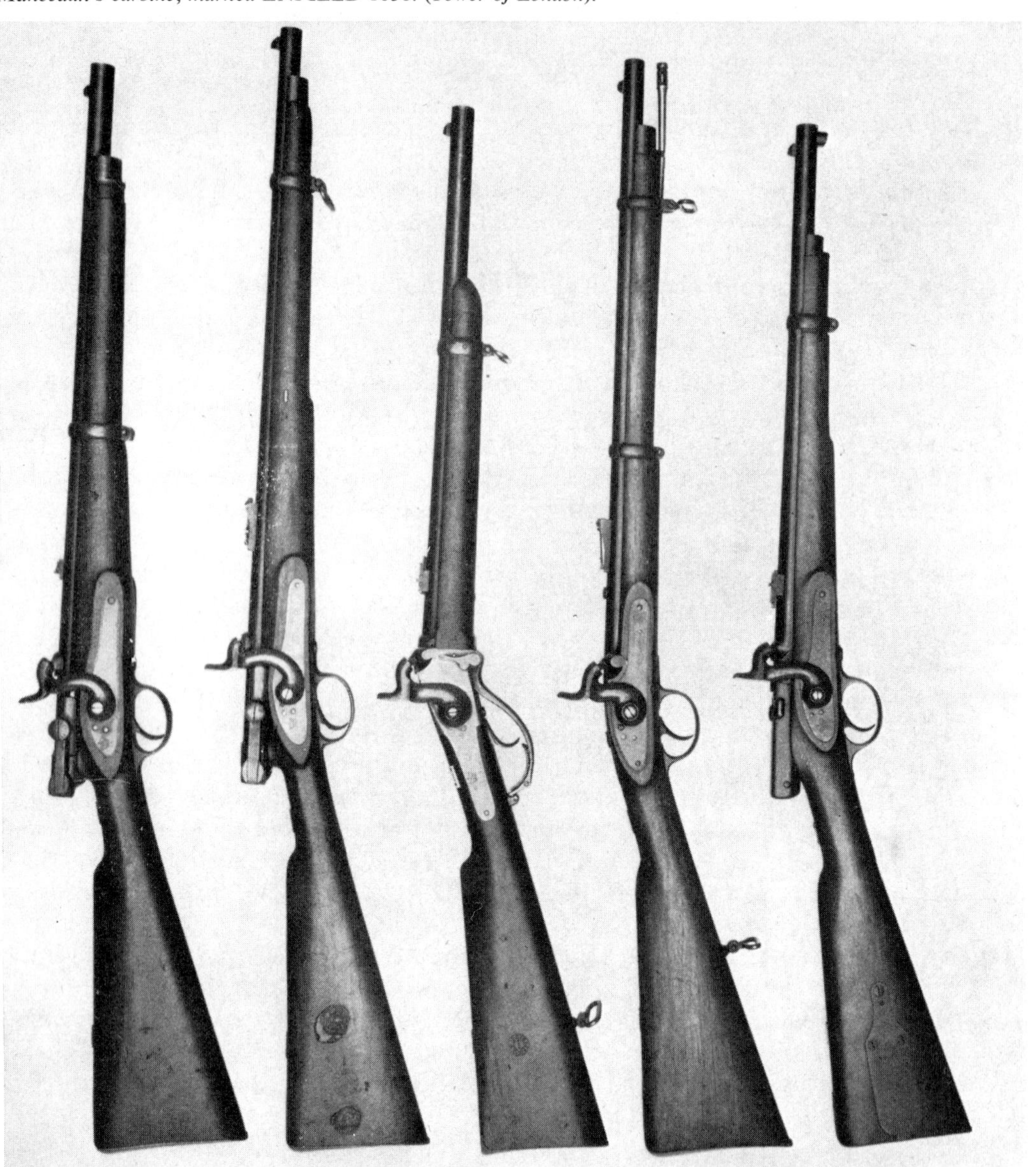

Plate 28 (Top) *Fine percussion target rifle by I. Riviere, using the box-lock patented by that maker in 1825; an unusual feature is the pistol grip, seldom found on English weapons.* (Bottom) *Baker flintlock rifle, with the characteristic brass patch-box lid set in the butt. This was the weapon issued to the newly formed Corps of Riflemen in 1800. (Bennett Collection.)*

Plate 29 (Top) *Merrill carbine dated 1861. This popular American breech loader saw service in the Civil War. The long arm, here seen raised, opened and closed the breech.* (Bottom) *English breech loading rifle by Westley Richards & Co., dated 1860. The breech was opened by the lug seen behind the hammer.* (*Bennett Collection.*)

Fig. 174: The Sharps rifles and carbines, patented in 1848, were first class weapons. The movement of the trigger guard in a lever action raised and lowered the breech block and exposed the breech. The mechanism, originally designed for paper cartridges, was later adapted for metal cartridges. (Tower of London.)

iron tube holding the charge was fitted into the breech. However, this type of weapon was rather expensive and complex for general issue and it was generally felt that the muzzle loader was sufficient for general purposes.

Later a number of breech loading pistols and long arms were produced, and some of these incorporated mechanisms which turned them into repeating weapons. One of the earliest of these systems, produced at the beginning of the 17th century, is known by the name of a gunmaker of Florence, Michele Lorenzoni. This ingenious system incorporates a double magazine in the butt, one holding powder and the other balls. Fitted to the lock is yet a third magazine which held fine grain priming powder. Situated by the side of the breech was a lever which rotated a breech block; to load the weapon the muzzle was lowered and the lever turned until the breech block lined up with each of the magazines. Powder and ball fell into the cavity, and when the lever was rotated again the powder and ball were brought into the firing position; at the same time the action primed the pan and cocked the mechanism. This same system was also used by an English gunmaker named John Cookson.

A very similar system was used by members of the Kalthoff family, who worked in Germany, France and the Netherlands. Kalthoff guns had two magazines, the one for balls being in a tubular cavity underneath the barrel; as in the Lorenzoni system, the powder was contained within the butt. Loading was achieved by means of the trigger guard, which was free to pivot, thus moving the breech block. The system worked well but was more complicated than the Lorenzoni mechanism and does not seem to have gained general acceptance by the military, although some were issued to members of the Royal Danish Foot Guards in the middle and later parts of the 17th century. Breech loading systems of several other forms were used, but it was in 1776 that probably the best known of all breech loading rifles was introduced.

Patrick Ferguson saw military service in Germany with the Royal Scots Greys, and was invalided home in 1760; he later joined the 70th Regiment of Foot and served in the West Indies, where he suffered ill health and was again invalided home. Captain Ferguson, as he then was, realised the difficulties involved in loading a tight-fitting ball and wad, and appreciated only too well that this was time-consuming. He sought some means whereby a ball and loose powder could easily and quickly be inserted at the breech end. To achieve this he fitted a screw plug which passed vertically through the barrel and was attached to the trigger guard. As the trigger guard was rotated the plug, cut with a large thread, was withdrawn to expose the open end of the breech.

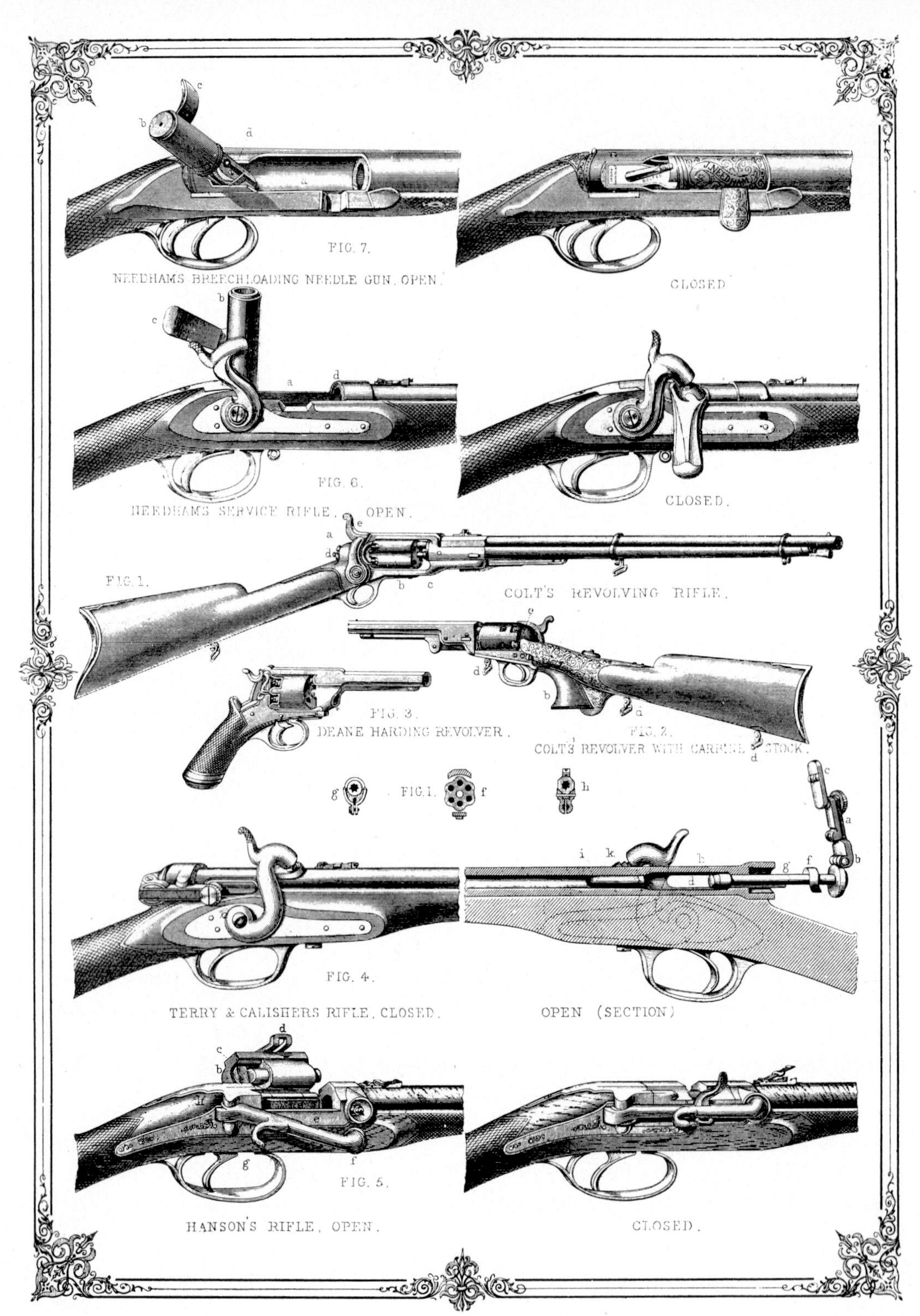

BREECHLOADING AND REVOLVING RIFLES.

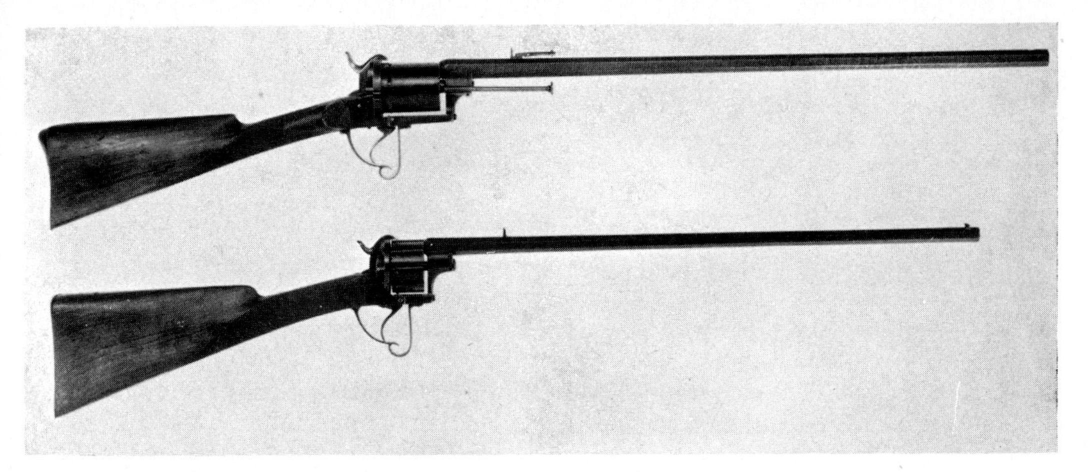

Left, *Fig. 175: A page from the 1860 edition of the* Book of Field Sports, *illustrating some of the weapons on the market at that time.*

Above, *Fig. 176: Pinfire cartridge revolvers. The upper weapon is Belgian and dates from about 1860; it has six chambers and measures 45½ inches overall. The lower piece, of the same vintage, measures 41¾ inches overall; it bears no marks of any kind. Both are double action weapons.* (*Winchester Gun Museum.*)

One turn of the trigger guard was sufficient to lower the plug; the bullet was then placed in the hole and the powder poured in behind it. A quick turn of the trigger guard screwed the plug back up, and apart from the necessary priming the weapon was ready for firing. Although the system was not new, Ferguson certainly staggered a watching audience in June 1776 when he carried out a demonstration which, if the account is to be believed, was undeniably impressive. It is recorded that despite high wind and rain he fired four shots a minute for four or five minutes on end; and although he soaked the weapon, it fired again in less than half a minute. He hit a bullseye at a hundred yards lying on his back, and he missed the target only three times during the entire course of the demonstration—a very impressive display, sufficiently so for the rather cautious Ordnance to place an order for 100 of his rifles. Ferguson was placed in command of a hundred men and undertook their intensive training. He fought at the battle of Brandywine Hill in the American War of Independence and it is recorded that the rifles did sterling work and helped to achieve victory. Ferguson himself was wounded, and sadly his group was disbanded. Despite the incapacity caused by the wound he formed a small corps known as The American Volunteers, and carried out many raids and reconnaissances. In 1780 Major Ferguson was made Inspector General of Militia in Georgia and Carolina, and whilst commanding a battalion of this Militia he was killed at the battle of King's Mountain on 7th October 1780.

Although examples of the official Ferguson rifle are extremely rare, perhaps a little more common are those civilian models made for volunteers and sportsmen by some of the great gunmakers of London. Despite its unquestioned success the Ferguson rifle was dropped by the authorities, and the breech loading system was abandoned until its reintroduction with the Snider system in 1864.

ALTHOUGH the virtues and advantages of the breech loading system were well known and understood, the big problem was that of gas leakage. Any system which utilised breech loading had to provide some means of access to the breech; this necessitated some moving part, which in turn meant that it was almost certain that there would be gaps through which would leak a certain amount of the gas formed by the explosion, with a consequent loss of power and a falling off in the efficiency of the firearm. Durs Egg, the famous London gunmaker, produced some breech loaders for the Ordnance in which the breech tipped up and allowed a paper cartridge to be placed in position.

Possibly one of the best of the earlier breech loading systems was that produced by Samuel Johannes Pauly, a Swiss-born inventor who worked in France and England. He patented a breech loader in 1812 which was far in advance of its time, having an internal firing pin which was cocked from the outside, and a breech which opened either with a lever or a tip-down barrel; but the greatest innovation was his centre-fire cartridge with brass head and paper body, in effect the equivalent of the modern shotgun cartridge. Ignition of the charge was achieved by a very small amount of percussion material set centrally in the base, which was bevelled to seal the breech when it was closed. It is claimed that at one demonstration Pauly fired 22 shots in two minutes.

Pauly's work pointed the way to the solution of so many of the gunmakers' problems. It fell to another Frenchman—von Dreyse—to take another step by producing, around 1827, a muzzle loading weapon which used a long needle to fire a cartridge. A lead bullet was fitted with a percussion compound in the hollow at its base, and this was detonated by a long, slim, sharp-pointed needle which passed through the powder charge and struck the cap—the flash then exploded the powder. In 1837 he produced a far better breech loading version of the weapon, and the Prussian Army was so impressed that they adopted it in 1848; in the Danish war of 1864 and the Austrian war of 1866 it contributed greatly to the swift Prussian victories. In 1866, Chassepot of France produced a bolt-action rifle which was adopted by the French Army; although basically similar to that designed by von Dreyse it had a shorter firing pin which was less likely to break or bend, and it proved itself to be a very satisfactory rifle. In America possibly the best known of breech loading weapons was that designed by Christian Sharps. When the trigger guard on these weapons was depressed it pulled down a block to expose the open breech, and into this was placed the paper cartridge. As the trigger guard was returned to its original position the breech block rose up and its sharp edge sliced the edge of the paper exposing the powder inside. The primer was a separate item, and Sharps used several systems, finally settling for a disc which fell automatically on to the nipple as the hammer was released. The Sharps rifles and carbines saw a great deal of service during the American Civil War and in the opening up of the West; in the latter connection it will always be remembered for its use by the buffalo hunters. Good though the Sharps system was, it did require a separate primer.

In 1835 another Frenchman, Lefaucheux, took breech loading a stage further and produced a cartridge which had a paper case and a brass cap-like head. A percussion cap was fitted inside the brass head and when in position was situated just below a small pin which projected from the side. This pin-fire cartridge was breech loading, with the pin projecting through a small slit at the end of the breech. When the hammer was fired the pin struck the percussion cap and so fired the main charge. However, it was obviously liable to accidental firing should one of the pins be struck; the system was somewhat limited by virtue of its built-in vulnerability. The next improvement was to deposit a small layer of percussion compound at the brass end of the cartridge around the circumference; this was the rimfire cartidge. Here the percussion hammer struck directly on to the base of the cartridge to explode the fulminate. However this system too had its limitations, for the case had to be soft enough to respond

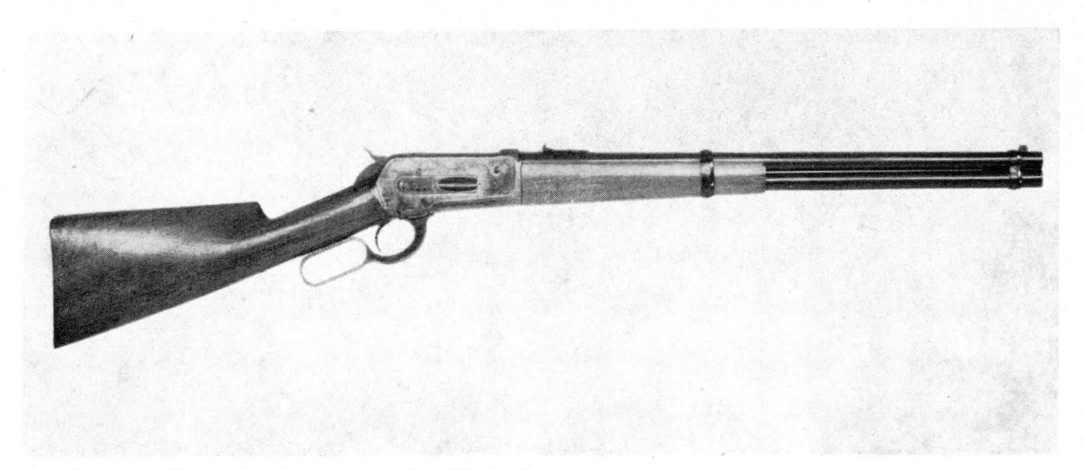

Fig. 177: Probably the best-known magazine rifle in the world is the Winchester. This is the 1886 Carbine, which fired a ·45 round, giving it a useful "commonality" with many of the hand guns of its day. The tubular magazine under the barrel was loaded through the gate visible in the right hand side of the lockplate; the ejection, feeding and cocking action was initiated by swinging the lever behind the trigger guard downwards and forwards. (*Winchester Gun Museum.*)

to the impact of the hammer but heavy enough to withstand the explosive charge; and in general rimfire cartridges were restricted to weak or low power weapons. It was a rimfire cartridge that Smith and Wesson used for their first rear-loading revolver in 1857—the beginnings of the modern cartridge weapon.

It was with the centre fire cartridge that the main line of development was to progress. After Pauly's far-sighted design in 1814 development of the centre fire cartridge had been spasmodic. In 1829 Pottet, a Frenchman, patented a centre-fire, metallic cartridge with a centre-sited percussion cap in the base. This and other similar systems suffered from sundry disorders—particularly as the weak cases tended to split as charges were increased. In 1866 Colonel Edward Boxer patented a centre-fire, coiled-sheet brass cartridge which expanded to form a good gas seal but also contracted quickly for easy extraction. It was adopted for use in the Snider rifle and the Martini-Henry, although in the latter weapon it did cause extraction problems. In 1888 its design was changed and a solid drawn case was used. Here was the style which was to become basic, and although there were further improvements and modifications, the true modern firearm had arrived.

The collecting of cartridge weapons is not easy for in Britain they are, with very few exceptions, required to be entered on a firearms certificate, and it is against the law to own one without such a permit. In many other countries the position is the same, and all collectors should check the legal requirements before seeking to acquire such weapons.

15

Flasks and Accessories

ONLY two pieces of equipment are required by the modern firearm user—the gun itself, and cartridges. There may be numerous extras which he can use if he wishes, but these are the only two absolute essentials. However, life for his predecessors was far more complex. For the earliest hand-gunner or artilleryman there were four items of equipment—gun, powder, ball and ignition. It is not at all clear from contemporary documents and illustrations exactly how the guns were ignited, although the inference is that either a hot iron or a glowing piece of fuel was used. Both methods required a fire, and the earliest gunners had to have some means of starting a fire; flint and tinder were obvious necessities. If a heated rod was used the gunner's freedom of movement was obviously limited to the immediate vicinity of his fire—the rod cooled rapidly and had to be re-heated at frequent intervals. The glowing ember was slightly more convenient; smouldering moss or rag could be kept aglow in some sort of container for a reasonable length of time, granting the gunner a consequently greater mobility.

With the advent of the slow match life became much simpler for the gunner, who was now free to move about as he wished. The match was made of cord or tow, but as these materials, once lit, did not glow for very long they had to be treated in some way.

Fig. 179: Annular wooden powder flask inlaid with discs of ivory and mother of pearl, and fitted with an ivory-screw stopper. The two rings are for the carrying cord. German, 16th century. (Gyngell Collection.)

The normal method of preparing the match was to take the cord, normally supplied in lengths or skeins, and soak it in any one of a number of formulae, all containing saltpetre in some strength; after this soaking the match was dried and cut into convenient lengths. The 17th century musketeer carried his operational match aglow at both ends, so that should one be extinguished there was an immediate reserve to hand. The match was carried in the left hand with the two glowing ends sticking up between the fingers. Since the match had to be kept alight continuously if there was any possibility of action, the amount consumed during the course of a day could be quite considerable. Musketeers therefore had to carry spare lengths of match; some preferred to sling this from their belts, while others wrapped it around the brim of their hats, or stored it inside the hat. The musketeer naturally carried flint and steel with him at all times.

As described in earlier chapters, the matchlock was subject to many inconveniences, and not the least was its vulnerability to drenching by rain. To prevent this simple pierced tubes were made, often of pewter, and into these were slipped the glowing ends of the match. While the holes allowed free ventilation they were not large enough to admit the quenching raindrops.

Muskets were no light weight, for they stood more than five feet high and the four-foot barrel was very thick and massive. To hold this weapon in the aiming position for any length of time was beyond the capabilities of most men and it was therefore essential to have some means of supporting the barrel. Thus was evolved the rest, which was a stout stick of ash fitted with a ferrule at one end and a U-shaped metal arm

Fig. 180: A superb powder flask of the type common in the late 16th and early 17th centuries, with sides of intricately pierced and chiselled metal. (Victoria and Albert Museum.)

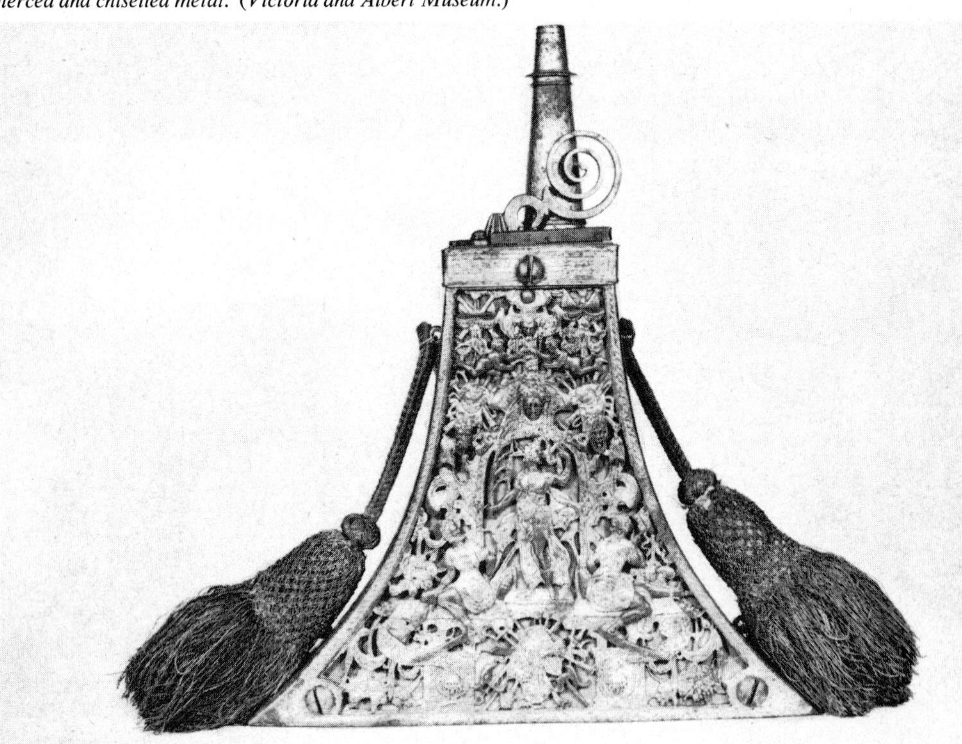

Fig. 181: An Indian belt with attached cartridge pouches; 19th century. (Reproduced by permission of the Trustees of the Wallace Collection.)

at the other. On the march the musketeer carried the rest rather like a walking stick, and when action was imminent the point was pushed into the ground and the barrel slipped into the U-shaped section at the top.

In the early days gunpowder had been a straightforward mixture of charcoal, saltpetre and sulphur in varying proportions; but it was found that when this powder was subjected to the jolting inevitable during transport over poor roads in springless carts, there was a tendency for the gunpowder to separate into its component parts. This simple mixture also deteriorated because of its rapid absorption of moisture, and was consequently slow burning, leaving heavy deposits in the barrel. It was found that if a very small percentage of water was added and the mixture was then forced through a sieve, the grains were far more stable and less absorbent. This blend, known as corned powder, was also found to be much quicker burning. With early artillery it had been a simple matter to prepare a number of chambers for the guns were breech loading; but for a variety of reasons handguns were muzzle loading. This meant that powder and shot had to be carried in a container and used as required, and most musketeers carried a powder horn or flask. It is likely that the earliest examples were merely some form of leather bag, but the flask as a separate item seems to have emerged in the 16th century.

ONE of the simplest forms was that fashioned from a piece of cow horn which was boiled until it softened and was then flattened to a tapering rectangular section. When it had cooled and hardened the wide end was closed with a wooden block nailed into place. At the other end the tip of the horn was cut off and a tapering metal nozzle fitted. These nozzles had a spring activated cut-off which was fitted either at the base or at the tip of the nozzle. Later examples invariably had the cut-off mounted at the base, the nozzle being designed to hold a set measured charge. The procedure was to cover the nozzle with the forefinger, open the cut-off by pressing with the thumb, and then invert the flask allowing powder to run out and fill the nozzle. If the cut-off was now allowed to close and the flask was reversed the correct charge of powder was ready to be poured down the barrel. These horns were often decorated with incised patterns or simple hunting or military scenes.

Another popular form of powder horn used a Y-shaped section of antler which was hollowed and had two ends capped and a nozzle fitted to the third. One side of the horn had the roughness ground off and the flat surface was then chiselled or carved into a variety of shapes or scenes.

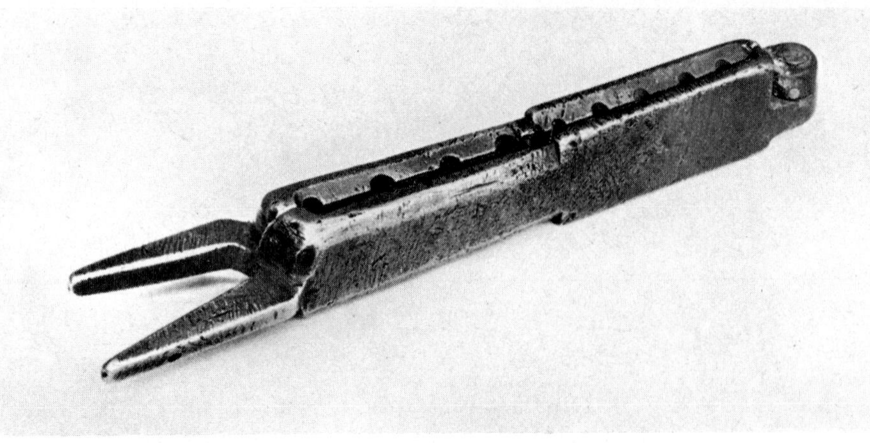

Above, *Fig. 182: 18th century bronze mould for casting four different sizes of ball and two sizes of buck-shot.* (*H. L. Peterson Collection.*)

Foot of opposite page, *Fig. 183: Nickel-plated brass nipple primer by G. & J. H. Hawksley; a few grains of powder could be fed through the funnel and exploded in a fouled nipple to clear it.* (*Bedford Collection.*)

In the late 16th and early 17th centuries another type of flask was in common use; this was basically triangular in form and was fitted with a fretted or chiselled metal plate on back and front. The main wooden body was often covered with velvet so that the material showed through the fretting. Smaller versions of this pattern were made to hold the much finer grained priming powder. Another but less common shape was the annular or "doughnut" style; these were usually of wood inlaid with bone or ivory plaques. This variety seldom had a measuring nozzle, a capped pourer being more usual.

The longest surviving style was that utilising an ordinary piece of cow horn, and these were still being used well into the 19th century. Some very desirable specimens are those which were carried by a soldier or sailor through a campaign and on which he engraved a map or battle scene, but genuine examples are rare. Far more common are the horns used by a master gunner to prime the cannon; these were basically just an ordinary section of horn with a conical brass end and spring clip. The other end was blocked with a wooden plug with a screwed stopper in the centre. Some bear government markings but others of the same pattern are quite plain.

During the latter part of the 18th century flasks were commonly of brass or copper and of oval section; in the 19th century the majority were pear shaped and were being die-stamped. Many were absolutely plain but others had a great variety of embossed patterns and scenes. The great majority were manufactured by British firms such as James Dixon & Sons, Frith and Sons, and Hawksley Sykes; and many were exported all over the world. Less common were the two or three-way flasks which served to hold not only powder but a number of bullets and spare flints. Many flasks had an adjustable nozzle which could be set to provide two or three different measures of powder. Large versions of the powder flasks were also made for use with sporting guns, and often held not powder but shot. Some were leather covered, while a few were of silver. Shot flasks often had an ingenious double cut-off in the nozzle which obviated the need for placing the finger over the end of the nozzle.

Asian flasks were produced in a greater variety of shapes than in the West, and many are made from the horns of sheep, goats and deer. The basic shape of the horn is often adapted to the design of the flask in an ingenious fashion. This is well shown in some Persian priming horns which used a double-curved piece of antelope horn fitted with a carved ivory head to give the form of a snake or monster. Indian gunners often carried a small all-steel priming flask.

Obviously the powder flask was a convenient device for measuring a correct charge but it was comparatively slow and liable to error. There were many who argued that it was much quicker to use devices holding measured charges and advocated the use of the bandolier, which was a shoulder belt from which were suspended a number of horn or wooden containers, each holding one correct charge for the weapon. The first appeared during the early part of the 16th century in Northern Europe, and their use soon spread across the world. Not only the small powder holders were attached to the bandoliers; many musketeers also used them to hold the priming flask, a bag of bullets and sometimes a spare length of match. The bandolier was largely abandoned by the 18th century, except in parts of the orient where it continued in modified forms. Probably one of the best-known versions is that used by the Russian Cossacks, with breast-pocket pouches each containing four or five bone tubes each holding one charge.

The cartridge was a great step forward, since even the bandolier of measured charges required a double operation; powder had to be poured down the barrel, and the wad or bullet driven home with the ramrod. The cartridge eliminated one action, since it contained both bullet and powder, and with the introduction of the flintlock there was an increase in their use. However, the adoption of cartridges meant that the soldier or hunter had to have some means of carrying them. Sometimes it was no more than a bag slung from the shoulder, but later on it was usually a leather or japanned metal case in which was a wooden block drilled with a number of holes each holding one cartridge. With the adoption of the percussion system yet another container became necessary to hold the caps, and generally this was a small pouch secured to the waist belt. Caps were small and rather awkward to handle, but for the sportsman

Below, *Fig. 184: Selection of combination tools; those in the top row were for flintlock weapons, and the remainder for percussion arms. The examples in the bottom row incorporate ingenious main-spring clamps. (Blackmore Collection.)*

Right, *Fig. 185: A set of armourers' tools carried in about 1820 by J. Delpire, armourer to the 7th Swiss Regiment of Royal Guards of the French Army. (Blackmore Collection.)*

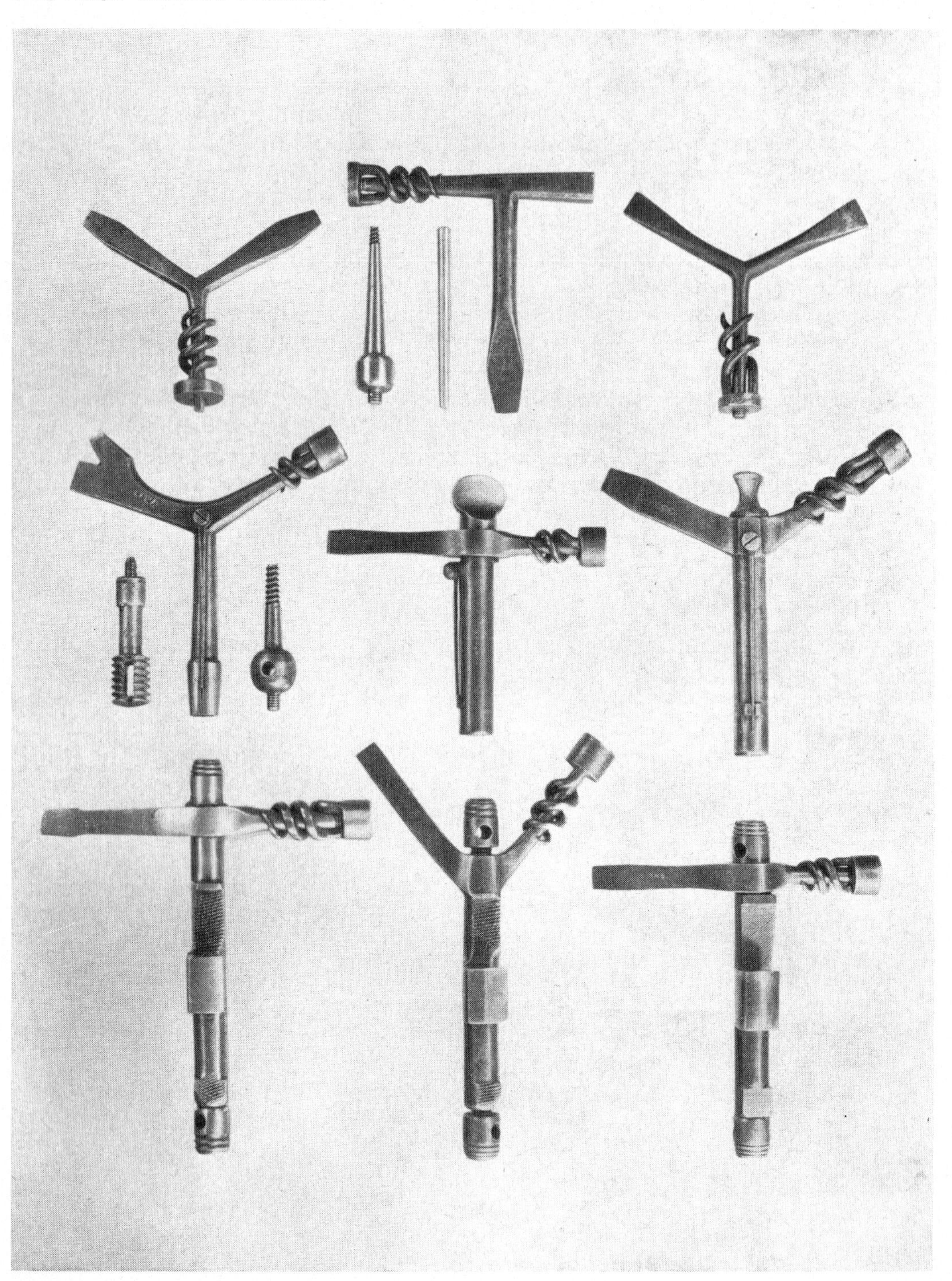

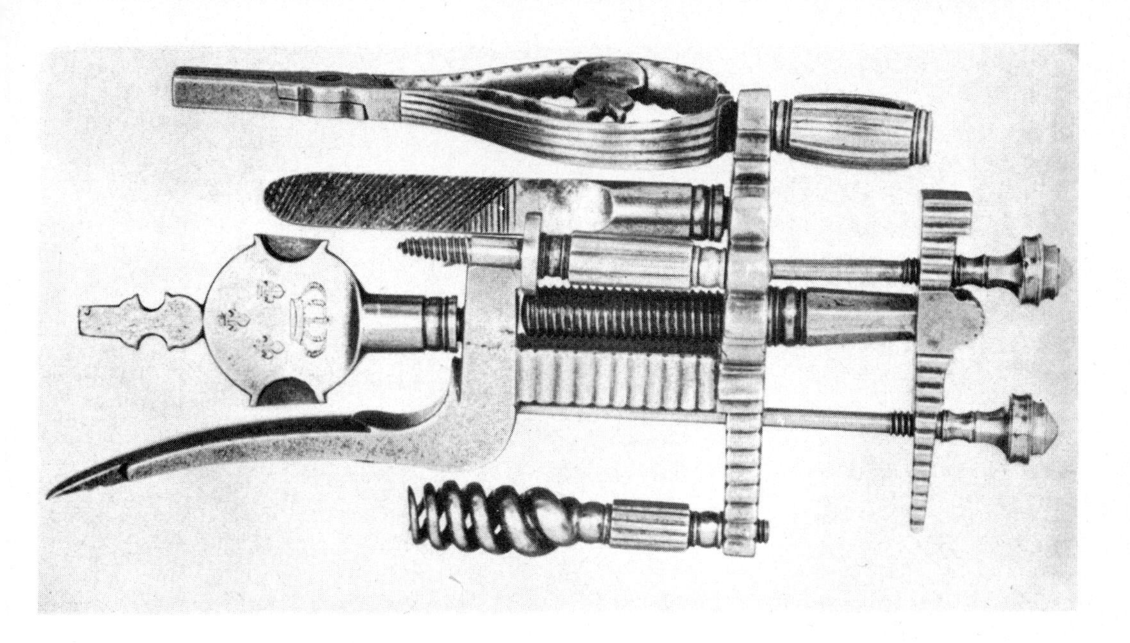

able to afford extras there were cap dispensers. Basically these consisted of a spiral channel which held the caps, to which a small spring-loaded arm applied pressure. At one side was an opening just big enough to hold one cap, which was placed over the nipple; as it was removed the pressure of the spring moved another up to take its place.

ALTHOUGH the paper cartridge was commonly available, any soldier or sportsman might well find himself in a situation where he was unable to obtain a fresh supply. To meet this emergency many pistols and revolvers were sold complete with bullet mould and powder flask. As early as the 14th century there are references to brass moulds, and this material was still being used when they became obsolete in the 19th century. Those early examples which have survived seem to suggest that the majority of moulds of the 16th and 17th centuries were of the "gang" variety, and cast not one ball but several at each filling. Essentially the design of the bullet mould remained unaltered throughout its entire history; it comprised two leaves, or arms, hinged at one end, which fitted closely together. Cut into the two leaves were hollows which were either round or conical, and running along the top was a small channel connected by narrow vents to each of the cavities. Lead was heated in a small crucible, and when at the right temperature was poured into the channel. Lead has a low melting point and also cools rapidly, so that within a very short time the mould could be opened and the line of bullets, all connected like a bunch of grapes, could be removed. The connecting arms were then clipped off and the ball polished smooth. In the 18th century a further improvement was brought about by fitting the mould with a sprue cutter to trim the excess tail—usually two sharpened edges on the arms of the mould which could be used as scissors. From the 17th century the "gang" mould gradually went out of fashion, until by the latter part of the 18th century most moulds cast only a single ball and were equipped with a cutting edge for trimming. With the advent of the revolver it was common practice to supply bronze moulds which could cast two

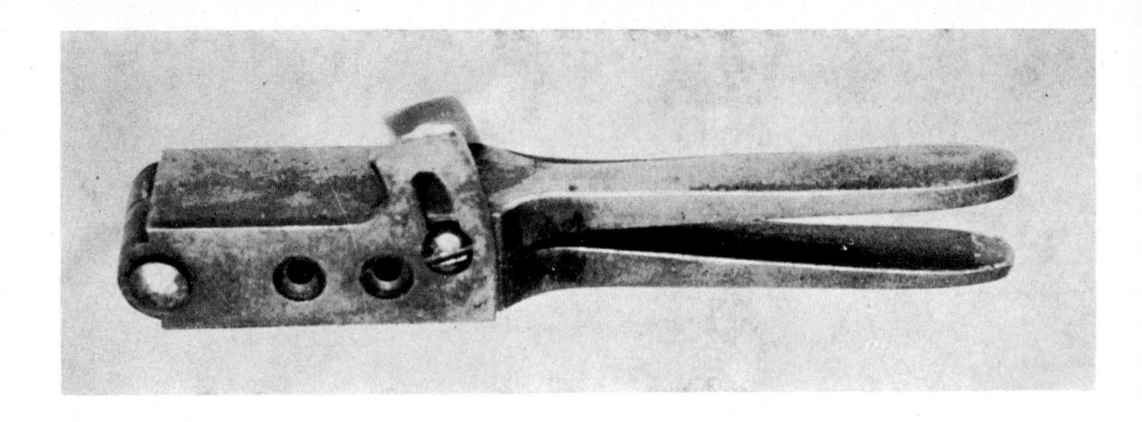

Above, *Fig. 186: Bullet mould for a Navy Colt of 1851, with two pouring holes for a conical or round bullet. The top pivots to cut the sprue from newly cast balls.*

Foot of opposite page, *Fig. 187: Delpire's tools dismantled—see Fig. 185. They comprise pliers, screwdrivers, worms, a file and a hammer.* (*Blackmore Collection.*)

bullets—one round and the other conical. More complex moulds were needed to cast bullets for weapons such as the Jacomb's rifle which used a hollow-nose bullet. Most of the later bullet moulds were fitted with a moveable plate which served as a simple funnel and sprue cutter. A slightly tapered hole sat neatly over the cavity, and when the lead had set this plate was swivelled to one side and cut off the sprue or tail.

ONE of the variables which concerned the early gunner was the quality of his powder, a very important factor since the force of the explosion depended on quality. For accurate shooting it was desirable to have some means of assessing the explosive qualities of the powder, and to do this the gunner used a powder-tester. This was a simple device which gave only a relative reading, since there were no absolute standards of measurement for the explosive qualities of gunpowder; but at least it enabled the user to make comparisons. These powder-testers or *éprouvettes* used all forms of ignition and the design was by no means standard, but the majority comprise some form of spring-loaded arm which pressed against a short chamber or barrel. Into this tiny chamber a pinch of powder was placed and the lid closed. If the powder was then exploded the force pushed back the plate, which being attached to some form of pointer gave a relative reading.

For the gunner using a wheellock weapon it was essential to have a key or spanner to wind up the mechanism. Some keys were extremely decorative, and some were made to double as screwdrivers and powder measures.

These then were the basic essentials for any sportsman or dueller; and the cased sets of the late 18th century normally included, apart from the pistol, a bullet mould and powder flask. The later cases of percussion revolvers almost invariably contained in addition some form of oil bottle, commonly of white metal and seldom more than an inch or so high. The top unscrewed for filling but the neck also had a separate stopper the end of which had a small spatula which could be used to transfer tiny drops of oil to the vital spots. Many of the cased percussion revolvers, as well as some flintlocks, contained a cleaning rod which was sometimes a double-purpose tool; it could serve as a ramrod, and the end might be detachable so that it could be changed into a jag or worm. This was a single or double corkscrew attachment which could be inserted into the barrel and turned so as to engage with a jammed ball. Once a good grip had been obtained it was comparatively simple to withdraw the ball and empty out the powder.

Cased percussion weapons also carried with them a supply of caps and these were usually in a small proprietary tin. The name most commonly seen on the tin was that of Joyce, a chemist who largely cornered the market in the early 19th century. In the case of rifled weapons such as French duelling pistols there was also a small mallet which was used to tap the ramrod to drive home the tight-fitting ball.

With the more sophisticated percussion revolver there was a need for one or two extra tools as nipples often broke and had to be replaced. Many cases carried small circular ivory or bone boxes which normally held at least one spare set of nipples. To unscrew the nipples a key was supplied, and in the simplest form this comprised a wooden handle and a short straight shank with a square-cut hole at the end. With English revolvers these nipple keys often have a pin screwed into the handle for cleaning nipples. Many of the nipple keys were adapted to incorporate other attachments, so that the same tool could be used as a nipple key or a screwdriver, and many have small hollow caps at the end of the arm which hold a spare nipple. For armourers attached to units in the British Army combination tools were issued comprising a wrench, screwdriver, nipple key and sometimes a spanner. These combinations are not new, for they were known in the 17th century; some of these early examples are delights of mechanical ingenuity, utilising the absolute minimum of space for the maximum number of items. Small hammers, chisels, screwdrivers, clamps, prickers, and pliers were all compressed and united in a variety of very ingenious designs.

In order to dismantle a lock it was necessary to remove the mainspring which was normally too powerful to be compressed manually. The lock was put to full cock

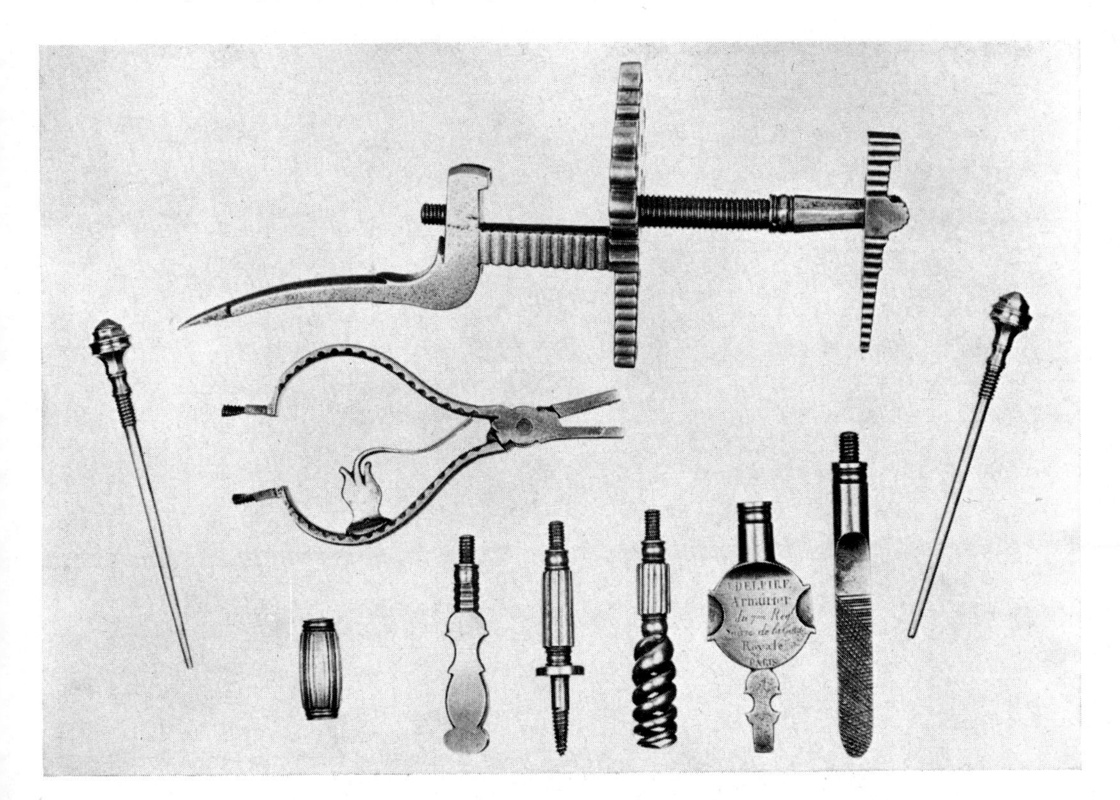

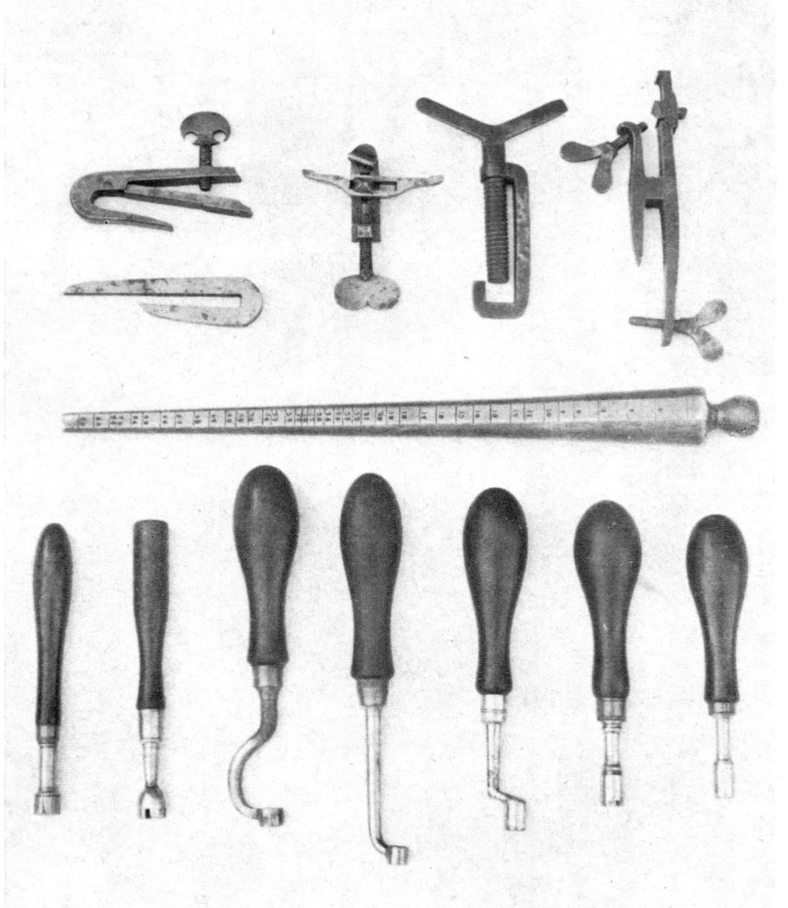

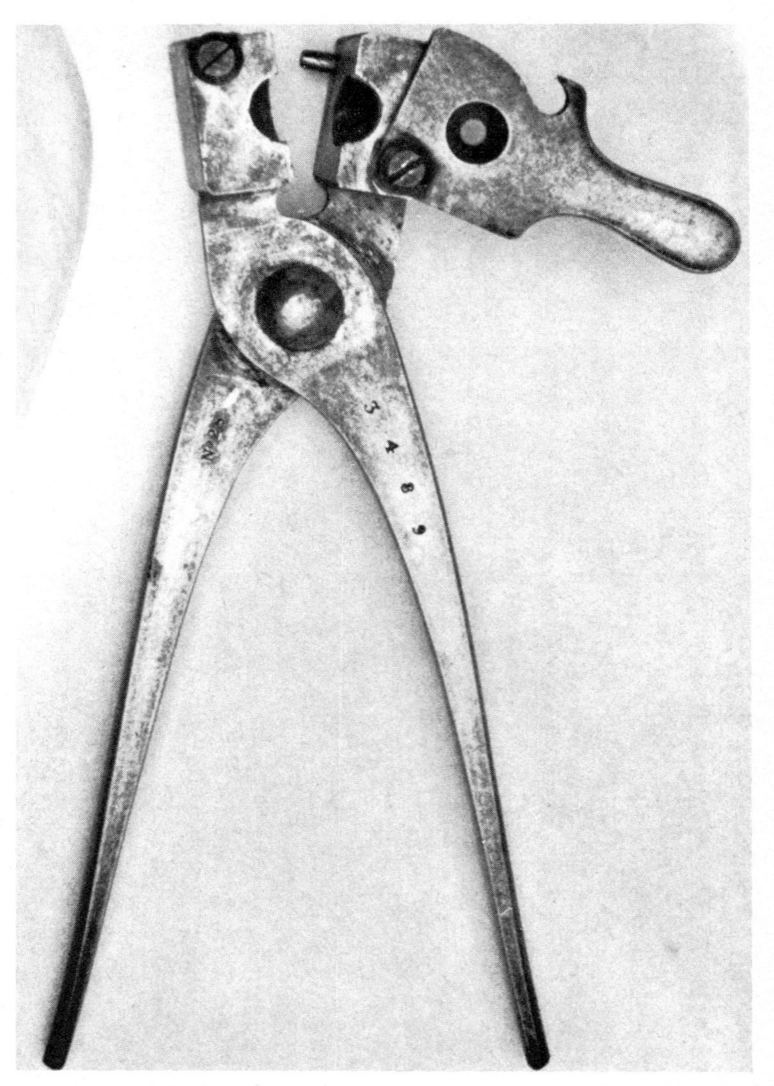

Right, *Fig. 188: Bullet mould for the ·577 Enfield rifle in the open position, showing the cavity and swivelling top plate;* circa *1860.* **Above,** *Fig. 189*: (Left to right) *Selection of spring clamps used when stripping down lock; barrel gauge, for determining diameter of bore; and a selection of nipple keys. (Blackmore

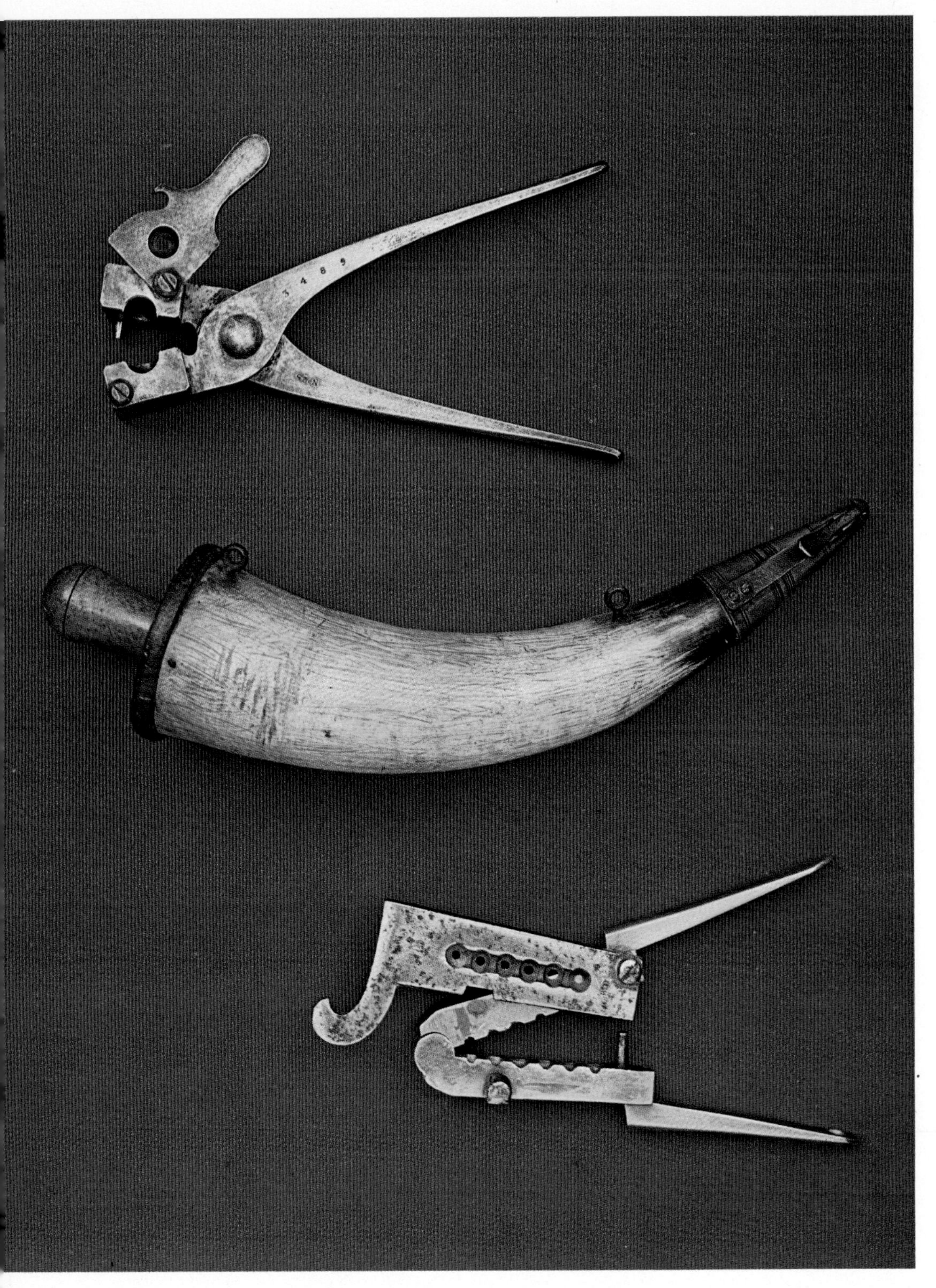

late 30 *Steel bullet mould for ·577 Enfield rifle. Master gunner's powder horn. Brass bullet mould, for casting six alls at a time.* (*Gyngell Collection.*)

Plate 31 *Accessories*. (Top left) *Nipple Key*. (Top centre) *Shot measure. T-shaped nipple key. Combination tool. Oil bottle*. (Centre) *Nipple key. Screwdriver. Cap dispenser. Barrel key. Powder flask*. (Bottom) *Charge holder. Mainspring clamp. Combined powder and shot measure in brass.*

and the mainspring was gripped between the jaws of a small screw vice. This clamp held the spring compressed and if the lock was now put to half cock it could easily be removed.

Nipple primers are a comparatively rare accessory but they do occasionally come on the market; they are in essence tiny powder flasks. A small nozzle fitted over the nipple and a few grains of powder were insinuated into the nipple vent. If a cap were now placed on the nipple and fired the resulting minor explosion effectively cleared any blockage of the nipple.

Sundry other odd items may also be found in cased sets, such as small wire brushes for cleaning the barrel, but these are essentially the same as the modern article.

With pocket pistols and Queen Anne type pistols another attachment which may be found is the barrel key. These were of two forms; the commonest slipped over the barrel and a small square slot cut at the bottom of the circular hole engaged with a lug beneath the barrel and so ensured a good grip. Less common was that resembling the carriage key, which was a T-shaped bar with the square end tapered so that when it was pushed into the muzzle it engaged with the notches cut therein.

LIKE the revolver and the duelling pistol, the more expensive shot gun or fowling piece was also cased. Normally the barrels could be easily detached from the stock and frequently a second set of barrels was included in the case. These long cases were often of leather secured by a long strap and from the shape necessary to accommodate barrels and stocks, are often known as "leg of mutton" cases. Some cases were produced in exactly the same style as for pistols and revolvers, that is a wooden case with green baize lining and the inside divided by a number of straight wooden fences. The powder flasks and shot flasks for long arms were naturally larger since the charge required was far greater. Apart from shot flasks there were also shot measures which had a short ebony or oak handle and a small cylindrical measure at the end. Many could be adjusted to give three or four different measures of shot. Another earlier method was the use of charge holders which were normally double-ended metal boxes with spring tops. Each section could be filled with the correct charge of shot and these containers were carried in the pocket ready for instant re-loading.

There was some controversy amongst sportsmen as to the best method of carrying shot. Some favoured the use of a shot flask whilst others preferred the shot belt, which comprised a hollow leather tube to one end of which was fitted a nozzle operating in exactly the same way as that on a shot flask. This was filled and slung either across the shoulder or around the waist according to preference, and used in exactly the same way as a shot flask.

Another item found in both revolver and sporting gun cases was the wad cutter—a punch with a circular, sharpened end. This punch was placed on the material and then given a sharp tap with the hammer to cut an appropriately sized disc of material. Patches for rifled weapons were usually cut from paper, cambric or calico and then greased with sundry substances. If round balls were used the patch was placed, greased side down, over the muzzle; the ball was placed on it and the two pushed down the barrel together with the ramrod. In the case of sporting guns the wadding was thicker, usually of pasteboard; and contemporary writers suggested that the larger the bore, the thicker should be the wad.

For the keen marksman anxious to preserve his barrel from all possible damage there were muzzle guards which clipped over the muzzle during loading and ensured that the ramrod did not rub against or damage the grooves of the rifling. Similarly there were sundry patented protectors which slipped over the muzzle and sights to ensure that the latter would not be knocked or bent in any way. To protect the nipple and hammer there were protectors in the form of small metal collars designed to fit over the nipple; the tops had a thick leather pad so that the hammer might be snapped down without fear of cracking nipple or hammer.

An accessory found in a few revolver cases was a separate detachable stock which fitted to the butt of the revolver and enabled it to be fired from the shoulder. They usually engaged with a couple of small lugs set on the sides of the revolver frame and locked into position by means of a screw which either engaged with the butt or merely exerted a pressure when adjusted.

For the later cartridge makers a great variety of tools were produced; these are rather specialised and comprise cap removers and crimping tools to fold in the end of the cartridge. They are still fairly plentiful and reference to appropriate books on hand-loading and cartridge-making will provide full details.

In the days when the slaughter of game was considered a virtue the number shot was often so excessive that it was difficult, if not impossible, to remember; and a number of mechanical game counters were provided whereby the busy sportsman could keep a check of the number of birds, deer and rabbits shot during the day. These were produced in a number of patented forms but nearly all comprise some form of dial and pointer.

The carrying of firearms was always something of a problem; early hand guns were occasionally fitted with a ring at the end of the stock and literally hung round the neck. The matchlock musket seems generally to have been carried over the shoulder and there is little evidence of slings. However, with the adoption of the flintlock musket the sling became fairly general and, of course, has remained standard up until the present day, varying only in details. The majority of handguns were intended either to be carried in the pocket or tucked in the belt, and many were fitted with a belt hook, a metal bar attached to the stock on the side opposite the lock. From quite early days horsemen carried their pistols in holsters attached, not to the man, but to the horse. Early engravings show the majority of personal pistols tucked on to a shoulder belt but in the case of horsemen a pair of leather holsters were affixed to the front of the saddle across the horse's neck. Some were all leather but others had the bottom tip covered with a brass or steel cap (see Plate 10, *Signature* 5). The top was covered by a leather flap which could be strapped down into place. Personal holsters did not appear until the 19th century. The earliest seem to have appeared with the pepperbox, and with the advent of the percussion revolver they became common items. Leather holsters for cavalry troops were normally worn on the right with the butt facing forward. This is a sensible arrangement, for a rider uses the right hand for the sword or for holding the reins. Most holsters were fitted with a leather flap which fastened over the top. The open holster so popular in Western folklore often had a small leather thong which was slipped over the hammer, since there was obviously considerable danger that the weapon would slip out of the holster. Carbines were often secured by means of a bar and ring fixed to the stock on the side opposite the lock. The ring was attached to a spring clip which in turn was secured to a shoulder strap. Sometimes this arrangement was replaced by the so-called bucket holster which was fastened to the harness; the carbine was slipped into this and often secured by a strap.

Individual accessories may still be found in many odd boxes and corners and are often not recognised for what they are. Powder flasks are easily spotted, unless they are oddities such as the multi-nozzle type used with the early Paterson revolvers; but clamps, keys and punches may well be discarded as "junk". However, it behoves the collector to be very careful, for replicas of flasks and bullet moulds are now being produced in bulk and if aged or worn, accidentally or not, it is sometimes difficult to recognise them as reproductions. Cases often lack an odd item and it is well worth acquiring any individual accessories that become available; later they may well complete a cased set.

Fig. 190: A plate by H. Miles in his "Book of Field Sports", *1860.* (Top, left to right) *Shot belt with 2 lb. capacity; powder and shot flasks; patent cartridge carrier.* (Centre, left to right) *Powder horn; cased Westley Richards "double" gun; cap dispenser.* (Bottom, left to right) *Game basket; complicated pocket knife for sportsmen; cartridge box, similar to contemporary military type.*

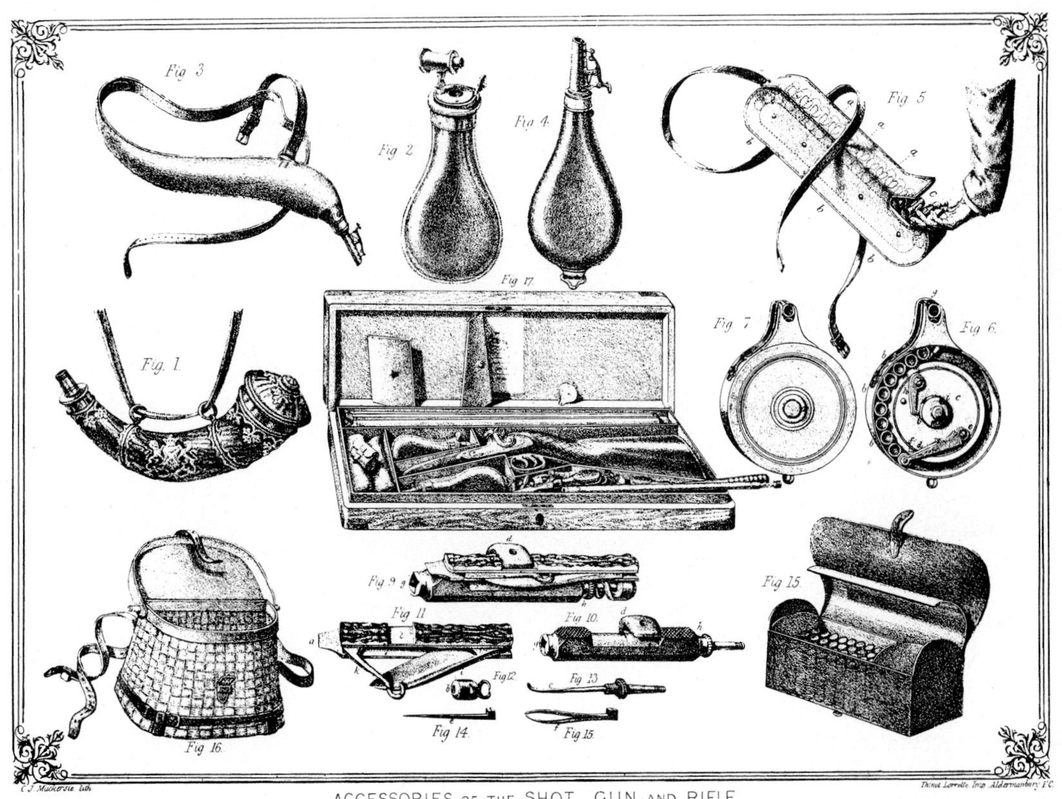

16

Manufacture and Identification

UNTIL the second quarter of the 19th century gunmaking was essentially a craftsman's job. Each part of the gun—lock, stock and barrel—was the work of one or more craftsmen working together to produce a unique finished article. This situation changed completely with the advent of mechanisation, and factories were set up capable of turning out hundreds of identical specimens. The earliest gunmakers were almost certainly armourers and weaponsmiths who looked on guns merely as another job; but as the demand increased it is reasonable to assume that some of them began to specialise in this field of construction, leaving aside their more conventional weapon and armour business.

In England gunmaking was largely the province of blacksmiths, since cannons and hand cannon were usually cast or welded. With the appearance of the wheellock there arose a demand for a degree of skill not possessed by the average blacksmith. There came, too, a demand for decoration and embellishment; and here lay the beginnings of the specialisation that was to become a feature of later gunmaking. The early Spanish gunsmiths claimed that they were unique in that each could manufacture all parts needed for a firearm.

Fig. 191: The flintlock from a late 18th century "Brown Bess" musket stripped down to its basic components; each of the 18 pieces was hand made and hand fitted.

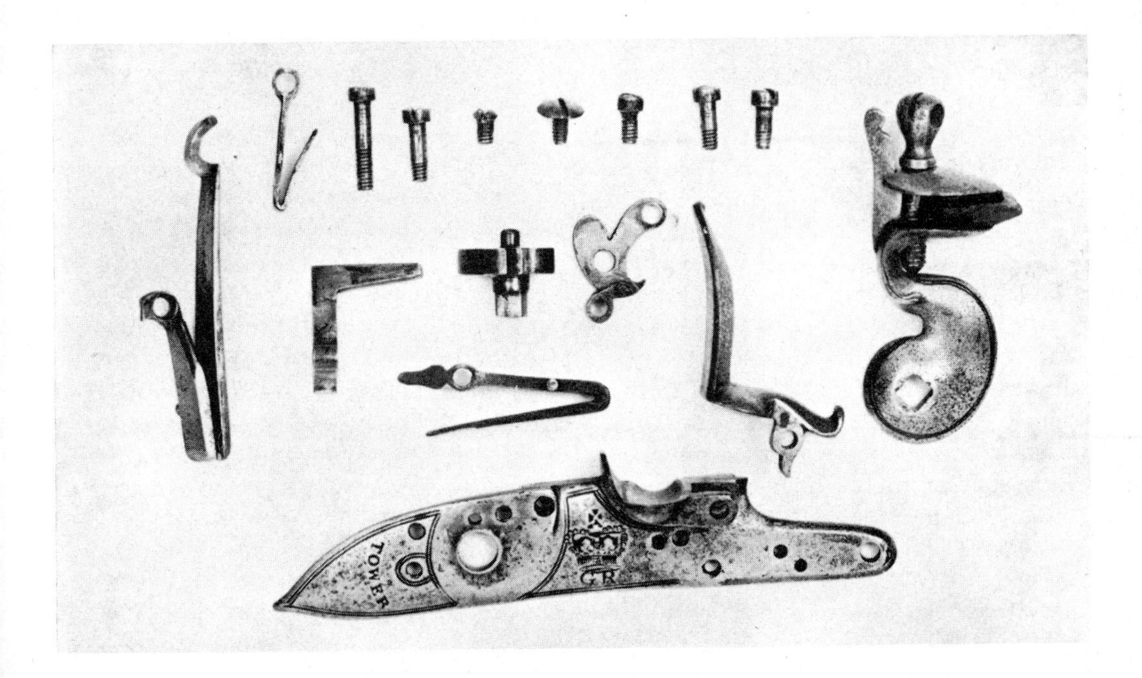

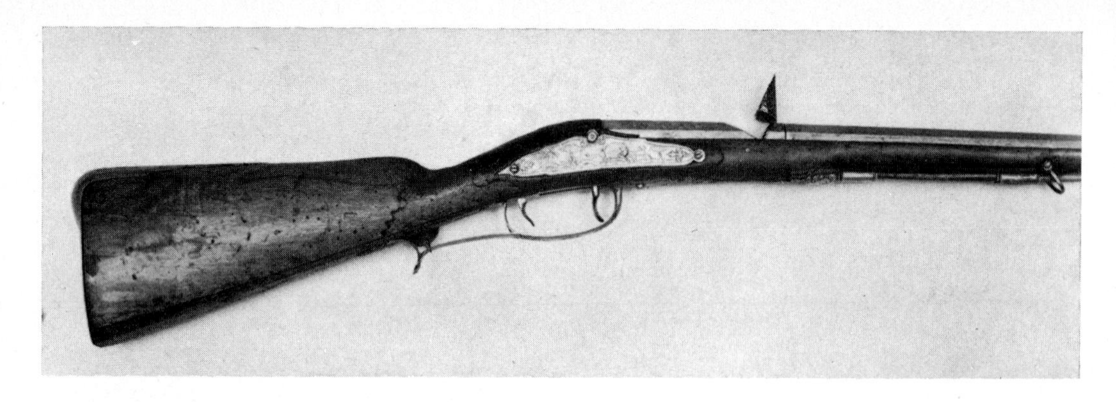

Fig. 192: Some guns with the flintlock mechanism entirely enclosed were produced during the second quarter of the 18th century, mostly in Germany. The triangular piece extending above the breech is the steel, which was closed down when the action had been primed. The action was cocked by the forward trigger. (Tower of London.)

Self-interest and communal protection led to the growth, during the Middle Ages, of the trade guild. This was a combination of local craftsmen who united to prevent the craft from becoming overcrowded, as well as ensuring that the public received work of a reasonable standard. In London these guilds were very powerful indeed and strenuously guarded their privileges. However, in 1637 a group of craftsmen sought permission from Charles I to break away from the Blacksmiths and to set up a Gunmakers' Company, and this privilege was duly accorded to them in March 1638 when the King granted them a charter.

Officers of the Company were elected and thenceforward only those who had served the approved apprenticeship and completed the trade tests were officially allowed to set themselves up as gunmakers in the City and environs of London. Established gunmakers took on assistants who were taught the trade, and when these apprentices had completed their training they were expected to submit an example of their work as their "master piece". If the work submitted was up to standard the applicant was elected as a Freeman of the Company. Apprentices usually served for seven years and for two years as a journeyman, although this latter period could be remitted on payment of a fine to the court.

One of the most important functions of the Gunmakers' Company was the proving of barrels, which were tested to ensure that they were safe. The normal practice was to load the barrel with an overcharge of powder and explode it, and if it had not burst or exhibited any other fault it was accepted as being satisfactory. This procedure has been recorded as early as the 14th century in Switzerland, and by the 16th century was common practice over most of Europe. Barrels which had been proved were marked, usually by means of a punch. The barrel was also examined visually, and the fact that this test had also been carried out was often indicated by a separate mark. It is not clear whether in the beginning proving was merely visual or by the exploding of a charge.

Stringent though these tests were it was possible for the unscrupulous or thoughtless maker to alter the barrel after it had been proved, and this was a difficult practice to control. To overcome this there grew up the system of double proof; first view and first proof were carried out when the barrel was in its rough state, and the second was performed with the barrel in its finished state. Before the creation of the Gunmakers' Company the Armourers and the Blacksmiths had assumed the responsibility for proof, and marked barrels with a crowned "A" and a crowned "P" or, in the case of Blacksmiths, with a crowned hammer. In 1638 the Gunmakers' Company started a set procedure at their proof house, which was situated in that part of London known as Whitechapel, not very far from the Tower of London and the Minories where so many London gunmakers had their premises. At this proof house the satisfactory guns were stamped with a crowned G.P. for "gunmakers' proof" and a crowned "V" when they had been viewed. Firearms belonging to makers who were not freemen of the Gunmakers' Company had their weapons proved and stamped with the letter "F". The weapons submitted for approval were those intended for the civilian market; military barrels proved at the Ordnance warehouse on the Tower quay were struck with crossed sceptres—a device which was adopted during the reign of William III (1694-1702).

Although the manufacture of firearms had been largely a London monopoly until the first half of the 17th century, the exigencies of the Civil War with its greatly increased demand stimulated a number of gunmakers to set themselves up in Birmingham. From a small beginning in 1639 the trade had developed sufficiently by 1643 for that city to be supplying large numbers of weapons to Parliament's army. Birmingham gradually increased in importance, and by the 19th century London was established as the centre of the select gun trade while Birmingham was the supply centre for the raw materials and the more ordinary weapons. In 1813 the gunmakers of Birmingham arranged for their own private proof house to be built, and in order to distinguish their proof from that of London they adopted as their mark a crowned "V", for the view, and crossed sceptres above "B.C.P."—Birmingham Company proof. These marks were stamped on the barrel and, in the case of revolvers, on the cylinder.

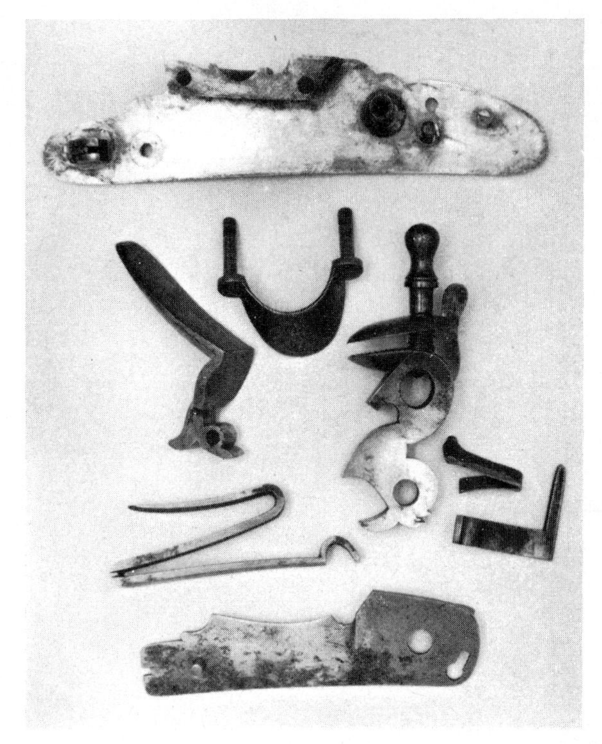

Fig. 193: In 1785 the renowned Henry Nock designed and produced a flintlock which used no screws at all, being held together by two plates; this Portuguese copy was made in 1791. The device was far simpler than the conventional pattern of lock, but was adopted on a limited scale only. (Tower of London.)

THE output from the Birmingham and London gunmakers was sufficient for normal demands; but the increasing size of armies during the Napoleonic Wars forced the British Government to look outside their own trade suppliers, and they purchased large numbers of muskets made for the East India Company by tradesmen not normally employed by the Ordnance. This position was unsatisfactory, and some steps to regularise, simplify and standardise the supply of military weapons were taken as early as 1804, when a Royal Small Arms factory was established at Enfield Lock in the County of Middlesex, not far from London. For the next half-century its output was comparatively unimportant, but in 1854 the shortage of weapons and the Crimean war aroused public opinion and forced the Government to take more interest in the supply of small arms. A Select Committee of Members of Parliament and others was set up to consider the problem, and, as already described in *Chapter* 14, evidence was heard of methods of firearms production in the United States, with Colonel Colt's revolvers as one of the items studied. The report of this committee suggested that all evidence pointed to the fact that machinery could replace the old hand work. It was decided that the factory at Enfield should be used experimentally to test out the feasibility of firearms construction in quantity by the use of machines. The manager appointed was one J. H. Burton, who had for a time been at the armoury at Harper's Ferry in the

Fig. 194: A superbly made and decorated pair of flintlock pistols by Henry Hadley, a London maker, dating from about 1775. They are etched, and the blued barrels are inlaid with gold. The escutcheon bears the arms of Charles, Third Duke of Marlborough. (*Tower of London.*)

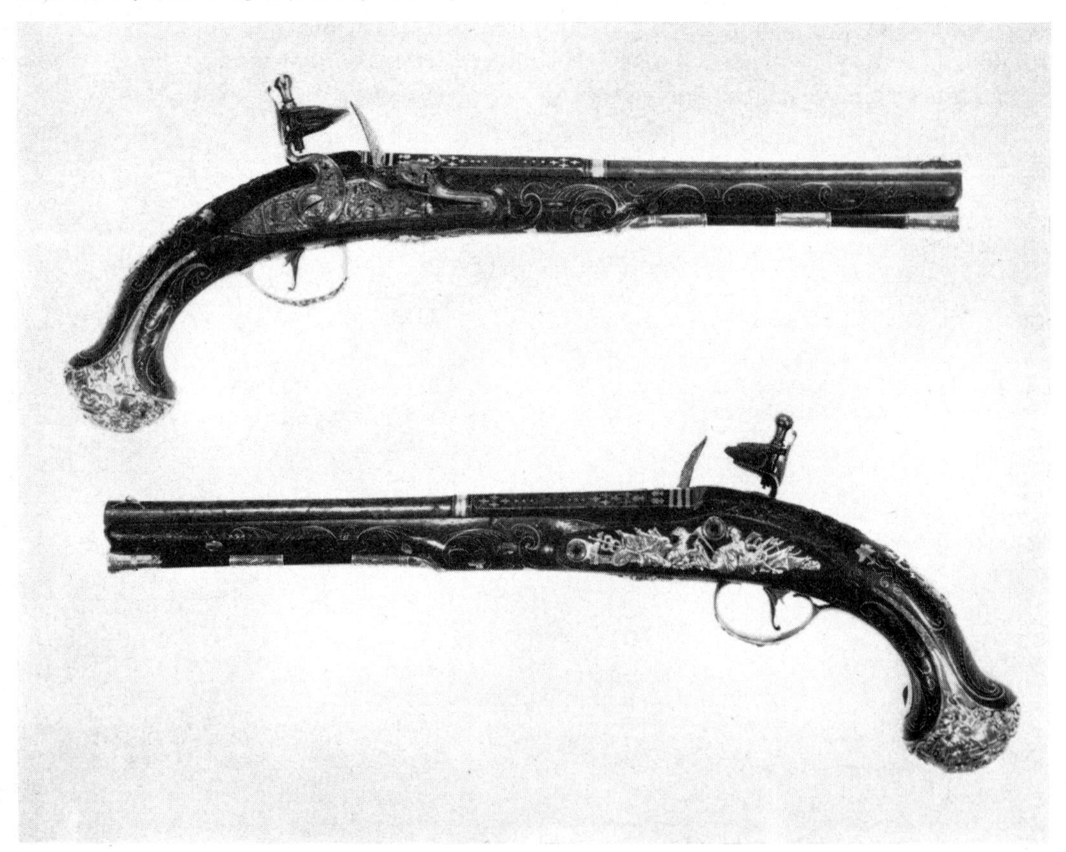

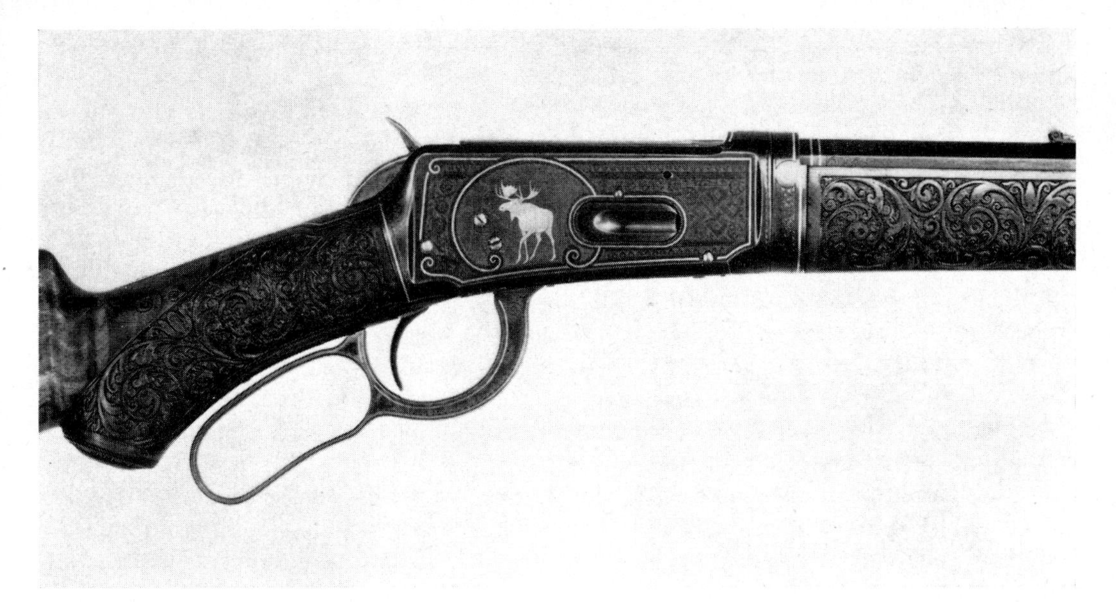

Fig. 195: A modern example of the decorative gunsmith's art; the stock of this Winchester Model 1894 is carved with intricate scrollwork, and the metal areas are engraved with patterns and a bull moose. The plain grooved plate is the magazine loading gate. (*Winchester Gun Museum.*)

United States. The new machinery was set up and production was started with the Pattern 1853 rifled musket, usually called the Enfield Rifle. Experience soon showed that the mass production worked well and saved enormously on costs, and for many years Enfield supplied the greater proportion of British military firearms; the factory is still in production today.

IN France the gunmaking industry had been centred at St. Etienne, Paris and Charleville; and the barrels at St. Etienne are described as being proved as early as the 17th century. Rules of proof were first laid down in France in 1729 and did not apply to civilian weapons, but in 1810 Napoleon extended proof rules to the whole of the French Empire; military arms were to be stamped with an "E" for *éprouve*, often surmounted by a crown. In Paris the proof mark was a reversed "E" and "P", whereas St. Etienne used crossed leaves somewhat reminiscent, at first glance, of the crossed sceptres of Birmingham. As the rules of proof applied to the whole of the French Empire the Belgian arms centre of Liège had to conform, and their proof mark was the letter "E", as required by Napoleon, and the letters "L.G." encompassed in a small oval. Over the years the mark underwent a number of changes including a re-introduction of the earlier one which used a formalised tower, part of the City of Liège's arms. These proof marks form a very useful aid in identifying weapons, since most of them are known and recorded; for example, Antwerp used a hand, Vienna a shield with a cross, and Suhl, a great arsenal town, used the letters SUL.

The procedure for the actual proving of the barrels was basically the same in all areas. Barrels were measured and assessed for quality of workmanship, and loaded with a stipulated charge depending upon the bore. The barrels were then placed in an enclosed chamber and fired, one after the other, by means of a chain of powder. If still satisfactory they were stamped as proved. This was normal procedure for first proof but for final proof, in Birmingham at least, the barrel was fired again individually. During the early part of the 19th century Joseph Manton introduced a further test whereby the barrel was filled with water under great pressure. It was found that any minute pinholes were easily discernable with this hydraulic pressure system.

THE earliest guns had the barrels cast in bronze or brass, but later they were made of thin metal plates which were rolled to make a tube. In order to give these thin tubes additional strength they were reinforced by strips of iron which were then secured by rings around the outside, building the whole assembly up to a fairly solid barrel. This method was satisfactory for artillery and the larger weapons but obviously had serious limitations when applied to the barrels of pistols and muskets. For the smaller weapons the first method of construction was apparently to drill from the solid, a procedure recorded well back in the 14th century and certainly a common practice throughout most of the 16th century.

Yet another method commonly adopted for pistol barrels was to use a sheet of iron, usually thicker at one end than the other. When the long rectangular piece of iron had been correctly sized and thickened it was folded around a carefully shaped bar, the mandril. The two edges were overlapped by half an inch or so and then carefully heated and hammer-welded together, section by section. The outside of the barrel was then filed and polished, and a breech plug tapped in at the thicker end. In the case

Fig. 196: Typical trade label, in this case that of William Parker of Holborn, London. Circa *1800. These labels were commonly fixed inside the lids of gun cases by makers and retailers.*

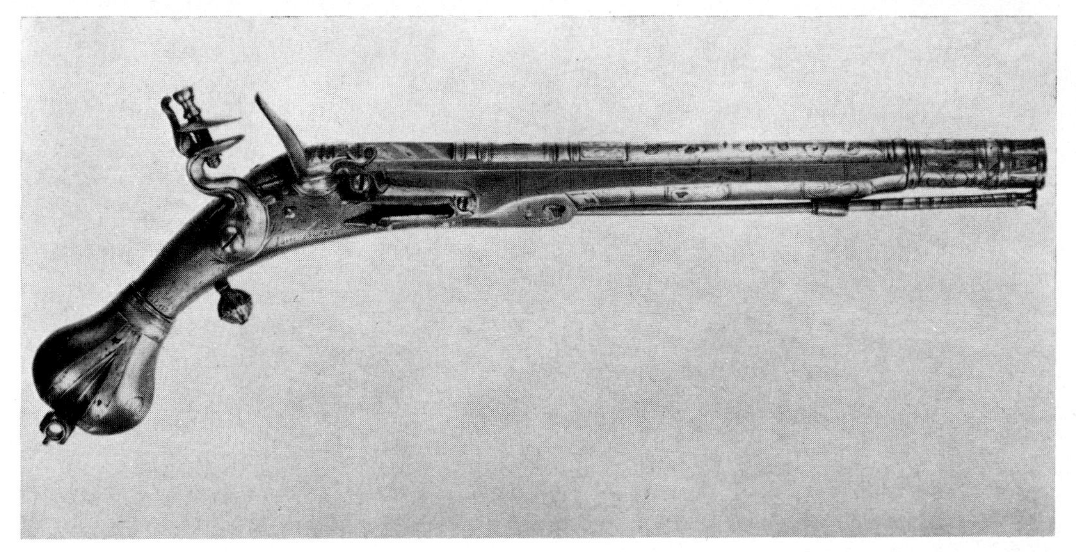

Fig. 197: A Scottish pistol with an all-metal stock and a heart-shaped butt, made by John Burges of Elgin in about 1700. Most Scottish pistols have the ball trigger. (*Tower of London.*)

of Continental pistols and muskets this completed the barrel, for it was secured to the stock by bands; but with British firearms lugs were then welded on to the bottom of the barrel ready to receive the pins when they were passed through the stock to hold the barrel firmly in position.

During the late 18th and early 19th century many of these processes were mechanised, and the "skelps", which was the name given to the rectangles of iron, were produced by rollers adjusted in diameter to produce the required shape. The plate was then made into a cylinder heated to the correct welding temperature; a rod or iron was placed inside and it was passed quickly through rollers which resulted in a quick, even welding of the entire seam.

While these basically simple techniques of barrel-making were quite adequate and satisfactory for general use, the hunter and fowler demanded an article of better quality with greater strength. In Spain in the mid-17th century gunmakers acquired a reputation for the quality of their barrels which they were to maintain for many years. Spanish barrels were made not from a long bar but from a number of small tubes. For this the best raw material was thought to be horseshoes which had been in use for some time. The rhythmic pressure of the hoof was, in effect, cold hammering, which produced an extremely good quality steel. Small flat plates were carefully lap-welded, that is edge to edge, until the entire length of the barrel had been built up. The whole piece was then worked over, traditionally at least 32 times, until it had acquired a uniform composition of good quality steel. So highly prized were Spanish barrels that they were frequently imported by European and British gunmakers, and to sell their barrels many gunmakers marked their products with spurious Spanish marks in the hope that the less discerning sportsman would be misled.

A system of construction probably first introduced at the beginning of the 18th century was even more complicated. Essentially the system involved winding a bar, which was made up of a mixture of iron and steel, around a core. This form of construction was known as "twist", and was probably Oriental in origin. It is often said

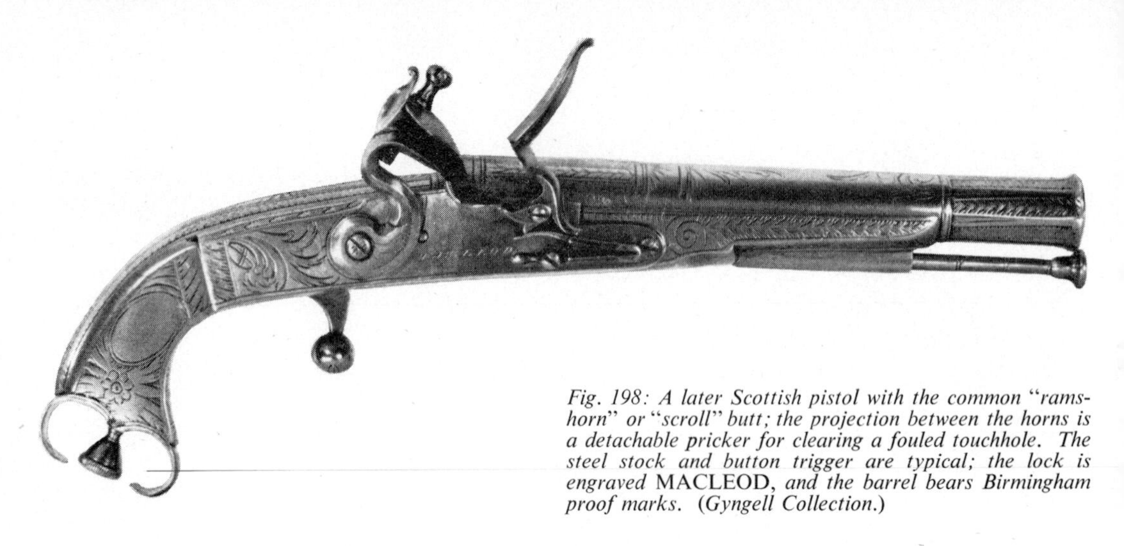

Fig. 198: A later Scottish pistol with the common "rams-horn" or "scroll" butt; the projection between the horns is a detachable pricker for clearing a fouled touchhole. The steel stock and button trigger are typical; the lock is engraved MACLEOD, *and the barrel bears Birmingham proof marks.* (*Gyngell Collection.*)

that the fashion may be traced to the siege of Vienna in 1683 when numbers of such barrels were captured from the Turks. These were mounted by the Austrians on ordinary stocks and found by the sportsmen of Europe to be extremely strong and efficient. Most British barrels were made from the steel in horseshoe nails which were imported from the Continent. First they were sorted and polished and then mixed with a certain proportion of steel, and the mixture was melted and "puddled" together. The metal was then drawn out and hammered into bars of appropriate size which were passed through rollers. The iron produced was of very good quality and free from specks, but was rather soft. The bars were then rolled out until they were several yards long and about half an inch wide; the thickness depended upon whether they were intended for the main part of the barrel or for the breech, in which case they would be thicker. The rod was then twisted into a spiral which was heated and slipped on to a cylindrical iron rod; this was banged up and down so that the edges of the spiral were united. Another spiral was placed on top and the process repeated until the appropriate length of tube had been formed, when the whole barrel was forged over.

For even better quality barrels the softer iron was formed into a sandwich—as many as 25 alternate bars of iron and mild steel, each about two feet long, two inches wide and a quarter of an inch thick. These were beaten and drawn into a rod $\frac{3}{8}''$ square, which was cut into lengths of five or six feet. A piece was heated, one end was held firmly in a vice, and the other was twisted round and round, a process which naturally shortened the overall length of the rod. If a number of rods were being used for the barrel construction they were twisted in alternate directions, so that when joined the surfaces of iron and steel would produce a most attractive finish. This style of working was said to produce a "Damascus barrel" because of an apparent similarity to the style of metal work used in Oriental sword blades allegedly made in Damascus. Differing patterns could be produced by variations in composition, the direction in which the twist was made, and the way in which the pieces were united. A number of these styles were given their own names—"imitation Damascus", "stub twist", "laminated iron", "stub Damascus", "charcoal iron", "twopenny iron" and "sham damn". This last was described by "Stonehenge," a famous 19th century sportsman, as being "too bad even for our general dealers, and it is solely used for guns made for exportation"!

When the barrel had been made it was rough-bored by a long square bit which was rotated at speed while being cooled by a constant flow of water. The outside of the barrel was ground on a very wide, engine-powered grindstone; the workman leaned against a wooden board suspended over the wheel and, holding the barrel on a long iron rod, adjusted the degree of grinding by the pressure exerted against the wheel. Many rough-finished barrels were then sent to London to be "set true" and completed by the fashionable London gunmakers. The end of the barrel at the breech was tapped, and the breech plug screwed in. For double-barrelled guns the two were then secured by means of a rib which was brazed, or hard soldered, at the breech end and soft-soldered along the remaining length, since the degree of heat required to braze the entire length of barrel would have been so great as to have damaged the temper of the metal.

THE stock was normally of walnut, although ash and maple were also used as were some of the more exotic woods. For best results the wood had to be well seasoned, and it was generally reckoned that it should have stood for at least two or three years before being used. In the case of expensive guns the stock was made to measure, and the customer might well take several fittings to make sure that the stock dropped just the right amount, was set at just the right angle to the barrel, and so on. This job was the responsibility of the stocker, who would also let the barrel and lock into the wooden

Fig. 199: This lock was designed by Sir Howard Douglas in 1817; the two pairs of jaws each held a flint. If one piece broke the jaws could quickly be loosened and rotated to bring the second pair into position. The system was not adopted on any large scale except in the case of cannon locks. (Tower of London.)

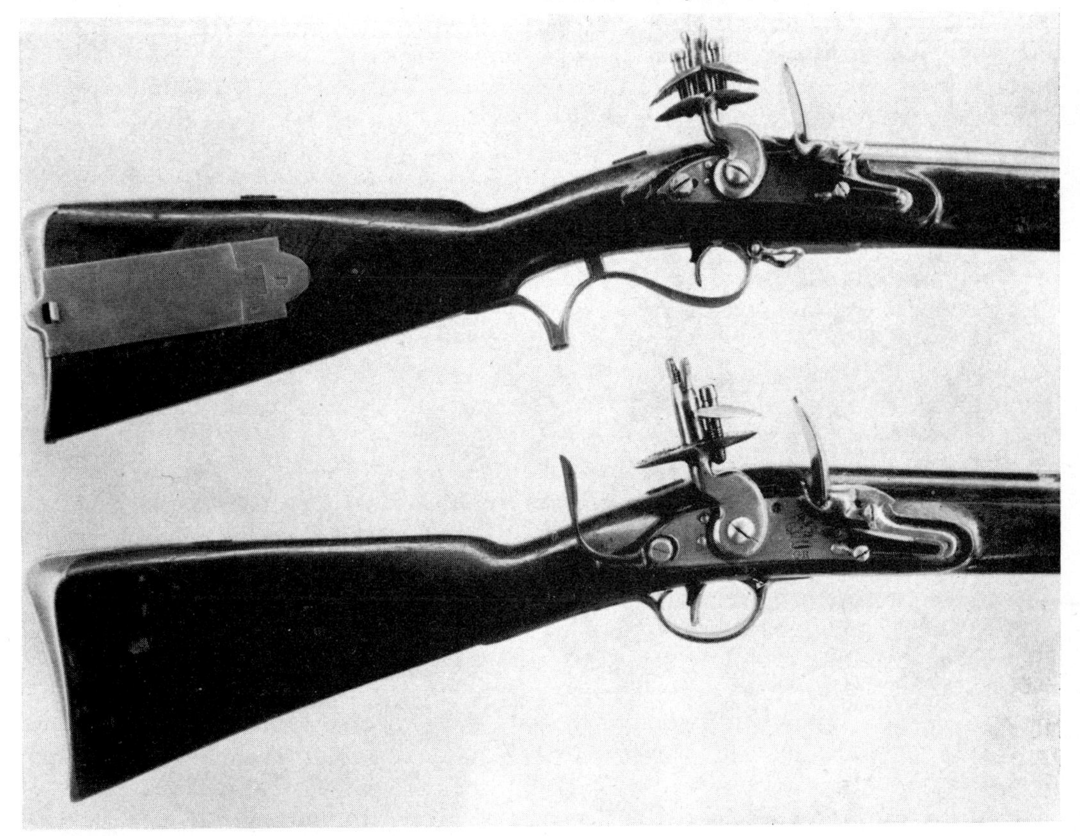

Fig. 200: Workmen in the barrel-boring, straightening, turning and polishing shop of "Mr. Charles Reeves's Implements of War Manufactory, Toledo Works, Birmingham". An illustration from the Illustrated Times *of June 28th, 1862.*

stock. When the stock had been cut and made to the correct measurements it was coloured with cold drawn linseed oil and alkanet root. When thoroughly dry it was varnished with a solution of shellac in spirits of wine. At first, of course, all this was done by hand, but later machines mass-produced stocks. The stocker was considered to be a very important member of the team and in 1841 a writer suggested that they could earn between £4 and £6 a week—in those days an uncommonly good wage. When the stocker had finished his job the pieces went to the next craftsman, the "screwer together", who let in the furniture—ramrod pipes, trigger guard, butt plate and side plates. As his title suggests, he also put in all the screws.

Now the weapon passed to the "detonator", who was responsible for fitting the lock and finishing the external part of the breeching. Next the "maker off" shaped the stock, finished the fore end, and did any carving that was required. The main part of the job was now completed, but there was still some considerable finishing off; the stripper and finisher took the whole thing to pieces and fitted new screws, and did any trimming that was required while the lock finisher did the same for the lock, which was then stripped down to its component parts ready for the next step. The polisher and hardener now dealt with the barrel and any other parts. The barrel was engraved and would probably be browned; in this process the surface was treated with any one of a number of chemical solutions which, in effect, produced controlled rusting. It also emphasised the pattern of the twist and produced a most pleasing effect. When the rusting had reached the required level the action was stopped and the delicate light reddish-brown surface would resist further rusting; should it be scratched or damaged then rusting would take place. The lock and other furniture would now be polished, engraved and hardened. This was done by taking the various parts and placing them in a large open pan filled with animal charcoal. Many of the gunmakers had their own private formula, but old leather, bone and ivory dust were great favourites. The mixture was heated for about an hour at red heat, and when the pan was taken from the fire the contents were thrown straight into a bucket of water. In this way the surface of the metal, being the most quickly quenched, was turned into steel, and this gave a hard surface as well as a delightful blue colour. A similar result was achieved by immersing the various gun parts in a bowl of molten lead and tin alloy.

This, then, was the more or less standard procedure for the construction of an 18th or 19th century firearm. With the advent of the percussion revolver and percussion musket machinery began to play a more important part, and drop hammers, lathes and borers increasingly took over the work normally done by hand; but there was still a degree of individuality, for the great majority of weapons were hand-finished.

If decoration were added then specialists would be called in. In the case of the earlier, highly ornamented firearms these specialists were engravers, chisellers, and carvers, and all would play their part in producing a finished weapon of superb decorative qualities. Many of the craftsmen marked their work with their initials or symbol, and some of the earlier weapons of the 16th and 17th centuries bear the marks of the barrel maker, the lock maker, the stockers and even the chisellers, somewhere upon the weapon. A very popular method of decoration was engraving, and this method continues today on most quality weapons. Colt produced engraved cylinders on most of his percussion models by the use of dies, and only a selected few were actually hand-engraved. In the case of Deane Adams revolvers and other English percussions the engraving seems to have been largely hand-executed. One feature which was often added by hand was the name and address engraved on the lock and sometimes on the barrel. At first glance this might be thought to identify the maker with certainty, but in fact it only identifies the retailer. He *may* have been the maker, but possibly merely bought his parts from Birmingham or London and had them assembled at his shop. However, some of the better-known names were unquestionably makers in their own right; Joseph Manton, Durs Egg, William Parker, Henry Nock, John Dafte, Ketland and many others will soon become familiar names to the collector who takes any interest in English pistols or long arms.

IDENTIFICATION of date and place or origin will, to the new collector, seem extremely difficult, but it is very much a matter of practice, observation and experience. The more weapons the collector sees and handles, the more competent he becomes in assessing the age of an antique weapon. Obviously a percussion weapon will not date before about 1810, while a flintlock could be dated anywhere between about 1620 and 1820, although the chances are it would probably be an 18th century example. A wheellock could well be of any date between 1550 and 1700 in the case of the later German wheellock rifles. Matchlocks are almost certain to be Oriental in origin and these are virtually impossible to date with any degree of accuracy, although it is a reasonable generalisation to say that the majority of them are probably 19th century.

If an English pistol is under consideration then such features as the butt cap help to narrow down the date: flattened ends to the butt suggest the 17th century; long spurs up from the butt cap suggest early or middle 18th century; small spurs or none at all suggest late 18th or even early 19th century. Construction methods varied over the years, and if the screw for the barrel tang goes up from the bottom of the stock to connect with the tang it is almost certainly a late 17th or early 18th century weapon. Carving on the stock would again suggest early 18th century origin. Plain stocks with cross hatching on the butt are a feature of the end of the flintlock era.

If the weapon has certain distinctive features such as an all-metal stock, this suggests either a Balkan or a Scottish origin. There is little likelihood of confusion

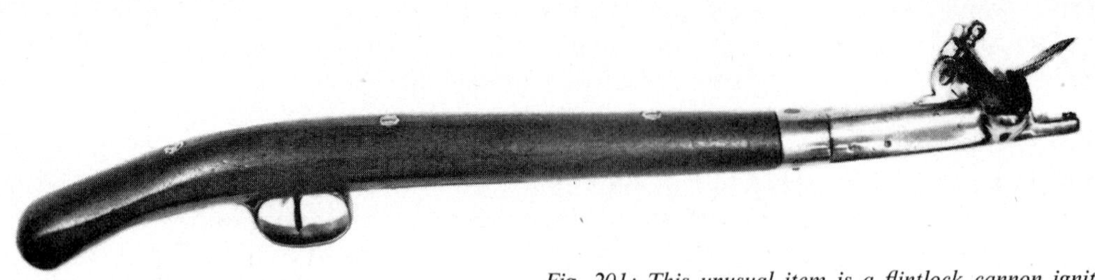

Fig. 201: This unusual item is a flintlock cannon igniter with a brass frame. The device, essentially a flintlock mounted at the end of a stock, was held with the lock adjacent to the touchhole of a cannon and fired so that the sparks struck the priming. (Kellam Collection.)

since the Scottish pieces or at least the later and less rare ones, have very characteristic ramshorn butts which are unique to the Scottish pistol. The style of lock will again give a further indication; a miguelet lock (see *Chapter* 3) suggests a Mediterranean origin.

Style of decoration is often a useful indication, but this applies largely to the earlier examples which few collectors will be fortunate enough to handle. Proof marks mentioned above are, of course, another very useful guide. Many makers have been listed together with the approximate dates they worked, but research is continuing apace and many of these dates are becoming far more definite.

It is unfortunate, but nevertheless one of the facts of life, that the increased demand for antique weapons has stimulated a number of the less scrupulous collectors and dealers to produce pieces which are not genuine; and the new collector must be constantly on his guard. It is not always easy to be certain as to the authenticity of a piece, for special circumstances alter cases; but there are one or two points which are worth bearing in mind. Examination should always be made of the area around the barrel tang and lock, for any refitted barrel or lock is likely to require some cutting of the stock which can only be disguised with difficulty, and some indication is often to be seen, especially if the lock is removed.

Other features such as government or regimental markings will help in dating, but there are few better guides than experience, and every opportunity to handle and examine specimens should be taken. However, it is not easy to acquire such experience and for the majority of collectors opportunities are very severely limited. For those lucky enough to be within reach of an auction room which specialises in sales of antique weapons there are excellent opportunities for handling the lots. Visits to museums are valuable but only in a limited way, since they cannot provide an opportunity to handle the weapons. Reliable text books are a useful aid, but while they offer some general guidance they are unable to illustrate all the minor features or describe the "feel" of a weapon which is such an important factor when assessing the authenticity and quality of a particular piece.

Antique firearms are becoming an expensive collectors' item and one should, therefore, be very wary before making any purchase. The weapon should always be examined thoroughly and close attention should be paid to all the metal work for signs of welding, replacements, fresh engraving or chemical treatment. Ideally one would like to strip the weapon and examine the inside of the lock and stock. In theory,

Plate 32 *A sample barrel, illustrating the process of heating twisted bars of iron and steel together to form a flat ribbon of metal which was, in its turn, twisted round a former.* (*Durrant Collection*).

Plate 33 *A French percussion pistol with a characteristic style of butt and trigger guard; and* (bottom) *a most unusual percussion pistol of circa 1830-35, the barrel inscribed* Missilieur à Vienne. *The concealed hammer is cocked by pushing the trigger forward.* (*Durrant Collection.*)

of course, the dealer should have no objection to one doing this but obviously it is not always practical and every collector has to take an occasional chance. Certainly mistakes will be made but this is inevitable and must be borne with as part of the price one pays for an interest in antique firearms. As some consolation it can be pointed out that except in the case of an absolute catastrophe, the value of almost any weapon will have appreciated enormously in a few years' time.

Fig. 202: An interesting group of firearms, all of which are associated with the General Post Office. The pair of flintlock pistols and the blunderbuss are by J. Harding, and were issue weapons for mail coach guards; the small knife-pistol, a most intriguing piece, is also marked G.P.O., *with the Royal Cypher of Queen Victoria. (Kellam Collection.)*

INDEX

Numerals in ordinary type refer to page numbers; *italic* numerals refer to monotone illustrations, and numerals in **bold** type to colour plates. Certain general terms are indexed under their first mention.